ALLAN JONES

TOO LATE TO STOP NOW

MORE ROCK 'N' ROLL WAR STORIES

BLOOMSBURY CARAVEL

LONDON · OXFORD · NEW YORK · NEW DELHI · SYDNEY

BLOOMSBURY CARAVEL
Bloomsbury Publishing Plc
50 Bedford Square, London, WC1B 3DP, UK
29 Earlsfort Terrace, Dublin 2, Ireland

BLOOMSBURY, BLOOMSBURY CARAVEL and the Diana logo are
trademarks of Bloomsbury Publishing Plc

First published in Great Britain 2023

A catalogue record for this book is available from the British Library

Library of Congress Cataloguing-in-Publication data has been applied for

ISBN: TPB: 978-1-4482-1825-7; eBook: 978-1-4482-1824-0

2 4 6 8 10 9 7 5 3 1

Typeset by Newgen KnowledgeWorks Pvt. Ltd., Chennai, India
Printed and bound in Great Britain by CPI Group (UK) Ltd, Croydon CR0 4YY

To find out more about our authors and books visit www.bloomsbury.com
and sign up for our newsletters

For Steph, Carol, Colin and Tom

CONTENTS

Introduction

Are We Rolling?

I meet a stranger in a bar, that's how it starts. It's April 2016 and I'm at Dingwalls in Camden Lock, not quite the same venue as the original Dingwalls Dance Hall that I remember in its mid-1970s heyday as an after-hours favourite of the pub rock crowd, many of them at some point associated with Stiff Records. Nick Lowe, Dave Edmunds, Ian Dury, Jake Riviera, Dave Robinson, Lee Brilleaux, BP Fallon, Larry Wallis and Sean Tyla are all back then bar jockey regulars. Tonight, it's packed for a farewell show by the American country rock band Richmond Fontaine. The band are splitting up after 12 years of some-times remarkable music that I've written about often in *Uncut*, the monthly magazine I edit for 17 years before checking out in June 2014, almost exactly 40 years after I first rock up at *Melody Maker* as a newly recruited feature writer/reporter, a wholly unexpected new gig.

Meanwhile, back in the new Dingwalls, I'm joined at the bar by someone who doesn't introduce himself but says he recognises me from my picture in *Uncut*, presumably the by-line mugshot that makes me look like the kind of hillbilly nitwit who ends up divor-cing his sister, marrying his mother and burning down a barn full of cows. He's kind enough not to dwell on this and tells me instead that he's a long-time *Uncut* reader, going back to the first issue with a glowering Elvis Costello on the cover. Before that, he was a regular reader of *Melody Maker*. What he wants to know now is why since retiring from *Uncut* I haven't put out a book. He mentions the 'Stop Me If You've Heard This One Before' stories I wrote as a back-page feature in *Uncut* for nearly as long as I was there. In these, I revisit

1

the adventures of a previous life on *Melody Maker*, the equivalent of stories told around a pub table. Colourful encounters with Lou Reed, David Bowie, Leonard Cohen, Van Morrison, Neil Young, The Sex Pistols, Elvis Costello, R.E.M. Why not a collection of them?

As it happens, a publisher's recently been in touch. He's keen to do something with the stories but seems increasingly attached to the idea of turning them into a comic strip. We have a series of very enjoyable lunches, but I can't see this going anywhere. Anyway, Richmond Fontaine are about to go on. The feller says I might find a better home for the stories with the company he works for. He hands me his business card, tells me to get in touch and disappears into the crowd. I'm on a train home when I have a proper look at the card. It introduces me to David Ward, then UK Sales Director of Bloomsbury. Really? This might be worth following up.

I give it a couple of days and email David Ward, wondering if he'll even remember our chat. He does and asks me to send some stories to Bloomsbury's Editorial Director, Jayne Parsons. A couple of phone calls later, she offers me a contract and a little over a year after that *Can't Stand Up For Falling Down* comes out. The book collects revised, rewritten and remixed versions of nearly 80 stories from the original 'Stop Me If You've Heard This One Before' features. The bulk of them are from my early years on *Melody Maker*, generally a raucous time when every day is like being thrown into the deep end of something that doesn't appear to have a bottom. You sank, or you didn't. Sheer bluff at times keeps me afloat.

When I turn up on my first day, I'm not really expecting the *MM* office to much resemble the party room on a Led Zeppelin tour, dolly birds in hot pants with platters of cocaine a glittering alternative to the traditional tea lady and her rattling trolley. But I'm still surprised by the relentless hum of labour. There's no music, not a lot of chat. Just the constant clatter of typewriters. My first impression is of a Hong Kong sweatshop, underpaid garment workers running up tracksuits and tank tops, 17-hour shifts, pissing where they sit. Is there some sensational breaking news I haven't heard that's sent the office into such an apparent frenzy? Not really. This is what it's like a lot of the time.

MM's weekly issues then typically run to 80 pages. The paper's format is huge, at least big enough to run up a flagpole and pass for a fair-sized flag. The type size is tiny. The thing eats words, can't get enough of them, and is always hungry. As I quickly discover, it's not unusual to write three or four features a week, plus umpteen album and live reviews. The turnaround on features is often so quick, there's no chance to transcribe interview tapes. You hotfoot it back to the office to type up an interview with Sweet, say, by fast-forwarding the tape and plucking out whatever decent quotes come up. There's no time to think about what you're going to write. You just do it, before dashing back out to interview Lemmy, Mud, Van Morrison, Sparks or Leonard Cohen. Welcome to the golden age of the UK music weeklies!

In any typical week, you might end up interviewing Elton John, Eno, Screaming Lord Sutch and someone from Hawkwind. The next week, it might be Bryan Ferry, Showaddywaddy, Kool & The Gang and Frankie Valli, who I interview in his suite at the Dorchester with a spectacular view of Hyde Park and west London beyond it. There's an invitation to stay for drinks, brandies on a couch to follow, Frankie at that point fondling my ear and starting to purr. The brandy was going down a treat, too.

It never lets up. I throw myself into whatever's happening like I've joined an early line-up of The Replacements or run off with a Wild West show. Being on the road with a band – piling into a van, onto a coach or tour bus and setting off for who knows where with The Clash, the Feelgoods, Rockpile, The Attractions, The Blasters, The Damned, whoever – was always the best part of it all. I'm soon racking up as many air miles as road miles, especially after Richard Williams replaces Ray Coleman as *MM* editor in 1978. Richard sends me everywhere. Covering XTC alone, there's a trip to Philadelphia and New York for a New Year's Eve show at the Beacon Theatre, as special guests of Talking Heads. The next year, we're in Australia. Not long after that, I join them for an epic road trip across Texas, New Mexico and Arizona, into California and on to Los Angeles. My last jaunt with them finds us in Venezuela, where they play at a huge sports arena in Caracas to an audience made up mainly of machete-wielding riot police and tear gas. There are times when I wonder if Richard has a side hustle as a travel agent.

In some ways, *Can't Stand Up For Falling Down* was a fan letter – bashful, unsigned – to the weekly music press, at least as it was when I joined *MM* in June 1974. There was later a sometimes sour, fractious rivalry between *MM* and *NME*. There was no lack of competition between the papers in the mid-1970s, either. But there seemed definitely a greater sense of fraternity, camaraderie, whatever you want to call it. A feeling that whatever we were in, we were in it together. You saw the same faces at gigs, festivals, album launches, after-show parties, record company blow-outs. Exclusive access to acts didn't seem to be a big thing. If a big-name American band or artist was in town for a day of press, you'd turn up for the interview and find yourself in a queue with Charles Shaar Murray, Chris Salewicz or Roy Carr from *NME*, Giovanni Dadomo or Pete Silverton from *Sounds*, David Hancock or Rosalind Russell from *Record Mirror*.

Nick Kent, already an *NME* legend, is untypically aloof. I don't get to know him at all until February 1986 when after a final falling-out with *NME* he calls me at *Melody Maker* where I am now editor. He wants to know if he can maybe do some stuff for *MM*. We meet at a pub near the British Museum.

It's a wet night, lots of rain, generally freezing. Nick turns up like he's arrived late for a fetish party, scantily dressed in a black PVC mac with a fake fur collar that looks like it's been attacked by giant moths. As emaciated as he is, the coat is at least two sizes too small for Nick. The sleeves end just below his elbows. There's only one button on the front. He's not wearing anything under it apart from skin that's turning blue as we speak. He keeps dropping his cigarette. He's shaking badly and possibly not just from the cold. His hair has the windswept look of a Ronette in a seafront breeze. He reviews Elvis Costello's *King of America* for the next issue of *Melody Maker*. He gets his handwritten copy in on time and the following week reviews the singles. He delivers his copy in a carrier bag full of scraps of paper, his reviews handwritten on them, which I then have to type up for him. The following week, he comes into the *MM* office to pick up some more albums to review and says he's off to meet up with Iggy Pop. I haven't seen him since.

The stories in *Can't Stand Up For Falling Down* stuck mostly to the format in which they originally appeared in *Uncut*. Some of them were rewritten, remixed or otherwise buffed up. But nearly all of them were short, 1,500 words or so, history as anecdote. I started writing the stories that now appear in *Too Late To Stop Now* during the first Covid lockdown in 2020, mainly because I didn't want to come out

4

of self-isolation empty-handed, as it were. I imagined people using their enforced seclusions learning to juggle or play the harpsichord, becoming fluent in Welsh, Amharic or Pawnee. It seemed the least I could do to knock up some tales and in writing them I let the stories dictate the length of their own telling, unrestricted by word count. Where whoever I was talking to was more than capable of telling their own story – Chrissie Hynde on The Pretenders, Elvis Costello on being Elvis Costello, John Cale on The Velvet Underground, Wilko Johnson reminiscing about Canvey Island and the early days of Dr Feelgood – I was happy to give them the floor.

A lot of the stories are again from those early *Melody Maker* years and a lot of them feature people who were involved with Stiff. Nick Lowe, Wreckless Eric, The Damned, Elvis Costello. There are also more than a couple of passing references to the label's charismatic co-founder, Jake Riviera, who writes his own notorious legend as Costello's sharp-tongued, two-fisted manager. I actually meet Jake for the first time not long after joining *MM*. I'm sent one Friday night to The Marquee to review a French prog rock band called Ange. I fear a flute was involved, certainly a Mellotron; probably a bass player in a scoop-necked T-shirt with belled sleeves, satin loon pants and clogs. Anyway, the support band turns out to be Alberto Y Lost Trios Paranoias, Manchester's answer to National Lampoon, playing their first London show. They're hilarious and when I spot a couple of them later in the bar, we start chatting. One of them, the drummer, Bruce Mitchell, who becomes a mainstay of the Manchester music scene, is in somewhat bitter humour about the fact that the band have had to pay The Marquee to play tonight. What the fuck's that all about? It's called Pay to Play and is everywhere rife, exotically coiffured assistant editor Mick Watts explains when I get up on a soapbox about this at the next *MM* editorial meeting. Mick adds that if I feel so strongly about the whole thing I should write a feature about it, interview some of the people affected. I get in touch with the Albertos. My *MM* colleague Geoff Brown, an early pub rock champion, suggests I also talk to someone called Jake, the manager of pub rockers Chilli Willi & The Red Hot Peppers.

We arrange to meet in a pub near *MM*'s Fleet Street office. Jake blows into the bar like he's turned up late for a fight and can't wait to get stuck in. He's got the pub rock cowboy look down pretty pat. Black western-style shirt, jeans, cowboy boots, a slick quiff, Ray-Bans. He's also abuzz with a bristling urgency, some barely contained energy. As promised by Geoff Brown, he's got opinions about everything. When it comes to the music business, most of them are scathing. He's got nothing but angry contempt for major labels, cloth-eared A&R men, greedy promoters, dodgy agents. He talks non-stop for about two hours. I'm merely a highly amused audience and handy source of refreshment. He sounds like he wants to bring down the entire temple, but says he has a better business plan. What's that?

'Infiltrate and double-cross,' he says, piling into another pint of cider.

More than anything, Jake seems like he gets things done. I'm not surprised when he turns out to be one of the prime movers behind The Naughty Rhythms Tour, a pub rock showcase for Chilli Willi, Dr Feelgood and Kokomo. The Feelgoods come out of the tour already on their way to briefly becoming the biggest band in the UK. Chilli Willi make a more modest impact and soon split up. Jake joins the Feelgoods as tour manager, before borrowing £400 from Feelgoods' singer Lee Brilleaux to start Stiff Records – 'Undertakers to the Industry' – with Graham Parker & The Rumour manager Dave Robinson. Soon, Stiff's HQ in Alexander Street, west London, is a hip and happening place to be. The label's first release is Nick Lowe's 'So It Goes' in August 1976. In October, they release The Damned's 'New Rose', produced by Nick, the UK's first punk single.

In 1977, when things are jumping at Stiff, Malcolm McLaren and his crowd have their own scene going somewhere across town. You'd see them around, McLaren usually looking down his nose, like someone reading a menu, a lot about him reminiscent of a fragrant fop in a Restoration comedy. The Stiff lot by comparison are more like something out of *The Lavender Hill Mob*. Wideboys and schemers, maybe. But at least they're getting records out while the haggling McLaren is holding out for a big bucks major label deal for The Sex Pistols. It's all theatre for Malcolm, but with one thing and another the Pistols are on their third label by the time they finally put out an album. If McLaren had signed the Pistols to Stiff in the summer of 1976, Dave Robinson would have immediately locked them in Pathway Studios with Nick Lowe and wrung enough singles out of them by the end of the year to have a Greatest Hits album in the shops for the post-Christmas record-token market.

By 1996, I'm done with *Melody Maker*. Britpop has been the big noise in town for a while. The publishers expect maximum coverage. If current sales are anything to go by, though, you'd have to say what's left by then of *MM*'s readership preferred us when we were writing about Butthole Surfers rather than Blur. Two successive issues covering Oasis at Knebworth together sell less than an issue a couple of years earlier with an American band called Thin White Rope on the cover that I'm not sure anyone outside the *MM* office had even heard of.

MM publisher Alan Lewis's answer to continually declining sales is to remake *MM* for a much younger readership, as if our current readers are all Van der Graaf Generator fans who forgot to cancel their subscriptions when *MM* stopped covering prog. This is clearly going to have to happen without me. *MM*'s publishing MD Andy McDuff indulges an idea I have for a film magazine. A week before a dummy I work on and off for about nine months with *MM* art editor Norman McLeod is scheduled to be sent to the printers, two rival publishers announce they're launching film magazines that will be out before whatever we come up with. *Uncut* as a film magazine is doomed. We've been working on the dummy film issue with Alan Lewis, by now the IPC editorial director who's played a crucial role in the recent success of *Loaded*. He knows Norman and I would probably rather eat each other than go back at this point to *MM*. He reminds us we still have a week before the original deadline to send a dummy to the printers. Maybe I can think of something over the weekend that Andy will want to publish.

That night in the pub, I draw up a features list and flat plan for what *Uncut* becomes. A music and movie magazine. Norman gets it as soon as I explain it to him on Monday morning. We rescue what we can from the original dummy, add a pile of music features and over the next four days knock out 148 pages. When Andy and Alan Lewis see what we've done, they give us another week to complete a 164-page dummy issue that's sent out by a research company to test the reaction of 200 readers. After a couple of weeks they're asked if they'd buy it if it was on sale. Enough of them say they would for IPC to greenlight *Uncut*'s launch in May 1997. As I write, in May 2022, it's just celebrated its 25th anniversary and is in many ways better than ever, although film has long been abandoned as an essential part of the editorial mix.

The last three stories here are from the end of my time on *Uncut*. By convenient narrative coincidence, they return me via an admittedly scenic route to three bands that nearly 50 years earlier took up a lot of my attention. Former Dr Feelgood guitarist Wilko Johnson had recently been diagnosed with terminal cancer when we met for what I expected to be the last time in April 2013. Dire circumstance had not rendered him sentimental, contrite or apologetic about a career that had started so explosively with the Feelgoods, the band he was forced out of at the height of their success. He wasn't short on bitterness and bafflement at his treatment by people he thought were his friends. Forgiveness was clearly beyond him.

The three surviving members of The Clash assembled in September 2013, around the release of their career-spanning *Sound System* box set, to look back on who they had been, Joe Strummer a ghost in the room. In 1976, Clash manager Bernie Rhodes puts a fist in my face and tells me that in six months no one will remember The 101'ers, the band he's recently strong-armed Joe Strummer into quitting to join The Clash. In July 2014, they're the first band I write about as a freelance contributor to *Uncut*. Talk about coming full circle, the end becoming the beginning.

Back at Dingwalls, Richmond Fontaine are plugging in. The lights are going down, the amps are humming. The show's about to start. Time for some thanks. First, to Kathy Archbold. If Kathy hadn't seen the ad for the *MM* vacancy she then encouraged me to apply for, I would probably have been stuck for the next 30 years in the mail order department of Hatchards bookshop, retiring eventually to bachelor accommodations in Penge with an inscribed clock and a labradoodle named Roddy. As many thanks go to Ray Coleman, who didn't so much give me a job as a life. Thanks to Mick Watts for pointing out that there's more to writing than putting one word after another and hoping for the best. For once, I was listening.

I'd already put together a pretty good record collection by paying attention to whatever Richard Williams recommended in *MM* before he left to work for Island Records. What an unlikely outcome to end up working for him when he replaces Ray Coleman as editor in 1978. Almost from the moment he arrives, he seems to think the office is a quieter space when I'm not there and keeps finding some pretty far-flung places to send me. I'm surprised, therefore, when he asks me to

8

edit *MM*'s new front section, something called 'After Dark', five or six pages I have to myself and whatever I want to put in them. I'm suddenly commissioning writers and photographers, editing copy, writing headlines and blurbs. It's a hint of things to come and something else to thank Richard for.

Thanks, also, to Andy McDuff, for taking a chance on *Uncut*, and Alan Lewis, who suggested the 'Stop Me If You've Heard This One Before' stories as an alternative to a more conventional editor's letter. That worked out pretty well. Robert Tame did an amazing job as *Uncut*'s first publisher during the frantic six weeks we had to put the launch issue together. Many thanks to Phil King for digital research and *Uncut* editor Michael Bonner and Paul Ward at NME Networks for their cooperation. David Ward appeared from nowhere and started the ball rolling that Bloomsbury Publishing Director Jayne Parsons has now twice taken over the line. Thanks to both. Thanks also to Caroline Guillet at Bloomsbury for her diligent oversight and patience. BP Fallon has been an extraordinary part of my life since 1974. Thanks, man, for the adventures, stories and more. Ring them bells for the psychedelic lightning storm otherwise known as Carol Clerk, legendary *MM* news editor, a pub partner and pal for thirty years. Put your hands together, including the people in the back, for Colin Irwin, a friend from my first days at *MM*, 50 years ago, who died as this book was being finished. Let's see some hats in the air, too, for illustrious lensman Tom Sheehan, *compadre* on so many unforgettable jaunts. What larks! And to Stephanie Jones, thanks for it all and a lot more.

ELTON JOHN

London, June 1974

It's Monday morning, the start of my third week on *Melody Maker*, when we gather for an editorial meeting. Heavily fragranced editor Ray Coleman sits at the head of the conference table, the man in charge. He's flanked to his left by news editor Rob Partridge, a man who's rather admirably turned finding ways of doing as little as possible into an art form, a major retrospective opening soon at Tate Modern. To his right sits assistant editor Mick Watts, resplendent today in a new safari jacket with enough pockets to fit his record collection. Ray's attention is now suddenly demanded by Rasputin-haired production editor Mike Oldfield. Mike's been going through the page plan for the new issue and there's apparently a page that needs to be filled. We're a feature short.

MM's top brass start bickering about who's to blame for this calamity, not a pretty sight. Does eternally jolly features editor Chris Welch have anything to fill the empty page, something handily already written, held back for such an emergency? Of course not. Everything we write goes straight in the paper. It's like feeding a fucking furnace. This is a bit of a problem. Today is *MM*'s press day. All our pages have to be written, subbed, laid out and signed off by 5.30 pm to be sent to the printers. Mick Watts asks Chris what interviews we've been offered. Is there anything we can turn around quickly enough to avert the evidently looming catastrophe? Chris searches through a pile of papers, discovers a press release and waves it about like Chamberlain, back from Munich with reassuring news about peace in our time.

Elton John has a new album out. Does the sequined short-arse never take a break? He's at the Dorchester today talking about it to anyone who's interested, among whose company I would not immediately include myself. *MM*'s been offered an 11.30 am slot with the fabled entertainer. Chris quickly confirms it's still open. It's 10.30 am now. Plenty of time, according to Chris, for someone to get over to the hotel where Elton is holding gaudy court, have a quick chat with the colourful showman about his new album and hotfoot it back to the office to knock out 2,000 words before the pubs open. I'm wondering what chump they'll send to interview Elton when I realise someone's talking to me.

'You're not busy,' Mick Watts says, with a malevolent smirk. 'You can do it.'

What? I haven't even heard the fucking album!

'Don't worry,' Mick says blithely. 'He probably can't remember making it.'

'Tell him how much you like it. You won't be able to shut him up,' Chris Welch tells me. 'The piece will write itself.'

Not much later, I step into the vast expanse of Elton's temporary digs at the Dorchester, the furthest parts of which are probably in different time zones, with their own border checks, possibly their own climates. Elton bounds out of the bathroom, like someone bursting out of a cake. Surprise! He seems overdressed for a Monday morning. He's not wearing a dress made of bananas or a wig in the shape of a South American cathedral. But he has the look of a pampered boy dressed by his mother for a party, possibly involving clowns, who calls his father 'Papa'. There's an abundance of frills. Whatever – he couldn't be friendlier if I was paying him the equivalent of the annual gross national product of Canada as a daily stipend for being my new best friend.

When he shakes my hand, he brings my whole arm into it, like someone pumping water from a well. He invites me to sit next to him on a large sofa. 'Sit, sit!' he says urgently. 'Drinks!' he shouts then, someone announcing an attack by Apaches, hostiles swarming over adobe walls. There's a lot of clanking as Elton trundles a drinks trolley as big as a medieval war machine across the room. He pours champagne into enormous goblets you have to drink from two-handed, Viking style.

'Time for another,' Elton says, refilling his suddenly empty glass.

I'm relieved to see a copy of Elton's new album on the table in front of us. It appears to be called *Caribou*. Is it a concept album about reindeer? Has Bernie Taupin written a song cycle about elks? I'm tempted to ask, but I don't want Elton to know I haven't heard the thing. Instead, I pick up the rather garish sleeve and merely repeat the title. 'Caribou.' It's not even a question, but Elton starts reminiscing excitedly about the studio in Colorado, somewhere in the Rockies, where he recorded the album. It sounds like he's describing a recent holiday, a winter break involving ice-capped peaks and jolly outings on snowmobiles. I let him ramble on. It's better than nothing. Then he gets a bit shirty about the press, how he's not taken seriously in the UK, a target for constant criticism, snide opinion, somehow not much loved. He finally declares a wholly unconvincing indifference to what people think about him and pours us another two pints of champagne, then grabs another bottle.

'Always good to have one ready to go,' he says, plunging the bottle into an ice bucket big enough to bury a dog in. We get back to business, the room taking on a warm, furry glow. He makes some disparaging remarks about Black Oak Arkansas and The New York Dolls that should keep *MM*'s letters page humming for a couple of weeks, and all in all things seem to have gone reasonably well, only the one hissy fit. We don't seem to have been talking very long, although I notice there are two empty bottles on the table and it's nearly 1.30 pm. I really should be getting back to the office. Elton's not having it.

'There's another bottle!'

He's right. There is. We decide to polish it off. I settle back with another large drink and remember Chris Welch telling me the piece would write itself. It's nearly 2.00 pm.

He'd better be fucking right.

Roy Harper

London, November 1974

The first time I see Roy Harper's name in the music papers, it's in a small feature on him in *Melody Maker* that appears in the folk section, stuck right at the back of the paper, just before the loon pants ads.

It would have been late 1967, perhaps early 1968. The article describes him as the UK's answer to Bob Dylan. The protest Bob, not the plugged-in hepcat Bob became. I imagine the worst. Someone in a denim cap – you know the sort – a chunky fisherman's sweater, sandals and a harmonica rack. The type you might find, in other words, playing 'With God on Our Side' around a CND campfire, some bewhiskered twat with a banjo unable to resist joining in. A potentially field-clearing 'The Lonesome Death of Hattie Carroll' the next song on the playlist. He doesn't seem like my thing at all.

Then someone gives me a copy of *The Rock Machine Turns You On Vol. 1*. The mind-blowing 1968 CBS sampler features tracks from some already established big hitters, including Dylan, The Byrds and Simon & Garfunkel. But there's lots of new stuff, too. Tracks from recent albums by Leonard Cohen, Moby Grape, The United States of America, The Electric Flag, Spirit – not to mention Elmer Gantry's Velvet Opera.

There's a track by Harper, too. A song called 'You Don't Need Money'. It's a kind of busker's stoned reverie about getting by on not much more than good vibes and enough hash for the next joint. Its sunny, slapstick utopianism is undercut however by a sarcasm that makes it ever more appealing. A line about time spent in 'the Paris of Che' is as evocative of the May '68 student uprising as baton-wielding gendarmes, tear gas and croissants. I can't stop playing the thing and become even more greatly enamoured of Harper when I get the album it's from, *Come Out Fighting Ghengis Smith*. This is just the start of a longer infatuation with Harper and his music. Over the years to come, he's often a light that fills the darkest room. The best of his records come to mean as much to me as anyone's ever have. Especially the run of albums he makes for Harvest between 1970 and 1975, including *Flat Baroque and Berserk*, *Stormcock*, *Lifemask* and *HQ*.

The first time I see him is in August 1968, at the National Jazz & Blues festival, held that year at Kempton Park racecourse in Sunbury-on-Thames. He comes on to join The Nice, who back him on a noisy version of an unreleased song called 'Hell's Angels', Roy on electric guitar. Then, in late April or early May in 1969, I see him at a folk club in the small South Wales town of Bridgend, on a blustery Sunday night. The club is in the bar of a pub run by some Welsh boxing champion and the few locals there look themselves like they've spent time in the ring, taking blows to the head and face that have left them with flattened noses and various other cranial dents and cavities. A hard-looking crew, in other words, and not much, I assumed, like Harper's usual crowd.

Anyway, Roy comes on to audible gasps and disbelieving stares. I remember his long blond hair, a swashbuckling moustache, a sash of some kind, an outlandish tunic and most clearly the boots he's wearing. They look like something you'd more typically see on someone herding yak on a far-off steppe or tundra, somewhere to the east of the Kirghiz Light, to which he's attached by a complicated arrangement of ribbons and leather straps that wind around his feet and legs to just below the knees.

Years later, when I get to know Roy a bit, I find out the boots were given to him by David Bowie, who's sported the spectacular footwear as part of his costume for the one-man mime show about the Chinese invasion of Tibet he performs on T. Rex's 1969 tour. At the time, I just wonder where I can get a pair and whether I'll be allowed to wear them to school.

The first thing I notice after the boots is that Harper seems to be totally stoned. It is at the time a condition I've only read about, various experiments with grilling banana skins inducing nausea rather than nirvana. Harper, though, seems so genuinely high even air traffic

14

control couldn't get through to him. He's somewhere it looks like it might be a lot of fun to be, and I frankly can't wait to get there myself. There's a lot of giggling and an inclination to conversational digression, a lot of talking. Roy, in a manner it would probably be fair to describe as rambling, seems keen to tell us about his day so far and then the day before that, working his way backwards through time to what if he carries on like this will be its very beginning.

He's on stage for nearly 20 minutes before he even starts his first song, which when he plays it is mesmerisingly brilliant.

He's not done talking, though. Nearly everything he goes on to play is either prefaced or interrupted by lengthy preambles and thoroughly windy interjections. Some of what he has to say is occasionally even vaguely connected to the songs that follow. About halfway through the set, four or five songs in, I guess, given all the chat, he announces a new song that I've read about and now can't wait to hear. It's called 'McGoohan's Blues', partly inspired by *The Prisoner*, the cult TV series devised by and starring the actor Patrick McGoohan, after whom the song is named. When it appears on Harper's next album, *Folkjokeopus*, it clocks in at just shy of 18 minutes. Tonight's version is at least twice as long

He's only a few minutes into it when he stops, brow furrowed, something clearly on his mind.

'I was just thinking about what I wrote there,' he says of a line in the song, and is off on another conversational tangent, a train of thought heading down the tracks to an unspecified destination. After about ten minutes of this, we're starting to wonder if he's forgotten he was playing a song and whether when he does remember he'll have to start again from the beginning.

'I just felt I needed to explain what I meant by that line,' he says then and having said it astonishingly enough picks up the song at the very point he left it and goes on to complete it faultlessly, with only two or three comparatively brief further digressions.

It's because of shows like this that Harper's often described by the music press as erratic. He's nothing of the sort. I see him a lot over the next few years. This is what he's always like. A Harper concert that proceeds in an orderly manner from one song to another without interruption is as rare as a tap-dancing fish. There's a show at Cardiff's

Grand Theatre when I don't think he finishes a song all night, most of the gig given over to lengthy musing on this and that. His fans love nights like this. But they don't help him sell a lot of records.

This means most people entirely miss the series of albums that Harper makes between 1968 and 1975, records of increasingly vaulting ambition that makes them emblematic of a time in which adventure is everything. New sonic territories there for the taking, as it were, as if in a land rush. They are pioneering days and Harper's wild poetic imagination and articulate indignation make him a standard-bearer for the counterculture of the time – quixotic, stoned, outspoken. He's very much a child of 1960s utopianism, but always bristles at being taken for a hippie, when he shares a more adhesive attachment to the freewheeling Beats and their hipster kin.

Similarly, he comes up through the folk clubs, although calling him a folkie risks reducing him to hopping like a three-legged dog. For Harper, as much as Dylan, the folk scene is a convenient route to a larger stage, one big enough in Harper's case to accommodate what's fast becoming the oceanic swell of his music. 'Circle', on *Genghis Smith*, is a hint of what's yet to come, a ten-minute autobiographical opus that combines elements of conventional songwriting with spoken-word monologues, music hall skits and a lot of funny voices. It's not much like anything you would have heard, even in 1968.

'McGoohan's Blues' is the first of his confrontational long-form songs, the template for epics like 'I Hate the White Man', from 1970's *Flat Baroque And Berserk*, 'The Same Old Rock' and 'Me and My Woman' from 1971's landmark album *Stormcock*, and the all-consuming 'The Lord's Prayer', which took up an entire side of 1973's *Lifemask*. Harper's music in these years makes fans of Led Zeppelin, Pink Floyd, Pete Townshend, Kate Bush and Peter Gabriel. Celebrity big guns turn out for his Valentine's Day Massacre show at The Rainbow on 14 February 1974. His backing band includes Jimmy Page, Ronnie Lane and Keith Moon, who turns up dressed as a Butlin's Redcoat. Robert Plant, a vision in leopard-skin lurex, is also to hand. As is John Bonham, who during one song dances around the stage in a red jacket, bowler hat and black tights.

The show's great in many ways. But I think I prefer Harper solo, sitting on a stool with an acoustic guitar, stroking his beard, moustache, whatever, maybe a small string section conducted by David

Bedford. Still, the occasion provides Harper with some great stories. One I remember involves Keith Moon, a helicopter, 'Legs' Larry Smith and a suitcase belonging to Moon full to the brim with a multiplicity of uppers, downers and pills that take you places they don't have names for yet.

By 1977, punk is upon us. Harper is cast adrift. He's dropped by Harvest. His wife runs off with the violinist Nigel Kennedy. He loses his house, goes bankrupt, disappears into what he later describes as a 20-year exile in the west of Ireland. There are more albums, although only hardcore fans listen to typically confrontational songs like 'The Black Cloud of Islam' and 'The Monster', an indictment of Tony Blair as a war criminal that appears on 2000's *The Green Man*, which turns out to be his last album until 2013's *Man & Myth*.

Anyway, the lack of recognition he's endured is one of the first things we talk about when I interview him for the first time in November 1974, one of many encounters that follow over the next few years. We're in the backroom on the ground floor of 32 Alexander Street that Dave Robinson uses as an office and mostly seems to live in when Stiff rent part of the building from Harper's managers, Peter Jenner and Andrew King, otherwise known as Blackhill Enterprises.

The first thing Roy does when we sit down is light a joint and smoke it. I help out here and there. It's pretty strong fucking gear. Malawi Trip Weed, or something. It's certainly a cut above the crumbly hash that would leave you coughing at student parties, everybody else in the room vibing out, glassy-eyed to the Moody fucking Blues. At least I remember to press record on my tape recorder before things get too psychedelicised. A not unpleasant paralysis rather quickly overcomes me. I feel quite soft. For a moment, I think I've turned into a quilt, a duvet. A cushion, at least.

Roy's enjoying the sound of his own voice and seems happy answering questions I haven't asked. Which means I get by mainly by nodding at hopefully appropriate moments while I try to figure out where and who I am. Whatever we're smoking's having no obvious effect on Roy so far. Me? I feel like a non-league footballer, out of his depth in a Premiership eleven, adrift and confused. The game passing me by in a bit of a blur. This shit is for real. I try to tune into whatever Roy's talking about.

'I think I've done some fucking great work,' he says, Roy rarely in my memory prone to underestimate himself or his music. 'And I just can't understand why it hasn't received the acclaim it deserves. I can see maybe why, though. The mass of the public aren't into being told what's going on. They aren't into thinking for themselves at all. They just want something they don't have to think about. And that's exactly the rubble they're fed.

'I think it has a lot to do with the way people are conditioned to fall into line, to not overstep the mark and ask questions. It's all about knowing your place and that's a terrible place to be. You're made to feel inferior. That everybody else is better.

'I was brought up just like that,' he goes on, taking another hit of the dope I'm now convinced is strong enough to paralyse a small bison. 'I was brought up to believe everyone was better than me. That the man next door was better than I could ever be. The thing is, when I was growing up, I thought the man next door was a complete cunt.'

He takes another hit, a deep drag that makes him apparently reflective.

'The thing is,' he says, a bit of drift in his voice, 'I still think the man next door's a complete cunt.'

A sigh.

'I don't know,' he says. 'Maybe I should just, you know, fucking move.'

A slow exhale.

'What do you think?'

I try to muster something resembling a reply. But I feel like I've just swallowed my own eyeballs, the Malawi Trip Weed by now having deposited me on the far side of senselessness, Roy waiting for me there with a cackling laugh and a joint on the go. Which is the way I always remember him when I can remember anything at all.

CHRIS FARLOWE

London, August 1975

'Look at this,' Chris Farlowe says, holding something wrapped in soft cloth and offering it to me for my cautious inspection.

'A genuine SS bugle,' he goes on, his voice dropping to something resembling a conspiratorial whisper, an appreciative murmur, as if he's afraid he'll wake the thing. 'Bloody luvverly, innit?' he says, louder again now, the kind of north London bark you might hear in a street market somewhere not far from here, someone raffish selling fruit from a stall with a cheeky line in chat-'em-up banter, a hit with the ladies, saucily inviting them to feel his plums, arf-arf.

''Ere,' he's saying now, handing me the bugle, delicately, like someone passing a baby to safe hands in a lifeboat, the *Titanic* sinking beneath them, waves lapping around their ankles on a tilting deck.

I take it from him, hoping I don't drop the thing and dent it. It is indeed beautiful, in a wholly terrifying way, the bugle I now have in my hands creepily engraved with a Third Reich eagle. Holding it makes you wonder where, as it were, it might have been blown, and by who, on the far-off fields of war.

'Travelled a hundred miles last night just to get it,' he says, carefully lifting the bugle back out of my hands, like it's an unexploded bomb he thinks I might set off.

'Bloke I bought it off got it in 'Amburg at the end of the war. The SS cleared out of this building and left all their bleedin' musical instruments. Must've been the 'eadquarters of the regimental band.'

We are standing on either side of a counter in Call to Arms, the military memorabilia shop Farlowe owns and runs on Islington Green. There are myriad medals in glass cases, regimental patches,

19

Nazi flags, decorated with the hideous swastika, odious symbol of the fallen Reich, assortments of weapons hanging on the walls, sabres, knives, bayonets, swords, things I can't put a name to that at one time were probably used to cudgel, bludgeon and pummel.

Propped on the counter to his left is the tail fin of something I imagine was shot down in some savage dogfight over the South Downs by some noble hero of the Battle of Britain. One of the plucky few of Churchillian legend, who keep the Hun at bay during the dangerous summer of 1940, when the skies are daily black with Dorniers.

I think Chris Farlowe is even now telling me how it came to be here, but I'm unaccountably tuning him out. All I can hear is static and when I look at him, he's starting to flicker and before I know it, I'm in front of a bulky old Ekco television set, and because it's Friday night, I'm watching the music show *Ready Steady Go!*, live from London, the weekend, as they used to announce, starting here.

Chris Farlowe's on stage belting out a song by Mick Jagger and Keith Richards called 'Out of Time' that Jagger's produced with a Spectorish flourish for Andrew Loog Oldham's label, Immediate. It's June 1966, and 'Out of Time' is number one, a palpable smash, in the vernacular of a time when for a couple of years Farlowe and his band, The Thunderbirds, are popular fixtures on a hot London club scene and Chris is feted as one of the greatest voices in British R&B.

I can see him still, on the *RSG* stage, shoulders hunched like someone who's spent time in a boxing ring, something about his pugilist swagger that hints at body blows and uppercuts. He's dressed in a suit he looks like he might burst out of, buttons popping, perhaps to blind one of the adoring dolly birds in the audience. His oddly equine features make him look like his face has been caught in a trouser press.

'Them was great days,' he says now, snapping me out of my reflective drift. 'Like in 'Amburg in the early days at the Star Club, with The Beatles and Tony Sheridan an' all that, I mean, they was hard times. We had to nick things from supermarkets to get a bite to eat. But playing over there was the thing, you know.

'At that time, the Star Club was booking people like Fats Domino, Jerry Lee Lewis, Chuck Berry, Ray Charles, and to be on the same stage as that lot was really something, because we were nobodies.

And the money wasn't too bad, either. I think we must've been getting, like, 30 quid a week. That was 'eavy bread in them days.

'In England, when I started my band, we'd get about 15 bob a night, and I'd 'ave to work as an apprentice carpenter. And I was only getting a quid a week pay for that. We did months at a time in 'Amburg, then come back over 'ere, do a couple of months around the American air bases. A great schooling, it was. Just think of all the bands that came straight out of that and into The Flamingo and all them clubs down the West End. Straight down there and on into oblivion some of them.

'It was a great scene, though. I loved those days,' he goes on. 'I wish it was like that now. You know, go down to any club in the West End and see a really great band. Everyone was mates, you know. We'd have various members of The Beatles come down and sit in with us. And the Stones would be around, everyone just coming down to sit in with us. Great days, great days.'

They came to an end, though, due to what Farlowe describes ominously 'as aggro with the management'. I'm not sure who he's talking about, and he is not inclined to go into further detail, adding only that when in 1969 he disbanded The Thunderbirds he moved for a year to New York, playing gigs there with Janis Joplin, Hendrix and a few dates with Joe Cocker at The Scene Club. He'd seen Cocker at Christmas and jammed with his band. As far as Farlowe is concerned, rumours about Joe's drug-addled decline have been exaggerated.

'He seemed fine,' he says. 'Luvverly guy. Great singer. And it's up to Cocker what he does, no one else. I'd never say to him, "Look man, you're fucking yourself up." If he's 'appy, leave him be. I mean, you wouldn't tell Van Gogh how to paint just cos he cut his fuckin' ear off.'

But back to Call to Arms, and his bugles and bomber parts.

With his solo career on the slide, Farlowe joined jazz rock blusterers Colosseum in 1970. By 1972, he was fronting heavy-handed progrockers Atomic Rooster. More recently, he's played a rare headlining show at The Lyceum, with a band featuring former Thunderbirds guitarist Albert Lee, bassist Pat Donaldson, drummer Gerry Conway, Madeline Bell on backing vocals, and a repertoire that includes Alice Cooper's 'Only Women Bleed' and Barry Manilow's 'Mandy'. A live album recorded that night and another show at The Marquee will be released in November. Otherwise, he has not been much bothered by the attentions of record companies over the last decade.

'It's a different world now, the music business,' he says. 'I barely recognise it. You talk to a label these days and it's not long before some berk wants to know about your image. Image? I never had a fuckin' image. I had a voice. There was a time when that was enough.

'That's why this place is a great sideline for me,' he says, standing there in Call to Arms. 'If things get a bit strained or depressed, as they often do in show business, I can walk straight in 'ere and talk to people who've got nothing at all to do with that world. They'll be dead ordinary blokes and they'll bring in their daggers and knives and we'll 'ave a good old natter and it calms you down, know what I mean?'

SCREAMING LORD SUTCH

Chatham, January 1976

A couple of weeks into the New Year I'm sitting at my desk in the *Melody Maker* office when the phone rings.

'Allan Jones?'

Who's calling?

'Screaming Lord Sutch.'

Wha-at?

'Screaming Lord Sutch.'

That's what I thought he said.

'Know who I am?'

Well, yes.

'We're off to a good start, then,' he says, a cheerful man with a bus conductor's chuckle. 'Time for a chat?'

Turns out something I've written recently in *MM*, I can't remember what, has made him laugh and he's calling to say hello. Which he does, and then carries on talking for about 45 minutes. He's a veritable conversational threshing machine, chewing up everything in its oncoming path. What a chatterbox! Give him a garden fence and someone to talk to over it and you'd probably need a stick of dynamite to blow him back into the house. He leaves so little space for interruption, it's like he's leaving a message on an answering machine. I may as well be down the pub.

He seems relentlessly upbeat, a little manic; someone whose idea of fun is setting fire to his hair, squirting people in the face with water from a plastic flower, falling out of windows. You imagine him in a house full of whoopee cushions, stink bombs and a random assortment of buzzers and such devices that give you an electric shock when you shake hands. Anything for a laugh, all that. By the time I put the phone down, my head's spinning like a plate on a stick and I've apparently agreed to go see him at a gig he's got that weekend at The Ash Tree, a pub in Chatham, wherever the fuck that is.

I spend the afternoon going through old Sutch press clippings from the *MM* files. They tell quite a story. He started off playing the 2i's in Soho, where Tommy Steele and Cliff Richards made their names. He's a bit too wild for the coffee bar scene and, nicking a new image wholesale from Screamin' Jay Hawkins and adding a bit of music hall slapstick and a dash of Hammer Horror, he becomes Screaming Lord Sutch. He's got a hot band called The Savages. At various times, the line-up includes Jimmy Page, Nicky Hopkins, Jeff Beck, Jon Lord, Noel Redding, Mitch Mitchell, Ritchie Blackmore and a drummer named Carlo Little, who's an inspiration for the young Keith Moon and other fledgling tub-thumpers. Some of these people appear on his 1970 album *Lord Sutch and Heavy Friends*, produced by Jimmy Page, which in a BBC poll years later is voted the worst album ever made.

His first single is produced by Joe Meek, a raucous track called ''Til the Following Night' that features clunky sound effects and the kind of screaming that used to get Yoko Ono bad reviews. Like every other record he releases, it sells poorly. He gets by for a while on an ever more outrageous stage act. Themed tours become a bit of a speciality. Screaming Lord Sutch and the Roman Empire has the band dressed up as Roman soldiers. No one's paying much notice, though. As desperate as ever for attention, he forms the National Teenage Party in 1963, the forerunner of the Official Monster Raving Loony Party that he starts in 1983. He stands for parliament at a 1963 by-election in Stratford-upon-Avon, on a ticket calling for such things as licences for cats and, it was said, goldfish, votes at 18 and the introduction of local commercial radio. The party's slogan is: 'Vote For Insanity – You Know It Makes Sense'.

As a National Teenage Party candidate, he stands against Prime Minister Harold Wilson in the 1966 general election in the PM's own Huyton constituency in Liverpool. He stands for election to parliament 39 times, losing each time, a record. It gets him on the telly a lot, though. Sutch at the hustings in top hat and leopard-skin jackets, festooned with rosettes as big as dartboards, beaming on stage with other candidates as the results are announced. As in his showbiz career, he's always somewhere near the foot of the bill.

He's not short of other stunts that keep him in the news. There seems to have been a time, in fact, when he was never off the front pages of the newspapers, Fleet Street continually agog at his antics. Here he is parading with a posse of naked dancing girls along Downing Street. Now he's setting sail dressed as a pirate in 1964 from Tower Bridge in a converted fishing smack called *The Cornucopia*. His destination Shivering Sands Army Fort, a disused Second World War fort nine miles off Herne Bay where he sets up his own pirate radio station.

I also come across a *Melody Maker* review of his 'Jack the Ripper' single from March 1963, another Joe Meek production.

'Nauseating trash – that's the only description we can apply to Screaming Lord Sutch's 'Jack the Ripper',' *MM* thunders. 'It's a sordid saga with all the horror squeals. Is this really music? No. It's undiluted tripe. We smashed the record after one play. And we hope you never have the misfortune to hear such dire rubbish!'

Chatham on a Saturday night has a grim, post-apocalyptic look about it. The streets are deserted, barely a light on anywhere. Where is everyone? Have I missed something on the news about mass evacuations from the Medway area after some kind of airborne toxic event, panic in the streets of Rochester and Strood? The Ash Tree looms into view. It's a large place. Cheerless, with peeling plaster walls, timbered beams, a few people who look like they might kill you if you knocked over their pint.

Sutch is in what passes for a dressing room, sitting in his shirt and underpants on a rickety plastic chair he seems to have mistaken for a throne, holding court here in his Y-fronts. There are pipes everywhere, a low ceiling, a puddle on the floor. Something sticky and black that looks like it's leaked out a corpse. Best avoided, whatever it is. Various band members are sitting around on beer crates with the glum look of people used to such dire circumstance. They seem like a small band of survivors of I'm not sure what. Huddled together in a bunker, a city above them being strafed, bombed and otherwise destroyed.

'Is there anything to eat?' one of them asks, not much hope in his voice.

'Only if you've brought a net and a trap,' Sutch tells him.

This prompts some groaning from the lads in the band.

'Buck up, boys,' Sutch tells them. 'At least it's not Butlin's.'

He notices me, finally, standing there.

'The man from *Melody Maker*?'

As promised.

'Oi, let him have your chair,' he tells one of his band, the one with the sullen look of a moody bass player. 'Take a pew.'

I pull up a chair, sit down. I start telling him about my afternoon going through the *MM* archive. The pile of press clippings with censorious comments about his early stage shows, the bison horns, the axes. Outrageous for the time, rock with a splash of horror, fully a decade before Alice Cooper.

'I was the first one who done all that,' he says, lighting up at the memory. 'I was the first one ever to mix horror and rock'n'roll. I was the first one with long hair. That was what got me all my first publicity. I had hair 18 inches long. No one had seen anything like it. I used to play colleges and universities when all the students had bloody crew cuts. I was an absolute freak to them.'

Taking not so much a stroll as a full gallop down memory lane, Sutch recalls the days when The Rolling Stones used to support him. He was the star then, earning as much as £50 a week. The Stones were barely scraping by. Pianist Nicky Hopkins came to the Stones' attention playing for The Savages, his backing band. As did his drummer, Carlo Little. The Stones were keen on Carlo and asked him to join them, an invitation he turned down.

'Said he couldn't see them making it,' Sutch laughs. 'Thought they weren't that good. When they did make it, his hair fell out. Went completely bald. He put it down to stress and regret. Strange, hey? Still, that's the way it goes.'

We talk a bit about his political career, all those election campaigns. Had he just been taking the piss?

'I was perfectly serious,' he says. 'Totally serious. Even if everybody did fall on the floor laughing at me. Even stood against bloody Wilson to prove me point. It was an expensive business. But I put my money on the line because of my beliefs. And some of the things I stood for – the right to vote at 18, commercial radio – they eventually became government policies. When I stood against Harold Wilson, when he was prime minister, whenever he had a meeting, we'd follow the next night. Same hall, same crowd. They'd come along just to heckle me.

'It was great,' he says. 'I loved it. They'd shout and bawl. Like a live show, a gig, it was. I'd end up singing 'em a song and they'd all join in. Didn't vote for me, though.'

Showtime beckons, time for him to get into his stage duds. There's a top hat and a cape hanging from a hook on the wall behind him. Stage props, too; including a sword, a couple of knives, an axe. I get up to go.

'Come back after and have a drink,' he says.

I leave him to put on his trousers.

Not long after, The Savages come on stage. They plug in, tap microphones, turn up amps. The drummer goes boom-boom on his bass drum. The crowd make a few enthusiastic noises, but no one seems to be expecting much. The group take a sort of collective deep breath, a here-we-go-again fatalism about them. You wonder at what point headlining Shea Stadium stopped being part of their career dreams. On the other hand, tonight may be a big gig for them, a Woodstock on their date sheet. Whatever, they press on. Lead guitarist Neil Besmoori counts to four and they're off into a rowdy 'Roll Over Beethoven', followed by an impatient, rushed 'I Saw Her Standing There'.

'What key are we in?' the sax player asks before a raucous 'Tutti Frutti', the group starting without him but getting a few cheers from the beery crowd anyway.

The Savages start playing 'The Funeral March'. It's obviously meant to set an appropriate mood for Sutch's appearance. Sinister? Gloomy? I'm not sure. There's no immediate sign of His Lordship, though. The band play on. And on. Where is he? Half of fucking Chatham could have been buried by now. The crowd are getting restless. Have they been stood up?

But what's this? There's a commotion behind us. Some pushing and barging, the crowd making way for four burly men carrying a metal coffin. Lord Sutch is in the house! Or the coffin, anyway, I presume. The recently press-ganged pallbearers make their way through the crowd to the stage, onto which they sort of heave the coffin, like they're throwing a body off a bridge or the deck of a ship.

It lands, more or less upright, with a bang a rapper could sample as a gunshot. But there's a bit of bob and sway, likely worrying for anyone inside, before the thing settles. The lid appears to be facing the audience, but I'm not sure if the coffin's the right way up. If Sutch is indeed inside, he could be upside down, standing on his head, his blood rushing fast enough in that direction to bring on an aneurysm or at least a nasty nosebleed.

The coffin stands there, the band staring at it as it might start tap dancing or juggling cats. They're obviously waiting for something to happen. Anything at this point will do. There's a longish pause, muffled noises from within the casket. Then a squall of feedback that makes everyone jump, followed by a piercing shriek, something feral with its head upturned to the moon and howling. Neil Besmoori hits another riff and the agonised screams from the coffin take on human form and what we can hear now is this: 'I CAN HEAR YA KNOCKIN' ON MY COFFIN LID!'

Surely Sutch will now burst from the coffin like one of the vampiric dead. Instead, the coffin starts rocking violently, looks for a moment like it might topple, a struggle evidently going on inside. Now there's an enormous amount of kicking and thumping, someone putting their shoulder to a locked door. Then the coffin lid flies open, like the door to a storm cellar ripped off by a tornado, everyone inside whisked off to somewhere that isn't Kansas anymore. Sutch falls out, draped in a gold lamé cape that trips him up, nearly catapulting him into the crowd. He steadies himself, clearly a bit winded after kicking his way out of the coffin. At least he's out of the fucking thing, which means the set is at last underway.

What follows is more puppet show than theatrical spectacle, but it has its moments. A flaming brazier is wheeled on for 'Great Balls of Fire', the smoke pouring from it making the band cough and at one point obscuring Sutch completely. The blaze in the brazier looks worryingly like it might get out of control. You could roast a bear over the flames coming from the thing. Sutch runs off stage, reappears with a watering can, which he wields suggestively over the fire and then pretends to be pissing on the flames.

'This is a true story about a sex maniac,' Sutch shouts at the crowd, introducing 'Jack the Ripper', the song that so many years ago offended *Melody Maker*, which will climax tonight's show. 'Are there any sex maniacs here tonight?'

'Yeeeaaah!'

Sutch is now sporting a top hat and black cape. He's prowling the stage, trying to look as menacing as Jack the Ripper, scowling at the crowd with eyes for some reason crossed. Which makes him look more the village idiot than the Whitechapel butcher of Ripper legend. Anyway, he's now telling us that he's looking for Mary Kelly, his next victim. Mary Kelly's played by Sutch's wife, saucily decked out in hot pants and a see-through blouse. That's her on stage now with her legs in the air being disembowelled by Jack. Sutch stands over her with an enormous knife – his 'chopper', as he inevitably calls it – and then hacks away at the hapless Mary Kelly with murderous gusto.

I'd had a quick chat with Mrs S. on my way out of the dressing room, before the show. She'd mentioned her part in the act, how she was nightly carved up. Sutch apparently has been known to get carried away at this point, his stabbing and hacking taking on a dangerous frenzy.

'Thank God the knife's blunt,' she said. 'I don't get cut or stabbed. But I've been left more than once with some nasty bruising.'

Anyway, with Mary Kelly duly dispatched, Sutch now waits for the arrival of the police, over whom he will once more assert his evil superiority by making a daring escape. Something like that, anyway.

'Even the police didn't catch Jack the Ripper,' Sutch announces, clearly expecting the boys in blue to turn up on cue and give chase to him.

There's no immediate sign of the law.

'Even the police didn't catch Jack the Ripper,' Sutch announces for a second time.

There's still no sign of the constabulary.

'Even the police ...' he begins again. 'I SAID ... even THE POLICE didn't catch Jack the Ripper!'

Sutch stands there, like someone waiting for a bus or the end of the world, whichever comes first.

'Not even SHERLOCK HOLMES caught Jack the Ripper,' he adds, rather desperately, to no response from the wings.

Finally, one of the Savages appears, still buttoning up his tunic, helmet on backwards. He and Sutch proceed to duel. First with rapiers that look like they've been made out of coat hangers and then with large wooden broadswords that they just sort of wave at each other, like paddles. Sutch is now in possession of a very large axe. He chases the policeman behind a curtain. Sutch reappears, brandishing a flaming torch, clearly not giving a fuck about any health and safety regulations that might come into play here, or perhaps merely determined to burn the place down.

He starts waving the torch around with some abandon, like he's just caught sight on the horizon of the Spanish Armada and is sending a warning to England. He swings it above his head like a fiery lasso. He's clearly forgotten how small the stage is. The band back off quickly to a safe distance, a couple of them ducking beneath the flailing torch. Neil Besmoori's a bit slow to react. Sutch catches him with the torch on the side of the head, setting fire to his hair.

Lesser men would have panicked, run screaming from the stage, looking for a bucket of water to plunge their smouldering head into. Besmoori smothers his flaming hair with a towel and carries on like nothing's happened. After all, it wasn't as bad, as he tells me later, as the night Sutch set fire to the bass player's trousers. That was nearly a job for the fire brigade.

Back in the dressing room after the show, Sutch is as pumped as if he's just walked off the stage of the Hollywood Bowl. He's already out of his trousers. The band are packing their gear, in a hurry to be gone. Besmoori says he'll give me a lift back to London, if I'm going that way. I'm probably going to have to listen to his fucking life story on the way back, but I think I've missed the last train. So, OK.

Sutch is towelling himself down, looking damp and a bit worn. By now, he's been doing the same act for nearly 15 years. How much longer can he go on?

He doesn't really have to even think about his answer.

'Forever,' he says. Which turns out to be not quite true, although I'm sure at the time he believes it.

LITTLE FEAT

London, June 1976

Little Feat are due back in London to re-join the Who Put The Boot In tour, after two weeks in Europe during a break between the opening date of The Who tour at Charlton football ground and tomorrow's show in Swansea.

I'm supposed to meet them at 10.30 am on a Friday morning at the Montcalm, the swanky hotel in Marble Arch much favoured in those days by anyone signed to Warner Bros. There's no sign of them when I get there, although they were meant to be catching an early flight from Amsterdam. Eventually, someone from Warners turns up with the news that Little Feat are as we speak being held at Heathrow. The band are in custody and their impounded equipment's being searched for drugs, flight cases and amps and the like being stripped, much like the group themselves, and thoroughly frisked. He has no idea how long they'll be held, but says if I want to wait, he'll book me a room. There's a well-stocked mini bar and food on room service if I want it.

I could, of course, go back to the *Melody Maker* office, where work is waiting for me. Alternatively, I could, you know, stay here and have a few drinks, some nibbles and maybe a nap. I decide to stay and wait, trying not to take undue advantage of the record company's generosity, an intention that fails miserably, the stock of the mini bar much diminished by mid-afternoon, Little Feat still at that point being grilled at the airport.

It's late afternoon when they finally show up, in remarkably good humour and full of apologies for the long wait I've endured with what I hope seems impressive professional stoicism. Anyway, I'm here to interview them individually for a regular *Melody Maker* feature called Band Breakdown. To which end, they troop one by one into my room. Bassist Ken Gradney's first, followed by percussionist Sam Clayton, both veterans of Delaney & Bonnie. Next up is keyboardist Bill Payne, who formed Little Feat in 1970 with guitarist Lowell George and drummer Richie Hayward, their ambition, as he puts it, to sound like 'a tougher version of The Band'. Bill's very funny about Little Feat's early days, playing occasional gigs at strip clubs and generally being so poor he ended up sleeping on the beach.

The poverty that's dogged the band ever since is something that subsequently preoccupies somewhat surly guitarist Paul Barrere, who joined them in 1972. He'd been working up to that point as a waiter – 'make that a servant' – at a musicians' hangout called The Black Rabbit Inn while playing part time with a group called Led Enema. 'For the next year and a half,' he says curtly, 'I made less money with Little Feat than I did as an out-of-work musician and waiter.'

I don't really hit it off with Barrere who in a simmering hint of escalating tensions to come grumpily spends most of the interview complaining that Lowell gets too much credit for the band's music, which the moody Barrere clearly resents. I get on like a dream, though, with flamboyantly moustachioed drummer Richie Hayward, who's sharp, funny and has great drugs. 'We sent everything ahead of us,' he says, explaining why nothing came of the airport bust. 'It was all waiting for us when we arrived. Have some more,' he says, busy cutting up lines as long as a baby's arm.

He starts off by telling me about The Factory, the band he played in with Lowell before Little Feat. 'It was electric miasma music,' he says. 'We had a song called "Car Crash", which was an instrumental that sounded like every violated water buffalo in the world plugged into a Marshall amp.'

He then remembers The Fraternity of Man, whose line-up also included Lowell. 'I spent most of my time bailing them out of jail, where they were paying for their enjoyment of nefarious pharmaceutical pursuits and behaviour sub-standard to the ethic of The Daughters of the American Revolution. The music was revolutionary. An incitement to riot. Anti-police state and pro-pharmacology. Inane, really.'

Not long after The Fraternity of Man split, Richie formed Little Feat with Lowell, who'd just left Frank Zappa's Mothers of Invention, Bill

Payne and former Mothers' bassist Roy Estrada, who eventually quit to join Captain Beefheart's Magic Band. 'Beefheart offered Roy $350 a month,' Richie recalls. 'Which was exactly $350 a month more than Little Feat, collectively, were earning. Man, we were poor.'

We suddenly realise we've been jabbering wide-eyed for hours and I still need to speak to Lowell. We go to his room, knock on the door. There's no reply. Richie suggests I meet the band the next day in Swansea, where I can interview Lowell. The next day I spend a lot of time in Little Feat's trailer, drinking beer, smoking this and snorting that. I have a grand time, thanks for asking. But I still don't manage to get Lowell in front of a tape recorder. It's agreed with someone that I'll meet with Lowell at the soundcheck for Little Feat's show on Monday at the Hammersmith Odeon, which is a gas in itself. But Lowell disappears as soon as the soundcheck's done. I don't see him again before the gig, which turns out to be mind-blowing.

There's an after-show party for the band, though, at the Zanzibar, a swish cocktail bar in Covent Garden, at which Lowell is finally cornered. We find a table and against much background rowdiness from the partying mob have to shout to make ourselves heard to each other. Lowell's constantly distracted by a stream of well-wishers and other people he doesn't know, some of them offering him this, others that. A pretty waitress who catches Lowell's eye brings us round after round of exotic drinks, which we knock back like sailors on shore leave.

Lowell's already kind of what you might call out of it, although not as far gone as he looks like he might get. Whatever, for the next 45 minutes, he's great company. There are colourful anecdotes about his time with Zappa, The Factory, Sky Saxon and The Seeds, The Standells, The Fraternity of Man, Stephen Stills, Peter Tork, Jimi Hendrix and, of course, Little Feat.

'We're like a Jackson Pollock painting,' he says. 'You know the way a Pollock painting is never really "finished"? Pollock painted until he came to the edge of the canvas, that's when he had to stop. He then had a painting. When we're recording, we have a deadline to finish by, usually imposed by the record company. When we hit that deadline, we stop recording. It's the edge of our canvas. That's when we have a new album.'

33

Around now, he's finally dragged away into the seething crowd and the flashing lights, the pulsing maw of the teeming Zanzibar.

The next time I see him is also the last. It's June 1979 and I'm in New York with The Damned. The horrid little miscreants have just played a show at Hurrah's that ends with the band at war with the crowd who seem only to be there to jeer them for not being The Sex Pistols.

'You want anarchy?' Rat Scabies shouts at them, a drumstick stuck up one nostril, spraying muck from the other at the audience. 'You're fucking well going to get it.'

Captain Sensible, stripped down to his underpants, has by now swapped places with Rat and starts banging on Rat's drums. Rat plays the riff from 'Whole Lotta Love' on the Captain's guitar, which was probably last in tune when he bought it. Dave Vanian then reappears, as if out of nowhere, like he's just dropped down from the rafters. At which point they play 'Pretty Vacant'. Someone rushes the stage to wrestle with Rat, who smashes him over the head with what's left of his drum kit, most of which Sensible has already thrown into the crowd, followed by an amplifier that shatters one of the club's wall-to-ceiling mirrors. A rather lively evening, all told.

Hours later, me and the Captain are in a lift at the Gramercy Park Hotel, where the band are staying. Sensible is by now wearing a fluorescent pink rabbit suit complete with ears and both of us are screeching with laughter at something or other. The lift stops at the second floor. The doors open. I look up, still shrieking with laughter, and there's Lowell George, in town for the start of his first solo tour after leaving Little Feat.

Lowell steps into the lift, looks disbelievingly at Sensible. Before I have a chance to say anything to him, he backs out of the lift, looking baffled, possibly worried that he's having some kind of alarming psychedelic episode, every acid trip he ever took coming back to terrify him.

Two days later, Lowell dies of a heart attack in Washington, another good man gone. As he boogies up to the Pearly Gates, I hope a man dressed as a rabbit, swearing his head off in a lift in New York at five in the morning isn't the last thing he remembers from the life he's just left.

LOUDON WAINWRIGHT III

London, November 1976

Lunch with Loudon Wainwright III turns out to be long and hilarious, with a lot more drinking than eating, which seems to be the way he likes it. At one point, between courses and our third or fourth bottle of wine, we end up talking about the opening track of his debut album. The one with the photo on the cover of him standing against a wall, hands in the pockets of a baggy black suit, his hair severely cropped, looking like a Depression-era bank robber; a young man doomed to die in what for self-evident reasons is known as a hail of bullets.

The song's called 'School Days', and in it he returns angrily to unhappy times. '*In Delaware, when I was younger, I would live the life obscene,*' he sings in a keening voice, something close to a caterwaul. '*In the spring I had great hunger, I was Brando, I was Dean.*'

'It was the fulfilment of an adolescent fantasy,' Loudon says of the song, wondering where the waiter is with the next bottle of wine. 'My parents decided I should be educated at a private school. They delivered me to an Episcopalian boarding school in Middletown, Delaware. It was called St Andrews.

'Nothing ever happens in Delaware,' he goes on. 'Nothing. At the age of 16, I was deposited there and completely isolated. At 16, all you really want to do, let's be honest, is get laid. It's all you think about. People at 16 were probably getting laid everywhere, except of course in Delaware. I resented being at that school and used to have this fantasy of driving up to it on a motorcycle and screaming, "FUCK YOU, ASSHOLES!" That was my big fantasy, what I thought about when I wasn't thinking about getting laid.'

Loudon's just released *T Shirt*, his sixth album in six years. It's out now on Arista, his third record company to date in a career that was launched with comparisons to Bob Dylan, Loudon one of a slew of singer-songwriters in the early 1970s routinely heralded as something called the 'New Dylan'.

'I'm certainly not being called the "New Bob Dylan" now,' he says, ruefully acknowledging a general lack of album sales, despite the kind of reviews you'd want to frame if you were so inclined. 'I'm not even being called the "OLD Bob Dylan" these days.'

He reaches for his glass, evidently wondering where what a moment ago was in it has gone. Time for another bottle.

'That was a whole double-edged situation, that New Dylan thing,' he says. 'It was a compliment because I think Bob Dylan was, is and probably always will be great. But I don't think the comparison was ever particularly apt. I was never really the voice-of-a-generation type.'

He briefly wanted to be an actor. After escaping boarding school, he studied drama for 18 months in Pittsburgh, before dropping out and moving to San Francisco. He spent the Summer of Love there, getting stoned and tripping to the Dead in Golden Gate Park.

'From a hedonistic point of view, San Francisco in 1967 was the greatest,' he says, almost glowing at whatever memories he has of that briefly sunny time. 'But I was never really cut out to be a hippie. And in 1968, I was put off the idea completely. I was arrested in Oklahoma City for possession of marijuana. I was incarcerated for five days in a horrible prison. They really wanted to lock me up and throw away the key. I thought they would. But my father was working for *Life* magazine at the time and was kind of well known in the States. They found out at the prison and said, "Ah! We got ourselves the son of some hot-shit Yankee journalist here." I thought they were planning to ransom me. Anyway, my father flew to Oklahoma to bail me out. The thing was,' he says with a little grimace, the memory giving him an uncomfortable pinch, 'my father was working in London at the time. He had quite a flight. When they let me out, we had a, let's call it a talk. After that, I didn't want to be a hippie anymore.'

He eventually fetched up in Greenwich Village, playing the folk clubs where Dylan and so many others had started out. Among them,

Phil Ochs, a stalwart of the protest movement and radical activist, now fallen on hard, entirely terrible times. In April 1976, his career in ruins, Ochs hung himself at his sister's apartment in Queen's, New York.

'I understood totally why Phil killed himself,' Loudon says. 'He was so absolutely miserable. It was hell for him. His life had become intolerable. It's not my place to cite the reasons for his death. Things were probably happening to him that no one was aware of. But as an observer, from the point of view of someone who knew him in the last years of his life, he was one of the most fucked-up people I've known.

'I never knew him when he was successful, but in those last years he was a terrible alcoholic. I mean, you would have classified him as a wino. He would drink the cheapest rot-gut booze, like some Bowery bum. He was also hung up about his work as a songwriter. He hadn't written a song in years. His inspiration had dried up.

'On appearances, they were the reasons. He may have had a lot of other problems. But I know he was miserable about those two things. His drinking and not being able to write. I was in Atlanta when he killed himself. A friend of mine called from New York to tell me. I wasn't surprised. For Phil, by then, he was so far down that to get out of the hole he'd dug for himself would have taken a gigantic effort that was beyond him, really. His only escape was suicide.'

Our glasses are empty again. Where's that waiter?

'When I was younger, suicide seemed a very romantic thing to do,' Loudon says, almost snatching the bottle off the waiter when he appears and pouring wine into our glasses like he's trying to put out small fires at the bottom of them. 'Unless,' he adds, a cautionary note here, 'you blow your head off. In which case, it's just messy.

'As I've grown older it's no longer something I've entertained. I certainly don't see it as a way to a better world. It's not something I really think about. In fact, I try to think about The Void – if you'll excuse the expression – as little as possible. We don't know what the fuck is going to happen after we go. If we did know what was going to happen and were generally happy with it, maybe a lot more people would be killing themselves. Or maybe there'd be less, if we knew that what happens next isn't going to be that cute.

'Who knows? It's going to be great, or nothing or hell. We don't know. It may be really horrible when we die. In those circumstances,' he says, 'I'll settle for living a little longer without knowing, thanks.

'I mean, what comes next could turn out to be even worse than fucking Delaware.'

Peter Gabriel

London, February 1977

In September 1975, *Melody Maker* prints a letter from Peter Gabriel, addressed to his fans. He's got bad news for them. He's leaving Genesis, the prog rock heavyweights he's fronted for nigh on a decade.

'I had,' he writes, clearly disenchanted, 'begun to think in business terms: very useful for an often bitten, once shy musician, but treating records and audiences as money was taking me away from them.'

A pall falls upon the land, a prevailing gloom. There are soon reports, possibly exaggerated, of distraught fans reacting to the news by throwing themselves on funeral pyres, their burning howls heard from Kent to Kirkcaldy, Wick to Weymouth. I feel, however, much distanced from their caterwauling anguish, their flagellating woe. I mean, Gabriel's quit Genesis? I'm supposed to give a fuck?

Genesis, after all, loom large in my possibly unreasonable lexicon of prejudice, if only because they remind me less of a rock band than the bell-bottomed equivalent of the school chess team on an outing to an owl sanctuary. Oh, and one of them – Mike Rutherford, I think – has a face like the risen Christ after three days of post-crucifixion recuperation with his head in a trouser press. You imagine them cracking jokes in Latin on breaks from recording toe-tapping tracks for albums like *Foxtrot* and *Selling England by the Pound*, letting off steam by running around, slapping each other on the bum with slippers. Pillow fights in the dorm seem always a mere heartbeat away. As for their music, I'd rather listen to bagpipes.

Gabriel ends his letter on an ambiguous note, hardly reassuring to fans hoping that whatever he does next will sound as much as possible like everything he's done so far with Genesis.

'My future within music, if it exists, will be in as many situations as possible,' he writes, specifying none of them. For the moment, he was retiring, to reassess his creative options, many recently thwarted by popularity, fame, success. He was looking forward to rediscovering 'the hidden delights of vegetable growing', apparently a reference to a much-loved cabbage patch at his country pile, just outside Bath. There was some guff about exploring audio-visual presentations, virtual theatrics. A mention, too, of something called the Cosmic Cadet Force, although it's not clear if this is something he's organising or joining and, anyway, sounds like something best avoided.

A year of apparent inactivity quickly follows. Then, early in 1976, word gets out that Gabriel's recording a solo album. It's being produced, to the surprise of many, by Bob Ezrin, who has Lou Reed's *Berlin* on his CV but is best known for producing monster hits for Alice Cooper and Kiss. Another 12 months on and the record's about to come out, and *Melody Maker*'s been offered an exclusive interview with Gabriel to attend its release. News of the scoop is gleefully announced at an *MM* editorial meeting by violently cologned editor Ray Coleman, Ray this morning wearing a suit-shirt-and-tie combo of such unnerving fluorescence it makes you think he must moonlight at least a couple of nights a week as a Times Square pimp.

Ray is just as excited about the pictures we've been given to run with the forthcoming Gabriel interview, commissioned by Gabriel and taken by the celebrated Terry O'Neill. Lank-haired production editor Mike Oldfield now spreads them on the table. They're close-ups of Gabriel, his head submerged in bath water, bubbles floating past his face, pretty arty. The problem as far as I can see is that the parts of the pictures that aren't grey are deep black. I can't wait to see how visually incomprehensible they're rendered after being run through the creaking wheels of the apparently ancient press that weekly prints copies of *MM* so over-inked that reading them leaves you looking like you've just finished a shift at a Rhondda colliery. None more fucking black, and all that. Oh, well. When the cover's got Gabriel's name on it in one of *MM*'s more declamatory fonts perhaps one or two of his family will recognise who it is. Everyone else will probably wonder why we've put a screen grab from a hostage video on the fucking cover.

Still, we've got our scoop. Ray and weirdly coiffured assistant editor Mick Watts are happy. Tuning back into the room, they appear to have moved on from Terry O'Neill's pictures of Gabriel and are now apparently discussing who's going to interview the returning former Genesis frontman. This is a surprise. Surely, eternally genial *MM* features editor Chris Welch is a shoo-in for the gig. He's such a champion of prog rock, it's a wonder he doesn't turn up for work in a chariot, sporting a cape and a wizard's hat, preceded into the office by mushroom clouds of dry ice and a laser show. He's been writing about Gabriel and Genesis for years, the journalistic equivalent of one of the band's faithful retainers.

Which is a problem, it turns out, for Gabriel, who's keen to present himself anew, distance himself from who he was. To which end, he'd rather not be interviewed by an old ally, a familiar face, someone predictably on-side. He apparently thinks a comeback interview will be livelier with someone he doesn't know, who may not even be a fan. My name's come up, apparently. Ray and Mick don't look especially thrilled by this as a condition of getting the interview and Chis looks rather bemused, like a man getting home to find his house has been stolen, the whole thing, including the garden shed.

I start to splutter, a man drowning in his own bath water, clinging to a loofah like a lifebelt. My opinion of Genesis is barely a secret. Prog rock, that entire musical sinkhole, just isn't my bag. Made furious by something flippant I'd written about his Genesis spin-off band, Brand X, Phil Collins in a recent interview with Chris Welch has deplored my lack of manners, general rudeness and grubby opinions. Mine apparently a yobbish voice among *MM*'s usually deferential chorus line. Effectively lobbying for my immediate dismissal, he's somehow restrained himself from simultaneously calling for a public flogging. If Gabriel's anything like his former bandmate, one of us is likely to end up going through a fucking window before the interview's anywhere near over.

It's useless, of course. I've been around long enough by now to know I'm not getting out of this. I glumly receive from Ray a test-pressing of Gabriel's album; handed the thing, in fact, like it's the bone of a saint, a revered femur, tibia or sacred metatarsal. I expect to hate it, but don't. In fact, I like a lot of it. As I'm now telling someone called Peter Thompson, who I take at first to be Gabriel's butler but

turns out to be his publicist. He arranges my meeting with Gabriel
with the solemnity of someone selling a funeral plan. Apparently, I'm
to be at Thompson's West End office at 7.30 pm the following evening, which means I'll be lucky to be finished with Gabriel before the
pubs close. I feel suitably sacrificial.

And so here I am, sitting in an office with a small conference table,
some unremarkable furniture, sombre lighting. Gabriel's late for the
interview. I haven't seen Peter Thompson since I got here, about half
an hour ago. I don't mind being stood up. I'm just hoping that when
Gabriel arrives, he's not dressed like a fucking sunflower or wearing
a fox's head.

The door opens. Peter Thompson walks into the room, his manner
solemn, almost tremblingly reverential.

He extends an arm, the hand at the end of it making a come-hither
sign to whoever's lurking out of my sight in the doorway.

'Peter Gabriel,' Thompson announces, like he's presenting royalty,
possibly fighting an impulse to bend a knee or curtsy.

Gabriel makes his entrance, thankfully without overture or fanfare.
He walks past Peter Thompson, who retires from the room, closing
the door behind him. Gabriel's head is slightly bowed. Low enough,
at least, to end up looking at me through a fringe of hair. The eyes
behind the fringe are clear and sharp. You might call them penetrating.

I'd vaguely expected someone possibly in a catsuit. A cape, at least.
A hint in his costume of woodland folk, or mummery, his appearance
preceded by the tinkling of finger cymbals, the scent of joss sticks and
patchouli. He's decked out, however, in what looks suspiciously like
the staff-room drag of a woodwork teacher in an inner-city compre-
hensive. A woolly jumper, a plaid shirt under that, jeans. There's probably a jacket hanging somewhere with leather patches on its elbows.
He has an air about him of corduroy and pipe smoke. He sits down
at the table before I have a chance to check if he's wearing brogues.
It's too cold for sandals, surely. I take the chair opposite him. He leans
forward, shoulders hunched, elbows on the table, as if he's guarding
a plate of prison chow amid the roaring noise of a San Quentin mess
hall, warders rattling bars with batons, screams from a shivving in a
shower stall: all that hoodlum hum.

'Can I say something?'

I was rather hoping you would.

'About the new record, before we start.'

Go ahead.

He stares at me. Through me. At the wall behind me. He doesn't say anything for long enough for me to think I'm going to miss the last bus home as well as last call in the pub. Some days nothing goes your way.

'I just wanted to say,' he says finally, a plummily accented voice with a slightly broody undertow, a hint of Heathcliff in an Eton boater, something like that. 'The new album, I think it's simpler, more direct emotionally, more personal than much of what I've done previously, and I think it takes itself less seriously ...'

He pauses, leans sideways in his chair at such an angle he resembles a dog looking out of a car window.

'Why are you laughing?' he asks, sitting upright, abruptly noticing that I'm grinning like a cat with a bird in its mouth.

Perhaps because of the airy manner with which he's just dismissed everything he did with Genesis. I wonder what his fans will make of that. I can hear wood being piled. Flames beginning to crackle.

'But that's not what I said!' he says, the shocked reaction of a man who's just been told his wife's run off with a flamenco dancer. 'That's not what I meant, at all.'

Sounded like it.

'Well, it wasn't.'

It's not me he's got to convince. It's the fans who tearfully accepted him leaving Genesis to try out new things who are now being told he left because he didn't like playing with them and thought they were rubbish.

'That's just not the case,' he insists. 'Really,' he goes on, 'my problems weren't so much with the band as what happened to us. The success we had so badly wanted when we were beginning was, in the end, a trap. Once we'd achieved that massive popularity, we couldn't develop with any freedom. There were so many people involved and so much money involved in the band that it seemed a risk to change anything. Everything was geared to preserve us as we were. I wanted and needed to change.'

Basically, out of some politeness he'd like to maintain the fiction that his parting with Genesis was perfectly amicable, not the result of falling out with them. That he left the band on good terms, with a handshake and a pat on the back. A farmer's son going into the world looking for adventure and the promise of letters home from exotic postcodes. A weeping Steve Hackett seeing him off with the hem of a pinny held to trembling lips. I don't believe a word of it.

How desperate were you to leave Genesis?

'I wasn't desperate at all,' he says. 'I was very happy in Genesis.'

So happy, in fact, you left.

'Yes, well …' he says, not quite floundering, but clearly wishing we were talking about something else.

I mean, why persist with the nonsense that he'd left Genesis on a whim, to satisfy a passing fancy to make a record with people who hadn't played on *The Lamb Lies Down on Broadway*? There must have been a deeper dissatisfaction. I wonder how many times he'd found himself at loggerheads with the rest of the band before he finally quit. How many ideas did he have to compromise or abandon because the rest of the band simply didn't dig them, thought they were too far out?

You imagine Mike Rutherford's Christ-like chops bristling at one far-out Gabriel notion too many. Disparaging tutting from the rhythm section. All of them keen to get back to work on some fiddly bollocks they've been cooking up like swots in a chemistry class. According to Gabriel, the majority opinion prevailed in Genesis in every circumstance. Increasingly a minority of one, Gabriel must often have been overruled, his ideas sidelined if not entirely jettisoned. Wasn't this the case?

He takes a moment to think about what he's going to say next and then just says it.

'There were ways to, let's say, manipulate the democratic machinery that existed in Genesis and there were certain things I was able to say in different songs. But it was always,' he admits, 'a struggle. I'd have to drop in an idea and let someone pick it up and develop it and hope I'd have a chance to revise it later. There were all sorts of games that went on. Very silly, unnecessary games. And because I used to get all the publicity, there was a lot of resentment and jealousy, which didn't make things any easier.'

This is a bit of a surprise. With their O levels and Boy Scout proficiency badges, you'd have expected Genesis to be a bit too bright, wised-up and otherwise above such petty frictions, claw-your-eyes-out envy, hissy fits and sundry tantrums. Tony Banks threatening to hold his breath until he bursts after not being mentioned in a review concentrating more on Gabriel's onstage antics and theatrical get-ups. The fox's head, a cape with bat wings, fluorescent make-up, all that.

'They are, basically, intelligent people,' Gabriel says. 'But that doesn't mean they were above certain kinds of pettiness. When I was credited in the papers with something they'd written, they'd get upset. Sometimes,' he says, and seems to be wincing at the memory of one row or another, 'they'd get very upset. It's a fundamental human reaction,' he goes on, a sage old yogi. 'It had an effect on the group. It did cause some friction. Especially towards the end. By the time I told them I was leaving, we were no longer quite the friends we had been.'

Had it come to the point where for commercial reasons they didn't want him to go, but at the same time couldn't wait to see the back of him?

'That may well have been the case,' he says, looking uncomfortable, a quisling slump to his shoulders. 'Let's just say it didn't end well,' he says, head down, wringing his hands in his lap like a schoolboy in a headmaster's study, about to face the music. Miserable in his contrition, even if he's unsure what he's feeling so guilty about.

It seems time to move on and when we do, his sigh of what I take to be relief sounds like the universe deflating. As soon as we start talking about the new album, he seems all at once brighter, rather more bounce now in his conversational step. So much so, in fact, he quickly assumes the toothy enthusiasm of a children's TV presenter, someone with a sheepdog and a flair for the recycling of sticky back plastic. He's already telling me how liberated he felt, in the studio, with new people and no sign of his former bandmates and their attendant insecurities. But we're getting ahead of ourselves. How did Bob Ezrin end up producing the record?

'There was a list,' Gabriel says. 'His name was on it. I knew a lot of people wanted to work with him. The Stones, Bryan Ferry, Bowie. He came in for a meeting.'

Which presumably went well, since he got the gig.

'Not exactly,' Gabriel says, visibly wincing, shoulders hunched again, someone expecting a slap on the back of the head.

45

Go on, what happened?

'I felt I should tell him that I hadn't liked anything he'd previously produced.'

Diplomacy in action! How did Ezrin react?

'He just laughed. Told me not to worry, because he hadn't heard much by me that he liked. One or two of the people I'd previously spoken to had been positively fawning. I desperately needed to work with someone who wouldn't be afraid to stand up to me. I played Ezrin some of the things I'd been working on, and he suggested throwing them out because they were too complex. He was more interested in the emotion of the songs, the heart of them. He was right. I revised everything I'd written, took the better parts of some of the songs and simplified them. The album is better for that.'

Ezrin has a reputation as a studio tyrant, keen to be involved in everything, including the writing of the songs.

'Well, that was never going to happen,' Gabriel says, quite sharply. 'I wanted a producer, not a co-writer. I made that very clear.'

Ezrin turned up with his usual crew, including guitarists Steve Hunter and Dick Wagner, who'd played on Alice Cooper's solo albums and on Lou Reed's *Berlin* and *Rock 'n' Roll Animal*.

'They were quite a tough lot,' Gabriel says. 'I mean, these were guys who play on like 15 albums a year, or whatever. They turn up and if they like it, they play it, as they say. They're not there to analyse the music. They don't usually get too involved in the songs. They're there to do a job. But very quickly, I found, these guys were always around, coming up with ideas.'

Gabriel wanted at least one like-minded soul in the studio with him. A big fan, it turns out, of *(No Pussyfooting)*, the album Brian Eno made with King Crimson's Robert Fripp, Gabriel asked Fripp to also contribute to the album.

'He was there to support a friend, really,' Gabriel says. 'That was the original idea. A bit of moral support.'

How did the noted musical egghead fit in with Ezrin's musical mercenaries, that hard-assed outfit?

'Robert was perhaps used to, I don't know, a bit more dialogue in the studio,' he says, laughing at his own understatement. As I discover a couple of years later, Fripp's reputation as a theoretical windbag is not to be underestimated. No idea too trivial it can't be expounded

46

upon until the universe, reeling at Fripp's expositionary blather, simply collapses into itself, sucking all and sundry into murky oblivion. 'But as soon as we started recording, there was this great fat sound coming off the studio floor,' Gabriel goes on, like he's describing one of the minor miracles. 'No one could believe it, at first. I mean, Fripp and Hunter, the first time they played together, was quite unbelievable. Very strange. But very powerful.'

What seems to have surprised him most was how much fun the sessions were. He goes on about this at rhapsodic length, a conquistador back from the New World and keen that you hear all about it. This begs an obvious question. How fucking stuffy were Genesis recording sessions?

'Well,' he says, not even bothering to walk this one around the houses, just marching up to the front door and pushing through it, 'I don't want to give the impression that Genesis sessions were terribly formal. But one had to be very careful not to be too critical of someone's treasured little idea. The atmosphere in the studio was always very, I'd say, polite. Everything was taken rather less seriously on the new album. There was more spontaneity, more excitement. With Genesis, I can see now, the way the band approached its material was often at fault. Too often, they were more concerned with contrived chord sequences and tempo changes. The melodies and lyrics – which I was more concerned about – were always secondary. Much of the time, the arrangements were simply too busy. There was no spontaneity. At some point, we just stopped being exciting.'

The longer we talk, the more ways he seems to come up with of making me like him. A passing mention of Kurt Vonnegut sends him on a lengthy digression. He's read most of the books, digs what he's read. Much more of this and I'll be joining his fucking fan club. We chat a bit about a couple of tracks on the album, the Randy Newman-inspired 'Waiting for the Big One' and the doomy ballad 'Here Comes the Flood'. Both are about a looming apocalypse. Did he really think the end of the world was, as they say, nigh?

He seems to gather himself, as if wondering how best to reply. Then leans forward, shoulders hunched again. Something about his concentrated stare suggests he's about to muster up the beasts of Revelation, all those creatures with wings covered in eyes, a lamb with seven

47

horns, not to mention various archangels of the abyss and cats with machetes. I prepare myself for the worst.

'Not in an annihilating sense,' he says, finally.

This sounds vaguely reassuring, I suppose. I breathe a sigh of relief. No lakes of fire just yet.

'But I do think there will be changes,' he then adds, voice dropping to a frankly ominous whisper, such as you might hear just before heaven's trumpets bring down the stars and destruction and ruin become rife. I tell myself to get a grip, even as Gabriel proceeds to describe the future as he sees it taking shape. What follows isn't exactly QAnon in a kaftan and there's thankfully no reference to Jewish Space Lasers. But there's probably enough in what he has to say that would perk up a conspiracy theorist on a dull afternoon otherwise empty of omen, portent or sundry eschatological shout-outs.

There's much talk of 'vital new forces', potentially destructive; changes of consciousness, evolving states. The potential of the unleashed mind. A select few, the superior minds, will survive whatever turbulence lurks ahead. The people more finely tuned to the gusts of change, open to uncertified phenomena, alert to the messages only they and a few like them can hear. Adaptability will be key. For the rest of us, it's the usual slough of fucking despond and pitchforks up the arse.

'There are a lot of things happening,' he says, a swami glint in his lit-up eyes. 'In religion. In the fringe sciences. New ideas. New concepts that are beginning to change the way we live. The people who are more used to dealing with other states of perception will be better able to face and survive these changes. I'm sure there are certain powers that some of us possess, maybe all of us, but we haven't realised our potential for discovering and using them,'

What kind of powers are we talking about?

'Telepathy,' he says, and I wonder if I should have seen this coming. How are his own telepathic powers?

'Early days,' he says. 'I still have a lot of work to do,' he adds, a man flummoxed by the assembly instructions for a flatpack sofa bed. 'But I really believe we have these powers that we will eventually learn to use and then there'll be a new and better world.'

I feel lucky at this point that he hasn't tried to sell me a subscription to the Cosmic Cadet Force and move on.

Talk of idealism, collective opportunity and the chance to get weird takes us back to the bell-bottomed 1960s, early shows by Soft Machine and Pink Floyd affectionately recalled.

'I was still at school for part of that time,' he says. 'I'd sneak up to London, to the Electric Garden, or whatever it was called. I remember being really excited at the prospect of so many people from so many different backgrounds getting together and coming up with things which were, if nothing else, totally original.

'There was in those days such a positive atmosphere, generally an exciting approach to life. I think that's exactly what we need now. No one is fulfilling that obligation. This whole punk rock thing,' he says sniffily, sounding exactly like the reactionary old cunt I feared he'd be. 'That's certainly not fulfilling it. It's depressing. So many of these bands have been overexposed before they've had a chance to play their instruments with any competence.'

Here we go. The supposedly pioneering visionary casting a patrician's patronising glance at the grubby oiks making an impolite noise, whose immediate impulse is to somehow improve their manners. As if some etiquette involving the correct choreography of cutlery at dinner will somehow turn Johnny Moped into fucking Mozart. He has a further few thoughts on how to better the inferior soul, the paltry mind.

'I'm sure we'll come through these times, and we'll possibly emerge stronger and fitter and better,' he says, making me think of Leni Riefenstahl and trim young Aryans in gym shorts and jackboots. 'One of the things that would make us better and stronger, is, I think, adult education. A lot of people need to be taught how to rethink everything they know, because most people, they spend all their lives in one job, including people in bands, and their thinking narrows.'

Now it sounds like he's describing a kind of Maoist mass thought-reform programme. Was he really advocating sending musicians back to school?

'In a way, yes,' he says.

I hate to be pessimistic, but I couldn't easily see Rat Scabies or Captain Sensible rushing to join up.

'That's a shame,' he says, as burdened by disappointment as a Deliveroo rider with a meal for eight on his back. 'I very much like Buckminster Fuller's generalist approach.'

Who doesn't? But let's wrap this up.

Two years ago, Gabriel walked out on Genesis because they'd become too popular, and he found their success confining enough to reject it.

'It's an inevitable thing,' he says. 'Unavoidably, when you grow to that scale of popularity, you have to be realistic and appreciate that one is in a business of a kind. One is making a product to be marketed. And because of the number of people who become involved in the long-term planning of a successful band, it's very difficult to respond spontaneously to anything. There are few opportunities available to change direction or explore new ideas. Everything is too cumbersome. Too complex.'

He promises now that when he next tours, there'll be no costumes, elaborate staging, the kind of mummery and pantomime associated with Genesis.

'I'll live or die naked on stage,' he says, laughing. 'Although not literally,' he adds quickly. 'I'm not sure that would really be me.'

You wouldn't, you know, be tempted to let it all, as they used to say, hang out?

'Good Lord, no,' he says, an alarmed vicar invited to a swinger's party in a bawdy farce. 'I don't think so. That's not really my scene at all.'

My point, though, is that for all his talk about wanting to keep things in the future small scale, risky and adventurous, he's about to release an album whose almost inevitable success will make him popular all over again. What's he going to do then?

'It's possible, yes,' he says, 'that I'll end up in the same trap I've only just escaped from. If I do, I'll try to get out again. Only this time, now that I'm a solo artist, I guess I'll have to leave myself.'

He allows himself a small chuckle that suggests he knows he's given me a decent last line for the piece I'm going to write. The interview is over. I start packing my stuff.

'I've got a car downstairs,' he says. 'Can we drop you off anywhere?'

I check the time. 10.15 pm. There's a pub on the corner. A quick sprint from Peter Thompson's office will get me there in time for last orders.

I blow past Gabriel like someone running for a getaway car after robbing a bank, one of charismatic Dillinger's nimble boys, dapper in spats and a shoulder holster. Gabriel looks a bit startled at my sudden exit, raises a hand as if he might have something else to say, another point to make. Second thoughts, perhaps, about something he's said regarding Genesis. It's too late, though. I'm already gone.

If he's as telepathic as he thinks he is, he'll find a way to get in touch.

IAN ANDERSON

London, February 1977

What we have here is Jethro Tull overlord Ian Anderson, fairly lolling in an armchair, in what I'm tempted to call agricultural repose. Hands clasped behind his head, legs stretched out in front of him, feet on a low table; a farmer at rest in a kitchen lit by an oil lamp after a day's hard toil in a barley field or ploughing England's soil. There's a lot about him that suggests he may have arrived here in a wagon drawn by Shire horses, possibly stopping briefly on his way to be sketched by Constable.

I'm a little disappointed. When I turn up at the swish West End offices of Chrysalis, the label that's been putting out his music for nearly ten years, I'm rather hoping Anderson will be decked out in his usual stage clobber, the stuff he wears when he's fronting Jethro Tull. You know the look. Doublet and hose, tights, thigh-high boots, a codpiece, of course; codpieces, after all, being to Tull what epaulettes were to The Clash. He appears, however, to have entered his Country Squire period, presenting himself as a bucolic buck with Romany trappings – a brocade waistcoat, thick corduroy breeches, neckerchief, the kind of boots you'd wear for a good hike across intimidating moorland or an afternoon grouse shooting.

The cigarette holder is an unexpected touch. But you wonder if the scene wouldn't be more complete if he had a pair of Irish wolfhounds at his feet, a plucked pheasant on a platter within easy reach, a mug of mead in his hand and a wench on his knee. A Peggy, Meg or Moll, big hipped and bouncy, breasts like beach balls, a noisy handful after a firkin of ale. Behind him, on top of a TV, sits the sleeve for the new Tull album, *Songs from the Wood*, roughly the amped-up equivalent of the music they use for Maypole dancing. There's a bowler hat next to it and I know that if he puts it on, I'm going to laugh out loud.

'Are you in good cheer?' he asks, more than a little about his rip-snorting locution that puts me in mind of a knighted thespian declaiming something shouty by Shakespeare. He turns out to be loquacious to a fault, one florid sentence after another in the conversation that follows, all of them windy enough to blow a steeple over. He sounds like someone who's used to being listened to, and if not always understood at least obeyed. It's like he expects everything he says to be accompanied by the pealing of church bells across the land, the hoisting of bunting, street parties and marching bands. Whatever he goes on to say is actually accompanied instead by much beard-grooming and whisker-tugging. More than once, he twirls the ends of his moustache, a silent-movie villain nimbly tying a trembling heroine to a railroad track, ripe with sadistic relish.

'Will you sit?' he now wants to know.

Did he think I was going to fucking stand for as long as it takes to interview him? I sit myself down.

The walls of the room we're in are decorated with a lot of Tull memorabilia – posters, album sleeves, gold records. An early press shot of the original Tull line-up brings on a flashback.

It's August 1968. I'm with three school friends at the annual National Jazz & Blues Festival, held that year at Kempton Park racecourse in Sunbury-on-Thames, before moving in 1969 to the permanent site we are more familiar with in Reading. There are bands galore on the bill whose music we already love; familiar names from *Melody Maker* we've listened to and read about, but not yet seen. Among them, Traffic, The Nice, The Jeff Beck Group with Rod Stewart, Ten Years After, Tyrannosaurus Rex, Joe Cocker and The Grease Band, The Crazy World of Arthur Brown, Deep Purple, Jerry Lee Lewis, Taste. There's a Sunday afternoon folk concert, with Fairport Convention, one of their first shows with Sandy Denny, and headlined by The Incredible String Band. It's mind-blowing stuff for four 16-year-olds from South Wales, our first festival. A season ticket for the weekend is the equivalent of just £2.50. Talk about getting your fucking money's worth.

So far down the bill their name barely makes it onto the festival posters is a group almost wholly new to us, who make as much of an impression as any of the big hitters. They're called Jethro Tull, and they turn out to be a blast. They're still a ferocious blues band at the time, raw and exciting. Their eye-catching frontman is Anderson, a wild man then, in a ragged overcoat, waving a flute like a baton, an unkempt cheerleader. The crowd on the whole loves them and I like them well enough to get their debut album – *This Was* – as soon as it comes out. I stick with them through the two that follow, *Stand Up* and *Benefit*.

After that, and quickly, come the codpiece and the concept albums. *Aqualung*. *Thick as a Brick*, basically a single 43-minute track, split over the two sides of the album, a conceit they repeat on *A Passion Play*, the album that follows. These vast musical landmasses prove unaccountably popular, albums going platinum on pre-release sales alone. The more overblown the albums over the years become, the more popular the group seem bafflingly to get, especially in America. In the early 1970s, they're up there as a live draw with the Stones, Led Zeppelin and The Who.

Recent times have been a little more testing. Album sales aren't quite what they were. Even some of their former champions in the music press have turned on them. *A Passion Play* is so epically obtuse it even infuriates *Melody Maker*'s normally chummy Chris Welch. Someone who rarely has a bad word in any circumstance to say about anyone, Chris is moved to unexpectedly harsh words about it; a family pet suddenly baring its fangs. Add to this the fact that for the gobby punks now starting to grab the headlines, Anderson and his band are no more than a joke. No wonder that when I meet him, Anderson has a rattled, angry air about him.

We've barely started when he starts complaining about the current music scene. All those uncouth punk bands and their crude manners, lack of respect for their musical betters. As one of rock's most entitled elder statesmen, he's splutteringly outraged by the ragged-arsed and musically inarticulate. And what's become of the music press, he wants to know. Formerly so supportive, now cast in his opinion as mean-mouthed quislings, backstabbers, untrustworthy, treacherous?

I should have been expecting something like this. Anderson seems always to have thought Tull in many ways hard done by, never fully given their undoubted due, unfairly criticised when properly they should be celebrated, as adored by critics as prog rock headbangers in their millions. A bitter little song on 1974's *War Child* is said to have been prompted by a scathing review of a Tull show, written by *Sounds* journalist Steve Peacock, obliquely referred to in its lyrics.

More unpleasantly, at a concert in Los Angeles, he'd launched an apparently furious tirade against veteran *LA Times* music writer Robert Hilburn, provoked by an unflattering Hilburn review of a performance of *A Passion Play* at the Santa Monica Civic and evidently not forgotten. Hilburn has dared to criticise not only Anderson and Tull, but also their support band, Carmen, whose fusion of progressive rock and flamenco – yes, really; check out *Fandangos in Space*, their debut album – was clearly not to Hilburn's taste. Anderson was bracingly outraged.

'I must say, I hated the man's guts,' Anderson huffs. 'He'd been very nasty to a support group who'd toured with us once and shortly after – perhaps not as a direct result of his review – they disbanded. It was a group called Carmen.

'Hilburn said that their singer just banged a wooden pole on the ground whilst doing a tap dance,' he says, disbelieving still. 'He wasn't bloody tap dancing.'

What was he doing, then, if he wasn't tap dancing?

'What he was actually doing,' Anderson says, 'was a classical flamenco dance.'

An easy mistake to confuse one for the other, surely?

'Hardly!' Anderson harrumphs, glaring at me with a seadog's wild eye. 'It was something which he had perfected after years of training. It wasn't tap dancing. Nothing like it. And what he was doing deserved more than some smart remark which would imply to people who weren't at the concert that the man was a bloody idiot or a moron doing a tap dance. I thought it was an unforgivable thing to say. He was simply being cruel, which critics often are, usually for no good reason.

'He should have known better, and he didn't, which is also something I find typical of his kind. I merely took him publicly to task for it,' he goes on, sounding like Hilburn was lucky not to have been thrashed to within an inch of his life on the steps of his club.

Anderson's view of critics, then, is that they are, in most respects, loathsome creatures, probably of mean intelligence.

'Let's face it,' he says with lordly conviction, 'I'm a bit brighter than most of them. We both know that.'

Moving on from what other people think of him, which he anyway imperiously ignores, is he capable of self-criticism?

'Of course!' he announces, flinging his arms before him like he's about to burst into song, an aria delivered from an alpine peak.

Then what did he make now of something like *A Passion Play*, the album that had so exercised Chris Welch and Robert Hilburn, a crude allegory involving the afterlife?

He gives me a look like he's just noticed half my face is missing.

'CRUDE?' he actually splutters. 'Crude? No!' he says, and I think he's going to spit out a tooth. 'I wouldn't say it's crude, no. I think some of the songs are perhaps reasonably naive and simplistic in terms of what I'm writing today. But I'm not saying that's a bad thing. There may be some songs that I'm not, looking back, happy with and wish I hadn't done them in a certain way. I wouldn't write them in the same way today. I'm, in fact, incapable of writing them in the same way. Arguably, if I did them today, they would be too refined and too sophisticated to work in the way they obviously worked for the people who liked, and continue to like, the record in its original form.

'At the same time,' he says, sounding a bit clenched, 'I'm still not very happy with that record, actually. I never was. For technical rea-sons. It's a rotten record in terms of production, which was basically my fault. I take full responsibility for that deficiency.'

If he's looking for sympathy, he's knocking on the wrong fucking door. Let's move on. Does he have a tendency to take himself too seriously?

'Again, no.'

He points to what he calls the 'ribaldry' of his songs, which is not the same, really, as self-effacement.

'I am no more than a jester,' he says, and I expect him to stand and make a low, swooping bow, bowler perhaps in hand.

'And like a jester,' he says, 'you always have to beware of falling foul of the ruling entity.'

I think he's talking about his fans.

'Be they the king or the duke, or whoever. There's always the ulti-mate audience you have to play for.'

Now he sounds, blimey, like he's talking about God, also likely to get an on-stage ticking off for giving him a bad review.

'You seek to amuse them first, to draw them in,' he goes on, eyes narrowing a little, his voice dropping almost to a conspiratorial whis-per. 'Then, when you have their attention, opportunities arrive to speak to them pertinently. It's useless, though, to antagonise them. You'll lose your bloody head.'

This last bit sounds suspiciously like he's wormed his way back to what he persistently describes as the pernicious inconsistency of music writers, how they can't for a moment be depended on for sup-port, succour; as if, say, giving a bad review to a poor new album by a band you've previously liked is somehow malicious, erratic, a kind of treachery. Why's he so fucking hung up on all this? What's up with Anderson and people like him, who are suddenly behaving like swooning French aristocrats in a tumbril on their way to the guillo-tine or the Romanovs in Urals exile, waiting for Bolshevik bayonets. An endangered species, soon to be extinct. It's fucking pathetic.

Whatever disparaging critics and loudmouthed punks think of his music, Tull still sell millions of albums. Look at those framed discs on the wall! The Sex Pistols and The Clash will never between them sell as many records – at least two albums on the wall certified platinum before they were even in the shops. Why's he worried about what Gaye Advert or Sid Vicious think about his band? Why does he get so wound up about the music press? For someone so convinced of his own artistic infallibility, it makes him sound a bit insecure.

'I am NOT insecure,' he almost bellows. 'And I resent the sugges-tion I am,' he says, waving his cigarette holder like it's a wand he can tap me on the head with and make me disappear, possibly in a puff of smoke, leaving only a sizzling absence where I'm now sitting. 'And I don't have a hang-up about the music press.

'I do get some good reviews, you know. From time to time, any-way,' he says, chuckling, an attempt at humour that falls rather flat. 'I'm not anti-press. I don't have a fixation with bad reviews. That's not the case at all. Sometimes, I'll be angered by something, but I don't let it affect me in any overwhelming sense. And one thing people never stop to consider is the fact that very often the unthinking praise of a record or concert can leave you more heartbroken than the meanest words of criticism.'

Why's that, then?

'Because you are often praised for doing the wrong thing,' he says, 'or you are praised for a part of a record to the exclusion of the whole and the part of the new record that is probably praised is likely to be the part that reminds the critic of something you've recorded previously, which implies that he hasn't come to terms with the newer things on the record. This in turn implies they haven't come to terms with the changes in the music.

'But I absolutely insist upon making different records. I do what I do,' he says grandly, someone quite above the muck and clutter of things. 'And damn anyone who should expect anything different of me.

'Damn them, I say.'

A 'Gadzooks' or two wouldn't have gone amiss here, or a riding crop slapped against a meaty thigh for vigorous emphasis.

Instead, he gets to his feet, the interview apparently over. He makes a grand fuss of assembling himself for the great outdoors.

As he bids his leave, the last thing he does is put on the bowler hat, a moment I had long been dreading.

As predicted, I laugh out fucking loud.

LOU REED

London, April 1977

When I turn up at the offices of Arista Records to interview Lou Reed for the first time, I'm taken aside and told quite firmly that certain questions I may have for Lou are off-limits. I'm particularly discouraged from asking, for instance, anything about The Velvet Underground, David Bowie, Andy Warhol, the much-lambasted *Berlin* album and just about anything else of conspicuous interest. I'm not quite sure what this will leave us to talk about, unless Lou's developed a recent passion for needlepoint embroidery or cattle farming about which he might care to wax lyrical for however long I get with him.

It turns out that by some remarkable chance, I hit it off with Lou. There's an obligatory barrage of colourful abuse, a well-practised nastiness that makes me laugh rather than terrorise me, which seems to be his intention. It makes for a bumpy first 20 minutes. Then, he suddenly softens, offers me a drink, pouring startlingly large measures of Johnnie Walker Red into a couple of glasses and handing one to me, leaving the top off for immediate refills and sending out for another. He seems to be settling in for the long haul.

I decide to ignore the instructions I've been given and ask him whatever the fuck I want. Which I do, Lou quickly getting into it. Any excuse to talk about himself, it seems, and he's off at a gallop. We talk about The Velvet Underground, Andy, Bowie, *Berlin* – 'The way that album was overlooked was probably the biggest disappointment I ever faced.' Eventually, we get around to the notorious *Metal Machine Music*, a double album of relentless feedback, by general agreement unlistenable. I review it for *Melody Maker* when it comes out in August 1975 and can't decide whether it's a Warholian prank, a conceptual joke or the brutal fulfilment of Andy Warhol's advice to The Velvet Underground to always leave their audience wanting less.

Lou laughs when I mention the album and the reaction to its release.

'RCA didn't want to release it,' he says, opening the second bottle of Johnnie Walker Red, filling our glasses. 'They thought it would be detrimental to my career, which was a notion that made me laugh. When have I ever done anything that someone didn't think was detrimental to my fucking career? They took it off the market after three weeks. You couldn't get it anywhere. It was so fucking fabulous. It was so exciting. No one else was doing anything that could have got that kind of reaction.

'Everything had become so fucking boring and predictable. Then along came *Metal Machine Music*. It was like a fucking bomb going off. It was like Andy's *Soup Cans*. I mean, the idea in and of itself was good. Brilliant, even. But for the full impact, you had to go through all the motions of execution.

'Everyone thought I was mad. They thought it would really finish me. Kill me, you know. Initially, the reaction was, "We don't want any more Lou Reed records." I said, "Fine. I won't make any more." Then, of course, they turn around and say, "Aw, c'mon, Lou. You don't mean it. You can't do that." I said, "What do you mean? You said you didn't want any more Lou Reed records." And they said, "Please." And I said, "Maybe." Then I put out *Coney Island Baby* and they hit that on the head as well. I love it. We were right back where we started.

'These people are too fucking much. They want me to make record and when I do, they tell me I'm a fucking parody of myself. But who better to parody? If I'm going to mimic anyone, it might as well be Lou Reed. I mean, I can do Lou Reed better than anyone, and a lot of people try to sound like me. Some of them have even made a lot more money than me by sounding like Lou Reed.

'Anyway, RCA had their guys taking the album out to the Top 40 radio stations. Can you imagine the look on some guy's face when he brings it to some programme controller and says, "Hey gang, anyone wanna listen to Lou Reed's new album?" And they're expecting, you know, fucking "Walk on the Wild Side" or something. And they put it on and it's just this fucking noise. They go, "Get that the fuck off. Get it the fuck out of here.' It's the worst thing they've ever fucking heard.

It's like a contagion. It's poisoning them. It was fucking hysterical. Excruciatingly funny.

'They take it to CHUM radio in Canada. Like the fucking Canadians are going get it. It's not a moose or an elk or ice hockey, so the fucking Canadians aren't going to get it. The fucking Canadians don't get anything. But they take it to CHUM radio, anyway. The guys at CHUM are like, "Is there something wrong with the record? It doesn't sound right. Should we try another side?" And they turn it over, and it's the same fucking thing. The same relentless fucking noise.

'That record is the closest thing I've ever come to perfection. It's also the only record I know that attacks the listener. Even when it gets to the end of the last side, it still won't fucking stop. You have to get up and remove it from the fucking turntable yourself. It's impossible to even think when the thing's on.

'It destroys you. You can't complete a fucking thought. You can't even comprehend what it's doing to you. You're literally driven to taking the miserable fucking thing off. You can't control that record. You have to go wherever it goes, which is basically – well, who the fuck knows? It depends on the weather.

'It's total gibberish, from start to finish. Half of it's backwards. What we did when we recorded it in Quad was to flip over the tape of the first side and just play it backwards to get the second side. We cut it to exactly the same length. It had to be the same length by definition. If it's that long forward, it's that length backwards.

'It didn't sound appreciably different, so we stuck with it. When I went to the RCA studios to cut the thing in Quad, I said to the guy who was in charge of the technicians, "Whatever you do, don't tell them that all we're doing is playing the tape backwards. That won't be technical enough for them. Make up some kind of complicated technical reason and then get them to do it." And that's what he did.

'I was really excited, you know, about recording it in Quad. There were only two Quad systems in New York at the time, so I was delighted. I ran over to a friend of mine and I told him I'd jived RCA into letting me have a crack at their Quad system and we listened to the tape, and he said, "Quad? It's barely in fucking stereo."

'It's not even balanced properly, that record. You can't even balance the fucking thing. If you wear headphones, sometimes the sound will dip over and take you with it. It's like someone hitting you on the side of the head. It's marvellous. Complete fucking gibberish. But I can invent such wonderful technical reasons for everything about it.

'Like those symbols on the back cover. Those DB symbols and kilo-hertz signs? I showed them to another friend of mine and asked him what I'd written. He told me that one quarter of side one, from what I'd written, could only be heard by dogs and after that nothing living or breathing that he could think of would be able to hear anything.

'He said, "Is that what you meant to say?"

'I didn't know. I'd just picked up a copy of a stereo magazine and copied out some symbols. I didn't have a fucking clue what they meant. My friend was astonished. "It's total gibberish," he said. "This sign means animals with high sensitivity can hear it. But the rest means that nothing human or otherwise can hear it. Is that really what you meant to say?"

'I said, "Yes. That's exactly what I meant to say."

'And he just said, "Congratulations."'

Wreckless Eric

London, September 1977 | Lisbon, August 1979

Talking about great singles, at the time of which I'm writing Stiff have just released another one: Wreckless Eric's 'Whole Wide World'. Even the square old daddios who supposedly call the shots at *Melody Maker* are hip by now to what's coming out of 32 Alexander Street, so when I make a pitch for a feature on Eric at an *MM* editorial meeting, I get the nod to go ahead without the usual drawn-out war of ghastly attrition, only features editor Chris Welch making mild protest at losing a page he's no doubt ear-marked for a chat over a pint and a pasty with some old muso mate who used to play bass in Humble Pie.

I call Jake Riviera at Stiff to set up an interview. Stiff receptionist Suzanne Spiro answers.

'Jake can't come to the phone right now,' she tells me.

Why's that?

'He's having a row with Rat Scabies.'

Now that she mentions it, I can hear an uncommon amount of shouting and swearing in the background that sounds like the dress rehearsal of an off-Broadway production of *Who's Afraid of Virginia Woolf?* or something shouty like it. Jake and Rat are going at it like squabbling fishwives. What a racket!

Suzanne says she'll get Jake to call me back as soon as he's finished with Rat.

Ten minutes later the phone goes. It's Jake, sounding a bit hoarse.

'What?' he asks, coming quickly to the point.

I tell him there's a page in next week's *MM* for a piece on Eric if he can hook me up.

'I'm on it,' Jake says, banging the phone down before he's finished talking. Not much later, he's back on the blower. I can meet Eric the following afternoon. He gives me the address of a pub in Wandsworth, where Eric will apparently be as soon as the doors are unlocked.

The next day, I find the pub and walk into the public bar, a room filled with sunlight pouring through leaded windows. There's an old bloke in a parka to my right, sitting on his own at a table and staring absently at I'm not sure what, lost apparently in drowsy reverie, a glazed look in his wistful eyes. At the far end of the bar, there's a younger bloke. Eric, I presume. He's wearing sunglasses and a white mac, buttoned to the collar. There's what I take to be a guide dog complete with harness asleep at his feet. This is a surprise. I don't remember Jake mentioning anything about Eric being blind.

I approach him with some caution, wondering how best to get his attention without startling him, possibly also making his faithful pooch start growling, barking or biting. I say his name, a rising inflection meant to suggest a harmless enquiry.

Eric?

No response.

Eric? A bit louder this time.

Again, no response.

ERIC? Louder still, hopefully not too shrill.

Still no response.

Fuck me. Is the little twat deaf as well as blind? Where's this going to end?

There's a commotion behind me. It's the old bloke in the parka, clearing his throat; the sound of a drain being sucked clean.

'Bob?' he finally gets out, hand hovering as if to pat the head of something that's not where he expected it to be. He reaches behind him for what turns out to be a white stick that he now taps against the leg of his chair. 'Bob!'

At this point, the hound at Eric's feet rouses himself with a bit of a snort from what had seemed like a profound slumber. He's on his feet in an instant. Ears aloft and tail wagging, he trots towards Blind fucking Pugh, or whoever the old geezer is. The aged feller reaches into a grimy parka pocket for some treats, savoury nibbles or whatever, that he now feeds to the self-styled Bob, who collapses contentedly on the carpet and, whiskers twitching, resumes his nap.

'Are you the man from *Melody Maker*?'
This is Eric. At least he can fucking speak!
I tell him I am the man from *MM*.
'Great,' he says. 'Fancy a drink?'
Love one!
'Me, too. Pint of lager, please.'

It's only a little after opening time, but it looks like Eric's already had a few drinks, possibly more. I get us a couple of pints anyway, the first of rather too many for our own good as it turns out, the afternoon that follows going on for what seems a very long time. I sit opposite Eric, who takes off his sunglasses and looks at me with some intensity.

'I was born in Newhaven. Lived next to the railway station,' he then announces, like he's giving a statement to the police.

Why's he telling me this?

'I've never been interviewed before,' he says, a little body squirm and shoulder hunch meant, I presume, to indicate some aversion to interrogation. 'I don't really know what I'm supposed to say. Ask me a question. I'll tell you anything you want to know.'

OK, what was he doing before he signed to Stiff and shortly after found himself in the studio making 'Whole Wide World' with Nick Lowe at the controls

'I was a quality inspector in a lemonade factory,' he says. 'But I had to leave because I was going deaf. The bottles made such a lot of noise coming down the conveyor belts. There'd be, like, three miles of bottles, rattling. I'd go home every night with the noise ringing in my head.'

Previously, it now transpires, Eric had been an art student in Hull.

'I had ambitions to become a sculptor,' he says. 'But I spent most of my time playing rock'n'roll or on the council rubbish tip, collecting things. I've got a letter that says I have the freedom of the Hull City Corporation Rubbish Tip,' he adds, stopping short of presenting the document with the flourish of a magician pulling a rabbit from a hat by its ears.

At art school, he was in a 1960s R&B covers band called Addis & The Flip Tops and also worked with free jazz drummer Eddie Prévost.

'I knew a lot of jazz musicians then. Played guitar in a trad jazz band, delved a bit in free form and that,' he says, sounding somewhat

65

wistful for long-gone days of atonal caterwauling. 'They thought I was too strange, though. One day I threw a chair at a wall and after that I never went back.'

Moving to London, he got a job as a part-time cleaner at British Home Stores, which he didn't really like. Then came the gig at the lemonade factory, which he had to leave because he was going deaf. Which is when he thought it was time to launch his pop career by getting a record contract.

'I'd read about Stiff,' he says, 'and they sounded pretty gullible, so I spent the weekend getting pissed and made this demo tape on the Monday morning.'

After another couple of drinks, he then set off in search of Stiff's west London HQ.

'I thought they'd have a big office in an office block, but when I got there, there was only this grotty little shopfront, full of these odd-looking people. I walked straight past. But they'd all seen me. They were all gawpin' out the window. I was trying to act sensible, but I was really a bit pissed. But they'd seen me, that's my point, so I couldn't walk away.

'So I walked in like a clockwork man. This big bloke came up to me and said, "What can we do for you?" And I looked up at him and just said, "I'm one of those cunts who brings tapes into record companies." Then I turned around and walked out.'

Two days later, Stiff called and the next thing you know Eric's up there at Pathway Studios with Nick Lowe, recording 'Whole Wide World', which Eric had originally written as a reggae song. Nick had other ideas for it.

'He kept going on about Jonathan Richman,' Eric says, possibly still baffled by what Nick had in mind. 'Talked a lot about him all the time. I went around my girlfriend's flat, and her flatmate had all these Jonathan Richman albums. Her name is Ruth. She's a very trendy girl and she'll think it's marvellous if you mention her name. Anyway, I caught up with Jonathan Richman. But I couldn't remember why Nick Lowe wanted me to listen to him. I'm a bit distanced from recording the single, actually. I had to go fishing.'

Sorry, Wreck?

'Fishing,' he says. 'I have a half-share in a fishing boat in Hull. The *Crusader*, it's called. It's in the agreement that I have to vanish once a year and go fishing in the North Sea. So immediately after we recorded "Whole Wide World", I went off to fish. Didn't come back until mid-February.'

I'm frankly having a hard time picturing Eric in a sou'wester on the pitching deck of a trawler ploughing the intemperate waves of the North Sea, fishing for haddock, cod or whatever marine edibles scoot through those dour waters. I mean, looking at him, you wouldn't let him near a fucking duck pond without a lifebelt. Eric, however, seems to be nostalgically missing the briny whiff of gutted fish, the lashing winds, the calloused banter of hearty trawlermen. I bid him move on from maritime reverie.

On his return to London, he thought he'd better get another job. He went to the Manpower agency, who got him some work 'taking down shelves in one room and putting them back up in another'.

'I mention this,' he says, 'because I started writing "Semaphore Signals" [the B-side of "Whole Wide World"] one afternoon on the job. We'd cleaned out this room and we ended up sitting in a pile of out-of-date documents. We found this drawing someone had done of the boss of this office. He had this big willie with scabs all over it and it was all deformed. It was a childish drawing. Evidence of a sick mind, I thought. "Whoever did this," I remember thinking, "is obviously mentally disturbed." And then I pinned it on the wall, so it would be the first thing the boss saw when he came back to the office.

'Anyway, it gave me the idea for the song, and I wrote it on the way home from work on the bus. It was a 77 or a 168. No, it was the 61. I remember having to sit on the side seat for most of the journey. Then I got home and finished it off on the kitchen floor.'

Turns out that as a songwriter, Eric's both prolific and easily inspired.

'I read a lot,' he says. 'Reading's always an inspiration. Have you seen the new *Woman's Own*? There's a marvellous article on Max Bygraves, who I think is wonderful. Trouble is, I tend to read things as I find them. Last week, I caught myself reading a copy of the *Daily Express* from April 1974. I found it at the bottom of the wardrobe. Still,' he says, 'it's nice to know what's going on in the world. As a writer, you have to keep up.'

The landlord's been shouting at us for a while to drink up and leave, clearly regretting the four pints he sold us minutes before ringing the bell for last orders. He's a burly man with what you can tell is a limited amount of patience. We finish our drinks as quick as we can, the landlord glaring at us. Stepping outside the pub, Eric trips, bounces off a lamppost and asks me if I want to go back to his place. Are we dating now?

Turns out he's got band practice this afternoon. From what he's been telling me, the group he's just put together features former Kilburn and The High Roads sax player Davey Payne, who goes on to join The Blockheads, Ian Dury's then-girlfriend Denise Roudette on bass and Ian on drums. Sounds like a lively combo, so I'm in. We head off to Eric's place, stopping briefly at an off-licence for as much beer as we can carry without having to hire a fucking pack mule, camel or llama to ferry the plentiful booze. Denise and Davey are waiting for us outside Eric's pad, Denise with news that Ian can't make the practice.

'He can't play the fuckin' drums, so it's not like we'll miss him,' Eric says, leading us into what I presume is his front room. I expect to see newspapers on the floor with front-page news of Mafeking's relief or the sinking of the *Lusitania*. Eric cracks open a beer, straps on a guitar, turns on an amp. Denise and Davey are ready to go. Eric takes them through a few numbers that turn up on his first album, including an early version of 'Piccadilly Menial'. Eric then gets stuck into a rowdy version of 'Whole Wide World', Davey Payne honking along, Eric, by now quite carried away, gets his feet caught on the carpet and ends up in a heap on the floor.

This appears to be the end of the afternoon's band practice. We crack open some more beers, drink them and crack open some more. Pretty soon, we head back to the pub, where the landlord visibly sags when he opens the doors and finds us waiting outside, tongues lolling in anticipation, like camels at an oasis, thirsty after a sprint across the Sahara.

There are lively times aplenty to come with Eric a few months after our first encounter, on the Five Live Stiffs tour with Elvis Costello, Nick Lowe, Ian Dury, Larry Wallis, Dave Edmunds and more. Then on the Be Stiff tour, the one on the train, and sundry gigs before and after it. Immoderate drinking is usually involved. In August 1979,

I get a call from Dave Robinson at Stiff. He's just signed a licensing deal with the Portuguese label Nova Records. Nova are apparently so thrilled with the deal, they're holding a party to celebrate. They have in fact hired a boat to sail 300 guests around Lisbon harbour. They've asked Stiff to send out a representative. Dave, laughing out loud, tells me he's sending Eric and wants to know if I'm up for going, too. Which of course I am. Eric, me and *Melody Maker* lensman Tom Sheehan fly out to Lisbon a few days later.

We're met at the airport by Sergio, point man and trouble-shooter for Nova.

'Yes! Yes!' he whoops colourfully. 'It is me. Is it shining also in London?'

Sergio drives us to our hotel and over drinks in the bar tells us we should be at the harbour by 6.00 pm and then leaves us in the bar, where we spend the rest of the afternoon. By the time we rock up at the quayside, it's 6.30 pm and the boat is getting ready to sail. Our collective vision of the gallant cruiser or spectacular galleon we had imagined would be waiting to carry us around the harbour beneath a pale romantic moon is immediately shattered when we fall out of our cab to be confronted by a rusting old tub bobbing in the disturbingly choppy waters. They're still loading the ancient tug with food and drink as we trundle up the gangplank.

Electricians are struggling on the main deck with a large neon sign advertising the liaison between Stiff and Nova. A crew of roadies in cute little sailors' hats are fiddling with amplifiers and a drum kit. Apparently, we're going to be entertained this evening by a Lisbon group called The Necromats. Sergio from Nova suggests tentatively that Eric might, you know, if he's in the mood, want to play a few numbers with them. Eric gives Sergio a malignant, squinty look and tells him to fuck off. Sergio replies with a crushed, pallid smile. We wander off in search of a drink, the decrepit craft moving now with a series of groaning shudders away from the dock.

'Bloody stupid, if you ask me, having a piss-up on a fuckin' boat,' Eric moans. 'I'm bound to fall overboard.'

Sheehan is similarly dubious about the entire enterprise. Tom, in fact, lives in fear of the sea and its uncharted depths, almost as if being this near to so much watery vastness will end up with him haunting wedding parties with an albatross around his neck.

'Twice around the harbour and straight into the nearest bar for a decent drink, I reckon,' the crusty old lensman mutters, the dock disappearing in the darkness.

'I reckon we should wind up the Portugeezers, cause a lot of trouble and get slung off the boat,' Eric says, not wholly helpfully. We settle with some beers in the hopefully safe haven of one of the forward cabins, where we are approached by someone who turns out to be the bass player with The Necromats.

'How long will you be in Portugal?' he asks Eric.

'Dunno,' Eric says. 'What time's the next flight back to London?'

'Are you going to sing?' the bass player from The Necromats asks Eric.

'Why?' Eric asks him back. 'Does it look like I'm about to burst into fuckin' song?'

The night drags on and Sheehan, as ever, becomes noticeably nervous about the beer running out before we make landfall. Time, therefore, as he puts it, to 'liberate the bar'. To be on the safe side, we grab as many beers as we can – virtually a crate-full each, about all they have left – and make our way aft, if that's what the arse-end of the boat is called.

''Old up,' Sheehan says then. 'We're being followed.'

Indeed, we are. A bunch of would-be local hard cases whose general look seems derived from early press shots of The Vibrators are what you might call on our tail.

'What do these fuckin' 'erberts want?' Sheehan wonders as we turn to face them, Eric so loaded with beer bottles he rattles when he moves, a clanking noise that possibly takes him back to the lemonade factory where he nearly went deaf.

The apparent leader of the group that's been following us, let's call him Punk 1, steps forward.

'Give me your beers,' he demands.

'Bar's over there,' Sheehan tells him.

'Bar is closed,' Punk 1 says. 'You take all the beer.'

'Give us your bee-ers!' the punks now start shouting in clearly thirsty unison. 'Give us your bee-ers! Give us your bee-ers!'

One of the punks starts spitting at Eric.

''Ere,' Eric says, giving the punk a truly nasty look. ''Ave you ever thought of getting a job as a garden hose?'

'*Que?*' says the punk.

'I said,' Eric says, 'do you want a knee in the bollocks?'

'We are the punks! We are the punks!' the punks are now yelling. 'Give us your bee-ers.'

'Sod the fuck off,' Sheehan tells them.

'Baader-Meinhof! Baader-Meinhof!' the punks now inexplicably start chanting, just as Sergio and some of his Nova chums appear on the scene. They wrestle the punks away, Sergio full of apologies for their behaviour, the punks glaring at Eric and following us at a glowering distance for the rest of the boat ride.

Some time later, the boat pulls back into the dock. Sergio and the Nova boys lead us down the gangplank, at the end of which Punk 1 and his crew are waiting with obviously malevolent intent. Punk 1 advances menacingly on Eric, who by now has had more than enough of this lot and their antics.

'I've been wanting to do this all fuckin' night,' Eric says then, grabbing Punk 1 by the lapels and headbutting the troublesome little squirt, not quite the behaviour Sergio might have been expecting from Stiff's ambassadorial presence.

'He has hit me in the head!' Punk 1 starts wailing, like a fundamentalist at an ayatollah's funeral or a distraught fan of a K-Pop starlet called too early to eternity's gate. He then collapses on the dock, making a dreadful noise.

Sergio looks on, aghast.

'Bet you wish they'd sent Lene Lovich now, eh?' Sheehan says to him.

'I think so, yes,' Sergio says. 'Very much, indeed. This is too much madness.'

'You have killed him!' one of Punk 1's mates, let's call him Punk 2, is now shouting.

'If he was dead, he wouldn't be making so much fuckin' noise,' Eric says of Punk 1 and his unholy lamentations.

Punk 2 then lunges at Eric, who promptly aims a kick at him that would have sent a ball sailing over the Stretford End. When Eric's boot makes somewhat thunderous contact with Punk 2's testicular region, Punk 2 is momentarily lifted off the ground and then doubles over in what appears to be considerable agony. Someone from Nova

71

hits him over the head with a bottle, adding to his woe. Scuffling pandemonium quickly breaks out, bringing with it the attention of three local policemen, gendarmes, whatever they are, who turn up in an epidemic of epaulettes, dinky hats, at least one flamboyant moustache and some disco chest hair. They take Eric aside, exchanging stern looks.

Tom steps in, hoisting his camera. I doubt any of the policemen can understand Tom's psychedelic cockney banter, but after some initial reticence, they're soon posing for pictures with Eric, like Hoover-era G-men with the bullet-ridden Dillinger. They then let Eric off with a finger-waving caution and shoo away the now battered punks.

Sergio wants to know if we'd like to go with him and his lads to a nightclub. Tom and Eric decide to go straight back to the hotel bar. One of Sergio's mates looks pretty lit-up, however, and I suspect at least one of them is packing coke, which turns out to be the case. I go off with them, even as Tom and Eric get in a cab for the hotel. Pretty soon, we're lolling around in an upholstered booth at the aforementioned nightclub, quaffing drinks and tooting up like cartel sicarios on a Tijuana mini-break from the usual drug-trade mayhem.

I guess I make it back to the hotel at some point, because that's where I meet Eric and Tom the next morning, in the lobby. At some point the previous evening, we've apparently agreed to appear on a local radio show. We get a cab to the radio station, where we're warmly greeted by the show's producer, who makes the mistake of offering us drinks as soon as we arrive, bottles of something called Super Bock. We've had a few by the time we go on air and carry on drinking during the show that follows, getting merrier by the moment.

Things seem to be going reasonably well, up to the point that our language gets a little too colourful for early-morning radio and the DJ swiftly ends the interview, appalled by some off-hand remark about Bruce Springsteen that makes him splutter, then choke like he's just swallowed a small dog. His producer looks stricken, bad news just in from his oncologist. Next thing you know, we're in the street, the DJ apologising profusely to his English-speaking listeners as the radio station doors slam shut behind us.

We stand there for a moment, wondering what to do until our flight, later that afternoon.

I suggest we might go sightseeing.

'What's in Lisbon?' Eric asks.

He's got me there.

'Place across the road looks like it's opening,' the eagle-eyed Sheehan says, with a nod towards what looks welcomingly like a bar, where a chap in an apron, shirt sleeves rolled, is putting out tables, arranging chairs around them. Tom and Eric are soon making themselves at home in a couple of them, Tom ordering the first of the umpteen rounds that see us through the morning and most of the afternoon.

The flight home's a bit fucking lively.

The Damned

Middlesbrough, November 1977

The night before goes from bad to what you might call worse, a quick drink after work getting monumentally out of hand, to the extent that I wake up the next morning in a hotel room in Maida Vale, in the company of people I don't appear to know and certainly can't remember meeting. I feel like doing not much more than spending the next week staring at a wall and dribbling but realise through a murk of returning consciousness that I have shortly to be at the west London HQ of Stiff Records, where I'm supposed to meet The Damned. They're playing a show tonight in Middlesbrough – MIDDLESBROUGH! – and with typically reckless disregard for what's left of my physical well-being, I've volunteered to go with them for a larky on-the-road feature for *Melody Maker*.

Anyway, I stumble around the room putting bits of myself back together, wondering what one of my shoes is doing on top of a wardrobe. No one else is moving, but from the ungodly amount of snoring, moaning and groaning I'm sure none of these people are dead, whoever they are. About now, the bathroom door opens, someone walking into the room who turns out to be Frankie Miller. Oh, yeah. It's starting to come back to me now. Frankie looks like he might have spent the night in a wind tunnel set to maximum blast.

'Still alive?' he says.

Just about. You?

'Touch and fucking go at the moment,' he says, looking around the room. 'Is there anything left tae drink?'

I stumble into the early-morning cold, twitching like Joe Strummer's leg, fall into the back of a cab that takes me to Alexander Street, where

Stiff have their offices. As usual it's bedlam in here, but this has nothing to do with The Damned, who are nowhere to be seen, although it's been impressed upon me that we need to make an unpleasantly early start. I'd spoken the day before to the band's tour manager, Ron. And this Ron had gone on at some length, in fact, about the need for me to be at Stiff not long after the crack of dawn. So here I am, but where is Ron? Where are the fucking Damned?

I sit in the Stiff office, fuming, a sullen silence my only response to the busy mayhem around me, telephones shrieking like alarm bells now and people shouting at each other. After considerably more than a while, a curious-looking cove wanders in off the street, looking baffled beneath a battered black bowler, an overcoat easily three sizes too big for him hanging heavily from his lankily emaciated frame. Turns out this is Robert 'Lu' Edmonds, enlisted a couple of months ago at the insistence of Brian James as The Damned's second guitarist, a recruitment that immediately worsened the relationship between James and drummer Rat Scabies, the latter jumping ship altogether on a recent European tour. Rat's been replaced by the dapper Jon Moss, who goes on to rather better things with Culture Club.

That's Jon, by the way, coming through the door behind Lu, followed in turn by the black-caped Dave Vanian, who looks like I feel, which is to say death with a hangover. The vampiric Vanian is limping badly and is soon telling us in gruesome detail about a growth he's discovered on his thigh.

'What happened?' asks Brian James, who's also now turned up. 'Get bitten by one of yer bats?'

James guffaws rawly at this vague stab at humour, and there is much sniggering from the hapless Lu, whose hungry look is increasingly disconcerting. He keeps staring at me, as if he's wondering whether my head will fit in his fridge. Such morbid ponderings are duly interrupted by the arrival of Captain Sensible, who's preceded by more clanking than you might hear at the London Dungeon, the Captain decked out in sundry chains and padlocks.

'Get yer fucking hair cut, you hippie cunt,' are his first words to me. 'Let's go to the pub,' are his second, on being told that Ron's yet to turn up. Over ensuing drinks, the Captain briefly describes the auditioning process for Rat's replacement.

'Most of the people who phoned were cunts,' he says. 'First thing we asked them was if they was the best drummer in the world. If they paused, we'd hang up.'

An unbelievable three hours after we were supposed to have left Stiff, we are finally off in the general direction of Middlesbrough, a lengthy journey made virtually unendurable by the wretched Sensible, whose pathological inability to settle down means that every passing minute is occupied by some desperate prank or mischievous jape. To which end, there's much farting, giggling, flicking of blazing matches and the dropping of lit cigarettes down the necks of unsuspecting victims.

'Something's burning!' screams the band's minder, Marty, somewhere just outside Birmingham.

This isn't news to me. My fucking hair is on fire, thanks to the pyromaniac antics of the clearly unstable Sensible. I turn around in my seat and slap him as hard as I can on the side of the head.

'Why did you do that?' he whimpers.

I give him another smack, much to Lu's gurning amusement, my hair smouldering and smoke filling the van.

By Sheffield, everyone's calmed down a bit and the Captain's telling me an amusing story involving Elvis Costello. The Damned and Elvis and The Attractions were returning by coach from the Bilzen festival in Belgium. Elvis had apparently got howling drunk the night prior to departure and the next morning was bundled onto the coach, a bilious wretch. Jake Riviera – then managing both Costello and The Damned – made it clear to the delinquent Sensible and the equally disruptive Scabies that under no circumstances were they to attempt to tease, torment or otherwise molest the suffering Elvis.

'Then Costello fell asleep,' the Captain recalls with an evil little grin, horns sprouting from the side of his head. 'With his mouth open.'

He's chuckling like a bastard now.

'Anyway,' the Captain continues, 'me and Rat tipped an ashtray into his mouth and then set fire to his shoelaces. He woke up with his feet on fire, started screaming and nearly choked on the dog-ends.'

The memory of this hilarious incident keeps the Captain sniggering until we get to Middlesbrough, when things turn bleak again. We're sitting in a cold, miserable dressing room backstage at the Town Hall when the woman who's promoting tonight's show announces gravely that there are punks fighting in the hall and her bouncers have lost control. Now she mentions it, there is an awful racket coming from the adjacent hall that I'd thought was probably the support band. Turns out it's the audience, who sound like they're in the slow process of demolishing the building, taking it down brick by brick, knocking holes in the walls with their heads, that sort of thing. The promoter scurries off to see what's happening.

Brian James saunters into the dressing room, glugging from a bottle of vodka, his second or third of the day so far, by my unofficial reckoning.

'What's it like out there?' the Captain asks him.

'Remember that place where we had to barricade ourselves in the dressing room because them skinheads wanted to kill us and Vanian saved the day when he went completely fucking mental and bit that bloke and freaked everyone out?'

'Yeah.'

'It's a lot fucking worse than that.'

'Tell me you're havin' me fucking on,' Sensible pleads. 'Please.'

Here comes the promoter, back from the front, wringing her hands and looking as stricken as someone who's just seen their own death foretold, evidently not a pretty sight. There's an air about her of hyperventilation and panic. Things are apparently getting more than a little out of hand, according to her breathless report. Her bouncers are losing control. Calamity evidently beckons, civilisation itself about to collapse, we are led to understand from her alarmed account. She makes it all sound more like the fall of the Ming Dynasty than the pissed-up antics of a bunch of brain-dead local yahoos. But there's no consoling the poor woman.

She beseeches the Captain to intervene. She wants him to address the crowd, reason with them, calm them with a few words that will appeal to what's left of their better instincts. I can't help thinking she must be fucking desperate if she's relying on Sensible and his probably untested diplomatic skills to bring order to what seems the prevailing chaos.

'You're going to have to go out there and tell them,' she instructs the Captain, 'that if they don't behave, like, there'll be no more poonk in Middlesbrough.'

'Too fucking right there'll be no more punk in Middlesbrough,' Sensible fairly wails in reply. 'If we go on and that crew start throwing fucking bottles and looking for a fight, there'll be no more punk in Middlesbrough and no more fucking Damned, either. I'll be gone so fucking quick it'll be like I was never fucking here.

'I may be a cunt,' he says. 'But I'm not fucking stupid.'

PETER COOK

London, December 1977 | December 1978

When my friend Al Clark quits England for the sunnier climes of Australia, he becomes a film producer and wins a shelf-full of awards for ...*Priscilla, Queen of the Desert*. At the time of which I'm writing, though, Al's head of press at Virgin Records. In which capacity he calls me up one afternoon to tell me that Virgin will shortly be releasing an album called *Derek and Clive Come Again,* by Peter Cook and Dudley Moore.

This is of course a sequel to the notorious, scandalously funny *Derek and Clive (Live)*, originally recorded by a hugely pissed-up Pete and Dud in 1973, but not released then because of its spectacularly ribald content. In the censorious opinion of many, it's not much more than blatantly obscene. It certainly sets quite remarkable standards for colourfully imaginative lewdness. The album is, however, much bootlegged and hugely enjoyed by people for whom terminal illness and the more intimate parts of Jayne Mansfield's anatomy are a source for rib-cracking mirth. It's eventually given an official release in 1976.

Anyway, with ...*Come Again* about to come out, Al now asks me somewhat casually if I'd like to interview Pete and Dud. In Bermuda.

He has to fucking ask? Too fucking right, I would.

I'm already imagining myself on a beach, lots of white sand, an endless blue sky overhead, sipping a rum-based cocktail from a glass as big as a bucket, palm trees swaying in a gentle evening breeze. A bit of calypso in the near distance.

There's a pause now, which is unusual when you're talking to Al. He's so rarely lost for words. For many years, a simple telephone call with exciting news of a forthcoming Hatfield and The North or

79

Henry Cow album is merely the prelude to a discursive chat that usually consumes the better parts of many afternoons. Right now, he sounds a bit, I don't know, evasive. I get the feeling there's something he's not telling me.

This duly turns out to be the case.

He now makes clear that while Pete and Dud will, as advertised, be in Bermuda, I certainly won't be joining them in the sun-drenched tropics, jauntily attired in recently acquired beach clobber. Along with an invited party of sundry hacks, I'll be asking them questions from the rather less exotic climes of Richard Branson's front room in the house he has at the time, just off the Portobello Road.

I arrive to find the place packed with quaffing hacks. Most of them seem to be from the Fleet Street papers. The *Daily Mail*, the *Daily Mirror*, the *Telegraph*, the *London Evening Standard* and the *Guardian*, among them. They fall upon the bar like jackals on a wounded gnu.

Bossily officious, Al now demands our attention and calls the room to order. He announces that Pete and Dud will soon be available for interrogation via what turns out to be a bit of a wonky transatlantic link. I'm suddenly not buying any of this. I suspect, in fact, that Pete and Dud are probably no closer to fucking Bermuda than we are. More likely, I'm beginning to think, they're upstairs, lurking in one of Branson's fucking bedrooms and chuckling like chimps at the buffoons downstairs.

There's suddenly a lot of static on the transatlantic link. Then Peter Cook's voice, bleary in what I presume we are supposed to imagine is a clear-skied Bermuda morning. Some light-hearted banter and a lot of swearing ensues. Then the man from the *Guardian*, a morose-looking fellow in a green cardigan, weighs in. He wants to know how much money Pete and Dud made from *Derek and Clive (Live)*.

'I'm afraid I can't discuss such deeply personal matters,' Cook replies. 'I'll talk cheerfully and at length about masturbation. But not money. I don't think we should bring such personal matters into the public eye.'

Someone else asks what the new album is 'about'.

'The usual,' Cook answers. 'Sex,' he goes on. 'And cancer, of course.'

Was there a link between the two?

'Well,' Cook says thoughtfully. 'They both occur during our lifetimes.'

'Going back to the dirty subject of the money you earned from the last album,' the man from the *Guardian* interrupts, to jeers from the rest of us who are more interested in sex, wanking, cancer and the private bits of dead Hollywood actresses, 'do you expect it to be the biggest sum of money you've earned in your working lives?'

'I certainly hope so,' Cook says eagerly.

'Do you think that it's right that you should have resorted to filth to be successful?'

This again from the man in the green cardigan, clearly on a mission, a moral crusade, to expose and condemn here.

There's a pause, silence for a moment on the line.

'You're not by any chance from the *Guardian*, are you?' Cook then asks, and you can almost hear his eyeballs rolling, a hint of frosty disdain in his imperious tone.

Things wind up not long after.

Fast forward to almost a year later. Virgin are about to release a third Derek and Clive album, *Derek and Clive Ad Nauseum*. Somewhere a man in a green cardigan is having outraged palpitations. Meanwhile, I'm walking down a lane in Hampstead to Peter Cook's house. I knock on the front door, which Peter Cook opens. He's one of those tall people who seem even taller than they are because however much they are inclined to stoop, they still end up towering over you, in a kind of carrion hover. He's lanky enough to pass for an exclamation mark with elbows and knees.

He's wearing a cheerful Fair Isle jumper, V-necked, sleeveless, a pale checked shirt and loosely knotted tie. He's also sporting an ill-advised new perm that makes him look like the raw-boned centre half of a struggling Second Division football team, famous for mistimed tackles, errant back passes and the hoofing of the ball the length of the pitch to the big feller up front. His trousers rather sag on him, exhausted, like he's been wearing them since he had legs. He hitches them up. With a swoop of a wing-like arm, he beckons me inside, pointing in the direction I should now go. He gives me a huge smile that seems to take over most of his head, eyes aflame beneath all those curls.

81

I walk into what memory insists I describe as a kind of conservatory that's more like a sultan's love nest, a pasha's padded recess. There seem to be a lot of cushions in quite a narrow space. To my right, there's a couch. Possibly wicker. It's certainly covered in cushions. There's a low glass table in front of me with candlestick holders that look like hookahs that give the little room the air of a shisha bar or a casbah drug hole. Cook takes a seat at the head of the table, motions me to take a seat to his left. I don't think he's stopped smiling since he opened the front door. It's like the hinge that works his lower face and jaw has had some kind of spasm and locked him into this weirdly grinning look. I also realise he hasn't said a word since I arrived. He rummages around under the table, and then plonks a bottle of vodka on the table between us. He finally speaks.

'Drink?' he asks, filling a very large wine glass with vodka. He splashes some tonic into the glass and hands it to me before pouring an even larger measure with even less tonic for himself. He goes at the drink like a thirsty dog at a puddle.

'Don't let me get ahead of you,' he says. 'I'd rather not get drunk on my own.'

We are soon talking about a track on *Ad Nauseum* called 'The Critics', which turns on the people who on the one hand indignantly lambaste the language he and Dudley Moore use on the Derek and Clive albums, while simultaneously applauding the deployment of the same expletives in something like Harold Pinter's *No Man's Land*. Shortly before recording *Ad Nauseum*, Cook had seen a TV version of Pinter's play starring those ennobled thespians, Sir Ralph Richardson and Sir John Gielgud.

'It isn't an attempt to justify the album or the Derek and Clive thing generally,' he says. 'If that's what you're getting at. It's just that you get all these complaints about language on the television. And there at 10.30, which is reasonably early, you have all these "fucks" and "shits".

'And because it's Pinter, coupled with these two distinguished knights of the theatre, it's somehow more tolerable. A "prick" is apparently acceptable if it's in Sir John's mouth. Sir Ralph can handle "arseholes" with delicacy and taste. It's acceptable because it's Pinter and two beloved thespians. It's bullshit. An example of the worst double standards. I also found it a very boring play. The only entertaining

82

thing about it was Sir Ralph's ability to fall down, which I thought he did exceptionally well. Marvellously agile for his age.'

And what of the critics who think swearing a lot for money is a bit off.

'It's a ridiculous proposition,' Cook says, pouring what's left of the vodka into our glasses. 'Of course, I want to make money from these records. Practically everything I do is to make money. If I'm entertaining the public, I want to make money out of it. The only thing I do that I don't make money out of – and I wish I did – is charity work. So, I certainly don't do much of that.'

He's scrabbling under the table now, looking for something and beaming when he finds it.

'I knew I had another one somewhere,' he says, screwing the top off another bottle of Smirnoff. 'Not leaving quite yet, are you?'

GUY CLARK

London, September 1978

When Guy Clark walks into the room, he makes me want to go for my gun and start shooting. Which is to say, my first impression on meeting him is that he looks like he's just walked off the set of a Sam Peckinpah western. There's a lot about him that's saddle-worn and creaky, like he's ridden all night to get here. Something about him also suggests single-minded cussedness, wild behaviour behind a drink. Easily riled, you might further speculate. Quick to find his temper with irrelevant fools and anyone standing on his shadow.

You imagine him at a table in the corner of a cantina near the border. Bob Dylan counting cans of beans on a shelf, tequila and a Colt on the table in front of him. Warren Oates and L. Q. Jones in close and whiskery attendance. Bo Hopkins outside, watering the horses. Everyone looking suitably leathery and a bit mean. Flies buzz. There's a dog barking somewhere, a posse closing in.

The night before, he'd made his UK debut at the Hammersmith Odeon, opening for Emmylou Harris & The Hot Band, three years after RCA released his debut album, *Old No. 1*. It's an album I reviewed for *Melody Maker* when it came out, gushing over incredible songs like 'Texas, 1947', 'Desperados Waiting for a Train' and 'Let Him Roll' and their cinematic evocations of the West Texas he grew up in. He lived with his grandmother, back then, in the desert town of Monahans, where she ran a ramshackle old hotel. A lot of grizzled old codgers had their digs there and their lives eventually made it into Clark's songs.

'"Desperados Waiting for a Train",' he says, lighting a Pall Mall, the first of many he gets through in the next hour or so. 'That was

84

written about this old fellow, he was like my grandmother's boyfriend. He was an old oilman. He'd drilled wells all over the world, including the first well they ever drilled in Venezuela. He'd been a wildcatter and a drifter. The song is about his separation from the past, the life he lived. It's about him waiting around to die.'

There's a song called 'The Last Gunfighter Ballad' on his second album, *Texas Cookin'*, that was similarly inspired.

'My grandmother's hotel,' he says, 'was full of these crusty old oil-field workers and old cowboys. This one old guy who taught me to play dominoes had been in the US Cavalry. He was about 80, maybe older. I must have been eight or ten. He'd seen the whole gunfighter era. That song is about his memories. He's looking back in the song with distaste, because he knows it wasn't the romantic era it was cracked up to be.

'At the same time, there's a yearning for that past. Because it gave him his moment of glory. It was his time. It's all he's got to hold on to. But he knows there was no romance. The gunfight, the stands in the street. They were brutal. It was just survival. If you were called out, you just shot the other son of a bitch in the back if you had a chance. The code of chivalry was bullshit. You just killed the other guy, and it didn't matter how.

'I'm really fascinated, I guess, by history and time passing,' he goes on. 'The things people see in their lifetimes. I have this idea for a song I've wanted to write for a long time. My mother's mother, she came from Kentucky in a covered wagon into the Indian Territory, which is now Oklahoma. She was a girl of just 12. That's a hell of a long way to come in a covered wagon. That woman lived through the Indian wars and died in an old people's home. Before she died, one of the last things she saw was the live broadcast of the moon landing. She lived to see men walking on the moon within 80 years of coming into the Indian Territory in a covered wagon. That to me is extraordinary. To see that in one lifetime. Those extremes of history.'

The albums we're talking about were both great, *Old No. 1* a classic of its kind. Not a lot of people heard them, though, and he finally had to buy his way out of his RCA contract before he was tempted to march into their offices looking for trouble and the dramatic despatch of available executives through the nearest windows.

'We had all kinds of problems with them,' he says of RCA, who are clearly not among his favourite people. 'There were problems with the budgets for the albums, having the money to do things right. They didn't know what to do with me, is the simple fact. That's the whole story, right there. They didn't know how to market the records. They wanted me to go to Nashville and make a nice country record. Which of course I had no intention of doing, even if they'd tied me to a horse and dragged me there. I mean, to hell with that.

'I wasn't what you might call a priority for RCA. They were too busy selling Elvis Presley records and making a star of John Denver, I guess.'

We talk a little about his friends, David Allan Coe and Townes Van Zandt, the latter a stone genius songwriter and hard-drinking hell-raiser. Was Townes as self-destructive as his legend allowed?

'Townes is Townes,' he says, picking his words carefully. 'He lives the way he lives and that's the end of it. It's his choice, his life. He lives it the way he wants to. I guess that's as much as anyone can do.'

What of the colourful David Allan Coe, self-styled Mysterious Rhinestone Cowboy? What were we talking about there? A caricature, a fantasist, what?

'A lot of people misunderstand David,' Clark says, lighting another Pall Mall. 'I know him well and consider him a friend. You have to understand, he has a very high sense of theatre. If he decides to be someone, he becomes that character from his heels to the top of his head. When I first met him, he was in a motorcycle gang. He had the leather jacket, the chains, the boots, the colours. Bikers were the people he wanted to be with. So, he became one of them.

'Then he went through that Mysterious Rhinestone Cowboy trip. That was something else. God. Right now, he thinks he's a pirate. He lives down in Key West. Has himself a sailor's hat and a Captain Ahab beard. He's real crusty-looking. If you didn't know him, you'd think he was a real old salt, he's so far into that role.

'I remember one time he decided to become a Mormon. He went around dressed like a preacher and had three wives. That was pretty far out.'

Was it true that Coe had killed a man in prison by beating him to death with an iron bucket for getting too – how to put it? – getting too familiar with him in the showers.

Clark laughs hard enough to make himself cough. 'Sputtering' is the word that comes to mind.

'Well,' he says, still laughing. 'There are a lot of stories about David. And a lot of them are true. He had had a pretty hard time. He had been in prison. Let's just say he's seen it all and done most of it. But he's in show business now, and good luck to him.'

JOE COCKER

London, January 1979

Joe Cocker's in London to promote his new Allen Toussaint-produced album, *Luxury You Can Afford*. According to his record company, Cocker is for the first time in years free of the alcoholism and heroin addiction that for so long has sadly made him a bit of a laughing stock, and which he has been lucky to survive. When he turns up for his interview with *Melody Maker* lugging three bottles of champagne and a crate of Carlsberg, he does not, however, seem entirely like a man at home with notions of sobriety.

'Compliments of the management,' he cackles, popping a bottle of Bollinger. 'Tuck the fuck in,' he guffaws, allowing a hint of the party monster that had threatened to consume the career he had made for himself from humble beginnings in Sheffield, where he makes his musical bones in the early 1960s as a raw-voiced singer on the Northern club circuit with Vance Arnold & The Avengers. By 1964, he's signed to Decca, but his debut single, a cover of The Beatles' 'I'll Cry Instead', is a flop. Cocker returns to his day job as a gas fitter for the East Midlands Gas Board, teaming up a year later with pianist Chris Stainton to form The Grease Band, who have a minor hit in 1968 with woozy soul stomper, 'Marjorine'.

What changes Cocker's world is its follow-up, a roaring gospel version of The Beatles' 'With a Little Help from My Friends', with Jimmy Page on screaming lead guitar, that tops the UK charts in November 1968. I remember seeing him that summer, when over the August Bank Holiday, I go, as previously mentioned, with three school friends to what then is still called the National Jazz & Blues Festival, which later finds a permanent home in Reading.

We arrive to find the festival on Friday night swarming with be-quiffed rockers, here to see Jerry Lee Lewis tearing the house down in spectacular fashion. My friends and I are agog. On Saturday afternoon, we get great seats to the left and only rows from the front of the stage, where Tyrannosaurus Rex are now playing, Marc Bolan, sitting cross-legged on a little rug, thrashing away on an acoustic guitar, Steve Peregrin Took banging away on some bongos. Deep Purple are on next, I think. Then the stage, as I remember it, is full of people and at their centre, making an incredible noise, is a burly man wearing what used to be called a granddad vest, with a voice that even without the rickety PA could have been heard in the next county. This is Joe Cocker and The Grease Band, Cocker looking like he's just landed on stage after being shot out of a cannon. Dishevelled and deranged, even at 24, he could not be described as fresh-faced. His increasingly hysterical physical gyrations are frankly a bit scary – his body seemingly beyond his control, much writhing and squirming that quickly becomes a trademark.

When he delivers almost exactly the same performance of the song the next year at Woodstock, it becomes a highlight of the movie that follows and brings him into the orbit of Leon Russell, with whom in 1970 he puts together Mad Dogs and Englishmen, a 21-piece band that rampages wildly across America, playing 65 shows in 57 days. The tour results in a best-selling double live album and a hit film, but leaves Cocker physically shattered, an alcoholic recluse with a ruinous heroin addiction that turns him first into a clown and then nearly kills him.

The young John Belushi, then a rising star on *Saturday Night Live*, makes an early name for himself with a cruel, wickedly unsparing impersonation of Cocker on a song called 'Lonely at the Bottom' that many find too distasteful for words. Cocker is so strung out at the time, he finds it hilarious and agrees to appear with Belushi on *SNL*, where they duet on 'Feelin' Alright'. Cocker emerges from the performance as a spaced-out wreck, someone to be pitied. 'I could have sung him offstage,' Belushi tells American rock magazine *Crawdaddy*. 'He just didn't have it. He really attracts slime. Bad people.'

Much to Cocker's credit, he's magnanimous about Belushi's savage send-up. 'I got on quite well with him,' he says of Belushi. 'He told me he used to terrify his mother, rehearsing his impersonation of me in his front room. She was going to have him committed. She thought he'd gone berserk.'

Joe pours us some more champagne, knocks the tops off a couple of bottles of beer, tells me about a meeting he had with Jerry Wexler, who was in line to produce the new album. Things did not go well.

'I freaked him out,' he says, shaking his head, perhaps taken aback by his own behaviour. 'I met him, and he started telling me what songs I should be doing. I'd already picked the fuckers. There was an immediate collision. The usual conflict. I ended up dropping my pants and showing him my latest dose of clap. I'd just been to the clinic and had a really bad dose. I said, "Take a look at this, baby." He just went, "Oh, my God." We ended up deciding not to work together.'

He now recalls being taken to dinner by label boss Jerry Moss, when he was still signed to A&M. Moss had been particularly critical of Joe's recent *Stingray* album.

'I thought, "Right, I'm going to really freak out this old fucker." I'd got these bright red shoes and boot polish to go with them. I turned around and crammed all this red boot polish in my mouth and turned back around to face him. I said, "Jerry …" – I just managed to get the word out – and then I went, "Yeeeurrrghhh", and dribbled all this revolting red shit out of my mouth. Went all over him. The fucker was covered in it. The man didn't bat an eyelid. Just reminded me that I still owed A&M $400,000. I'd just had a bill from the Inland Revenue for £65,000. I told him to join the fucking queue.'

There were serial run-ins on the new album with Toussaint. As far as Cocker was concerned Toussaint was spending too much time in the studio rapping with the band when Joe thought he should have been behind the mixing desk.

'I said to him, "Hey, Al, when do you start operating the faders and that?" I mean, he's supposed to be producing the fucking record, not fucking chatting all day to the fucking band. He said, "I don't do that shit. I got an engineer to do that." I said, "Fuck that, man. You can't trust these young buggers." But he wouldn't listen.

'I'm not a moody guy, but when you're looking at that huge piece of glass in the studio and you're trying to sing your fucking heart out, it's fucking disturbing, man, when all you can see is people running in and out of the control booth delivering fucking takeaways.

'I ended up asking them to set me up with a microphone behind a brick wall. They were all shaking their heads and going, "What have we done to upset him now?"'

As for Belushi's comment about the kind of parasites who exploited him, Cocker admits there was much unfortunate merit in the suggestion that he'd brought about his own ruin, via a tendency to blunder unplanned into his own future, which often, he wearily confesses, involved poor choices on his part of managers, lawyers and business partners, who took ample advantage of his addled gullibility.

'It was the times, man,' he says, 'and the people I allowed myself to be surrounded by, who sucked the fucking life out of me. This is a ruthless business. Folk aren't concerned for your well-being. You're just someone they can make a fast buck out of and they're not satisfied until they've stripped you of everything.'

We talk a little about Donny Hathaway, a friend of Joe's, whose recent suicide has deeply affected him.

'Threw himself from a fucking window,' Cocker says. 'I cried my bloody eyes out. I've never been that crazy. But who knows, when the point comes and you black out like that, what you might do?'

Joe gets a bit maudlin now, no doubt thinking about his own brushes with disaster, which have been legion. But let's leave him, though, as we found him, with a drink in his hand and a room full of laughter, looking back at the dark times he had been lucky to escape.

'You can't afford to dwell on shit like that,' he says. 'There's no bloody point. You do what you do, and you pay the price. Fuck it. Let's have another.'

And we did, and a couple more after that.

JOE ELY

RAF Bentwaters, Suffolk, May 1979

Then paint me this. A flash of neon against a tumescent Suffolk sky, a lot of black up there and fighter jets screaming in from the coast. We're standing outside something called The Phantom Club. It sounds like the name of a South Side blues joint in 1940s Chicago, Otis Spann on piano, Little Walter blowing into a harmonica, Muddy Waters making the earth move. The Phantom Club we have here, however, is in fact part of a breeze-blocked entertainment complex on the US airbase at Bentwaters, in Suffolk, home to the USAF 81st Tactical Air Command Fighter Wing.

In a Scorsese tracking shot, starting now, the camera follows us through The Phantom's doors, down a couple of corridors, into a bar, out the other side and into a large room full of people and noise. There are tables everywhere, much whooping coming from them. Most of the airbase seems to be here tonight at The Phantom, for a show by the Texas country singer Joe Ely and his band. That's them on stage now, burning through a song called 'Did You Ever See Dallas from a DC9 at Night?', written by Joe's friend Jimmie Dale Gilmore and originally recorded by The Flatlanders, a legendary Texas trio that featured Joe, Jimmie and Butch Hancock, another great songwriter. They're just finishing a set anyone who was there is probably still talking about. The crowd won't let him go. There's a huge cheer when he leads his band back onstage for another encore.

'Hey,' he says then, wiping a hand across his face, looking like he's just been hosed down in somebody's shed. 'If we're gonna play some more, you gotta dance on the tables.'

Which everyone does.

At the time of which I'm writing, Joe's just released *Down on the Drag*, produced by Bob Johnston, the follow-up to two even better albums, *Joe Ely* and *Honky Tonk Masquerade*. None of them have really sold, however many five-star reviews they've had. This is all before Joe becomes some sort of talisman for The Clash, especially Joe Strummer and Clash tour manager Johnny Green, who eventually quits The Clash to work for Joe. But even The Clash's well-meaning patronage when it comes does nothing for his record sales.

'A lot of people are worried because I don't sell a lot of records,' Ely says after the show at The Phantom Club, nursing a beer at a table in the corner of the bar back at his hotel, hat tipped back, now lighting a cigarette and squinting through the smoke.

'Don't bother me so much. I don't really care about sellin' records, tell you the truth,' he says. 'Don't really think about it too much. I'm a guitar player and a singer and a songwriter and a fool and a vagabond. If MCA decided to drop me tomorrow, it wouldn't be the end of my fuckin' world. I'm a hell of a sign painter. I cook a mean fried chicken and I ain't too proud to wash dishes. I don't give a flyin' fuck. I don't give a shit. To me, a record company is nothin' but a pawn shop or loan shark.

'As long as there's opportunities for me to hit the road and play different places, I'll take 'em. I'll be gone, man. If the records sell, fine. If they don't, that's fine too. People who buy records are a fickle bunch. If one of my records was a hit, well, hallelujah, I'd buy Madison Square Garden a beer. In the meantime, I ain't gonna worry. There's more important things to do. Let me get a couple more drinks here.'

Joe's soon in something like full swing, full of great stories. He tells me about growing up in Lubbock, Texas, hometown of Buddy Holly. How he hit the road when he was in his late teens and hasn't looked back.

'I was lookin' for somethin', don't know what,' he says, lighting another cigarette, calling for more drinks. 'Guess it was just somethin' I had to do. Maybe I read a little too much Kerouac. I don't know what it was that kept me travellin'. Guess gasoline was cheap back then. I just knew I couldn't stay around Lubbock. I knew there was a different wind that blew out in the desert and in the pines and I wanted to hear it.

'America's the kind of place,' he goes on, 'that if you live there and really want to see it, it's not like you're going to do that on a two-day drive. If you get a wind of somethin' somewhere else and you're lookin' for the source of it, you may have to go maybe 800 miles to New Orleans and then follow the old Mississippi to Chicago, which is another 1,200, maybe 1,500 miles. It's like endless spaces. And places take you places.'

He tells me how he wrote a song called 'Because of the Wind' in the back of a boxcar outside Toledo, Ohio. How his father worked on the Santa Fe Railroad. How he hung out in Lubbock with ramblers and street poets and hard-luck drinkers. How they taught him songs they'd picked up on their own travels. How he started playing those songs himself, digging into the east Texas blues for inspiration.

'I've played just about all over,' he says, a fresh drink in front of him, another in his hand he's still working on. 'From Faith City missions to cafés and backstreet bars and street corners. I'll tell you a hard place to play. The corner of 34th Street and 6th Avenue in New York City. I was 19 the first time I went to New York. Played on the street and in the subway. Made just enough to eat the next day. Played the Staten Island Ferry, too. Saw John Lee Hooker playin' the ferry one time. There was just a few folks gathered around him. There was a lotta other people asleep. A lotta people who were pissed off. A lotta people wishin' they were somewhere else.'

As we've been talking, I've become keenly aware of a group of what I take to be local businessmen of some kind sitting across the bar from us. They're corpulent types, straining the seams of their suits, thick-necked and red-faced from drinking. There's a lot of backslapping, shoulder punching and crotch grabbing, accompanied by much guffawing, hoarse laughter and shouting. Ties are coming off, never a good sign in certain types. They look like the kind of shire Tories who support the death penalty and national service and get their kicks from public floggings.

'Oi! Cowboy!' one of them, let's call him Mr Fucking Angry, shouts at Joe. This gets a big laugh from his lardy mates.

Joe carries on with whatever story he's telling me. But I catch something in his eye, a hardening that wasn't there a minute ago when he was making me laugh at something that had happened to him once in Laredo.

'I said, Oi! Cowboy! Got any Wild Turkey?' Mr Fucking Angry, getting worked up, shouts at Joe. Ignored again, he gets to his feet, clearly fuming and coming our way. Tom Sheehan's been taking some pictures while I've been talking to Joe. He's between me and Joe and Mr Fucking Angry, who now barges him out of the way. He's now just a few feet from where I'm sitting with Joe.

'Oi! Cowboy! I said, "Got any Wild Turkey?"'

Fuck me. This wasn't funny the first time he said it. Joe puts his drink down, seems about to say something to Mr Fucking Angry when Tom comes back into the shot.

'There's no wild turkeys around 'ere, mate,' he tells Mr Fucking Angry, putting enough Camberwell into it to sound like one of Charlie Richardson's South London Torture Gang. 'But there's a lot of fuckin' great bores.'

Oh! Nifty wordplay under pressure from the legendary lensman. Mr Fucking Angry now squares up to Tom. They go head-to-head like boxers at an ill-tempered weigh-in. Joe just sighs, like he's been here before. He tilts his hat over his eyes, a nice cowboy touch, gets up, stands to face Mr Fucking Angry.

'Help you, Hoss?'

A tense moment follows. Tom is between Joe and Mr Fucking Angry and Mr Fucking Angry's mates. They're beginning to stir a bit, too. A few of them are on their feet.

I've been hoping to sit this one out. My right arm's in a sling, nursing a painfully broken elbow. I'm not going to be much use if current circumstances take an unpleasant narrative turn. I reckon, though, that if Mr Fucking Angry or one of his mates goes down, I might be able to kick them hard enough to keep them there until someone breaks my other arm and I start whimpering like a seal pup in the shadow of a baseball bat. Anyway, we're all on our feet now, me standing next to Joe, everybody standing around the room like we're on a fucking Leone film set, everyone squinting and waiting for someone to shout *action!*

'Are these guys seriously lookin' for trouble?' Joe asks quietly, looking over my shoulder at someone walking into the bar who nobody else has spotted.

Looks pretty much like it.

'Then maybe they oughtta meet my man Bo,' Joe says.

I know who he's talking about. I met Bo earlier. At The Phantom Club. He's somewhere north of six foot, with a pair of shoulders it would take a couple of days to walk across. We're having a drink at the bar. I notice he only has one thumb. What happened to the other one?

'Got bit off in a barroom brawl in Waco,' Bo says.

I'm not sure what exactly he does for Joe, but room-clearing duties may be high on his CV.

Heads turn as Bo walks into the bar, big enough to block out the sun. A couple of Mr Fucking Angry's mates already look like they're standing in the shadow of an eclipse. Bo stands there for a moment. He's clearly seen this movie before. He takes in the scene in front of him with a practised barroom scan, like he's checking for his missing digit or, more likely, deciding who if it comes to it he'll hit first. Bo now has a tooth-loosening look about him.

He walks over to Tom. Puts a hand the size of Texas on Tom's shoulder and his enormous bulk between Tom and Mr Fucking Angry's mates. They suddenly seem a little less leery. A couple of them are already sitting down. The others back off a bit, then a bit further.

'Trouble, Joe?' he finally asks Ely.

'Not my call,' Joe says, looking straight at Mr Fucking Angry, who starts to deflate a little, then a lot. You can almost hear the hiss as he grows visibly smaller. Tom makes ungracious shoulder-bumping way for him as he goes back to his mates, more than one of them putting on their coats, all of them gawping at Joe's man Bo like they've never seen a Texas neck-breaker before.

'Don't look like it,' Joe now tells Bo, sitting down, tipping back both his hat and his drink.

'Where were we?' he asks me.

Laredo.

'Oh, yeah,' Joe laughs. 'Well, what happened there was …'

ROCKPILE

Cambridge | Manchester | Leicester, May 1979

This is the house in Shepherd's Bush that used to belong to record producer Tony Visconti and his wife, winsome Welsh warbler Mary Hopkin. When they moved out, it passed on to Jake Riviera, highly combustible manager of Elvis Costello and Nick Lowe. Nick then moved in with Jake, installing a studio in the downstairs dining room.

You join us on a particularly balmy Tuesday evening. Jake's prowling the upstairs living room, where Nick's sprawled on a couch, listening to Jerry Lee Lewis and scribbling something in a notebook. We're waiting to be picked up by Rockpile tour manager and general Riviera scapegoat Nigel Buchap. Rockpile have a show tonight in Cambridge, at the Emmanuel College May Ball. Nick's not looking forward to it.

'I hate these functions,' he says, haunted perhaps by flashbacks of playing too many of these things with his old band, pub rock veterans Brinsley Schwarz. 'We were always doing them in those days,' he goes on, staring into his own past and not enjoying the sight. 'They really are the most horrendous affairs, May Balls. Bloody miserable, by and large. Just an excuse really for all these bloody students to get damned unpleasantly pissed. It'll be absolutely grim.'

Jake goes to answer a knock on the front door.

'And have you noticed?' Nick asks, a bit of wonder in his voice here. 'There's always a steel band. You never see them anywhere else.'

We can hear Jake talking to someone downstairs, laughter.

'The organisers lock you in a room,' Nick is going on. 'With as much bevvy as you can drink. Which is the only compensation. Then you go on at, like, eight in the morning, and by then of course you're dreadfully pissed. All you can see is this horrible crew of drunken students, vomit dripping down their dinner jackets and ball gowns. It looks like *Come Dancing* in a fucking abattoir. Absolute fucking nightmare.'

Jake interrupts Nick's litany of woe with the sharp command to get downstairs, now. Nigel's down there with the Welsh half of Rockpile, Dave Edmunds and drummer Terry Williams. We jump in the van, Nigel at the wheel, and head off to Enfield to pick up guitarist Billy Bremner. Where will we find Billy? In his local pub, of course.

'He won't be having a drink, though,' Dave says.

'Good Lord, no,' Nick agrees. 'Not Bill. Not having a drink. Not in his local. Damned unlikely. If he's there at all, he'll be in a quiet corner discussing the European economic situation with a group of industrial chemists.'

'And he won't be having a drink,' says Terry Williams.

When we get to his local Billy it turns out isn't having a drink. He's having two. Pints with brandy chasers, more than a few of each down the hatch before we arrive. In fact, Billy looks like he's been here since the pub opened. In 1923, according to a sign over the door.

It proves somewhat difficult to budge Billy from the pub before closing time, not that I remember anyone trying very hard. We reluctantly join him for a drink. Just to be sociable, you understand. Jake mentions that on a recent fraught visit to meet Peter Grant to discuss Dave Edmunds' contract with Led Zeppelin's Swan Song label, he'd heard that Zeppelin in preparation for their forthcoming bash at Knebworth would be rehearsing for a full six weeks.

Nick nearly falls off his stool.

'Six weeks?' he says, incredulous. 'It would kill me to rehearse for six days. This band never rehearses. It's a miracle if we do a fucking soundcheck.'

'It would split the group up,' says Terry Williams. 'Four days and we'd be at each other's throats,' he adds a little gloomily. 'Three, maybe.'

Some while after this, we're driving down a dark lane, towards what we take to be the lights of Emmanuel College. There's a large wooden gate at the end of the lane, manned by a crew of surly-looking security guards. They don't seem in a hurry to open the gate, which makes Jake a little impatient.

'I'll just get out and have a quiet word with them,' he says.

Which he then does.

'OPEN THIS FUCKING GATE OR WE'LL DRIVE THE FUCKING VAN STRAIGHT FUCKING THROUGH IT!' he screams at the startled security men, who back off like they're being attacked by a polar bear.

'Good to see Jake finally coming out of his shell,' Dave says as we drive into the college grounds, a night of unquiet mayhem ahead of us.

Excuse the bags under our eyes and the dull thumping between our ears, but we didn't get back to London from Cambridge until 7.30 am this morning. It's now just after 12.00 pm and we're on our way to Manchester, where Rockpile will start a short tour at the Free Trade Hall. Nick is suffering.

'Nige,' he whines. 'I badly need a Coke and a paper.'

'Thirsty and hungry?' buzzes a despicably bright Billy Bremner. 'That's the way to start the day.'

It starts to rain.

'If it's raining, we must be going to Manchester,' the guitarist says, talking to people who aren't really listening. 'Did you know,' he asks chirpily, 'that Manchester's the only city in Britain where they have lifeboat drills on the buses?'

Granada Television, based here in Manchester, have recently been filming a documentary on Nick and Dave. It's eventually called *Born Fighters* and follows the making of Nick's *Labour of Lust* album and Dave's simultaneously released *Repeat When Necessary*. It's an often-hilarious insight into the traumas, tantrums, drunkenness and frustrations of making the records. We've been invited to the Granada studios to see a rough cut.

We gather in a small viewing room and watch Nick on screen.

'The hardest thing in the world is to produce a three-minute rock'n'roll song,' he's saying, through a haze of cigarette smoke, drugs and strong drink. The state he's in, you can fully believe him. He looks like writing a note to the milkman would be beyond him, let alone writing a song. He's as strung out as a washing line. And why is he wearing a fucking cowboy hat?

'Very new wave, that hat,' Nick says, probably wondering the same thing and wincing at the playback. On screen, he's now directing Dave

Edmunds through a guitar part he wants him to play that Dave looks like he's got doubts about. He suggests leaving it for the moment, coming back to it later.

'Nah!' Nick shouts at him. 'Let's nail it right now. Just play like you've gone mad. Don't worry about it. It's only a fucking guitar solo. We're only making a record. It's not going to change the world.'

'You weren't drunk when they filmed this, were you, Nick?' Billy asks Nick, who's looking around for a rock to crawl under until all this is over.

The penultimate scene in the film was shot one night at Dave's flat. He and Nick are both fairly well gone. Nick is in one of his tortured, introspective moods.

'I should be writing the … the soundtrack for life,' he exclaims, apparently delirious, waving his arms around like he's on the deck of an aircraft carrier, signalling frantically to a squadron of fighters coming in to land. 'Something the milkman can whistle in the morning.'

Edmunds looks at him dubiously: 'Take it easy, Nick.'

'You don't know how I feel!'

'And I don't give a shit,' Edmunds, on screen, tells Nick.

'That's his problem,' Dave tells the camera, or whoever's pointing it at him. 'If we have a day off, Nick doesn't go home. He'll be out boogieing.'

'I wouldn't be seen DEAD boogieing,' Nick says, offended, alarmed at the very thought. 'But I know I'm going to snuff it. I know.'

Edmunds, in the film, rolls his eyes. He's heard it all before.

'You should try boring yourself to death,' he suggests to Nick, who's becoming ever more befuddled.

'My dad,' Nick says, close it seems to tears, 'my dad bombed Jerries every night for five years.'

'Jesus fucking Christ,' Billy says in the playback room. 'This is like watching a documentary about a fucking mental home.'

'Oh, dear,' Nick says, stricken by his own performance. 'What is my poor old mum going to say when she sees that?'

A couple of nights later, we're in the bar of the Holiday Inn, in Leicester, after a show at the De Montfort Hall. Before they settle in, I remind Nick and Dave that I need to sit them down for an interview.

I suggest we go up to my room. Dave says he'll get some drinks to take with us, goes to the bar, comes back.

'I thought you were getting some drinks,' Nick says to the empty-handed Edmunds.

'They'll bring some up,' he tells Nick, and we go upstairs to my room. Ten minutes later, there's a knock at the door. It's the barman and a porter with our drinks. Two crates of beer, a bottle of vodka and four bottles of wine. Nick visibly brightens.

'That should see us through a couple of hours,' he says, pouring more wine into his glass than it will actually hold.

Several hours later, the room is thick with cigarette smoke and laughter. The vodka's long gone, there are two empty wine bottles on a small table besides the bed where Nick is stretched out like a garrulous corpse, ubiquitous Senior Service dangling rakishly from his lips. Dave is at the foot of the bed, uncorking another bottle of plonk, and struggling to remember when he first met Nick.

'I can remember meeting you,' Nick, prone to sentimentality in his cups, tells Edmunds. 'You were my hero. I was in total awe of you. I remember when I was first in a group, and I heard Dave with Love Sculpture on John Peel's show. I thought it was the most fan-fucking-tastic thing I'd ever heard in my life. Dai was my absolute hero.'

'Please, Nick ...' Edmunds says, embarrassed.

'You were, man,' Nick gushes. 'I remember one night, Brinsley Schwarz were recording at Rockfield and we'd done a version of a Chuck Berry song ...'

'"Don't You Lie to Me". I remember that.'

'You thought it was great, and we really got off on that, because you were such a mystery figure. You actually mixed that track, and another one, "Home in My Hand". It sounded fantastic. We couldn't believe it.'

'I don't even remember it coming out,' Edmunds confesses, a bit baffled.

'Oh,' Nick says, trying to light a fag. 'We never released it. We thought, "It doesn't really sound like us." And we dumped it.'

Nick pours himself another half-pint of wine.

'We didn't really become friends, though, until I produced that Brinsleys album,' Edmunds says, trying to plot a chronological course to the present.

'*New Favourites*, yeah,' Nick remembers. 'But we still weren't chums. It was only when you moved to London from Rockfield that we started knocking about together.'

'That's when the shit really hit the fan,' Edmunds recalls. 'I was going through a divorce. I came to London, and I was really down. I was drinking a hell of a lot. Some people breeze through a divorce, but some people end up in a mental hospital. I didn't get that bad, but it was still a huge upheaval. I was really hitting the bottle.'

'Dai's problem,' Nick interrupts, 'was that he had no real mates. He'd been living in, like, seclusion at Rockfield. Never came out of the studio. People were rather in awe of him. There was no one close to him who could say, "Look here, Edmunds, old chap, you're really fucking up your life, pull yourself together, man." People were scared to say anything to him.'

'At least you called me up and asked if there was anything you could do to help.'

'Basically, that was because I wanted to learn things from you, Dai,' Nick laughs, spilling his wine and dropping his cigarette on the floor, where it burns a small hole in the carpet. 'I was always coming up with things like, "'Ere, Dai, you know that handclap sound on that version you did of "Needle in a Haystack"? How did you do that?' And he'd go, "Oh, it's a delay spring, a very short delay spring."

'And I'd go, "Oh, yeah. Of course, it is." I didn't know what he was talking about, but the next time I was in the studio pretending to produce someone, I'd turn suddenly to the engineer and say, "HEY! Give me some delay spring on this!" And I'd just sit there and hope to God I hadn't just made a complete idiot of myself. And the engineer would say, "Fine, yeah." And sure enough, out would come the same handclap sound.

'I must say,' Nick goes on, 'that I basically wasn't much help at all to Dai. When he was telling me about his divorce and all his endless problems, I was just trying to nick all his fucking ideas.'

'We never had any real plans to work together,' Edmunds says, moving things along, 'until I got a deal with Swan Song and we were out drinking, standing at a bar somewhere …'

'It was The Nashville, a Graham Parker gig,' Nick suddenly recalls.

'I remember I had a terrible hangover and I said to Nick, "I've got to make an album, have you got a song for me?" And he just said, "Let's write one." I'd been trying to write songs for years, and I'd never been able to. We were at the bar of The Nashville, trying to come up with an idea for a song. I said, "No one's written a song about the weekend since Eddie Cochran, let's do one about the weekend." We were at the bar, actually writing it. We went into the dressing room, the quietest place we could find, and Nick scratched it out on the back of a cigarette packet. By the end of Graham's set, we had "Here Comes the Weekend". I'd been trying for years to write a song, you know, and suddenly I was doing it.'

God knows what time it is by now, but I notice there's only one bottle of wine left. Time to start on the beers. Nick, quite spectacularly drunk by now, is pouring most of the wine into his glass and having a moan about not being what he calls 'fashionable', citing criticism of his new album, *Labour of Lust*, as evidence.

'Nobody thinks I'm hip anymore,' he says, somewhat sorry for himself.

'Get a grip, Nick,' Edmunds advises sagely.

'But it's true,' Nick blearily laments. 'The album was terribly slagged. But who cares?' he asks, trying to put a brave face on things. 'The only people who read reviews of my records are the people who write them, me and my mum.'

'The album's still selling,' Dave tells him.

'Oh, yeah,' Nick laughs bitterly. 'It's crawling up the charts with a fucking anvil around its neck. But I still think I'm streets better than most people making records today. All these very serious people trying desperately to look thin. They're all crap. I mean, whenever I hear Siouxsie and The Banshees, I think, "Come back, Curved Air, all is forgiven." I'm much better than any of them, whatever anyone else says.'

'That's telling them, boyo,' Edmunds roars, almost falling off the end of the bed.

'It's true, Dai, don't fucking laugh.'

'But that's the point, Nick,' Edmunds says, grappling with Nick for the wine, Nick reluctant to let go of the bottle. 'What it all comes down to is this: if you can't laugh, fuck it. And if you can't fuck it, laugh.'

Nick looks at Dave, stunned, as if he's just been told one of the secrets of the universe, a truth imparted from the invisible lips of God.

'Dai,' he says, incredulous. 'You're fucking marvellous. I love you, man.'

'Easy, Nick,' Edmunds says, finally wrestling the wine from Nick's white-knuckled grip. 'Easy, boy.'

JUKE BOX JURY

London, June 1979

'Jesus, Jonesy, what the fuck's up wi' you?' Bob Geldof asks, expressing the kind of concern he will become famous for years later when far more deserving cases than me become the focus of his urgent attention.

The state I'm in when we meet at the BBC studios in Shepherd's Bush is anyway entirely self-inflicted, no need really for the ubiquitous sympathy Bob will eventually bestow upon Africa's starving millions. I've merely been on the road for a week with Rockpile and only just arrived back in London after an all-night interview with Nick Lowe and Dave Edmunds in a Leicester hotel room.

We go down to the breakfast room after we finally wrap up the interview.

'Full English, Nick?' Dave asks.

'Full Smirnoff, I think,' Nick says, wandering off to see if he can find someone to open the bar.

'What the hell,' Dave says then, going after Nick, giving up on breakfast. 'Why not?'

Christ in the wilderness was ne'er so sorely tempted as I am now to follow them. Duty calls me back to London, however, where I've just fetched up at the BBC's Bush Theatre – now Shepherd's Bush Empire – because in their broadcasting wisdom the Corporation's decided to bring back from the dead the TV pop show *Juke Box Jury*. Readers of a certain age may share dim memories of the show's 1960s heyday – Saturday nights around the blazing familial hearth, rain on the windows, the weekly ritual of the football results, followed by *JBJ*. The show weekly features a panel of guests, a mix of people with records in the charts or otherwise members of popular beat groups and so-called celebrities usually recruited from the twilight world of what used to be known as Light Entertainment, who are played the new singles and asked for their hopefully amusing comments and whether in their opinions said singles will be either a HIT or a MISS.

To enliven the proceedings, mystery guests lurk backstage while the jury pontificates on their records. They are then wheeled out to either backslapping congratulation or hostile embarrassment, depending on which way the vote's gone. The original host of the show was the sleek David Jacobs, who had the air of a disbarred barrister or a Harley Street surgeon, struck off for a history of absentmindedly leaving forceps and surgical swabbing in the sewn-up stomachs of unfortunate patients. He's been replaced in this new incarnation by Noel Edmonds, a man who always seems to be wearing someone else's head.

As soon as I hear the programme's being relaunched, I'm on the phone to the BBC press office to see if I can attend the inaugural recording. Which I apparently can't, the press clearly unwelcome. I then bump into Geldof at some after-show jolly-up and he tells me he's been invited onto the first panel and if I meet him at the Bush Theatre, he'll get me in.

Which is why I'm now standing at the stage door of the theatre, where I've just asked a doorman to find me Bob.

'Geldorf's not 'ere,' I'm brusquely told.

Where is he?

'Gorn out.'

I check the local pubs. No sign of Geldof. I go back to the stage door, where the doorman gives me a surly look.

''E 'asn't come back.'

I'm now approached by an elderly commissionaire.

'A fan of The Boomtown Rats, are you?' he asks sympathetically, adding that he saw Geldof arrive a little while back.

I nod eagerly. Give him what I hope is a winning smile. Tell him I've won a fan club competition to meet Bob. I'm supposed to rendezvous with him here, but haven't been able to find him and have no way of getting in touch. What to do? The commissionaire strokes his nose conspiratorially, disappears. He's soon back with a backstage pass. Minutes after that I'm sipping wine in the green room with Geldof.

Bob's wearing a ridiculous black-and-white checked jacket with big shoulder pads that makes me laugh out loud when I see him.

'What's so fuckin' funny?'

His suit. He looks like a clown or a third-on-the-bill music hall comedian whose career hasn't survived the passing of vaudeville.

'Fuckin' thanks a lot,' Geldof says, as ever easily affronted. 'That's exactly what I needed to hear, that I look like a fuckin' comedian.'

He seems to be having second thoughts about his imminent appearance on the relaunched show.

'If you write about this fuckin' thing,' he says, 'can you at least please emphasise that I was forced into it. That I had to be physically fuckin' coerced into doing it. You know, say I had no fuckin' choice or something.'

But you never turn down the chance of being on the telly.

'I know. I know,' he says. 'But don't make it too fuckin' obvious, you know. My fuckin' credibility's taken enough of a fuckin' bashing for the time being.'

Geldof's been invited onto the show because he's a dependable loudmouth with opinions to spare. The rest of the panel are the usual mixed bunch, in the show's grand tradition. It includes veteran BBC DJ Pete Murray, gameshow hostess Isla St Clair, then at the height of her popularity as the fragranced assistant to Larry Grayson on *The Generation Game* ('Shut that door!'), and trilling songbird Linda Lewis.

Pete Murray's dressed as if he's on his way to an RAF reunion. You can easily imagine him stationed at some Battle of Britain airfield in the grim summer of 1940. But not exactly one of the plucky pilot heroes of our darkest hour. A stranger, therefore, to bursting flak and burning fuselages. But a good man in the mess. Always ready to stand his round, or drop his trousers for a laugh. Someone in air command intelligence, perhaps, who pushes model aeroplanes around with a long stick on a table map covered with Luftwaffe flight formations. Known to his friends as Pongo, or something. He's been a staple of the BBC for so long, it's a shock to see him in colour. He's been around for as long as the test card and the potter's wheel.

There's something disturbingly pristine about Isla St Clair. Her skin looks like it's been vacuum-packed in clingfilm, like something you

107

might find at the back of the fridge but can't remember putting there. From certain angles her head glows like the landing lights of an alien spaceship. She reminds me of one of those old settees that came sealed in a PVC covering that were too hot to sit on in the summer and otherwise were cold enough to make you think you were lounging on a rapidly cooling cadaver. I'm sure the case is otherwise, but she gives the impression of someone with enough space between their ears to herd cattle.

Linda Lewis, meanwhile, looks like she's dressed for a night on the Reeperbahn. Geldof looks aghast at her skin-tight red satin pants.

'Where the fuck didja get dose trousers?' Bob asks her.

'They're Jim's,' she giggles. Jim is her husband, Jim Cregan. He plays with Rod Stewart.

'Jim's?' says Geldof, disbelievingly. 'Jesus. Where does he put his bollocks?'

'Same place you put yours, probably,' Linda says, and even Geldof is stuck for a reply.

'Thirty seconds to go if anybody wants to!' announces a waggish floor manager, and the panellists take their seats. They are introduced by Noel Edmonds as 'pop piranhas about to set their teeth into some of the new releases'.

The first record played is Supertramp's 'Breakfast in America', through which Geldof conspicuously fidgets. Pete Murray's asked for his opinion.

'I was going to say,' he waffles, 'it is, in fact, if I'm not mistaken, and you know more about these sorts of things than I do, I think this is the title track from an album that's 15 in the long-playing record chart, isn't it?'

Geldof looks at Pete like Pete's brains are dribbling out of his nose and gathering in a sticky puddle in his lap. Noel meanwhile has noticed Isla nodding her head vigorously at Pete's ramblings.

'Does that mean you agree, Isla?' he asks.

'It does, actually!' she beams, which gets her a glare from Bob.

'Breakfast in America' is now voted a hit. Unlike Art Garfunkel's 'Since I Don't Have You' – 'not a patch on "Bright Eyes",' Isla decides. 'The words are a bit miserable' – and Patti Boulaye's 'Disco Dancer', which the panel slate. As do most of the people interviewed on the seafront at Eastbourne.

'What would you do to improve the record?' one holidaymaker is asked.

'Smash it,' comes the terse reply.

This is all rather unfortunate. Patti is tonight's surprise guest and clearly upset.

She's brought out to face the jury who've so ruthlessly dismissed her new single, all of them squirming now, like people trying to get to sleep in a bed full of mice. She tries to put a dignified face on her humiliation. But it doesn't fit. Keeps pulling her smile into something more closely resembling a furious snarl. The panel seem relieved when she quits the set without biting anyone.

The grim charade winds to a thankful conclusion. I hit the bar in the hospitality room with Geldof, while the second in the new *JBJ* series is being filmed with panellists Annie Nightingale, Olympic swimmer David Wilkie, Joe Brown and choreographer Flick Colby.

Isla St Clair joins us for a glass of wine, head still shining. She hasn't enjoyed the programme at all.

'I didn't really know what I was talking about,' she confesses. 'It's not the kind of music I listen to at all. Now if they'd played me a Gerry Rafferty record ...'

Geldof's had enough by now and leaves.

'Remember to write that I was fuckin' forced to do it,' he says over a departing shoulder. 'At fuckin' gunpoint.'

I hang around the bar, talking to one of the production assistants on the show, who tells me how panels are selected.

'Basically,' says the PA, 'what you're looking for is a hatchet man. Like Geldof. A loudmouth. Then you want someone who's going to be benign. A Pete Murray type. Then you look for a bit of crumpet. Linda Lewis, say. Very nice. And then you get someone who doesn't know anything about the subject, like Isla St Clair or David Wilkie. Those are the ingredients we're looking for.

'But, you know,' he says, lowering his voice like he's about to share some dark secret, 'it's all bollocks, really.'

Which you'd have to say it truly, sadly is.

STING | THE POLICE

London, September 1979

It's a basement flat in Bayswater, just beyond the casbah rowdiness of Queensway. Sting is in the small front yard when I arrive. He's leaning against a whitewashed wall, arms folded across his chest, a telephone cradled between head and shoulder, an extension cord pulled through the open window of what I take to be the flat's living room. There's a movie director's chair beneath the open window, red canvas stretched over a wooden frame, Sting's name printed boldly in white letters across the back. Sting carries on talking, his chat interrupted now and then by a sandpapery laugh, a serrated chuckle. Two passing school-girls stop, one of them peering over low railings into the basement yard. She recognises Sting, waves, giggles, shouts something. Sting ignores her, finishes his business on the phone.

As soon as the receiver's back on the hook, the phone starts ringing again. Sting apologises for the further interruption, takes the call. It's someone from the Police office. The band's new single has been voted top of Capital Radio's Hit Line. Sting passes on the news with consid-erable glee and smiles to the tune of ringing cash registers. A roadie arrives with plane tickets. The Police are flying to Holland tomorrow morning for a television show at the weekend. They'll be back in London the following Monday to finalise preparations for a British tour following their recent headlining appearance at the Reading Festival. There's another telephone call that leaves Sting smiling even more broadly. He's just been told that *Outlandos d'Amour* has gone platinum in the Netherlands. He receives all this good news, the chart forecasts, album sales, general attention, with a kind of lip-smacking relish. He clearly loves the taste of his own success. And why not?

As he remarks more than once over the next couple of hours, nothing he's enjoying now was handed to him. To which extent, he's keen at every opportunity to remind you how far he's come, how just are the rewards for his hard work and talent, that singular thing. It's a pay-off, too, for the sheer relentless effort The Police have put in to get where they are now, even greater riches soon to come. Their second album, *Reggatta de Blanc*, is due out in a couple of months, international stardom beckons. Time, *Melody Maker* editor Richard Williams decides, for a feature charting their history so far, including commentary from each of the band, but with the emphasis on Sting, by now quite the heart-throb. Assistant editor Mick Watts also briefs me on what's needed. 'Use the opportunity,' he says, in reference to Sting, 'to take the measure of his ambition.' Is he quoting Shakespeare now?

Anyway, Sting leads the way into the house, to a small living room with a colour TV in one corner, a stereo in another. There are prints, photographs and paintings on the wall. It all seems very cosy. Sting settles into a large red velvet armchair, although you get the impression he'd be more comfortable yet on a throne made of skulls and the bones of his enemies, a snarling jaguar at his feet. He certainly has an imperious air about him, someone most at home in a room full of mirrors, surrounded by his own reflection. The clear eyes, the broad forehead, those cheekbones, a fictional assassin's cruel smile. It's vaguely the look of one of the minor Caesars, the kind who marries his sister to his favourite horse and races their children in the Colosseum as a warm-up to a headlining act involving the devouring of Christians by lions.

He sits upright in his chair, legs crossed, for most of the afternoon. His left hand is always near his chin, holding it or stroking it whenever he wants to look lost in thought, reflecting on a considered response to this question or that. His right arm is mostly languidly extended over the chair arm, as if he's expecting a kitty-hawk, kite or kestrel to fly through the window and land on it, announcing its presence with excessive preening and blood dripping from its beak. Absent avian interruption, you expect at least to see at some point a serpent of some kind coiled around the extended limb. As usual, I'm getting carried away. He's actually telling me how ordinary he is, how he lives here simply with his wife and young son in modest retreat.

111

'As you can see,' he says, scanning the room, a U-boat commander at a periscope, 'I do want things around me that I wanted as a kid. I wanted a house of my own. I wanted a car. I wanted to send my kids to a good school. I don't think there's anything phoney in those aspirations. I'm aware of the middle-class caricature. The ducks on the wall, you know. But all this is part of me. I try as far as possible not to disguise the fact that I am a home-loving, average home-husband. I have a wife. I have a child. I do have a family life that is quite normal. I don't see any point in trying to disguise it. I don't see any profit in trying to promote an image of myself as a kind of rebellious playboy.'

The very thought makes him laugh, that chuckle again.

'I mean,' he says, 'someone like Phil Lynott has this wonderful playboy image. A girl in every bed and all that. I think it's very funny. But people eventually start seeing through it. One day, the world catches you with your hair in curlers and there goes the image, blown away.'

I'm not really buying into any of this man about the house, blessed in the bosom of his family and happy with his simple lot in life bollocks. The chaste and humble image he has of himself isn't much in evidence, for a start, in the shots Adrian Boot takes of him for the story I'll soon be writing for *Melody Maker*, in which he poses, smirking, on a Huey Newton throne, draped by scantily dressed Bunny Girls. You sense there's not much he enjoys more than adoration. I ask him at one point how he felt recently on stage in front of 40,000 cheering fans at the Reading Festival.

'I felt like a god,' he says.

There's a low purr in his voice when he says this, and on his face the wholly smug look of a cat with its own podcast.

'And I loved it,' he adds, as if this might have been in any doubt, and takes a beat to savour the memory. 'I felt born for the moment.'

I have a bit of history with Sting. In August 1977, I get a call from a PR friend, Rick Rodgers, who's doing the press for a punk festival being held in a bullring in a place called Mont-de-Marsan, in the far south of France, near the Spanish border. The festival's headlined by The Clash, Dr Feelgood, The Damned and The Jam. Do I want to go? Rick doesn't have to ask twice. The day before we're due to fly out, however, Rick calls with a change of plan. The festival headliners will still be flying out, as scheduled. But the rest of us – support bands, photographers, journalists, anyone else – will now be going by coach, a two-day drive with an overnight stop in Paris.

The next morning, there's a banged-up old coach waiting for us outside the London Dungeon, near London Bridge. There are a lot of people standing around, loading stuff onto the decrepit old banger and generally giving off a collectively grumpy vibe. I'm surprised to find among them veteran guitarist Andy Summers, who I've known for a couple of years as a member of a great band fronted by radical singer-songwriter Kevin Coyne. More recently Andy's been playing with Kevin Ayers. What's he doing here? Turns out Andy's recently joined a punk band called The Police, formed by former Curved Air drummer Stewart Copeland, regarded as a bit of a joke by hard-core punks.

Andy introduces me to one of his new bandmates, a bass player from Newcastle named Sting, who follows me onto the coach, sits down next to me and on the way to Dover tells me all about himself. A tale of hand-wringing woe ensues. Sting has apparently given up the security of full-time employment as a teacher in somewhere called Cramlington, a mining village outside Newcastle, and moved to London with his wife and young son after being persuaded by Stewart Copeland to join The Police. Things have not gone well for them so far and he wonders if he's made the right decision, something he's still fretting about the next day on the long drive from Paris to Mont-de-Marsan.

The Police aren't terribly well received at the festival, where their performance is barracked by a meagre crowd. This means that on the coach back to Paris, Sting endures even greater agonies about what more than ever seems the reckless decision to give up his job and uproot his family. For what seems like hours, he bleakly contemplates a future he seems to be increasingly convinced he doesn't have.

'Should I just give up?' he finally asks. By now, I've had quite enough of his ceaseless bleating and tell him, yes, if he's so unhappy, he should probably walk away from it all. Quit The Police. Move back to Newcastle with his family. He could be back in the classroom by Christmas. He thanks me for my advice, says he'll think it over.

Two years later, here we are. Gold discs in his lavatory, Sting well on his way to his first million or two.

113

'It's undreamed of,' he says. 'Just this last year, we've been presented with financial problems that are just bizarre. Shall we become tax exiles? Shall I buy an estate in Ireland? It's fun, I must say. I mean, I'm not complaining. It's just that because we're a small group we've been able to keep costs down and make an extraordinary profit.'

The Police have recently been described as a successful small business, which made them sound like a grocery chain, or a retail outlet with a growing turnover and opportunities for commercial expansion.

'I know,' Sting says, 'that people criticise us for being a nice little business. Well, we are a nice little business. We're a damned good business. And we've made money because not only are we a great band, we're also very intelligent. We're not in debt, like most groups. Spending £100,000 on one album is something we avoided because we knew from the start that's just mindless.

'Most bands,' he goes on, tills chiming in the background, 'don't make money. They just squander it on producers and cocaine and lots of other bullshit. It's disgusting, really. There's so much idiotic excess. It goes beyond enjoyment, you know. Like, I heard this absolute horror story about the drummer with a well-known band, one of the biggest bands in the world. He apparently has this huge bag of cocaine on stage and at each gig, at the start of every number, he'll reach down and dig up a handful of coke and just sort of smear it all over his face. Just to get through the number. At the end of the gig, the roadies are crawling all over the stage, sniffing the Persian carpets which have got, like, thousands of dollars of cocaine all over them.'

He makes a suitably harrumphing noise, appropriate to his outrage.

'The waste is appalling,' he tuts eventually, like someone in middle management tasked with cost-cutting efficiencies and determined to do something about spiralling overheads.

Stewart Copeland puts his feet up on a record company desk and tells me how he spent most of 1976 'nursing', as he puts it, the idea of The Police. Punk is already happening, grabbing headlines. Stewart at the time is drumming with Curved Air, one of those badly dressed early 1970s prog rock bands like Wishbone Ash or Argent who seem to exist only to drive me to furious distraction whenever they're on *The Old Grey Whistle Test*, which seems to be most fucking weeks, their every appearance introduced with fawning reverence by presenter Bob Harris and his mustang teeth and hedgehog beard.

Stewart doesn't much like the idea of being left behind by a bunch of sweary teenagers in bondage trousers and torn T-shirts. But while he digs punk's energy, he doesn't think much of the music. He wonders, though, if there's an opportunity for a band that matches punk's velocities with solid musical chops that might muscle onto the scene and take it over. He's still thinking about how he's going to do this when Curved Air fetch up in Newcastle in late November 1976 for a couple of shows. A local journalist named Phil Sutcliffe who also writes for music weekly *Sounds* takes him to see a hometown band called Last Exit, who have a gig at Newcastle Polytechnic.

'It was terrible,' Copeland recalls. 'The band was a sort of sophisto Newcastle Chick Corea affair. Everybody was in their mid-30s, balding, and taking it all very seriously. The numbers were all seven minutes long and very intense. They'd moved the gig from a small hall to an even smaller classroom and everyone was standing at the bar, wondering where the band was going to play. There was no stage. There were two reading lamps on a desk. That was the light show. Every time someone walked into the room, you could hear their footsteps echoing on the floor. It was absolutely, incredibly awful.

'But they went down a storm. Just because of Sting. Because of his raps with the audience. Because of his singing. Because of his presence. The group was dire. They did all these really jazzy numbers that started with little swishes on the piano or cymbals …' He holds his head in his hands and laughs out loud at the memory. 'But Sting,' he goes on, 'had then what he has now. This fantastic presence. It was obvious he had enormous potential.'

Stewart returns to London with Sting's telephone number, convinced that whatever he does next will be better if he can somehow involve Sting, who at the time, if not for much longer, is happy enough with Last Exit and their jazz rock odysseys.

Sting, as he now tells me, has come to Last Exit after dropping out of a first-year English course at Warwick University.

'I was lost there,' he says. 'Totally lost. It just wasn't for me. I thought that leaving school meant getting rid of your uniform. I thought it meant freedom. Being at university wasn't freedom at all. It was more of the same in a different uniform.'

Back in Newcastle, he works for six months on a building site and then joins the Inland Revenue. There's a bit of theatrical hair clutching when he describes quitting the job before he's sacked. He's soon after enrolled at a Newcastle teacher's training college.

'It was a total lack of imagination on my part that took me back to college,' he says. 'I just didn't know what else to do. My life was falling apart around me.'

Music alone is a respite from his almost permanent state of woe. He remembers an uncle who emigrates to Canada when Sting is a nipper and leaves behind a guitar. When the uncle returns to Newcastle five years later, he finds Sting has made the guitar his own and has taught himself to play, strumming along to records.

'I'd listen to The Beatles, the Stones, The Kinks,' he says. 'Learning the chords to "Dead End Street" was a major breakthrough.'

He's 14 when he borrows some jazz albums from an older school friend, keen to expand his musical horizons.

'I didn't like any of them,' he says. 'But I thought listening to them would do me good, somehow. I'd listen to album after album of Thelonious Monk piano solos and I thought, "This is so awful, it must be doing me a world of good." Gradually, the music grew on me. It was the same with blues. I'd listen to loads of blues albums and I just didn't like them. But I persevered because I thought they were doing me some good, like taking medicine.

'Eventually, I grew to love things like that. But at first it was a real effort. I just endured them because I desperately wanted to be hip. There was an elite group of us in the sixth form. Very snobbish. We knew who John Fahey was. We'd heard of Thelonious Monk. We'd heard Jimmy Witherspoon. We were horribly precocious.'

He's 18 when he starts playing in bands, recently returned to Newcastle from that unhappy year at Warwick University. By now, he's disenchanted with rock and plugs into the Newcastle jazz scene. There's a pub called The Wheatsheaf where Tyneside jazzers hang out, older guys, getting drunk, swapping stories, holding informal sessions. There's a resident rhythm section with a bass player named Ernie who allows Sting to sit in on his instrument when he goes off for drinks breaks.

'He had this big double bass,' he remembers. 'I used to get up, play two numbers and get blisters that wouldn't go away for three weeks. Eventually, I got the hang of it. Learned to play.'

One night, Ernie doesn't turn up at The Wheatsheaf. Sting's asked to stand in and turns up to the gig with his electric bass.

'The band jumped into the modern world that night,' he says. 'It was the first time they'd ever played with an instrument that worked on electricity. They went crazy.'

He's soon asked to join The Rivermen, Newcastle's premier trad jazz combo.

'It was great,' he says, and you wouldn't doubt him. 'They all wore blue suits. They'd been together for about 20 years, which was the same age as the suits. But they were a great band. Trad jazz is regarded as a bit of a joke, I know. But it can be very exciting. Especially fast rags. I loved it.'

He has a low opinion of most of the local Newcastle rock bands, with their Led Zeppelin riffs, sub-Sabbath heavy metal histrionics, horrible clothes.

'Those bands,' he says, with quite regal disdain, 'they all had long hair and flared trousers, looked terrible and sounded worse. I was only 20, but I had no time for any of them. I was mixing with much older musicians. People who'd worked for years at their craft. I felt proud to be playing with them. It was a great experience. If I'd been in a rock band with long hair and loon pants, I wouldn't have learned anything like as much as I did.

'I was conscious that there was some sort of apprenticeship being served. I learned to read music, worked hard practising every day. I was still a student at the teacher's training college, but I was earning a fortune every night. I had a brand-new car. I was definitely the face of the college. Everyone used to come and see me play. There was, I think, a ratio of seven girls to one guy at the college …'

How did that work out for him?

'You could say,' he says with a knowing leer, 'that I was well looked after. I'll leave it at that.'

He gets a job teaching at a primary school in Cramlington, six miles north of Newcastle. He's there for the next two years.

'I felt really frustrated there,' he says. 'The other teachers, it was just a job to them. They didn't care for the kids at all. It was a very reactionary school, very conservative. It was hell, actually. There was no way the kids there were going to feel anything but resentment for school. I felt the same. I hated that school as much as they did.'

He pauses, hand to chin.

'I'm not sure what I accomplished as a teacher,' he says after due consideration of a question no one's asked him.

'But if one kid in that class becomes a musician or plays in a group somewhere, I think he'd have to be thankful to me for encouraging him,' he adds, possibly imagining a statue in the town square, public dancing on his birthday.

He's still teaching in Cramlington when he joins Last Exit, whose local success encourages him to bring the band to London, looking for a record deal. They play a series of support gigs at The Red Cow and The Nashville, where they open for Stiff signings Plummet Airlines. 'We blew them off stage,' Sting remembers with satisfaction. They also manage to get a gig at the LSE with Kevin Coyne and John Stevens' Away. Sting remembers that show especially, because it gets them their first mention in the weekly music press.

'Karl Dallas reviewed it in *Melody Maker*,' Sting says. 'There was a sentence about us in the review. I was thrilled. I remember thinking, "At last, we're a tiny microcosm in the rock business. At last, we've been recognised!" I've still got the review. I've got loads of press cuttings now, but that was the breakthrough.'

Last Exit take their demo tapes around the record companies. No one's interested in signing them, but Virgin offer Sting a publishing deal.

'It wasn't a particularly good deal,' he says. 'But I was so excited I took it. I thought, "At last. I'm a real songwriter." It was like a trophy that proved I was a songwriter. I could talk to people about *my publishers*. It was another great thrill.'

Last Exit return to Newcastle, most of them happy to make a reasonable living on a familiar circuit. Sting, however, is hungrier than ever for success on a larger scale, a bigger stage than Newcastle pubs. He wants to take the band back to London, where he's sure they can make it. The rest of the band won't give up the security they have in the North East. But it's time for him to move on.

On 12 January 1977, Sting leaves Newcastle.

'I packed in teaching,' he says. 'Packed everything I owned into a car and drove off. I'd just got married. The baby was six weeks old. It sounds dramatic and it was. My life suddenly just turned over. I said, "This is it." It was the only way to do it. We were all in the car with

118

the dog and we didn't have anywhere to go. We had a friend who had a flat in Battersea, so we went there. We slept on the floor of his living room for three months. It was awful.

'The only thing that looked hopeful was this group Stewart Copeland had called me about the week before we moved. I told him I'd see him in London.'

Stewart Copeland is living at the time in a two-storey apartment in Mayfair. He has a studio there, where he's been recording with Henry Padovani, a Corsican guitarist he meets at one of Curved Air's last shows. Curved Air have split by now, missed by no one. When Sting gets in touch and tells him he's moved to London, Stewart invites him to the studio to talk about his plans for the band that becomes The Police. Sting is extremely dubious about the whole thing.

'He was a typical provincial boy,' Copeland says. 'He thought he was going to be ripped off by everyone. He wasn't at all sure about the music, either.'

'Musically, I thought Stewart's ideas were shit,' Sting says. 'But the energy, the dynamism of the guy really affected me. I thought, straight away, "This is the bloke for me." Yes, I suppose I did see something of myself in Stewart. He's very egocentric. Very, very energetic. Very determined. Very intelligent. He recognised what was happening at places like The Roxy. He's an opportunist. Like me.'

Copeland's biggest worry is what Sting will make of Padovani when he meets him and discovers how musically limited the guitarist is.

'Henry only knew about three chords,' Copeland recalls. 'I used to say that in the very early days, when we first started gigging, that we had a 20-minute set and a 20-minute guitarist. He had a nice feel, but he wasn't technically very proficient. I knew Sting was a sophisto jazz musician and he was going to freak when he met Henry. Henry had never played in a group before and here was Sting about to turn up having played for years with all these old jazzers. God, I thought he'd go crazy. I don't know how we pulled it off, but we impressed him enough for him to come back to rehearse the next day.'

Copeland by now is fully immersed in punk, the music, the attitude. Sting isn't impressed by what he hears, won't open up to punk at all.

'He was a dreadful reactionary,' Copeland says. 'And it really showed in the early days. Which is one of the reasons we were never accepted by the so-called punk elite. One of the first gigs we did was at The Nashville. Everybody from the punk scene turned out for it. And Sting … Sting did this thing where he said, "All right, we're going to play some punk now, which means the lyrics are banal and the music is terrible." He just totally blew it. He didn't understand what he was doing then. God knows what he thought he was up to.'

'I was reactionary,' Stings says, conceding the point without argument. 'But that was just because I wasn't sure where we stood with all these punk bands. It took me a while. Stewart's enthusiasm carried me along for quite a long time, until I started contributing something to the group.'

'I knew it was going to take some time to acclimatise Sting,' Copeland says. 'For those first few months, Sting hated everyone he saw. We did some gigs with Johnny Thunders and The Heartbreakers. Sting hated them. We'd wander down to The Roxy, and he'd be going, "Jesus Christ, what the fuck is this all about? Who are these people?" A band would come on, and he'd be totally freaked out. But the crucial thing was that he was immediately competitive. He'd see these people and say, "Look at these guys. They're getting all this media attention and they're shit. I can do better than this fucking lot." He'd get wilder and wilder. He became very aggressive, very determined.'

Stewart makes himself furious, recalling the way The Police are dismissed as shallow opportunists by most of the other punk bands, whose attitude towards them is often sheerly hostile. Sting shrugs it all off.

'I met a lot of those punks,' he says. 'Joe Strummer. Paul Simonon. Rotten. We were never incredibly chummy or matey. I don't think we ever had much in common with those people. I never got to know them very well. We were sort of untouchables as far as they were concerned. We weren't allowed to mix with the in-crowd. There was an inner circle, and we didn't belong to it. We didn't even try to penetrate it. I wouldn't have minded being part of the in-crowd. But, you know, I wasn't going to lose my temper if Dave Vanian refused to speak to me one night at The Roxy.'

Whatever his indifference at the time to the sneering of the punk bands, there's a fair amount of gloating now that The Police are on the verge of world-conquering success.

'I love it that we stuck to our guns and eventually won through, yes,' he says. 'Our success in America is especially ironic. We were forced to turn to America, because here every door was closed to us. And then we went there, and we did it, where all the elite bands from England totally failed. And will continue to fail, I think. They have nothing to say to America that America wants to hear. They don't want to hear The Clash. There's a minority on the coasts, maybe, who think it's very fashionable to like The Clash. But the heart of America is the Midwest. That's the reactionary, conservative, Ted Nugent-loving territory you have to break to break America. And they don't want to listen to The Clash out there.

'You know,' he goes on, not so much warming to his theme as glowing with vindication and not a little spite, 'I really think groups like The Clash and The Sex Pistols had it too easy. They had such an easy victory. It was a walkover for them. And I'm sure it's not as satisfying as being right down there and then swimming up to the surface through all the shit like we had to. In many ways, that's probably why The Sex Pistols split up. It was all too easy for them. They were just catapulted up there without any problems. They were their own biggest problem in the end. They just couldn't cope. On the other hand, we've been through it all and we've grown with it. We crawled. Then we walked. Now we're running. And we'll keep running until we fall.'

Copeland, Sting and Padovani play their first gig as The Police at a club called Alexander's in Newport, South Wales, on 1 March 1977. Back in London, they drag themselves for a couple of dismal months around the pub circuit, the punk clubs. Anywhere that will have them, really. When they can't get their own gigs, they're the backing band for former Warhol actress and David Bowie publicist Cherry Vanilla. They release their first single on 1 May, a Stewart Copeland song called 'Fall Out'. Padovani struggles through the sessions at Pathway Studios. Copeland has to double on guitar. Sting simmers through the session, multiple frustrations coming quickly to the boil. There's a chance he might quit.

'We were starving, backing Cherry Vanilla for a fiver a night that she usually couldn't pay us,' Copeland says. 'And Sting was offered a job with Billy Ocean for 90 notes a week. I had to force the money out of Cherry Vanilla, really put her over a barrel. Just to keep Sting. He would have gone, I know. He's a real bread-head. He goes for the money. If it had looked to him that The Police were going to fold, he would have taken that job.

'I'm glad that happened,' Copeland says. 'Because now, whenever he says, "I wrote 'Roxanne', I am The Police", I can say, "If it wasn't for me, mate, you'd have joined Billy fucking Ocean." The guy who turned Sting onto the gig eventually took the job. The gig lasted four months. So, four months after leaving The Police, Sting could have been back in Newcastle playing in a pub with a jazz band.'

Two things more crucial than the pittance Copeland strong-arms out of Cherry Vanilla influence Sting's decision to stick it out with The Police. Stewart's brother, Miles Axe Copeland III, belatedly becomes their manager, and they get another guitarist.

Not long after 'Fall Out' is released, Sting and Copeland join former Gong bass player Mike Howlett's Strontium 90 for a Gong reunion concert in Paris. The band's guitarist is Andy Summers. He's a veteran of Zoot Money's Big Roll Band, R&B stalwarts of the mid-1960s London club scene and the band's brief psychedelic incarnation, Dantalian's Chariot. He's been a member of Eric Burdon's late-1960s Animals, studied classical guitar for five years in California, toured with Soft Machine. He's also the inspiration for Davey, one of the main characters in Jenny Fabian's steamy 1969 novel *Groupie*. 'I was knocked out by the perfection of his genitals,' Fabian writes adoringly. 'They were compact and beautifully symmetrical.'

More recently, he's been playing with Kevin Coyne and Kevin Ayers. He's a decade older than Copeland and Sting and clearly not your typical up-and-coming punk guitarist, obsessed with Mott the Hoople, Lou Reed and David Bowie, with a granny in a high rise overlooking the Westway. Copeland and Sting are nevertheless impressed. They ask him to join The Police. Summers is keen but wants them to get rid of Padovani, who he sees as nothing but a musical hinderance. Copeland and Sting at first refuse and they play two gigs as a four piece – the second and last at Mont-de-Marsan – before they agree with Summers and sack Padovani. Summers' old-school music mates are aghast at his new career move.

'A lot of people thought I'd lost my marbles when I announced I was joining this new wave band called The Police,' he says, opening a bottle of wine in the flat in East Putney where he's living at the time. 'There was definitely a certain amount of sniggering behind my back. Especially when the dyed blond hair appeared. That really was the big snigger. They might have laughed, but I didn't give a shit. Anyway,' he says with the bright relish of the recently vindicated, 'I'm obviously having the last laugh now. At first there were a lot of jokes. Now there's a bit of cap-doffing. I think we've earned it.'

There are times, early on, however, when he admits wondering if he's made the right decision, giving up the relative job security of regular work as a freelance session musician for the uncertain future of a new band that nobody seems to like. The first year is especially depressing. The Police play a mere dozen shows in the six months after he joins. He remembers glueing up posters in freezing snow for a gig at The Red Cow in Hammersmith. The group are starving, and he's being supported by his wife.

'I felt like I'd put my balls in my mouth and taken a big bite,' he says, and you wonder what Jenny Fabian might think of her favourite testicles being bitten, chewed and spit out in the rank disappointment of failure. What keeps him going is the single-mindedness now being displayed by Copeland and Sting.

'Stewart's great enthusiasm and drive was immediately conspicuous,' he says. 'He and Sting were overwhelming in their preoccupation with The Police. You just don't meet that many people with their kind of drive and energy.'

Miles Copeland has meanwhile been rebuilding his career after his British Talent Management company goes bankrupt in 1976. Like Stewart, he sees punk as an opportunity to get back in the game, launching Illegal Records with Stewart in 1977. Illegal release The Police's 'Fall Out' and on sublabels Deptford Fun City and Step Forward put out records by Squeeze, Alternative TV, The Fall, Chelsea and The Cortinas. By now, he's also managing Squeeze, and Illegal Records is morphing into IRS, among whose early signings is R.E.M. Miles is as ambitious as any of his acts, as acerbic, fast-talking and colourfully opinionated as Jake Riviera, with whom he has a fierce rivalry. He doesn't have time for anyone who's not as smart as him, which means just about everyone in the music business. Everything he

123

says is delivered as an imperative, a command. He's clearly someone used to giving orders and expecting them to be obeyed. He's been critical so far of what he's heard by his brother's band but is increasingly impressed by Stewart and Sting's conviction during these grim early months, their absolute confidence in what they're doing. He gives them £1,500 to record their debut album and then agrees to manage them.

'Sting on his own, but especially under the influence of Stewart, was not about to be put down by anybody,' he says. 'Sting has a very high opinion of himself. He has tremendous self-confidence. Stewart is the same. And with the two of them, the confidence in the group was doubled. It didn't matter to them that people were putting them down. That they were unfashionable. That most of the other punk bands looked down on them. They knew that one way or another, they would survive. That they would come through.

'Sting always knew that he was good. If someone came along and said that he was a talentless sonofabitch, he thought there was something wrong with them. If someone came along and said, "You're a loser. You're full of shit," he'd feel sorry for the guy. He knew that guy must be an idiot. He knew he had the talent to succeed. Sting always knew he was going to be a star. Like he knew and Stewart knew, and I knew that The Police were going to be enormous. Anyone could see that Sting was someone of obvious talent. An idiot could have seen it. The trouble with this business is that it often takes the idiots longer to open their eyes to the obvious.'

Because of Padovani's musical haplessness, Sting has been withholding songs that he now starts bringing to rehearsals, confident that Summers will know what to do with them. He also makes what he describes as a significant connection with reggae.

'I'd always wanted to make a connection between the energetic music of punk and more sophisticated musical forms,' he says. 'There was this amazingly aggressive music, full of energy, on the one hand, and I wanted to take it and bridge a gap between interesting chords and harmonic variations and this wild energy. And what eventually allowed me to do it was listening to reggae. Bob Marley, especially. I saw a rhythmic connection between the fast bass of punk and the holes in reggae. I got interested in trying to write songs that combined these apparently diverse styles. I think we succeeded with "Roxanne".'

Andy Summers clearly remembers that breakthrough moment.

'We were rehearsing in this piss-awful cellar in Finchley,' he says. 'It was freezing cold, and the rehearsals were going dreadfully. I knew that Sting had had the chords for "Roxanne" for ages. I remember him playing them for me once in Paris. We weren't getting very far with anything, so we said, "Let's have a go at that song." Sting had written the lyric by this time, and he sang it and we messed about with the chords. We changed it around, played it backwards and thought, "Mmm. Not a bad song. Rather good, in fact." Then Miles came along to see how we were getting on. He had this real punk-religious glint in his eye. So, we played him all the more obvious songs and he told us that mostly they were shit. Then we played "Roxanne" and he flipped.'

'I thought it was one of the fucking great classic songs of all time,' Miles says.

He takes it to A&M, where he's already placed Squeeze. When they release 'Roxanne' as their debut single for A&M in April 1978, it doesn't chart, but sells just enough copies to finance the band's first American tour. A third Copeland brother, Ian, a decorated Vietnam War veteran, has by now launched a booking agency in America called Frontier Booking International (FBI). He's started breaking British new wave bands in America and for their first US tour books The Police in every small club that will take them, wherever the fuck they are. Inner-city shitholes, boondock bars. The Police play them all, their reputation growing through word of mouth and a lot of hard touring, driving up to eight hours from one gig to the next, often playing empty rooms. It's gruelling but pays off when 'Roxanne' starts picking up airplay. By February, it's cracked the *Billboard* Hot 100, prompting its re-release in the UK, where this time it's a hit.

Miles remembers a turning point on the first American tour, a gig in Syracuse. There are four people in the audience.

'Most groups,' Miles says, 'would have said, "Shit. Fuck this." The Police went on and played one of their best gigs. Sting actually introduced the audience to each other. And one of the people in the audience turned out to be a DJ who was really blown away. The next day, he started playing The Police really heavily on his show. That gig turned out to be one of the most important they've ever played. That's why I think their success is such a tribute to their conviction. They see each gig as a challenge. They'll play anywhere, to anyone. They're prepared to do anything for success.'

As their audience grows and their popularity expands, Sting becomes an obvious focal point. He doesn't flinch from the spotlight.

'God, he loved it,' Stewart Copeland says. 'He took to it naturally. Comfortably. One might say casually.'

As The Police start racking up hits, Sting's even cast in a couple of movies. He plays mod leader Ace Face in Franc Roddam's version of The Who's *Quadrophenia* and has a cameo in Chris Petit's arty black-and-white British road movie *Radio On*. He's reluctant at first to audition for *Quadrophenia*. He thinks he's too old for a part he knows Johnny Rotten and Sham 69's Jimmy Pursey have already tested for. Eventually, he's persuaded to meet director Franc Roddam.

'I washed my hair, went down to the studio, met him and sat around for a bit discussing Hermann Hesse,' he says.

Hermann Hesse?

'Yes,' he says, as if he and Roddam would have had nothing else to talk about. '*The Glass Bead Game*, I think.'

What happened next?

'He suddenly said, "You're perfect. You look perfect." I got the job that day. It transpired during the conversation that followed that I was going to appear in a two-million-dollar movie, and I'd never even been in a school play.'

The cameo in *Radio On* is similarly gifted to him when his agent sends him along to meet Petit and the director casts him on the spot.

'I just sit in a caravan and sing "Three Steps to Heaven". It's not exactly *Ben-Hur*,' he says, although you imagine he'll be disappointed if he's not at least nominated for a BAFTA or some other thespian gong to add to the gold records.

'I'm not surprised that Sting has been successful in movies,' Stewart Copeland says. 'He looks great, and he has a real rapport with the mirror. He enjoys being looked at. But only when he's being Sting. People say that he's not wild, that he doesn't party after gigs. That's because he can only keep up the intensity of being Sting for a limited amount of time. Then he has to switch off. And he can only do that when he's alone in his hotel room. He won't even come down to the hotel lobby if he thinks there might be a photographer there.

He has to be Sting in front of the camera. He'd have to keep up the persona. That's his career. His whole art form is down to the way he looks. That's why I'm not surprised he's been a success in the movies. Everything about him you can see is part of his art form, and he really gets uptight if you try to get behind it. Because he really does put out a lot, all the time. He gives people plenty to look at and conjure with. And that should be enough.

'He's not exactly two different people, but there are differences,' Copeland says. 'Let me put it this way: when he shows up, he's on stage and when he's not on stage, he doesn't show up.'

Sting hasn't yet fully developed the habit of looking over the shoulder of whoever he's talking to, like he's scanning the room for someone more important he should be chatting up, Sting forever stalking bigger prey. It eventually gets to the point where his whip-pan over both shoulders of whoever's in front of him makes you feel like you're talking to someone watching a tennis match. The only person who gets his full attention is probably Miles Copeland, usually when they're talking about money.

Right now, though, in his basement flat in Bayswater, I'm increasingly aware of Sting glancing at what I presume is the wall behind me. We've been talking by now for over three hours. Maybe he's looking at a clock. As much as he seems to like talking about himself and his success, maybe our time's running out. Our conversation, meanwhile, has come something like full circle. He's been talking about growing up in the Newcastle district of Wallsend. He remembers growing up on a street dominated by the Tyneside shipyards, watching, amazed, as the great ships being built took shape at the end of his road.

'We'd watch them being built,' he says, a little incredulous still. 'Then after about six months, they'd fall into the river and disappear.'

Now he's telling me that after music, his great passion at school is athletics. He's a sprinter. The Northern Counties 100-Metre Champion. He's invited to race in the British National Championship. He comes third.

'Do you know what I did when I came in third?' he asks.

Train harder, to win the next race?

'No,' he says. 'I never raced again.'

I'm not sure if this is a self-inflicted punishment or some way of turning defeat into a perverse sort of triumph. Either way, it sounds a bit extreme.

'You're either the best or you're not,' he says with a kind of unflinching finality. 'I realised when I came third that there were two people in my age group who were better than I was. And there was no possibility of me beating them. So, I just stopped running.

'I didn't want to be part of the pyramid. I wanted to be on the top. I like to be the best. I only want to be the best. I enjoy being the best. I am an egoist. I wouldn't get on stage and do what I do if I wasn't. I'm extremely self-confident about everything I do.'

There's a point where single-mindedness turns to ruthlessness. Sting seems to have arrived there pretty early on.

'I can be very ruthless,' he says. 'I admit it. We're a tough band. I mean, we sacked a guitarist we all liked. We all loved Henry as a person. But because he stood in the way of our musical progress, we sacked him. It was ruthless. But it had to be done. We sacked him in pieces,' he adds. 'I started it and Stewart finished it.'

You can only imagine Padovani is lucky he didn't find himself being marched into New Jersey's Pine Barrens by a couple of Tony Soprano's boys carrying shovels and a chainsaw. Anyway, I'm conscious again of Sting looking at the wall behind me. The clock seems to be ticking. Quickly, then. What of the suggestion that his arrogance is boundless? That he has something of a superiority complex.

He stirs slightly in the red velvet armchair that looks like a throne.

'I know I'm arrogant,' he says. 'I don't need to be told that. Arrogance is a useful tool to me. If I wasn't arrogant, I wouldn't be as successful as I am.'

The viper coiled around his arm hisses and retreats to his shoulder, where it curls black-eyed against his ear.

'I think it would be false for me to be modest,' he goes on. 'I'm a great singer, and I know it. I'm a great songwriter, and I know it. Of course, this kind of arrogance will antagonise some people. There are some people who don't like me, obviously. I'm not beloved by everyone.'

There's a fluttering of wings at the window, a hawk's hoarse screech.

'But a lot of people,' Sting says, 'think I'm really rather a nice bloke.'

Even the fucking jaguar laughs at that.

BRYAN FERRY

London, September 1979

'I've realised for a long time that I've been disliked,' Bryan Ferry says, head coming up from a tastefully patterned earthenware dish piled high with cocaine.

'But it's only lately that I've realised I might actually be hated. It's an unpleasant situation,' he goes on, nose back in the coke. 'But one I think I can accommodate. I mean,' he says emphatically, 'if some people hate me, fuck them. I don't need them. I'm as good as anyone currently working in the field of rock music, and better than most, I think. If some people don't recognise that, then they must be pretty fucking stupid, frankly,' he adds with some feeling. Then sighs like he's just run out of steam, all indignation for the moment spent.

'More charlie?' he asks, even though we've been hitting it pretty hard for the last couple of hours, working our way simultaneously through several bottles of the rather fine wine served up by long-time Roxy Music 'media consultant' Simon Puxley. It's actually in Simon's swanky Holland Park digs that you find us currently lolling, Ferry preferring to stretch out on the carpet, me beside him, than to take one of the amply cushioned armchairs in Simon's prettily decorated front room. It's been two years since I last interviewed Ferry, at Air Studios, when he was rushing to finish his *In Your Mind* album and looking forward to the world tour that would follow. Since then, however, he's taken a bit of a personal and professional pasting. There was the public humiliation of Jerry Hall ditching him for Mick Jagger – 'What did people think I was going to do? Challenge Mick to a duel?' – reports of poor international sales for *In Your Mind* and the continued indifference of America to contend with.

There's recently been worse. A comeback single, 'Sign of the Times', has flopped badly after largely scathing reviews, the most venomous of which was penned by *Melody Maker*'s puritanical Chris Brazier. Chris is a lovely guy, but prone to bouts of self-righteous fury, at which point he tends to go off like a minister of the Pentecost, some hellfire pulpit-basher or fire-and-brimstone tub-thumper.

For Chris, and a lot of people like him, Ferry has no place in the post-punk landscape. He's become irrelevant, his playboy image now an embarrassment. Chris had been particularly incensed by a news report about Ferry moving into a £400-a-night hotel room, where he stayed for months during the recording of his new solo album, *The Bride Stripped Bare*, in Montreux. This is evidence enough for Chris that Ferry has long since parted company with reality, abandoned any sense of common value, a martyr to extravagance.

'I read that bloody review,' Ferry harrumphs noisily. 'It's all about this guy who supposedly spent £395 a night on a hotel room and consequently has nothing to say to humanity. What am I supposed to say to a charge like that? To think *Melody Maker* has someone like that writing for them. This is a paper I used to, like, deliver. Used to, like, buy every week. To think they have someone with insufficient brains, who believes that I'm dumb enough to pay £395 a night for a hotel room! He doesn't deserve to write the ads at the bloody back of the paper. You know: "Guitarist wanted. Hair. Image. No time-wasters." He doesn't deserve to be even doing that. Or even driving around to the bloody newsagents to distribute copies. What am I supposed to think about reviews like that? What kind of dumb people are they employing to write for *Melody Maker* these days?

'I mean,' he goes on, really no stopping him. 'God, you try living in a fucking hotel room, working on a new album. Trying to improve upon the last record and the record before that and you're digging within yourself to try and do something, to turn yourself and everyone else on. It sounds dreadfully like the old art-is-suffering number, I know. But there's an incredible pressure on you. My whole shirt was on this album. I don't need some ridiculous cub reporter criticising me for how much – and it was a hell of a lot less than he claimed – I was paying to stay in a fucking hotel room. He didn't write about the record. He wrote about me. And he even got that wrong. You can't get away with saying that I have nothing to say to humanity, man. That's just too heavy a thing to say about anybody.

'I'm tired of it,' he says wearily, reaching for the dish of coke. 'People are forever going on about me being in the gossip columns. But it's not as if I have teams of PR people rushing around trying to get me into the newspapers. At the same time, you can't have your lifestyle limited, or totally imposed upon you, by your audience. If some people in my audience were offended or put off me because I was being written about in gossip columns, then they should have realised that it wasn't something I particularly wanted. I mean, I did try to resist it.'

Come on, admit it. You loved it.

'You're right. I did. And perhaps it was slightly juvenile of me. It certainly works against me now. And I think that's unfair. I mean, look, I know Nigel Dempster [then the snooty social diarist for the *Daily Mail*]. If I meet him at a party, I'll talk to him. It's not that I want him to write about me in his column. I just enjoy talking to him. And I'd rather talk to him than some boring trade union official. But is any of this really relevant to the music?'

You brought up it.

'Yes, but only because Chris Brazier seemed obsessed by my play-boy image,' Ferry moans, long-suffering and easily hurt. 'Perhaps it had got out of hand. Who knows? But it was weird being criticised for having an image when the whole Roxy thing had been about play-ing with images. It's why a lot of people were originally attracted to the band. You know,' he says, and he's after that dish again, 'I've never confined myself to any limited social situation. If anything, I'm a social explorer. And to be castigated for that is really hurtful. Of course, it makes you more withdrawn, more sensitive to criticism. It's the price you have to pay.

'I realise that the more celebrated you become, the more notori-ous you become, then the more difficult it is for somebody like me to merely circulate. I can do it in New York, because nobody knows who I am. I'm not John Travolta. But here, there are limits. The only outlets tend to be uptown places. Café society places, if you like. But if you're seen in those places, you're accused of betraying your audi-ence. God, sometimes I just like a night out. Where am I supposed to go? Down the pub?

'It seems strange, too, that I should suddenly be deemed so unfashionable. To think now that people aren't buying my records because of my image is extraordinary for me. I can only think they may be unaware of Roxy and just think of me as some kind of playboy who occasionally makes records. They probably aren't even aware that I've been making a new album. They probably think,' he says with tired exasperation, 'that I've been off on someone's yacht.'

He sighs again, the sound of profound resignation or the *Hindenburg* deflating.

'Pass the charlie, would you?' he says then, looking for vague solace in another big hit of the much-diminished stash. 'Thanks. Sorry. I really shouldn't carry on like this.'

Although he does. For at least another hour; that earthenware dish I mentioned reduced to not much more than its tasteful pattern when we're done.

JERRY DAMMERS

Dublin | Belfast | Hemel Hempstead, November–December 1979 | London, August 1983

I'm sitting in The Specials' dressing room, backstage at the Dacorum Pavilion in Hemel Hempstead, talking to vocalist Terry Hall and the band's manager, Rick Rodgers. There's a table in the middle of the room, covered in the usual dressing-room debris. Cans of beer, overflowing ashtrays, a couple of bottles of wine, plates of sandwiches, sick and curling things, a couple of bananas in a plastic bowl. There's what looks like a pile of clothes someone might have dumped under the table, mistaking it for the doorway of a charity shop, that turns out to be Jerry Dammers, the architect of the 2 Tone revolution, mastermind of The Specials' spectacular recent assault on the charts, apparently asleep.

He's got a battered black overcoat pulled over him like a blanket, the collar clutched to his face, and seems oblivious down there to the chatter around him. The comings and goings of roadies, band members, a couple of fans brought in by drummer John Bradbury from the bitter winter cold outside. Jerry is part of the conversation I'm having with Terry and Rick until he announces that he rather badly needs a kip and without further ado crawls under yonder table, where for the last 20 minutes he's been snoring quietly and dribbling onto the sleeve of his overcoat.

At this point, I've spent two months chasing the dozing Dammers for a *Melody Maker* cover story. I first spend a week on October's 2 Tone tour, with The Specials, Madness and The Selecter. I spend as much time as possible with Jerry. But whenever I suggest something more than an informal chat, he finds an excuse to be somewhere else and quickly disappears.

Rick Rodgers is an old friend, a former independent PR, famously associated with the 1977 second Mont-de-Marsan punk festival of hilarious legend. He knows I'm still keen on talking to Jerry and calls me one afternoon with news that The Specials have a couple of shows coming up in Dublin and Belfast with Dr Feelgood. Talk about dream dates! Rick thinks there may be an opportunity here to get Jerry on his own for a proper chat that I take to *MM* editor Richard Williams. Richard makes a face like he's tweaked a hamstring when I mention the Feelgoods – where's this going to end? But he's been keen for weeks to follow up October's cover story on the 2 Tone tour with an even bigger feature on The Specials and 2 Tone, concentrating as much as possible on Dammers as the unlikely driving force behind the band and their label. I'm duly sent off to get the full story, or as much of it as I can.

I spend a lot of time shadowing Jerry over the next couple of days. In hotel rooms, hotel bars, pubs in Dublin and Belfast, at a couple of soundchecks, a trip to a Dublin radio station, a weird backroads taxi ride to Belfast airport that ends with us being pulled over by an army patrol, Rico Rodriguez losing it badly at the checkpoint. Jerry's in every way the best kind of company. Bright, funny, self-effacing and he doesn't take himself unnecessarily seriously, always a fucking blessing. You could tritely describe him as goofily endearing. The quick grin, the seal-pup eyes, the toothless smile. An eccentric, prone to comic mishap, slapstick and pratfalls. And there are times, you'd have to admit, when in a blur of motion, he does seem like a cartoon character, drawn by a child with a talent for crude animation. At the same time, he gives the unmistakable impression of someone on a mission, propelled by an unstoppable urgency.

Whatever – he remains, typically, elusive whenever an interview is mentioned. I do, however, spend a couple of hours in the bar of a Dublin hotel, talking to Rick about him. I also chat at length about Dammers in a pub or two and a room not much bigger than a telephone box at Dublin's Olympic Ballroom with Specials' guitarist Roddy Radiation and on the train the next morning from Dublin to Belfast with bassist Sir Horace Gentleman, a conversation that continues in a corner of a function room at the Europa Hotel commandeered by Dr Feelgood for a party after a sensational show at Belfast's Queen's University. But I still fail to get Dammers in front of a tape recorder and a notebook full of questions.

It strikes me that tonight may be my last reasonable chance of pinning Dammers down to anything like the interrogation I have in mind. I'm relieved, therefore, when he wakes up from his recent slumber, comes out from under the table, stands, stretches, dusts himself down and then surprises me by announcing that he's ready at last to talk, like he's handing himself over to the feds after a short manhunt. I almost expect him to offer his wrists to be cuffed. Anyway, Rick Rodgers has found us an empty space, somewhere in the Pavilion building. A grim room, brutally lit by overhead lighting strips, that seems to be a cafeteria or something, empty now and cold.

A few days earlier, in a Dublin bar, I ask Rick what he knows about Jerry's background.

'He doesn't talk about his family at all,' Rick says, above a raucous din at the other end of the room, where Lee Brilleaux is holding rowdy court. 'As far as I know, he's not very close to them. Possibly, he's a bit self-conscious about his background. He doesn't talk about the past at all.'

About all I know is that Jerry is the son of a clergyman, an Anglican dean, and that he was born in India and that when he was two, the family moved back to Britain, first to Sheffield before settling in Coventry, where Jerry grew up. At the time, his parents are living in Bristol. The first time The Specials played there, he went out for tea with them. He even invited them along to the gig, but typically didn't introduce them to anyone.

He squirms now under the cafeteria lights when I ask him about his childhood, that uncomfortable territory.

'I don't know what to say,' he finally admits. 'My father was a vicar. I grew up in a vicarage. It was a bit weird, a bit oppressive. I didn't like it. In fact, I hated it. It was very strict, and when I was about 13, I started to rebel against it. I refused to accept all the things my family stood for.

'I used to go a bit mad,' he goes on. 'I suppose when I was about 13, I was a mod. A mini mod. Then I grew my hair and ran away from home when I was 15. I went with a friend to Ireland, some island off the coast that John Lennon had bought, sort of a hippie commune.

135

I stuck it out for two weeks, went home and freaked out completely. I got badly into drinking and vandalism. I used to get really pissed up and put my feet through shop windows, things like that.'

One summer in Torquay, his career as a vandal ended abruptly.

'A whole load of us went down there on holiday,' he remembers. 'We were drinking scrumpy and got really pissed up. We were walking down the road and this car was coming toward us, so we stood in the middle of the road. But the car didn't stop. I got on the roof and started jumping up and down. There was a family of holidaymakers inside, looking horrified. I was jumping up and down and the roof of the car finally collapsed. I was arrested and fined £250. The judge said that had to be the last time I was brought before the court. It was.'

He'd been listening to a lot of music during this otherwise hooligan time. Everything, as he puts it, from 'Skinhead Moonstomp' and 'Liquidator' to Rod Stewart, The Faces and Slade. He decided to put a band together.

'I'd always wanted a group,' he says. '"Little Bitch", which we do now, I wrote that when I was 15. I wanted to be in a group from the moment I saw The Who playing "My Generation" on the telly. That was the best thing I'd ever seen. It wasn't the flash or the glamour of it. It was just the music. I wanted to be a musician. I love the music and I love making music. But I hate the flash. I hate the glamour.'

There was a band called Peggy Penguin and The Southside Greeks, whose repertoire was mostly old rock'n'roll numbers.

'After that,' he says, 'I was in a few more groups, playing around the working men's clubs. We've all done that. Roddy, Horace, Brad. Then I was in a country and western band for a bit, doing Johnny Cash numbers. Then there was a reggae band and a soul band and a funky soul band.

'I was writing songs, but none of the bands wanted to know. Only the rock stars you saw on the telly did their own songs. The kinds of bands I was in, they never thought they could possibly do that. You just had to copy what you heard on the radio or on the telly. And that didn't change, really, until The Sex Pistols came along.'

He left school at 16, with a single O level, in art. His mother encouraged him to apply to art school. The new academic year has already started, but he's offered a place at the art school in Nottingham.

'I got there after everybody else,' he says. 'I was nervous, because I didn't know anyone, and they'd all been there a couple of weeks. The first project the class did, they had to make a list of their likes and dislikes. Some girl said she hated people with half-mast trousers, white socks and winklepicker shoes. I walked in a week later wearing exactly that. The whole place burst out laughing. It didn't exactly do a lot for my confidence.'

He did his pre-diploma year in Nottingham, enrolling for a three-year Diploma in Art and Design course in fine art at Lanchester Polytechnic. Horace was starting his second year there when Jerry arrived.

'I remember him wandering about, looking very lost,' he tells me, on the train from Dublin to Belfast, the morning after the Olympic Ballroom show. 'I remember him sitting on his own in the first-year studio, not really knowing what to do.'

'I didn't really pay much attention to what was going on at the art school,' Dammers says. 'I only attended about two tutorials the whole time I was there. I just got on with what I wanted to do, which was making cartoon films.'

In college, he'd played with 'a lot of totally crummy bands'. When he graduated from art school in 1976, he was playing with a soul group called The Sissy Stone Band.

'We worked mostly around the local discos and clubs. We made about 30 quid a week, I think. We used to play all over the place. But we couldn't afford to stay in hotels, so we had to travel home every night from gigs. If you're playing in somewhere like Egremont or Sunderland and you have to travel 900 miles or something to get home, it gets a bit desperate.

'I used to do a lot of sulphate then, because I was so scared whoever was driving would drop off to sleep. I used to sit up front and keep them awake by chatting all night.'

He might still be stuck on that circuit if he hadn't been so inspired by The Sex Pistols.

'They were the only group, in a way,' he says. 'They were the first group a lot of us could really relate to, I suppose. They opened the door for a lot of people like me and Roddy and Terry. They were a real inspiration.'

At the time, he was making his own home demos, his songs a mix of reggae, ska and punk.

'I'd always loved reggae,' he says. 'Like, in Peggy Penguin, when I was 15, I was always telling them, "You play a reggae beat, you play a rock beat." They used to tell me to fuck off. But I always loved the idea of mixing reggae and rock. When The Clash and Elvis Costello came out, I was really mad, because they sounded so similar to what I was trying to do.'

Dammers' first demos were recorded with Neol Davies, who soon has his own thing going with The Selecter. Jerry remembers Horace from art school and one night goes to see him playing with a soul band called Breaker in a Coventry club and ends up asking him to help out on the tapes he's making.

'I went around to his flat,' Horace tells me somewhere between Drogheda and Dundalk on the train from Dublin to Belfast. 'He had this Revox set up in his front room and he said, "Can you play this?" He showed me what he wanted me to play, and it went from there. We got a nucleus of musicians together to record the demos and after we learned those songs, he said, "Well, I've got a few more." So, we did those, too.'

Horace was at first bemused by a lot of Dammers' ideas. He was from a mostly soul music background, has never played reggae before, the bass patterns Jerry teaches him initially baffling. When they start to make sense, he begins to appreciate Jerry's ambition, vision, whatever you want to call it.

'I began to see him as a kind of mad professor,' he says. 'Not an evil genius, something nuttier than that. He was forgetful and untidy. He looks like a shambolic figure, a bit of a mess. But I don't think I've ever met anybody as single-minded when it comes to getting what he wants. It's difficult to reconcile the first impression you get of him with the kind of determination he showed from the start. It took me ages to realise this was going to be a successful band. But Jerry believed it was going to happen for us from the beginning.'

A group eventually forms from the sessions in Jerry's front room. They call themselves The Coventry Automatics and the line-up includes Dammers, Horace, Lynval Golding on a guitar, Silverton Hutchinson on drums and a singer named Tim.

'That was the Automatics,' Horace says. 'Tim looked a lot like Lou Reed. We did about half a dozen gigs. We even got as far as

138

supporting Ultravox at the local Tiffany's, which seemed like an enormous achievement at the time.'

The rock academic Simon Frith, then a contributor to *MM*, saw their debut, recalled in one of his weekly Consuming Passions columns. 'The Automatics' first performance was just fine,' he writes. 'Tim sang from scraps of paper, Jerry couldn't get his keyboards on stage and played from the floor, facing his group like a conductor. The mood of the music was punk, the sound was reggae, and the group played then, as they play now, the best dance music you could hope to hear.'

Jerry is clearly less thrilled than Frith with The Coventry Automatics. Tim is soon gone. Jerry has his eye on a local singer named Terry Hall, who's just been sacked from a punk band called The Squad.

'Terry was hilarious in The Squad,' Roddy Radiation remembers, backstage at the Olympic Ballroom, the Feelgoods sound-checking in the main hall. 'They used to support my band, The Wild Boys. He used to jump into the audience, spitting at people.'

'Jerry wanted Terry in the Automatics,' Horace recalls. 'But Terry was very much into this heavy punk thing. He said he couldn't possibly be in a band with keyboards. He was well into all that punk stuff. Lou Reed. The New York Dolls. All that New York death wish business. He was in his element with all that.'

Roddy's Wild Boys are at the time going through line-up changes of their own and Roddy asks Jerry to join on keyboard. But the Automatics have started playing by now and Jerry turns him down and instead eventually recruits Roddy for the band that becomes the first line-up of The Specials, with Terry, Horace, Lynval, Silverton on drums and singer Neville Staple.

'I went to see the Automatics a few times,' Roddy says. 'They were already doing "Too Much Too Young" and "Dawning of a New Era". It was a good time just then in Coventry. There was a club called George's. It was a big, flash nightclub when it opened. But it got seedier and seedier. In the end, the only people who'd ever go there were punks. The Specials had a residency there. Marvellous times.'

It now turns out that Roddy had first come across Jerry as early as 1971.

'I was in this terrible group,' he says, 'playing bass. We had this weird long-haired guitarist. It was horrendous. Anyway, we were looking for a drummer. We got a message that there was a guy who wanted to audition for the group. It was Jerry. We went around to this vicarage to pick him up. He had this really battered drum kit that he had to keep in the garage because his mum wouldn't let him have it in the house. He was terrible. The worst drummer I've heard in my life.'

He met Jerry again during the early punk days in Coventry. It was a tight little scene, Roddy remembers. Everybody knew everybody else, and you kept running into the same people.

'I used to meet him in pubs a lot and we'd go a bit mad,' he says. 'Everybody knew Jerry from the crazy things he used to do. He's a legend of sorts in Coventry. He used to look like a puppet, you know, at one time. He used to wear this blue Beatles jacket, a red corduroy shirt and this mauve, knitted woollen tie. And he used to wear Rupert Bear tartan trousers and what were once pink brothel creepers.'

He remembers one night, going down to a Coventry club called The Domino. His own band, The Wild Boys, were on the point of splitting up.

'The Domino was basically a late-night loony bin,' he says. 'Jerry and the rest of them were there, his new band. We were all pissed, and they said they were going down to London the next morning to record some 24-track demos. They wanted me to play guitar on one of the tracks. I just said, "Yeah, sure." Then got drunk and went home. The next morning, they were outside the house in a taxi, someone was banging on the door, and I was in bed thinking, "Fuck me. They mean it."'

The Coventry Automatics' first London recording sessions are financed by Chris Gilbey, manager of Australian punk pioneers The Saints.

'All we got out of it was some cassettes,' Roddy says. 'I think John Peel may have played something we sent him.'

'We actually supported The Saints,' Horace remembers. 'It was an Easter Monday at The Marquee. No one came and we had to borrow ten quid off someone to get home.'

Nothing comes of their brief connection with Chris Gilbey, but Dammers, back in Coventry, now has another idea. Johnny Rotten has just left The Sex Pistols. Dammers is convinced he'll be able to persuade Johnny to join his band, newly rechristened as The Special

140

AKA. Jerry knows Roadent, a roadie for The Clash. Roadent knows Rotten and says he'll pass on some tapes to Johnny. Impatient for an answer, Jerry comes down to London, looking for Rotten. Somehow, he runs into Bernie Rhodes, manager of The Clash, and hustles Bernie for a support slot on The Clash's upcoming On Parole tour.

'Bernie said we could do the first two dates,' Jerry says. 'But I wanted to do the whole tour. I went to Joe Strummer and got him to come and see us and he said he wanted us to do the tour, all of it. Bernie still wasn't keen, but The Clash wanted us and that was enough.'

Rhodes took more notice of The Special AKA as the tour went on. There was talk at one point of him becoming their manager.

'He just couldn't make up his mind,' Dammers says. 'There were a lot of legal things going on. It got as far as contracts being drawn up and there were lots of arguments about that. Basically, we refused to sign the contract he offered us and that was that.'

Bleak months back in Coventry follow The Clash tour.

'We were rehearsing in the backroom of a pub during the winter,' Roddy says. 'We were all on the dole. I had about £1.50 to last me all week. The drummer would never turn up [Silverton was replaced at this point by John Bradbury]. It was pretty rough. Horace used to go out to collect wood for the fire. Jerry used to play wearing these old Steptoe gloves, the kind without fingers. I was sure we were going to split up. But Jerry was really determined that we kept it all together.'

By the start of 1979, The Specials have scraped together enough money to record 'Gangsters' and decide to release it on their own label, 2 Tone.

'It was as much a reaction to Bernie Rhodes as anything,' Dammers says. 'He didn't think we were any good. He had no confidence in the band. I was determined to prove him wrong. We didn't have enough money to record a B-side, we had The Selecter on that side. Neol Davies had made this tape about two years earlier, and we just over-dubbed a ska guitar and hey, presto! That was the Selecter B-side. And that's what gave us the idea of having more than just The Specials on 2 Tone.'

'I think Jerry always thought of 2 Tone as a label in the very widest sense, even when we first discussed it,' Horace says. 'I think he thought of it as something more than a vehicle for our own records. He obviously thought of it as a kind of figurehead, if you like, of a movement.

'A movement, obviously, has a lot more potential than one band. The Sex Pistols would probably have made it on their own. But if it hadn't been for The Clash and The Damned out there, backing them up, I don't think the impact would have been so great. Because The Sex Pistols seemed to be at the head of a movement, they seemed even more important. And that's very much what 2 Tone was intended to be. I really liked the idea of having a record label. It seemed to give the whole thing a greater unity. And one night, Jerry came around my flat and we sat around with sketch pads, trying to come up with a name and a design. Eventually, we came up with 2 Tone and the 2 Tone man.

'I think it's true to say that the label takes its identity from the personality of the whole group. But I think we saw it as just an outlet for our own records. Jerry was thinking beyond that, well before the rest of us.'

By March, 2 Tone have signed a distribution deal with Rough Trade. Jerry had planned to press up 2,500 copies of 'Gangsters'. Rough Trade persuade him to double the print run.

'Jerry at that point decided he was going to need some publicity if The Specials were going to sell 5,000 copies,' Rick Rodgers says. 'That's when he came to see me.'

Rick at the time has his own independent publicity company, Trigger PR. His main account is Chiswick Records and he's also worked with Little Bob Story and Motörhead and recently been managing The Damned. He's recommended to Jerry by Alan Harrison, a former lecturer at Lanchester art school, an old friend of Rick's, who'd tried earlier to get him interested in The Coventry Automatics. Jerry turns up at Rick's Camden office and plays him 'Gangsters'.

'That weekend I went up to see them in Coventry,' Rick says. 'I thought they were the most exciting band I'd seen in ages. Our relationship grew from there.'

Rick's not sure at first what to make of Dammers, his apparent vagueness, general eccentricity.

'To begin with, I wasn't sure he had that much going for himself,' he says. 'He still had his false teeth at the time. Whenever he talked to you, he'd be dribbling down the side of his mouth. It was quite difficult to talk to him and look him in the face at the same time. I'm still getting to know him, really. He's a very complex character, I think. I didn't realise at first how important he is to The Specials. That only became clear after I'd known them for a while. He used to stay at my place whenever they were in London, and gradually I got to know him. He used to talk about his plans, his ideas for 2 Tone. I began to realise he was really the heavy kingpin of the whole operation.

'It was difficult to see at first,' Rick goes on. 'But you don't find a band as strong as The Specials unless there's a really powerful individual behind them. And Jerry, I realised, was the axis of that power.'

'I think we'd all have to agree that Jerry got the band off the ground,' Horace tells me. 'He put the band together. Originally, we were doing all his songs. He organised everything. And if there was a final say, it was usually Jerry who had it.'

Roddy, however, contests Horace's view of Jerry as the mastermind behind The Specials.

'Horace would say something like that,' he says. 'Sir Horace Yesman,' he laughs, a little bitterness in there. 'It seems everyone thinks of Jerry as the instigator, the brains behind the whole operation. I don't think that's quite the truth. A lot of the ideas he uses are ideas that we as a group have come up with. And he just pools those ideas. The music is like it is because of the different people in the band, who are there because Jerry knew what they could contribute when he asked them to join. I don't think he planned it so the band would turn out like it has. You can't foresee how someone's going to play. I could have changed my style completely when I started playing with Lynval and there's nothing Jerry could have done about that.'

The afternoon in December after they blow the roof off the London Lyceum, The Specials are massing in the lounge of the Kenilworth Hotel in High Holborn, waiting for the coach to that night's show in Hemel Hempstead. I'm at a table in the corner, with Dave Jordan, the recording engineer who'd worked on The Specials' debut album, whose previous credits include The Rolling Stones' *Some Girls*. Dave's currently in charge of The Specials' live sound and goes on to co-produce *More Specials* with Jerry. He was working at TW Studios in Fulham when Elvis Costello turned up with The Specials. They intend to use the studio to record some demos, but decide to record the whole album there.

'It was Elvis's first time producing anything,' Jordan says. 'He didn't have a clue, really. But he was enthusiastic, had a lot of ideas and was basically the only person Jerry would listen to. There were one or two of the band who'd make suggestions, but he'd always argue with them. He's got this way of really wearing people down. He'll come up to you and blubber a bit and keep on at you until you agree with him. Most of the time, he was usually right, but if someone thought he was wrong they'd really have to prove to him what they thought wasn't right. He was absolutely determined about some things, though, and he wouldn't be talked out of doing them his way. There are only a few people whose advice he takes. Some of the band he won't listen to it at all.'

'He does tend to sulk a lot when he doesn't get his own way,' says Roddy on the coach to Hemel Hempstead. As the other main songwriter in the band, he has sometimes struggled to get his songs accepted by Dammers. 'I come in and raise my hand and Jerry says, "What do you want now, Rod?" And then he usually tells me to fuck off. I've had a few problems.'

The first thing Rick Rodgers does as The Specials' manager is get them back in front of an audience. They've barely played a gig since the Clash tour.

'That was Bernie's fault,' Rick says. 'He basically hid them away for six months. They were cracking up. They really needed to be seen. But Bernie kept them off the road. I brought them down to London and said, "Play anywhere and everywhere, wherever they'll have you."'

Rick books them into The Hope & Anchor, The Moonlight, The Nashville Rooms, The Music Machine.

'We did that whole circuit,' he says. 'We had them in London for two solid weeks. That's when it all started.'

There are soon almost as many record company A&R men as fans in their audiences. Open cheque books are waved at them.

'There were so many companies sniffing around that I realised we could sign a deal completely on our own terms,' Rick says. 'There was just so much competition.'

CBS are keen to sign them, but MD David Betteridge only wants the band, not their label. Chrysalis, however, agree to Dammers' demands to bankroll 2 Tone if it means signing The Specials. Some people close to the band wonder if it's all happening too fast.

'That was ridiculous,' Dammers says. 'I wasn't worried that it was happening so quickly. Why would I have thought that? We'd been working towards this for two years. We were penniless.'

In less than a year, The Specials have had four Top 10 singles, including a number one with 'Too Much Too Young', a Top 10 album, become one of the UK's top live bands, and inspired an entire youth cult. It will soon be 1980, a new decade there for the taking. What next, then, for The Specials and 2 Tone? How ambitious is Jerry?

Rick talks a lot about 2 Tone as an equivalent of Stax or Tamla, although even at the time this sounds a bit euphoric.

'I think Jerry will be happy with what we've got,' Horace says. 'We're where we wanted to be. We've got a record deal and our own label. I think he'll be satisfied with that. I don't think he's got a great masterplan for the future.'

'I don't think Jerry's going to stop until 2 Tone's taken over the world,' Roddy says, laughing.

And Jerry?

'I'd like our own 2 Tone studio, maybe a club one day in Coventry,' he says. 'Most of all, though, I just want to keeping making records that people like.'

For the next year, that's mostly what he does. Then it all blows up.

A thunderstorm breaks across north London. Rain smashes against the front windows of a semi-detached house on a quiet suburban street. It's August 1983, a late Friday afternoon. The light has just been sucked from the sky outside. It's been dark in here for the last couple of hours where I'm sitting in a gathering gloom with Jerry Dammers and John Bradbury, all that's left by now of The Specials as we left them in 1979, on the cusp, it seemed, of so much. It's two years since 'Ghost Town', their crowning moment, that eerie hymn to nowhere, was number one for three weeks, coincidentally the soundtrack to a summer of protest and riot, uprisings in Brixton, Toxteth, Bristol, all over.

Only the band know at the time how fraught everything has become between them. Exhausted by Dammers' dictatorial perfectionism during the largely unhappy sessions for 'Ghost Town', virtually the whole of the band eventually mutinies. Coming back from an American tour in October 1981, Terry Hall, Lynval Golding and Neville Staple quit to form Fun Boy Three. Roddy Radiation leaves to launch The Tearjerkers. Horace stays for a bit then falls out with Jerry when he joins a cult. Which leaves just Jerry and Brad, this afternoon's often bitter hosts, and a new line-up called The Special AKA.

Jerry's changed since we saw him last. The furry flat top's grown out. He's got his hair combed back in a kind of pompadour, a cool vintage look, matched by natty threads. A smart 1950s-style jacket over a crisp white shirt, pleated cream pants, expensive-looking loafers. Has he just joined The Style Council? We're here ostensibly to talk about the new Special AKA single, the suffocatingly uncompromising 'Racist Friend'.

It's the third single from the new band that Jerry's put together who were introduced by 'The Boiler', Rhoda Dakar delivering a six-minute spoken-word monologue about rape over a creepily jaunty instrumental track, the whole thing culminating in a full minute of Dakar screaming and sobbing. It's a long way from 'A Message to You, Rudy'. Its follow-up, 'War Crimes', is similarly confrontational, a nightmarish musical tract comparing Israel's invasion of Lebanon with Nazi death camps that strangely fails to get The Special AKA a spot on *Top of the Pops*.

I'm also this afternoon hoping for an update, however vague, on the album Jerry's been working on for the last couple of years, at a cost so far, some say, of £500,000. We come to that, briefly. What's consumed Jerry and Brad for most of the afternoon so far, though, has been a lingering and powerful sense of betrayal.

'To my way of thinking,' Jerry says, shredding the filter from another of the Camel cigarettes he's been chain smoking since we started talking, an ashtray in front of him, overflowing with butts, 'Terry should have left to pursue a solo career, which is basically what he's doing now, and maybe left Lynval and Neville with us. Instead, he took them with him and fucked everyone else up. It was totally disheartening, because we'd all put in so much work and effort. It took so many years to build it all up. To see it all fall apart was incredibly disappointing.

We just had to start all over again. After all we'd done, it was back to square one. It was disastrous. The fact there have been so many gaps between the records since the split is mainly down to the difficulties in replacing them and Roddy. I thought we could have followed through from "Ghost Town", but the momentum was lost when they left.'

He separates another fag from its filter, something to do with keeping his hands from Terry Hall's throat, you imagine.

'I thought that I had some security with The Specials,' he goes on. 'I thought I was in a position where I'd be able to keep producing records with the same team of people for years.'

A big shrug of his shoulders, a sigh.

'The thing is,' he says, 'it's still not clear to me why they left. I think to put it all down to one reason is difficult. Money was probably an important factor. The fact that I wrote most of the material and I earned more than them. I think they probably thought that was unfair. I don't know whether it was or not. But I think that was their basic grievance.'

'The thing about the split,' Brad says, nursing a Red Stripe, tensing up, 'was that it was all engineered very subtly. It wasn't blatant. I can't ever remember thinking, "Well, this looks like the end." It all just fizzled out. We got back from America, and they'd already agreed with Rick Rodgers that they were going. And they went.'

'A lot of the blame rests on Rick's shoulders,' Dammers says, a lot of anger in his voice. 'I mean, there was Rick Rodgers and them three. He was definitely engineering a split within the group. They planned the whole thing during the American tour and when we got back, they did it. They left.'

What of their claim that Jerry had become too autocratic, a dictator in the studio, determined to have his own way at every turn. He doesn't deny it.

'It's true,' he says. 'On "Ghost Town", you wouldn't believe the effort that went into me trying to get the band to play the thing the way I'd written it. I arranged everything on that record, even wrote the bass line. And Lynval, he didn't know any of the chords I wanted him to play. I had to show him the shape of all these diminished chords, the way I wanted the guitar part played.

'I always thought there was a lot of room for everyone in The Specials,' he goes on. 'A lot of it was quite free. It wasn't all composed by me. People had a lot of room for solos. But with "Ghost Town", it was a song that meant a lot to me, and I sat down and wrote the whole thing out as I wanted to hear it. I suppose it did cause problems, yeah. Because I can be dictatorial. That's a big problem. Because if I've got something in my mind and I want someone to play it exactly the way I can hear it, I'm not afraid to be a dictator. There's no way around it that I can see.

'But it's not something that came naturally to me. It's not a role I particularly wanted. That's the ironic thing. It's just that I had to learn to be ruthless. Especially when the band was first getting off the ground. I had to be strong as the leader. Later, I tried to let everyone have a say. Unfortunately, that's when the whole thing fell apart.'

'I still think the biggest shock,' Brad says, 'was Horace leaving.'

'Yeah,' Dammers says. 'In a way, I felt more disappointed with Horace because I thought he'd remain loyal. But we fell out over the cult he joined. I didn't feel too strongly about it until he tried to pressure everyone else into joining. Then I had some pretty grave arguments with him. Because these people, this cult, they were trying to recruit people off the dole with promises of jobs. They were just brainwashing people. The effect it had on Horace was terrible. It became unbearable in the end. But, you know,' he says, resigned to it all, if far from happy with the way things turned out, 'that's all in the past and done with. That was The Specials. This is The Special AKA.'

And what of the album he's been working on for two years, at such expense? When's that likely to come out?

'It's been a nightmare,' he says. 'But we're nearly there. It's been slow, but there have been lots of problems, especially with mixing it. It's a bit like painting the Forth Bridge. You get to the other end, and you think you've finished, but then you notice you've left a bit out. So, you go back and dab a bit more paint on. Then you notice another bit that maybe needs another coat. The thing I've realised,' he says finally, 'is that nothing's ever finished. Eventually, whatever you're working on is just abandoned to the public.'

The album Jerry eventually drolly calls *In the Studio* doesn't come out for another year, by which time most of its tracks have already been released as singles. People feel a bit short-changed. Chrysalis seem to regard it as Jerry's *Heaven's Gate*, an expensive disaster, its dismal brilliance wholly out of step with the perma-tanned hen party pop has lately become. They refuse even to promote it. It charts modestly, but no one's really in the mood for its austere despondency. Is Jerry broken by all this, done in? I don't know. But it's the last album he ever releases.

Joe 'King' Carrasco

Austin, September 1980

He picks me up from the house on Wood Avenue where for the last few nights I've been sleeping on the kitchen floor and we roar off into blinding sunshine towards Montopolis, in the south-eastern suburbs of Austin. The bashed-up bright red VW Beetle hurtles through busy afternoon traffic like something that's been shot out of a cannon, Joe 'King' Carrasco at the wheel and talking up a storm when you wish he'd just keep his eyes on the fucking road.

'You ever kissed a Mexican girl?' he wants to know, hitting a kerb, head ducking beneath the dashboard, nose hard against the radio dial down there while he fiddles with the tuner, looking for a Mexican station, anything but the blaring hard rock we're currently listening to.

'I hate this shit,' Carrasco yells. 'Drives me fucking crazy.'

He looks up in time to avoid a purple Cadillac that screams past us, horn blaring, its driver furious and making it clear with a provocative hand gesture and lots of swearing we can't hear.

'Motherfucker!' Carrasco shouts back, smacking the wheel of the VW with enough force to send it across a lane of oncoming traffic. By now, he's given up on the radio, nothing on it he wants to hear.

'Whenever I listen to the fucking radio, all I ever hear is shit,' he shouts in my ear, over the distressing screeching of gears and brakes and whatever. He swerves around a stationary pick-up, whose driver, sitting there, looks at us, horror all over his face. We leave a coat of paint on the side of his truck and speed into the distance, like something infernal let loose on Austin's sun-blasted streets. 'As far as the radio's concerned,' Joe goes on, oblivious to the chaos he's causing,

'I'd rather listen to the static. It's a lot more fucking tuneful than Van-fucking-Halen. Christ, yeah.'

We're driving through Montopolis now, where Carrasco used to play in Chicano bands like Shorty & The Corvettes.

'That used to be a club called El Get Together,' he shouts, pointing at a derelict shack, paint peeling off clapboard walls. 'Great place until someone set fire to it.'

Another of his old haunts looms into view.

'La Villa Latina!' he shrieks, like he's just run into an old friend he hasn't seen for years. 'The men's room was back of the stage, so you'd be playing and there'd be a constant procession of guys walking across the stage to go to the bathroom. Weird, uh? Hey! There's Govale's. That was a hell of a bar. One time, playing there with Shorty, a guy came through the audience, swinging an axe. Hit a guy in the head with it. Caught him with the flat of the thing, fortunately. Didn't kill him. Kinda stunned him, is all.'

I am here with Carrasco partly on the recommendation of Elvis Costello. As a guest about a year earlier on Radio 1's *Round Table*, there to review that week's releases, Elvis plays a track called 'Jalapeño Con Big Red' from an album called, in turn, *Tex-Mex Rock-Roll*, by Joe 'King' Carrasco & El Molino. The latter are a crew of legendary Chicano musicians with names like Rocky Morales, Ernie 'Murphey' Durawa, Richard 'Eh-Eh' Elizondo, Speedy Sparks, Arturo 'Sauce' Gonzales and Al Castro, who in the group picture on the back of the album's sleeve look like they've just served time somewhere, which for some of them is actually the case.

'That kind of music,' Elvis says after playing the track, 'doesn't need any pretentious reviewers, or even DJs with their not very discerning taste, to tell people it's wonderful.' Not for the first time, Costello is right.

A few months later, Stiff supremo Dave Robinson sees Carrasco at a club in Boston. Later, he remembers Joe sweeping onstage, sporting a cardboard crown, a regal cape and a guitar with a 50-foot lead. Joe plays on the stage, on table-tops, on the bar, up the stairs, in the men's room and finally ends up in the street, dodging traffic. Dave immediately signs him to Stiff and the week before I meet Joe in Texas, they release a single called 'Buena', an album and headlining slot on the Son of Stiff tour to follow.

Anyway, I'm soon on a flight to Houston, where Joe's got a gig at a place called The Spitz, a punk hang-out with a reputation for much rowdiness, mayhem and general rough-housing. When I get there, Joe's giving the once-over to the heavy chain-link fence in front of the stage. In a couple of hours, it's all that's going to be between his new band, The Crowns, and Houston's hardcore punk stormtroopers. Joe gives the thing a shake and turns to a skinny little dude, not much of him at all, who turns out to be his manager, Joe Nick Patoski. He's quite a sight in his big sunglasses, gaudy floral shirt and voluminous shorts.

'Should hold 'em until the encores,' Carrasco tells him.

Patoski doesn't look so sure.

'If you get that far,' Joe Nick says.

As it happens, The Crowns do get that far into their set. They're about a minute into their first encore, which Joe had earlier insisted they would play whatever the audience reaction, when the first of the gormless local punks clambers over the wire fencing, others following, a horrible mutant swarm. Joe stands his ground at the edge of the stage, like noble Crockett at the Alamo. Joe's got his battered white Fender by the neck and wields it like a club against the punk invaders, catching at least one of the unruly horde with a truly memorable thwack to the head. He then disappears beneath a pile of bodies. Joe's still laughing about all this the next afternoon, as we head out of Austin in the band's beat-up Nomad trailer. We're on our way to something ominously called the Rockathon Festival, which is being held in a place called Helotes, in the hills somewhere beyond San Antonio. The Crowns are on a bill with a lot of local heavy metal bands. According to Joe, the audience are likely to be hostile.

'We get up there and start playing Chicano licks, they'll shoot us. There ain't gonna be no sunny side to it,' he says, clearly no stranger to gunfire at the kind of places he's played in the past, which cues up another story about playing with Shorty & The Corvettes.

'We used to play real shoot-'em-up places. It'd be like the fucking Wild Bunch, man. First place I ever played with Shorty, a couple of guys insulted the owner's wife. Man, he marched 'em into the parking lot, held a .38 to their heads and made 'em weep for mercy. Christ, yeah. I remember when we started El Molino, man. They were wild times, too. We were so unpopular, one time we ended up playing a deaf-mute institute. Only place we could get a gig. It was real wild. Bein' deaf and dumb did nothing for their tempers after a few beers. Another time, we played a New Year's Eve party for a buncha cowboys from a rodeo camp, and they were fucking nuts. Fight broke out, the bar owner went through a window. Cops showed up, arrested everyone 'cept the band. We were OK. No one fucked with us. We had a drummer always carried a big old .38. Anyone tried to fuck with us, he'd whip out his pistol and threaten to blow their damn heads off. He was a hell of a drummer, too. Only had the one leg, but he kept a mean beat.'

We're pulling up to the entrance to the festival now, up there in the hills somewhere beyond San Antonio. There's a bit of a fuss when the security guards want to stamp passes on our arms, hands, wherever we want. Joe's having none of it.

'You're not stamping me, man,' he says indignantly. 'No one stamps The King.'

We take a stroll around the festival site, such as it is, the sky beating down from an unblemished blue sky. The stage is a concrete block, overlooking a desolate picnic park. There are maybe a couple of hundred people scattered around, most of them apparently already drunk, stoned or otherwise out of their minds. There's a rowdy huddle at the foot of the stage, beefy oiks in baseball caps, sleeveless T-shirts, baggy shorts and shit-kicking boots. They're banging heads and butting chests to a band called Blac Dog, who are making an awful racket. Joe looks at Blac Dog, takes in all that hair, all those power chords and churning metal riffs that are making the crowd at the foot of the stage froth and drool. The crowd holler for more of the same as Blac Dog wind up their set with a lot of screaming, feedback and cymbal splashes.

'Hell,' Joe says, turning away from the belligerent horde The Crowns will shortly be playing in front of. 'They're gonna fuckin' hate us.'

He's right. They do.

Carrasco appears wearing a black-and-white vest and shorts, shades and a crown. The audience, down there at the foot of the stage, 12 feet below, are hostile from the moment they set unbelieving eyes on him. The Crowns have just started their second number, 'Houston El Mover', when the first cans hit the stage.

'Play some rock'n'roll,' some yahoo shouts.

'This is rock'n'roll,' Carrasco shouts back. 'Y'all too fuckin' deaf to hear it?'

The audience gets noisier. The Crowns get louder. Carrasco clambers on top of a rather wobbly-looking stack of speakers, scales a primitive lighting rig, races along the dangerously sloping lip of the stage. There are jeers, a lot of booing. More cans being lobbed, clattering on the stage around the band, a few near misses as they duck, dodge and dive. Joe's starting to look very annoyed. He finally snaps.

One minute, he's at the back of the stage. Then he's running, full pelt, for the front of it. He takes the monitors in a single bound and is then flying through the air, something ballistic, a be-crowned missile in harlequin drag; a worrying thing, you have to imagine, to see coming down upon you from the skies above. He lands with a thump on the hecklers, is immediately on his feet, swinging his guitar like a very big bat. The hecklers scatter, Carrasco giving chase across the picnic area, whooping and screeching at the retreating drunken miscreants, most of them falling over each other as they flee Carrasco's eternal wrath.

'Don't you ever,' he yells after them, 'fuck with The King!'

Later, after a photo-session outside the Alamo, we're driving back to Austin and the moon is up and the night is beautiful and clear and we're breaking out the beers and Carrasco is telling me how he got his name. When he first joined Shorty, he was still using his family name, Teutsch. The group couldn't pronounce it, so they gave him the Mexican name of Carrasco.

'They named me after this guy, Fred Carrasco,' Joe recalls. 'He was a legend. A bandit. A 70s Pancho Villa. They put him in Huntsville Penitentiary, and he tried to break out. Held eight hostages for two weeks in the prison library. The Texas Rangers said he'd never get out of there alive, even if it meant killing all the hostages. They told him he might as well surrender. But he wouldn't. So, they killed all the hostages, and, sure enough, Fred didn't get out of there alive. He was a real hero among the Texas Mexicans. They have a lot of songs about him. He was a dangerous man. He had a shoot-out with the cops at the San Antonio Hotel. Held 'em off for a couple of days, guns blazing.'

He took the title of King from a Chicano tradition, as a joke at first. Then it just stuck.

'It's a common Southern tradition,' he says. 'Lotta Cajun bands, the leaders wear crowns. Like Clifton Chenier. I'd seen this Chicano band, guy wore a crown, called himself El Rey de Texas, the King of Texas. I thought, "Hell, I wanna be a king, too." Originally, I thought of calling myself Joe "Count" Carrasco. But it didn't sound right. I thought, "Hell, be a king, man. Why stop at a count?" If you call yourself a king, you get to wear a crown. Counts don't. Some people just run when they see me. But what the hell? I don't care. It's just a gimmick, man. Vaudeville. Entertainment. I'm just a show-off. At least people pay attention when I wear it. I don't think it puts people off. Shit. Look at Sam the Sham. He wore a fucking turban, and he made it big.'

For about five minutes.

'Five minutes,' Joe laughs. 'Five years. It don't matter. One minute at the top is long enough. At least you can say you've fuckin' been there.'

Jon Anderson

St-Jean-Cap-Ferrat, the French Riviera, November 1980

Jon Anderson pours generous amounts of a rather good wine into glasses big enough to keep goldfish in. He passes a glass to me, takes a sip from his.

'Where were we?' he asks, his voice as it sounds on record, when he's singing. Soft, husky, a little wheezy; a gas leak with a Lancashire accent.

You were telling me about the 1979 recording sessions in Paris with Yes that ended with you no longer in the group. How you'd turned up at the studio, bursting as usual with all kinds of ideas that were coldly received. You were going to give me an example.

'I can give you a couple,' he says. 'One was a song about a dentist. They wouldn't even talk about that one.'

I take a big swig of my drink.

'The other was a version I'd rewritten of Randy Newman's "Rider in the Rain".'

You rewrote a Randy Newman lyric? What, to improve it?

'No,' he says. 'That wasn't the idea at all, to improve it.'

Then why rewrite it?

'To change the perspective of the song.'

How?

'My version was written from the viewpoint of the horse.'

You're fucking joking, right?

'That's funny,' he says, conspicuously not laughing. 'That's basically what Steve Howe and Chris Squire said,' he adds with a deep sigh, long-suffering, a martyr deflating, a visionary betrayed.

We're sitting in a lounge as big as a football pitch in the villa overlooking the harbour that Anderson has rented for the winter in

156

St-Jean-Cap-Ferrat, down there on the French Riviera. I'm here to talk to him about his new solo album, *Song of Seven*, his first release since – some say – being turfed out of Yes by mutinous bandmates, tired of his dictatorial bossiness, an excessive need to be in charge, his authority unquestioned. Tantrums to follow when his directions are refused, his ideas rejected, his way of doing things contested.

Anderson and his wife Jenny are out when I arrive at the villa by cab from the airport in Nice. I spend an hour with Jenny's younger brother, Garry, who's here with some friends. Unfortunately, Garry's got a copy of *Song of Seven*, Anderson's new album, and keeps playing the title track, the one with the children's choir on the chorus, an unbearable sound. I quickly feel like setting fire to the carpet, the flames spreading at speed up the curtains, taking all the fittings in a fiery rush, Anderson returning home to nothing but ashes.

Anderson duly arrives with his wife and new manager, Jannis Zographos, a gaunt-looking Greek with the elongated face of an El Greco saint about to be boiled alive, sawn in half or otherwise raised painfully to glory. He also manages Vangelis and throughout the time I spend with Anderson is forever lurking somewhere.

'Fancy a drink?' Anderson asks, small, charming, courteous, maybe a little wary.

'What are you reading?' he asks, noticing the copy of Michael Herr's *Dispatches* I've packed to reread on the flight this morning.

'I love a good book,' he carries on without waiting for an answer. 'I remember when Yes were touring America. After the gigs, I'd just want to get back to my hotel room and get really stuck into some Tolkien. Put on something by Sibelius and really get into it.'

I imagine him tucked up in a Hyatt king-size, dressed in pyjamas – perhaps a onesie – decorated with appliqued elves, with a copy of *The Hobbit*, perhaps *The Swan of Tuonela* playing in the background. I try to concentrate on the job in hand.

'This might interest you,' Anderson says, changing the subject.

Go on.

'When we came down here earlier this year, we stayed at the Grand Hotel in Nice until the villa was ready,' he says. 'Guess who I saw in the restaurant, on our first night. Having dinner.'

I couldn't have looked more blank.

'Elvis Costello!' he says.

Oh! How was he?

'He was very ...' Anderson seems a bit lost for words. 'He was very Elvis Costello, I suppose. I went over to introduce myself and he jumped up, looking very suspicious, and just glared at me. We didn't have a lot to talk about, really. I imagined he hated Yes and was embarrassed to be seen with me.'

Are you hurt when people don't like you or your music?

'You learn to live with it,' he says. 'Bands go through three distinct phases. When you start, you're unknown. People think you're hip. Then you become successful. That's the second phase. Then there's the third phase.'

What's that all about?

'Oh,' he says. 'That's when all the persecution starts. That's when you sit down and wonder what it is that you've done that's so wrong.'

Bands that become pampered superstars sometimes make targets of themselves.

'But we weren't always pampered!' he huffs, quite indignant. 'We weren't always superstars!'

He pours us more wine.

'People forget what we went through,' he says, calming down a bit. 'We were just like every other group, starting out. No money. Cheap digs. Sleeping in the van. It was no easier for us than anyone else. Just because we made a bit of money later on, we became targets for the kind of people who want to slag off anyone who's become successful. But we worked for it. Nobody gave us our success. We earned it. There was no reason for us to feel ashamed.'

We're on our second bottle of wine by the time we get back to the Yes sessions in Paris, in October 1979, when it started to become clear how adrift Anderson had become from the rest of the band.

'Very soon, the mood changed from enthusiasm to frustration to complete confusion,' he says. 'Things weren't coming together. It was difficult for everyone. When it's not happening, you tend to clutch at straws. Try this. Try that. Try anything. But nothing would hang together, whatever we tried. And then an obvious feeling of doubt and uncertainty spread through the group.'

He didn't take well to the rejection of nearly all the ideas he'd brought to Paris, once again expecting to dictate the band's future course.

'It's only natural that I should have been disappointed by their reaction,' he says. 'These were ideas I'd been working on to present to the band. I thought they'd provide the next step in the group's musical direction. I hoped the other members of the band would enjoy working on them. Evidently,' he says, somewhat tartly, 'they didn't.

'It was becoming more evident that we didn't fit together as a group as we had done before. We didn't seem to be working towards the same end. All the ingredients that make up the kind of group that's going along happily, making music that's interesting to each member of the band, these things were all missing.'

The band took an enforced break from the Paris sessions when drummer Alan White broke his foot at a roller disco. The atmosphere between them when they reconvened in February 1980 was even more rank and odious. By March, Anderson was out of the band.

Was he pushed, or did he jump?

'There was some ... uh ... gentle persuasion,' he says. 'But I don't think going into that in any detail is relevant. It just happened. They didn't ring me up and say, "Jon, you're fired." And I didn't ring them up to say, "Hey, I'm leaving." Things just weren't happening between us.'

Anderson is deft at self-effacement, presenting himself as misunderstood by disloyal band members, finally even betrayed. But why do I keep imagining him stomping his feet and holding his breath until he turns blue and gets his way?

How much of the breakdown between him and the band, in other words, was his fault? Former Yes drummer Bill Bruford, who quit the band after *Close to the Edge*, once described Anderson in *Melody Maker* as a tyrant. Was he?

The question provokes a long silence.

'I think I might occasionally have lacked ... tact,' he says finally. 'Sometimes, to get things done, you have to step in and say, "Right. That's enough. This is how we're going to do it." There has to be a line somewhere, and someone has to draw it. Sometimes, perhaps, I should have been more persuasive. But I remember reading something about Puccini, a long time ago ...'

You're comparing yourself to Puccini now?

'Only to the extent that he never got on with anyone,' Anderson says, rather airily. 'But that was counteracted by the pleasure people have derived from his music throughout this century and will continue to derive pleasure from his music for the rest of time immemorial. The point is, if you want to achieve something and you've got a strong will and you're determined to see something through, some people are going to get hurt or upset if they stand in your way.

'Bill Bruford saw me as a tyrant,' he goes on. 'So have some other people. There are times when I'd have to agree with that description. I think if I'd been more tactful on occasions, the work I was doing might have been better. Instead, I maybe caused resentment and the music suffered. I will admit, there was a time when I was difficult. It's something I went through. But all I ever wanted was what was best for the band and the music.'

Jenny Anderson appears. Time for dinner, apparently. We drive down to the harbour, to a restaurant with views of the Mediterranean and the starry sky above it. Anderson takes as long over the wine list as it would take to listen to *Tales from Topographic Oceans*, all four, dismal, life-sapping sides of the thing. By the time he orders, I'm thirsty enough to drink sand. The meal's very pleasant, though, and it's well gone midnight by the time we leave.

Back at the villa, the lights low, everyone else asleep, I guess, by now, Anderson pours a couple of brandies. We're talking about punk. The backlash against groups like Yes, Pink Floyd, Led Zeppelin; the supergroups with their dire pomposities, elaborate stage shows, all that spectacle and dreary theatre, self-regarding virtuosity and, in the case of Yes, stage sets that looked increasingly like the inside of David Icke's head. How had he dealt with punk's vitriol, the noisy hostility?

'More than anything,' he says, 'it strengthened my convictions about a lot of things. Possibly, there were times when I thought, "Leave me alone. I can do without all this." But I just kept on, anyway, and hoped it would all work itself out. I remember when the only question was, "What do you think of punk?" It wasn't easy to answer flippantly or quickly. You couldn't brush it off. It was happening and a lot of the music, I thought, was good and exciting, and I don't mean to sound patronising when I say that.

160

'But, yes, of course the punks hated us. But I always thought we were putting on a good show, wherever we played. As it happened, we were playing large halls, to large numbers of people and we were getting attacked for it. There was some confusion. You know, "Why are they knocking us?" We were a supergroup, yeah. But we were still working hard. We were still learning, looking for new ideas. New ways of presentation. Albums like *Topographic*, they took us into other areas. Got us thinking more about presentation. We got really involved in the visual thing.

'Admittedly, we did run at it like a bull in a china shop. First it was just slides. Then a dome over the drum kit that lit up. Then sculptures and shapes on stage. We got terribly criticised for that. But at times it was magical. Because we were successful, we were trying to give the public something bigger and better. A huge show.

'At the same time, you had Rod Stewart and The Faces, playing football on stage and having a great time. But they had their audience, and we had ours. I enjoyed reading about Rod Stewart and The Faces and I'd have loved to be like that. But you can only do what comes naturally to you. What were we supposed to do? Play cricket on stage?'

A question about Yes's early days, the scene they were part of when they formed in 1968, puts him in nostalgic mood.

'It was a great time,' he says. 'The Nice, later ELP, and the Floyd, Jethro Tull, Genesis, we were often in contact with them. We listened to their records, ran into them now and again. There was a time when I hoped we might all get together. Do a show, you know? This was just a dream of the times. Anything and everything seemed possible.'

Do you miss the idealism of those days?

'I think the idealism's still there!' he says, certain of it. 'It's just unfashionable to even talk these days about flower power. But that was a great era.'

He has a sip of brandy, sighs, remembering the days of kaftans and patchouli oil, joss sticks, incense, headbands, bell-bottoms and loon pants, the long-gone hippie Narnia.

'I wrote a song about it last year,' he finally says, waking from his reverie of more fragrant times.

He clears his throat, sits up, leans forward with his elbows on his knees, hands clasped. Closes his eyes, and fuck me, starts reciting the lyric.

'*The children of the flower time,*' he begins, '*have spread their wings and begun to fly/Those summer days are near/We breathe again …*

'That's the opening of the first verse,' he says. 'It's a reflection of those times. And maybe we're going into those times again. A lot of people still have all their original beliefs inside them, just waiting to flower again.'

Does he realise that to a lot of people all this will sound like embarrassing hippie waffle? Imagine there's no heaven, and all that.

'I really don't care,' he says, freak flag flying. 'I know it's not 1967. It's 1980. And it's a great time. A very exciting time. Things are moving fast, but everything has its place. Order is there, all the time. It just doesn't look like it to most people. Which is why they're cynical and hostile. But, you know, I thought it was great when Elvis Costello did that song, "(What's So Funny 'Bout) Peace, Love And Understanding". What is so funny about it? Nothing.

'That's why,' he says, 'I still believe in everything I believed in then. I stand with it and by it and for it and that's all there is to it.'

We both raise a glass to that, at least.

THE FABULOUS THUNDERBIRDS

Austin, April 1981

The Fabulous Thunderbirds have just released a new album, *Butt Rockin'*, a blistering thing produced by Nick Lowe. *Melody Maker* editor Mike Oldfield is on holiday, so as his assistant I'm briefly in charge. The first thing I do is send myself to Texas to interview them for what I've decided in Mike's absence will be an *MM* cover story. That's me and photographer Tom Sheehan now boarding a plane for Austin, where in a couple of days the Thunderbirds are playing a big hometown show, debonair Chrysalis PR Hugh Birley also in tow.

Transatlantic flights in those days are like flying pubs. The drinks keep coming until you can barely speak to order the next round. Somewhere over the vast Atlantic, Tom has to resort to scribbling our drink requests on any bits of paper that come to hand. Seems to work, though, and we're settling in for the long haul in a comfortable glow, Tom on first-name terms with most of the cabin crew, when the captain makes an announcement.

As far as I can remember, we were supposed to fly from London to Houston, and then on to Austin. Seems we're now being diverted to New York, where we have to change planes. We retire for several hours to a bar, waiting for a connecting flight to Chicago. We spend the flight to the Windy City knocking them back and have a few more in a bar in Chicago before getting a flight to Atlanta. We spend another couple of hours in a bar there, until we're called to board a flight to Houston.

Sheehan by now is talking in tongues, like a shaman at a voodoo exorcism, human bones rattling around his neck and snakes wrapped around his arms. There's another delay in Houston before our final

163

flight to Austin. We pass the time in a bar, just for the sheer fucking novelty. After something like 23 hours, we make it at last to Austin. Hugh Birley seems to be coping pretty well. But Sheehan and I struggle through the airport terminal like we're coming last in a three-legged race, our ankles tied together and our trousers around our knees.

We're hours behind schedule and relieved therefore when we run into Thunderbirds guitarist, the super cool Jimmie Vaughan, who's driven out to meet us.

He takes one look at the bedraggled mess we have become and suggests we might want to get something to eat.

'I'd prefer a drink,' Sheehan hiccups.

'We have places where you can drink and eat,' Jimmie says drily. 'We're pretty up to date here.'

He takes us to a Mexican restaurant, where Tom sinks ever deeper into sodden befuddlement.

'What's this, Jonesy?' he asks, bits of enchilada dangling from his fork. He's chewing on another bit of enchilada, brow furrowed, trying to put a name to the taste. 'It really reminds me of something.'

It's fucking cheese, Tom.

'Really!' He sounds surprised. Perhaps a little relieved it's nothing too foreign. Tofu, or something. Kale, maybe.

Now it's Jimmie's turn for a puzzled question.

'Y'all don't have cheese where you come from?'

'Of course, we have fucking cheese where we come from,' Sheehan tells him. 'I just couldn't remember what it tasted like.'

'Y'all couldn't remember what cheese tasted like?' Jimmie says, possibly wondering if he should have stayed at home and left us stranded at the airport until we were deported.

'Jim,' Sheehan says. 'I've been drinking for nearly a day and a half. I'm numb from the ankles up. Not being able to remember what cheese tastes like is currently the least of my fucking problems. Now, did you say we could get a drink in here, or what?'

Jimmie drives us to the Heart of Texas motel, where we'll be staying for the best part of the next week. Hugh Birley's rather tight travel budget means the three of us have to share a room. Not that Tom's in a hurry to settle down. There's a bar across the street called The Silver Bullet and a band on tonight by the name of Bert Rivera & The

Nightriders. Sheehan and I are at a table ordering a round of drinks before Hugh Birley's unpacked his toiletries.

The Silver Bullet turns out to be a lively sort of place, where they serve beer in pitchers big enough to pour the Dead Sea into. We only find this out after ordering several rounds at once, Sheehan living in something approaching eternal fear of someone shouting last orders without a drink in front of him. Which is how we end up with about eight pitchers on the table in front of us and not enough time to drink them all before The Silver Bullet closes at what seems just before dawn.

This means we've only had about three hours' sleep when Jimmie turns up to drive us to a bar for breakfast. Over beers and not much else, Jimmie outlines the plans for the day. When we're done here, we'll drive over to T-Bird drummer Fran Christina's pad and then on to Jimmie's house to pick up his wife Connie and some beer. After that, we'll be heading over to Thunderbirds bassist Keith Ferguson's place, where there's going to be a party.

The first thing Fran does when we get to his joint is to introduce us to his pet parrot.

The thing's name is Vito. The fucking bird is as big as pterodactyl, with the wingspan of something you might see soaring above Aztec temples on an Andes thermal. A bird of legend, anyway. A roc, perhaps. Whatever that is. Vito takes one look at Tom and starts squawking like it's trying to wake the slumbering dead or alert us to the fact the house is on fire. The room is suddenly a cacophony of avian screeching, Vito making all the noise, deafening ululations, high-pitched warbling, keening wails.

'Fuck me,' Sheehan says. 'It's Yoko fucking Ono.'

Vito lets go with another ear-piercing shriek, ruffles its feathers and shakes what I suppose are its hips like a belly dancer. It spreads its wings, bringing darkness to the room. Tom backs off, a target of Vito's killer stare. The bird takes flight, flies twice around the room, crashing into things. It lands on Tom's shoulder with a thud and starts pecking the startled photographer on the head. Vito's really going at it. I fully expect the winged beast to crack open Tom's skull, pluck out his brain and fly off with it in its beak.

I'd rush to the stricken lensman's aid, a comrade in arms, faithful to the end. But I'm laughing so fucking hard Jimmie and Fran have to hold me up.

We pull up outside Jimmie's place a little after this, Tom in a fearfully bad mood after his mauling by Vito. Jimmie's wife Connie's just off to a local 7-Eleven, to pick up the beer for Keith's party. I go with her. We're loading a trolley with as many cases of beer as it'll hold when Connie asks me if I've ever heard of legendary rock casualty Roky Erickson of 13th Floor Elevators fame. Of course I've heard of him. Why?

'That's him over there,' Connie says, pointing out a bedraggled individual who looks like he's just escaped from somewhere they never turn off the lights.

'He lives around here with his parents,' Connie tells Tom when we get back to her place with the beer.

'Little green people with aerials coming out of their heads, are they?' the sulking photographer asks, checking his scalp for bits of missing hair.

Keith Ferguson turns out to be a very large man with tattoos and a diamond in the shape of the Lone Star of Texas in a front tooth. Here he comes, strolling down the path from his front porch.

'Y'all want to come feed some dawgs?' he asks, picking up a bucket of raw meat.

He leads us around to the back of the house. Three big pit bull terriers are testing their muscles against their chains. Keith tells us these dogs are bred purely for fighting. They look appropriately ferocious, heads as big as bombs, teeth like chainsaws. That kind of thing.

'Would they attack us if they got loose?' Sheehan wants to know, possibly calculating how far he'll get with them in unleashed hungry pursuit before they catch him, pin him to the ground with their fabulous paws and start chewing his legs off.

Keith has reassuring news, however.

'They wouldn't attack nuthin' smaller than a horse,' he tells Tom. 'Y'all got nuthin' to worry about.'

We both take a step back anyway from the fence against which the hounds are currently smashing their heads, saliva splashing from their sagging jowls.

'These old boys ain't too bad, y'know,' Keith says, getting a bit sentimental. He flings a shank of something dripping with blood over the fence, where it's set upon by the dogs with a lot of worrying growling. 'They're jes' dumb, is all. Don't know how to do anything 'cept fight.'

Keith leads us back to the house, where his wife, the singer Lou Ann Barton, is directing operations in the kitchen.

'Beers are in the freezer. Wine's on the side. Vodka's on the table. You got it! Fix me one while you're at it, honey.'

I grab a bottle of Rebel Yell and follow Lou Ann into the garden. She stretches out on a recliner, sun bed, whatever it is. I take the one next to her. I sit down on the thing. The contraption suddenly snaps shut, catapulting me into a flower bed.

'If you really want to make a success of that thing,' Lou Ann says, 'I suggest you plant your butt somewhere near the middle.'

Much later, after Tom gets stuck up a tree and has to be coaxed down like a frightened cat, I find myself in someone's bedroom, sitting on whoever's bed it is and talking to Thunderbirds vocalist Kim Wilson about our mutual friend Nick Lowe.

'I've played with a lot of great people,' Kim says, rolling a joint with leopard-skin papers, a cool touch. 'But I tell you, out of all of 'em, the guy I respect most is Nick. We've done some great shit together, man. I tell you, man. Nick's Got It. That's why he's great. He's just fuckin' Got It. Like you gotta have It, right? Dig what I'm sayin'? Understand what I mean when I say It?'

Frankly, I didn't. But not to worry, Kim's now handing me the joint. Maybe that'll give me some answers.

'This is real wild Mexican shit,' Kim says as I take the joint. 'Don't go too hard on her.'

Of course, I completely ignore what Kim's just told me and start puffing on the joint like Thomas the fucking Tank Engine. I am quickly aware that I am no longer quite myself. Kim's chatting away although I'm not sure who to. It strikes me I might not remember too much of all this in the morning, so I wrestle my tape recorder out of my bag, which seems to be fighting me back as I rummage around inside it. I've got my tape recorder in my hands. But I have no recollection of how the thing works. I press a button and a cassette flies out, violently ejected. It hits me in the eye, nearly blinding me.

'If you don't know what It is, you ain't got it,' Kim is now saying, as if from a pulpit. 'You gotta believe in It or you won't get It. That's a fact,' he says, although I'm not arguing with him. Mainly because I can't fucking speak, the wild Mexican shit having quite an effect.

'You believe what I'm sayin'?' Kim asks a young guy with a shock of red hair who's mysteriously appeared at the foot of the bed like a fucking leprechaun or something.

'I believe!' he now testifies, a disciple.

'Well, you Got It, man!' Kim is thrilled with his convert.

'Anyone for a refill?' Sheehan asks, on his way to the bar.

'You Got It, man?' Kim asks him.

'I think I had it,' Tom tells him, although he doesn't have a clue what Kim's talking about. 'But I think I left it in the garden.'

'Whatever you do, don't lose It, man,' Kim tells him. 'You'll be fucked without It.'

Kim's now talking about what passes for the music business and has a few gripes.

'You go into a record company these days and there's always someone who wants to talk about the psychology of music. The psychology of the fuckin' music? What's that got to do with us? We just play the fuckin' blues, man. How come they're talkin' all this psychology shit to us? You wouldn't go to a fuckin' psychiatrist for dancin' lessons.'

The party rages on for quite a while at Keith and Lou Ann's. At some point, we move across town to somewhere called Soap Creek. We make a quick stop first at Jimmie's, where Jimmie, Kim, me and Tom squeeze into a small bathroom. Jimmie gets out a Bowie knife, pours a ton of coke on the blade and passes it around like a peace pipe at a powwow. Not long after that, we find ourselves in a club in the basement of the Stephen F. Austin Hotel, which we only quit when they throw us out a little before sunrise. Jimmie's still with us, but somewhere along the way we seem to have lost Kim.

'Don't worry about Kim,' Jimmie tells us. 'He'll show up.'

And he does. The next afternoon, we find him in a bar called Wylie's. He's still trying to put the events of the previous evening together.

'I know I must have had a good time,' he says. 'Because I woke up this morning and the backs of my eyeballs were soft.'

He adjusts his beret, smooths out his moustache. He's got a lime juice and a bottle of beer on the bar in front of him. A hangover tip from Nick Lowe apparently coming into play here.

'What does the lime juice do?' Sheehan asks, never knowing when this kind of information might come in handy.

'The lime juice?' Kim laughs. 'The lime juice don't do a thing. You just drink the fuckin' beer and it gets you drunk again.'

It did, too.

Nick Lowe and The Confederate Air Force

Texas, October 1981

This all starts when Nick Lowe sees a television documentary on something called the Confederate Air Force and decides he wants to join. What's the Confederate Air Force? According to the BBC2 documentary Nick watches, it's a private air force started in 1951 by a small group of American former airmen in the Rio Grande Valley in Texas and dedicated to the collection and preservation of at least one of every type of Second World War combat aircraft.

Every year, the CAF – whose newly sensitive membership changes its name in 2001 to the Commemorative Air Force – hold what's apparently an amazing 'airsho' at somewhere called Rebel Field, in Harlingen, on the Mexican border down there in south Texas, where they reenact major air battles from the last world war. This all has a special appeal for Nick. His father, Drain, is a Second World War veteran, at 24 an RAF Squadron Leader who in 1940 leads bombing raids over Germany. Nick after a few drinks is sometimes prone to go on at length about this, becoming usually maudlin when he compares his father's wartime heroics with his own paltry achievements. Producing Wreckless Eric and The Damned is hardly in Nick's downcast opinion the equivalent of Drain braving flak and enemy fighters on nightly air raids along the Ruhr. Nick's jaw drops further when he learns from the documentary that anyone who subscribes to the CAF at the 'airsho' is automatically accorded the rank of colonel. You can even buy your own uniform. This settles it. Nick's packing for the trip before the show ends.

Turns out that nearly everyone Nick knows has seen the same TV show and wants to go with him, including Drain and several of his old RAF chums. The first I hear of the escapade is in Amsterdam, where I'm covering a Carlene Carter tour for *Melody Maker*, photographer Tom Sheehan as usual in tow. Jake Riviera has flown in, mainly it seems to shout at everyone. We're in a bar when Jake mentions the trip to Tom and goes on to invite him along as a kind of official photographer.

I fall into a black-hole sulk, a place without hope, see myself standing like Mrs Miniver, teary-eyed at the end of a runway, a plane disappearing over the horizon, left behind. I'll be fucked if I'm going to miss this, however, and make a pitch for going along to chronicle the great adventure, provide a suitably evocative and humorous text to accompany Tom's pictures, something for everyone to remember the trip by.

Jake's not buying it.

What about something on the trip in *Melody Maker*, then? Nick's not exactly setting the charts afire at the time, so the music weeklies haven't recently been in much of a rush to cover him. I'm sure I can soften up *MM* editor Mike Oldfield with a couple of drinks and get him to commit some space to the trip in our Christmas double issue. A couple of pages, at least. We're usually desperate for copy to fill the thing.

'Make it three,' Jake says, 'and we're in business.'

What the hell? Sure. I'll deal with Oldfield later.

Which brings us a couple of weeks later to the Brook Green Tavern, a pub near Nick's old pad in Shepherd's Bush, where we meet, about 20 of us, at some ghastly predawn hour. We'll be going from here by coach to Gatwick airport, where Tom Sheehan will meet us for a flight to Dallas, where we'll pick up a second flight to Harlingen.

Time for a few drinks first, surely, and a chance to see who's here.

Down at the far end of the bar, The Attractions' Pete Thomas is in villainous huddle with Nick's drummer, Bobby Irwin. The lanky tub-thumpers appear to be sharing a moment of percussionist humour, a joke possibly with a punch line involving paradiddles, cymbal splashes and collapsing hi-hats, hilarious enough to make Pete laugh out loud, a braying noise that sounds like a mule having its ears cropped. Former Commander Cody and His Lost Planet Airmen guitarist Bill Kirchen now hoves into view. Bill's been in London for the last couple of weeks, recording an album with his band The Moonlighters, Nick producing. He's here because at the last minute Bobby Irwin's dad is taken ill and can't make the trip. Bill's stepped in but looks like he's already regretting what must now seem to him a wholly rash decision. He gives the room an apprehensive look.

'This may be the most dubious venture I've ever signed up to,' he says, although you would have thought his years with a wild man like Commander Cody have prepared him for just about anything.

Peter Barnes from Plantagenet Music, Elvis and Nick's publisher, is also here, along with Aldo Bocca and Neil King, engineers from Eden Studios where Nick does a lot of production work. I have a few words with Paul 'Bassman' Riley, who used to play with Pete Thomas in Chilli Willi & The Red Hot Peppers, the pub rock band managed by Jake before he forms Stiff with Dave Robinson. And here's Andrew Lauder, who as MD of United Artists signs Can, Hawkwind, Brinsley Schwarz and Dr Feelgood to the label. He later launches Radar Records with Jake and now runs F-Beat. He later makes an extra bob or two when his Silvertone label releases the first Stone Roses album. He now lives in the south of France.

Jake's here, of course, delivering a torrent of instructions to hench-man Andy Cheeseman, former child actor turned F-Beat enforcer. At the bar to my right, someone I take to be Drain Lowe is at the centre of a hearty crew who look like they're dressed for a morning on the golf course. There's no sign of Elvis Costello, though.

'Men in uniform, singing and drinking?' Nick laughs. 'Bit Hitler Youth for EC. He's probably packing his rucksack for a CND march as we speak.'

Nick introduces me to his dad.

'Pleased to meet you,' Drain says, a handsome man with a mous-tache. 'This is the Geriatric Squadron,' he goes on, bringing the rest of his team into it. 'If we go a bit quiet it means we haven't lasted the pace.'

'On the coach,' Jake shouts, frightening everyone. 'Now!'

There's a lot of running around as we grab our bags, finish what-ever we're drinking and clamber aboard.

Nick, Drain and his pals are already in the front seats, Jake and Cheeseman behind them, the seats through the middle of the coach already occupied. I make my way to the back of the bus, where Mossy,

Vom, Brendan and Roy Simmonds from the resident F-Beat road crew are comfortably sprawled. Pete Thomas and Bobby Irwin are last on board, Bobby already looking merry enough to break into song.

When everybody's in their seats, Andy Cheeseman starts handing out large paper sacks of grub. Are we going to stop on the way for a picnic? Sheehan will be furious if we're late. There are freshly made, rather posh-looking sandwiches and assorted nibbles in the bags that Jake has organised as a culinary alternative to the usual airline nosh, a thoughtful touch.

'Is there any wine with this?' Pete Thomas wants to know, rummaging through his sack, Christmas at the orphanage.

The coach pulls away from the pub, the traffic already heavy as we head into Hammersmith. We're soon moving so slowly, I'm frightened Jake will work himself up into a fearsome tantrum, force us all off the coach and make us walk to Gatwick with our luggage on our heads, like refugees escaping a war zone. Soon, we're not moving at all. At the back of the bus, everyone's quiet for a moment or two, wondering what to do next. Then as if in response to someone firing a starting pistol, the F-Beat road crew start handing out beers from a couple of crates they've liberated from the Brook Green Tavern in a triumph for forward planning. Someone's chopping out some lines of speed, coke, whatever. We all tuck in.

Nick, ever alert to pharmaceutical action, comes down the aisle.

'Dare I?' he says. 'I mean,' he goes on, looking over his shoulder. 'My dad ...'

'I'll have Nick's if he doesn't want any,' Pete Thomas says, always eager to help.

'Maybe just a quick one,' Nick says, before returning to his seat, where he immediately starts chatting to his dad. I hope he's not telling Drain the story about touring Scandinavia that includes an encounter on a motorway with a moose. We'll be in fucking Texas before he gets to the end of that one.

By the time we finally get to Gatwick, some of us are wild-eyed and very merry indeed. When Sheehan sees me basically fall off the coach in the company of Pete Thomas, Bobby Irwin and the F-Beat road crew, he fears the worst.

'Fuck me, Welsh,' he says, fairly appalled. 'Do you know what time it is?'

No idea.

'Eight o'clock.'

That late?

'In the fucking morning.'

Oh, dear. I may have peaked a bit early.

We somehow make it through check-in and security, everyone at Jake's uncompromising command on their best behaviour, even Pete Thomas. We then find Nick, on his own, looking a bit confused. Where are his dad and the RAF lot?

'They're already in the bar,' he says. 'Went rushing off to meet an old mate of my dad's. A chap called Len. A complete bloody hooligan. An absolute rascal. The Pete Thomas of the Battle of Britain. They're going to be such trouble, this lot.'

The British Caledonian flight to Dallas is called about four pints into a lively interval in the airport bar, where Pete Thomas has seemingly settled in for the rest of the day and has to be dragged out of it by Jake and Cheeseman, both of them swearing colourfully. On the plane, I fall into a window seat. Pete Thomas takes the seat next to me. We settle ourselves in for the long haul to come. Pete pulls a well-thumbed paperback from his bag, Charles Mingus's autobiography, *Beneath the Underdog*. This is a surprise. Given the open-bar drinks policy of transatlantic flights at the time, I hadn't expected to lose Pete to a book by an old jazzer, however distinguished.

'This?' Pete says, holding up the battered paperback. 'It's a great book. But I haven't brought it along to read.'

The book is thick enough to use as a pillow, but that can't be the reason he's got it with him.

'It's a decoy,' Pete explains. 'Jake will be around in a couple of hours,' he goes on, 'to check on how drunk we are. If we keep an eye out, we'll see him coming, stick our noses in a book and if we're lucky we'll convince him we haven't spent the entire flight so far getting totally pissed.'

And this will work?

'There's always a first time,' Pete says. 'Now where's the waitress?'

Pete goes into action as soon as the seat belt signs are off, flagging down a stewardess and sending her chuckling to the galley with his drinks order. She's back in record time, carrying a big tray with enough miniature bottles of vodka on it to have a game of chess with.

'We have more if you need any,' the stewardess tells us, a little sarcastically if you ask me.

'We'll be in touch,' Pete tells her. 'Cheers,' he says to me, as we knock the first ones back. The flight goes by in a vodka blur. Pete is notoriously indiscreet after a couple of drinks, a source whenever I meet him of hilarious tales from the Costello camp that usually end up in the *MM* gossip column, or whatever at the time passes for one. He's soon off on a round of Elvis stories that make me laugh so much that at one point my head falls off and rolls under the seat in front of me.

'Keep these to yourself,' Pete says, opening another couple of vodkas. 'Elvis knows there's a mole in the camp and he's pretty sure it's me. Don't laugh. He was talking about firing squads the other day. And I don't think he was joking.'

Some time later, Sheehan comes down the aisle, swaying like someone on his way home, still drunk, from a party. He's clearly had a few and appears to be speaking in Braille or reciting the Eucharist backwards, a high priest at a black mass. Either way, he's not making much sense.

The stewardess appears with a large bin bag, like she's on an afternoon shift at a Wetherspoons, and clears the now-empty vodka bottles.

'Same again?' she asks.

'If you insist,' Pete tells her, as Andy Cheeseman now approaches, rolling down the aisle like a Bowery beat cop looking for a bum to beat with a baton. He gives us a sinister once-over.

'Just checking,' he says and with a nod moves on.

Nick now stops by for a chat, drink in hand.

'I'm trying to pace myself,' he says, although he already seems a little unsteady on his feet and nearly ends up in an open luggage rack when we hit an upper-atmosphere speed bump. 'I have a mortal fear of ending up horrendously drunk in front of my old man.'

Nick makes his way back to his seat. Pete settles back with a cigar and a contented sigh, finishes off the last of his vodka, and wonders where the stewardess is with our refills. He suddenly sits bolt upright, like he's accidentally pressed a hidden ejector button and is lucky not to have gone straight through the cabin roof.

'Jake!' he says, as if the anti-Christ himself is upon us. Pete grabs his copy of the Mingus autobiography. I drop my book, fumble for the laminated safety manual from the seat rack in front of me and try to look engrossed, although its simple-minded instructions will be useless if the pilot turns out to be an undiagnosed manic depressive who puts us in a suicidal death-dive, we lose a wing, the engines explode, or the tail fin blows off.

'Afternoon, chaps,' Jake says, looming above us with a frankly terrifying smile.

'He's obviously pissed,' he says, giving me a nod, at which point I realise I'm holding the safety instructions upside down. 'What about you?' Jake asks Pete.

'I'm pacing myself,' Pete says, brightly.

'That's funny,' Jake says. 'That's what Nick said just before his dad had to help him into his seat.'

'You know what Nick's like,' Pete says, an innocent admonishing the fallen. 'Never knows when he's had enough.'

With this, the stewardess arrives with a trolley.

'Your drinks,' she says to Pete, handing him one miniature bottle of vodka after another until there's no room on our fold down tables for the cans of beer the stewardess is now unloading on Pete.

'That's nearly the last of the vodka,' she says. 'But there's plenty of beer, gin, wine and whiskey left.'

'I'll talk to you later,' Jake tells Pete with a murderous glare and then stomps off.

'Talk about being caught red-handed,' Pete says, pouring out a vodka, opening a can of beer. 'There's only one thing for it now,' he adds, knocking back the vodka, reaching for the beer. 'Bottoms up!'

There's a brief stopover in Dallas, where Pete Thomas goes missing. I'm beginning to wonder if he's collapsed onto the luggage carousel and might even now be going around the arrivals hall for the umpteenth time, trapped beneath his own bags. But no, he's merely stopped off at a souvenir shop where he's bought a cowboy hat. He strolls into the airport bar with the swagger of a man who's just changed his name by deed poll to Tex and surprised his friends by joining a rodeo.

'Ride 'em, cowboy!' Sheehan shouts over guffaws from everyone at Pete's appearance.

'If you've bought a horse to go with that fucking hat,' Jake tells him, 'I'm going to tie you up and leave you here.'

Pete gets a bit moody at this and pours a drink over his head, then another, I'm not sure why, until his new hat is a sodden mess, the brim collapsing damply and the crown awash.

'I was only trying to blend in,' Pete says, a man made forlorn after being laughed at by friends.

Then there's a welcome call for flight BN245 to Harlingen, and we're on the move again. Hours later, we check into our room at Harlingen's Rodeway Inn. Sheehan disappears at some speed into the bathroom where he has an unspeakable episode with the twanging stem of an undigested bay leaf that he's evidently wolfed down with the last curry he ate. The errant bay leaf has now – how to put this delicately? – passed through his digestive system, causing the legendary lensman some considerable alarm when he discovers it sort of hanging, dangling or protruding from his arse.

According to his vivid account, he gives the wretched thing a manly tug – and out it pops. At which point, he falls into a swoon and returns ashen-faced to the room, where he sits in a chair, mopping his fevered brow and taking deep breaths.

'Time for a drink,' he says, regaining some of his composure, the colour slowly returning to his cheeks, a ghastly intestinal catastrophe averted, if not easily forgotten.

There's an excursion for anyone who wants to go to somewhere called Reynosa, part of the Reynosa–McAllen metropolitan area that includes Harlingen, but on the other side of the Rio Grande. In other words, south of the border. It's not exactly Old Mexico, but I'm moved nevertheless to pick up a sombrero from a souvenir stall and try the thing on, hoping for a gay *caballero* look.

'For fuck's sake, Welsh,' a passing Sheehan says, giving me a slap on the back of the head. 'Put it back.'

The group we've arrived with seem to have scattered by now, Pete Thomas and Bobby Irwin leading a troop in one direction, Nick, Drain and Drain's RAF buddies wandering off in another. Jake, Cheeseman, me and Tom are looking for somewhere to eat and find a restaurant on a corner that looks a bit lively. We take a table in the middle of a room full of laughter, crowded with families on a night out, a mariachi band doing the rounds. Tom goes off to the men's room, possibly to check if there's been any further bay leaf action. When he gets back, there's a large platter of sizzling ribs in the middle of the table and we're already tucking in.

'Don't mind if I do,' Tom says, taking a seat, tucking a napkin into his collar with an Oliver Hardy flourish, pinkie extended. He picks up a rib, takes a delicate bite.

'Delicious,' he says, now chewing away at the rib like a beaver trimming a log. 'What is it? Beef? Pork?'

'Goat,' Jake tells him.

Tom freezes, mid-nibble.

'Goat?'

'Goat,' Jake repeats.

'You've got to be fucking joking,' Tom says, panic, disbelief and not a little horror in his voice. 'Goat?'

Tom drops the rib like it's just come alive in his hands and started barking at him. He's pale and hyperventilating.

'Jonesy,' he says, giving me a stricken look, gasping for breath, a man betrayed by someone he trusted. 'Tell me it's not goat.'

It's goat, Tom.

'Welsh!' he positively wails. 'How could you let me eat a fucking goat?'

He makes a horrible retching noise, like he's choking on one of Lemmy's old socks, spits a lump of half-chewed goat into his napkin, which he flings on his plate like it's contaminated. He's still hungry, though, and his prowling eye now lands on a small bowl of diced jalapeño peppers, ferociously hot.

'What are these little chaps?' he asks, scooping up a handful and popping them in his mouth like they're peanuts.

Tom's eyes are quickly watering, like he's just been teargassed. He's soon glowing like a nuclear reactor on apocalyptic blink, all the needles in the red zone. I wouldn't be surprised to see steam coming out of his mouth even as his tongue melts. He seems to be giving off more heat than the solar core, the sun's molten heart. Which makes him sizzle when touched, however lightly.

At least he's breathing again, although his gasping hysterics are turning heads at nearby tables. The waiters are no help. They're laughing as hard as Jake and Cheeseman.

I offer a word of sympathy, cruelly rebuffed.

'It's your fucking fault, Jonesy,' he finally splutters, wheezing like a Flaco Jiménez accordion solo. 'You made me eat a fucking goat.'

Boy, is he in a huff!

The celebrated photographer has barely cooled off when the cab from Reynosa drops us off at the Rodeway Inn, where we find Nick, Drain and Drain's Invincibles in the bar next door to our Texas digs. Nick soon decides he's had enough.

'A couple of them haven't had a drink out of their hands since we left Gatwick,' he says on his way out. 'They're killing me.'

Jake and Cheeseman are also quickly on their way, me following not much later. Tom decides he's going to stay for another couple with the veteran flyboys, several of whom he's been regaling with details that leave them aghast of the earlier bay leaf melodrama. The looks on their faces suggest they'd rather be facing ack-ack barrages over Essen or Gelsenkirchen. Tom barrels on, regardless.

A while later, the door to our room crashes open. Sheehan flies in, like he's been blown into the room by a grenade blast. I watch in amusement as the great man attempts to negotiate a safe passage to his bed, every couple of steps forward that he manages followed by as many the way he's just come. Which means at one point, he's back outside the room.

Eventually, he makes it to his bed, shedding clothes along the way. But when he gets there, he apparently can't settle. He gets up again, somewhat unsteadily, a bizarre apparition in his Kursaal Flyers T-shirt, figure-hugging bikini briefs and socks. There's a television set on the wall opposite the beds, fixed to a hinged bracket. Sheehan reaches up to turn the telly on but can't reach it. He drags up a chair and climbs on it, loses his balance and grabs at the TV, which now swings on its hinges into the wall, bounces back towards the befuddled snapper and smacks him on the head. Tom flies off the chair like he's been shot, goes arse over bonnet onto the floor, where he spins on his back like a breakdancer.

It doesn't end there. He gets to his feet like a newly turned zombie still working on his moves and staggers around the room like a sack of potatoes learning to walk. He makes it back to his bed, though, give him that. Unfortunately, Tom's now listening to a new Nils Lofgren album on my Walkman and singing along to all the fucking guitar solos. Will this day never end? I'm seriously thinking about calling the

F-Beat road crew to ask them to take him out to the desert and kill him when he mercifully falls asleep.

I'm turning the light off now.

Oh, what a beautiful morning! The sun's already blasting in the cloudless blue sky above the forecourt of the Rodeway Inn as we get on board the bus for Rebel Field and the CAF airsho. The F-Beat road crew come to the rescue again, handing out cold recuperative beers as we pull onto the highway, freeway, whatever it is. We pass a lot of music clubs, roadhouses, taverns, blues joints, bars. Single-storey buildings, most of them, usually with one set of doors and no windows, occasionally a sign advertising BEER AND BLUES.

'I love these places,' Nick says, quite wistfully, as another couple flash by. 'They look built for speed. I imagine they never close for more than an hour, just to hose the insides down. They're probably open again before the floor's dry.'

There's a great roar overhead. A vast shriek that sounds like the roof of the coach is being torn off. It's followed quickly by another ear-shattering explosion. Two F6F Hellcats, the kind that flew off American aircraft carriers in the Pacific War against the Japanese, are zooming above us, coming in low for landing. We must be getting close to Rebel Field.

We join a long line of cars, coaches, motorhomes, campervans, all kinds of RVs, moving slowly to the entrance to Rebel Field, where crisply uniformed marine cadets are directing the traffic. They wave us to the right as we go through the gates, and we drive into a car park as big as a parade ground and overlooking the site. The airstrip is slightly below us, down a long sloping path. There are a couple of large hangars away to our left, used now as a museum space for the CAF collection. To our right as we walk down the path, there are what seem to be office buildings and a souvenir shop. Beyond that and behind a white picket fence, an American flag dangling from a flagpole, is the CAF Officer's Club.

We stop at the shop first, where we sign up and become honorary CAF colonels. There are CAF baseball caps and uniforms for sale. A cap's enough for Nick. Tom, Cheeseman and Jake, however, come out of the shop completely togged up, like the fucking Village People, or something. In his Ray-Bans, braided cap and shirt complete with epaulettes, the swaggering Riviera looks like he's just led a military coup in a small South American country and installed himself as the man in charge, someone with an appetite for cocaine, machine guns and throwing political opponents into pools of crocodiles. ¡*Viva el presidente!*

We head for the Officer's Club, Jake marching in like MacArthur wading ashore at Incheon. The club is packed with crusty old types. Most look like they're dressed for a barbecue at a country club, a few of them, presumably veterans, in USAF garrison caps. There's a crew at a table, however, near where I'm standing at the bar, that catch my eye, old Texas money types, with buzz cuts and bolero ties, who look like they may in 1963 have chipped in to fund a presidential hit, images of Kennedy, Dealey Plaza and the Texas School Book Depository coming to mind rather too quickly for comfort. Most of them seem pretty past it, though, a few of them wheezing like the dilapidated horn section of a second-rate soul band.

We have a few drinks, then make our way through the crowd, down to the grandstands and spectator areas on the edge of the runway. The F-Beat road crew, that blessed congregation, have staked out a prime spot, where they've parked four large coolers full of beer. There's a rostrum down here, too, and it's occupied by CAF colonels Eddie May and Ray Norton, our masters of ceremonies this afternoon, who provide a running commentary on the airborne events that follow.

'Ladies and gentlemen,' Colonel Eddie now announces, his voice full of sombre inflections, 'we would now like to ask y'all to step into the giant chamber of imagination that is going to transport y'all back to the dark days of World War Two.'

Cue the sound of drums, marching feet. The crowd takes a breath.

'Germany,' we are now being told, 'is ree-armin', under the leadership of Aydolf Hitler. The swastika looms over Europe ...'

Whatever Colonel Eddie says next is entirely drowned out by the unholy fucking racket of a simulated blitzkrieg, the sky suddenly black with Messerschmitt Me-109s and Heinkel He-111s. They come over us in a rush, a malevolent horde. The crowd, clearly suckers for spectacle, give them a big cheer.

'Whose side are this lot on?' Nick asks, a bit bewildered.

'And so,' Colonel Eddie goes on, really getting into it, 'th'Nazi hordes swept through Poland, Holland, Belgium, Norway and Denmark. The French Maginot Line crumbled. Hitler's goose-stepping troops entered Paris. The British fought with their backs to the sea at Dunkirk. Poised on th'English Channel, the Führer demands Britain's surrender ...'

'NO FUCKING CHANCE!' yells Bobby Irwin, as defiant as portly Churchill, ready to take on all-comers. Pick your beach, street or field. Bobby's suddenly so full of the so-called Bulldog Spirit of popular legend I'm worried he might start barking.

Anyway, thus starts the CAF recreation of the Battle of Britain, a chapter of the unfolding conflict somewhat compromised by the absence of any British planes. CAF Colonel Johnny Williams has only that morning in fact crashed the Hawker Sea Fury that at the time is the only operational RAF warplane in the CAF collection. Pilot and plane had gone down in a ball of flames somewhere in the Rio Grande Valley. The CAF tribute to the Battle of Britain is therefore rather underwhelming. Over, in fact, in less time than it would take to scramble a squadron of Spitfires and have them in the skies over the White Cliffs.

'Is that it?' Nick asks, astonished, watching a lonely Messerschmitt flying through a cloud of smoke. 'Oh, well,' he says, wholly disgruntled. 'I hope we didn't keep anyone. I mean, they've obviously got a lot to get through. Pearl Harbor. Winning the war on their own. That sort of thing.'

'PLANES COMIN'!'

Colonel Eddie's not wrong. This is the afternoon's big production number, the Japanese attack on Pearl Harbor. The horizon is suddenly swarming with Japanese Zeros. The sleek fighters zoom low over Rebel Field, which is quickly aflame, great sheets of fire shooting skywards all over the airfield, explosions everywhere. It's like the end of a Metallica show. The noise is appalling.

'Shoot those bastards out of the fucken sky!' yells someone we don't know, a flinty-eyed old codger you can imagine as a young man taking fire off Tarawa or Guadalcanal, kamikazes homing in and nowhere to run.

What follows is chilling. A B-29 Superfortress trundles onto the runway, prepares for take-off. This is *FIFI*, sister plane to the *Enola Gay*, the B-29 that dropped the atomic bomb on Hiroshima. In *FIFI*'s

'I am no more than a jester…' Ian Anderson, London, February 1977.

'I'd go the whole wide world just to find yer…' Wreckless Eric in the front room of his Wandsworth flat, 1976.

'Infiltrate and double cross…' Jake Riviera outside Stiff HQ, Alexander Street, West London, July 1977.

'I wasn't what you might call a priority for RCA. They were too busy selling Elvis Presley records and making a star of John Denver…' Guy Clark, London, September 1978.

'Don't let me get ahead of you. I'd rather not get drunk on my own…' Peter Cook at home in Hampstead, December 1978.

'I allowed myself to be surrounded by people who sucked the life out of me…' Joe Cocker, London, January 1979.

'Nothing's ever finished. Eventually, whatever you're working on is just abandoned to the public…' Jerry Dammers, Coventry, February 1984.

'PLANES COMIN'…' Andy Cheeseman, Nick Lowe, Jake Riviera and Andrew Lauder at the CAF 'airsho', Rebel Field, Texas, October 1981.

'Wheels up! Let's 'ave at 'em…' Lee Brilleaux, Hammersmith Palais, London, 1976.

'All we ever asked for was the chance to be heard…' The Blasters' Dave and Phil Alvin, Los Angeles, 1980.

'What interests me most is the terror of the moment…' John Cale, London, December 1975.

'Dai was my absolute hero…' Dave Edmunds and Nick Lowe, London, June 1979.

'You can think too much, you know, and it can get a bit fucking evil…' Elvis Costello, London, 1989.

'There were lots of drugs…' The Pretenders' Jimmy Honeyman-Scott, me, Pete Farndon and Commander Cody, San Francisco, September 1981.

'You diggin' this, man...'
With Paladin, of the Oakland
Hell's Angels, San Francisco,
September 1981.

'They were still pushing their
gear around in a pram…' The
101'ers (Joe Strummer, Clive
Timperley, Richard Dudanski
and Dan Kelleher) outside
their squat in Orsett Terrace,
West London, 1976.

cockpit is CAF colonel Paul Tibbets, the pilot at the controls of the *Enola Gay* when it dropped the A-bomb on 6 August 1945.

'I had the honour of sittin' in that beautiful bird and flyin' it at Airsho 80,' Colonel Eddie says, like he's recalling a spin through the countryside on a vintage tandem, as *FIFI* banks into the turn that will bring it back to Rebel Field.

Four Hellcats now fly in tight company down the Rio Grande Valley in the Missing Man formation.

'Th'Missing Man formation,' Colonel Eddie tells us, choking back tears by the sound of it, 'reminds us of the brave men who never came back from their last mission. They paid the supreme sacrifice, laid their lives on the altar of freedom so that peace would prevail in this great land.'

As the Hellcats fly over the airsho crowd, one of them peels away, leaving a vacancy in the formation. As the three remaining planes continue their slow descent towards Rebel Field, the fourth begins to climb in lonely ascent. A solo bugle blows 'Taps', that lament for the fallen. Another old coot, nearby in the crowd, takes off his ball cap, looks for a moment like he's going to say a prayer and then throws back his head like the MGM lion.

'GOD BLESS AMERICA!' he fairly roars, loud enough probably that even the missing fucking man can hear him.

The fourth plane continues to rise, rise, rise, almost invisible to us now. The crowd is muted, heads lowered like they're at a graveside. There are pockets of throat-clearing, someone honking noisily into a dampening hanky, a general air of bereavement, loss. The bugle's last blue notes fade over Rebel Field. A great mourning silence prevails, settling on the crowd like a shroud. No one moves in the contemplative moment.

'Fancy a quick one in the Officer's Club before we go, Jonesy?' Tom suddenly pipes up, already on his way to catch up with Nick, Jake and Cheeseman. Pete Thomas and Bobby Irwin are already at the top of the hill, on the other side of the white picket fence, Pete saluting everyone he passes.

As it happens, I did.

THE BLASTERS

Texas, April 1982

Flying back from Texas after an eventful week on the road with Ozzy Osbourne that's included, among many other larks, Ozzy pissing on the Alamo and being arrested by irate Texas Rangers, I pick up a copy of a Dallas newspaper someone's left on the plane. There's an article on a band called The Blasters and a picture of them that makes me think it must have been taken on the day of their collective release from a chain gang or hardcore penitentiary. Angola, Parchman Farm, San Quentin, somewhere like that. They look like a tough crew. Anyway, it seems that the self-titled album they released the previous December on LA independent label Slash has become the season's big sleeper hit. Rave reviews merited only modest original sales, but it's soon climbing the *Billboard* chart, a surprise break-out hit, after being picked up by Warners.

From what I read about it in the Dallas paper, the album sounds like it might be fantastic. When I get back to London, I try to track down a copy. I call around the usual record shops. No one's even heard of the band. Someone suggests I try Rough Trade distribution, to see if they've got it on their books. They have! Turns out the album's been picked up for UK release by Jake Riviera's F-Beat label. A copy is soon on its way to me and when I get it, I can't stop playing the thing. Its 12 tracks run for barely 30 minutes, only one of them over three minutes long and most clocking in at a cough over two. It's not quite The Ramones turning up at Sun Studios one afternoon in 1955 and knocking out an album in a couple of hours with Sam Phillips. The Blasters don't yield everything to velocity, so much as come to the musical point with minimum fuss and maximum impact.

184

They cover Jimmie Rodgers' 'Never No Mo' Blues', complete with yodelling, Bo Diddley's 'I Love You So', Sunnyland Slim's 'Highway 61', Little Willie John's 'I'm Shakin'', revisit the Bakersfield Sound on a cover of Bob Ehret's 'Stop the Clock'. But it's the band's original songs, written by guitarist Dave Alvin, that really stick – 'Marie Marie', 'No Other Girl', 'Border Radio', 'Hollywood Bed', 'This Is It' and the battle cry of 'American Music'. Like Creedence Clearwater Revival's John Fogerty, Alvin clearly worships at the shrine of Sun 45s. He's not big on frills. His blue-collar heartbreakers are more rock'n'roll haiku than Springsteen aria. In fact, you could probably tattoo the lyrics to every song he's so far written on your back and still have room for a couple of Raymond Carver stories. No wonder Fogerty's keen on producing them.

The album still hasn't come off the turntable when a couple of months later, I get a call from Jake. The Blasters have been confirmed as support on Nick Lowe's next UK tour, starting in a couple of weeks. Before that, they've got some dates coming up in Texas, including a big show in Austin with Joe Ely. I take *Melody Maker* editor Mike Oldfield down the pub, buy him a few drinks and sing the praises of his visionary editorship loud enough to walk out of the place with a commitment to a cover story. I'm soon on a plane back to Texas.

I arrive at a motel in somewhere called Mesquite, in the drab boondocks somewhere outside Dallas, and walk into a room full of quiffs, bandanas, motorcycle boots, leather jackets and hard-nosed attitude. There's clearly a crisis afoot.

'They've put us in a dry fucking county,' Dave Alvin says, the band's disconsolate mood quickly explained. 'We can't get a drink.'

He goes on to say that bass player John Bazz and pianist Gene Taylor have just gone off in search of alcohol, or something like it. I get the impression that at this moment, they'd settle for brake fluid or swamp water. How far will Bazz and Taylor go to get a drink?

'Wyoming, if they have to,' Alvin says.

I have something in my bag that might yet save the day. I produce a bottle of Chivas Regal. The room reacts like they've just witnessed a magician pulling something spectacular out of a hat. A unicorn, perhaps.

'My eyes have seen the glory of the coming of the motherfucking Lord,' singer Phil Alvin, Dave's brother, says. 'Open her up and empty her.'

Which is exactly what we do, still no sign of the intrepid Bazz and Taylor when the lights go out.

The next morning, I meet up with Bazz and drummer Bill Bateman in the motel parking lot, the day already bright with spring sunshine. Bill is regaling *MM* photographer Janette Beckman, who's just flown in from New York, with some evidently colourful anecdote that I catch the end of.

'... so, Belinda's screaming at this guy. And he gets out of his car and walks over to Belinda, who's sitting in her car with the window open. The next thing I know, he's pulled a gun on Belinda. He's got it aimed at her head and he's got the hammer cocked and he's threatening to shoot her.'

'What did you do?' Janette asks, breathlessly anticipating, no doubt, some account of reckless heroism on Bill's part.

'I, er, took the number of the guy's car and called the cops,' Bateman rather sheepishly admits, scuffling his boot on the sidewalk.

I'm at this point shoved roughly from behind and turn to face someone sporting a beret, Ray-Bans and a satanic goatee. It's Gene Taylor, a squat ball of random provocations, possibly someone who can't walk into a bar without starting an argument that might end up with chairs being thrown and someone going through a window.

'She's got a camera, so I know she's the photographer,' Gene says with a nod to Janette. 'Since you're not in the band,' he says, giving me a poke in the chest, 'you must be the writer, I guess. But shit, I don't see a pen or a notebook or a tape recorder or any of that journalist shit. What the fuck are you?'

He stares at me like we're soon going to be rolling around in the car park trying to bite each other's ears off. Then starts laughing.

'I'm fucking with you, kid,' he says, giving me a slap across the face. 'Don't take it personal. I hate everybody. Journalists, especially. Only good thing I ever read in a magazine was when someone asked Jerry Lee Lewis what he thought of Dave Brubeck. Jerry Lee just said, "I play better with my dick."'

'Where are the fucking Alvins?' Blasters tour manager Wally Hanley now wants to know. We're already late for a meet and greet at a record company lunch in Dallas. Dave and Phil finally turn up, smoking Kools and grinning like a couple of hoodlums who've just beaten a felony rap on a technicality. A key witness going mysteriously missing, a trial collapsing, something like that.

'Let's go, people,' Wally says, herding his flock towards the band's van.

'Come on,' Gene says, grabbing my arm. 'The record company are paying. Bring an appetite and a good thirst.'

The record company reception turns out to be at a downtown Pizza Hut. There are some fans, waiting with albums to be signed, but they're outnumbered by the record company reps, a horde of tittering inanities, shaking hands like they're collecting fingerprints.

'At least they're not wearing satin tour jackets with our name on the back,' Phil says as we go inside.

'We had them put it in our contract when we signed to Warners,' Dave says. 'No. Fucking. Satin. Tour. Jackets.'

'Are you eating, sir?' a waitress asks as we commandeer a table.

'Just drinking, thank you,' Dave says, accepting a beer, signing an album cover, being waved at by the record company reps, who seem to have formed a chorus line, a high-kicking dance routine perhaps in the works here. Dave gives them a wave back.

'This is so fucking weird,' he says. 'A year ago, there wasn't a record company in the country that would piss on us. Now this.'

There's a lot of clapping and shrieking now from the record company reps, a couple of them hugging, like they've won a raffle or something. Dave, meanwhile, is telling me how two years ago The Blasters cut an album for the LA rockabilly label Rollin' Rock: 12 tracks, recorded over two days in someone's garage.

'You can hear the neighbour's dog barking all the way through one track,' Dave says, already working on his second beer, another couple of album sleeves being handed to him to autograph. They called the album *American Music* after one of Dave's songs, and pressed up 4,000 copies, one of which somehow makes it into the hands of Shakin' Stevens who has a UK hit with a cover of 'Marie Marie'. Encouraged, the band took the tapes of the album and some recent demos to whatever major label would meet with them. They were turned down by everyone.

'One guy listened to our tape and said, "I don't hear any songs",' Dave says, a bitter memory forming even as he grabs a couple more beers from the passing waitress. 'He's just been listening to, like, "Border Radio", and he couldn't hear any songs?'

They eventually signed to Slash, another independent LA label, and made the album that's brought me here, reworking several key tracks from their debut, Warners then signing them to a distribution deal that helps take the album into the charts.

'More pizza?' another waitress now wants to know, although we've been too busy drinking to eat.

'No, thanks,' Dave tells her. 'But we could do with a couple more beers.'

'Let me clear these first,' the waitress says, making a production number of sweeping what's on the table into a plastic bin bag, a clattering avalanche of empty beer bottles that draws alarmed looks from the record company reps and a big laugh from Gene Taylor, who's on at least his second pizza and even now is being handed a pitcher of beer by a waitress he seems to have made his own.

Dave's now telling me that Jake Riviera was also a fan of the first Blasters album. Liked it well enough, in fact, to invite Phil to play an acoustic blues set as support to Elvis Costello at a show in Los Angeles to promote Costello's country album, *Almost Blue*.

'Later, Jake took us backstage to meet Elvis,' Dave says. 'Some of us were even allowed to shake his hand,' he adds, tartly. 'He looked at me and said, "I'm a fan." I thought, "Why not?"'

Anyway, here's Dave, a couple of weeks away from a UK tour with Nick Lowe and something's obviously on his mind.

'Are The Stray Cats still big in England?' he asks, finally. Do I detect a hint of animosity here? I do. 'Jesus. Those shrink-heads,' he says. 'We play a lot of shows with a cat, he's coming in for tonight's show, Lee Allen. Lee played sax with Little Richard and Fats Domino. Man, he's on everything. The Stray Cats got him to play on their last album and then took him off most of the tracks. Brian Setzer said in an interview that Lee couldn't rock. What an arrogant, pimply little dickhead. Probably had hair down to his ass a couple of years ago. Probably has one Gene Vincent record and thinks he knows everything about rock'n'roll. Asshole. If The Stray Cats turn up to one our shows, they're dead. Man, as long as I'm in this business, I'll be trying to drive a nail into their coffin.'

One of the record company reps is calling for Dave to join them for some pictures. He groans when he sees the photographer, who's wearing a satin tour jacket, REO Speedwagon the name on the back.

'Hey, man,' Dave says to me, smiling back at the record company reps, getting up to join them. 'Don't hold any of this against us, uh?'

'Me and Dave grew up in Downey, a suburb out in East LA,' Phil Alvin says, drinking enough coffee to keep him awake for a week in the booth of the diner back at the motel in Mesquite, the sun coming through holes and tears in the blinds a waitress has just pulled down against the mid-afternoon glare.

'We had a cousin called Donna,' he goes on. 'Donna Dixon. A wild lady. Drove a '53 Chevy with flames painted on the flanks. Hung out at a burger stand on Eastern and Florence with Eddie Cochran. Donna used to babysit us, and she'd bring over a record player and a lot of rock'n'roll records. Sometimes she would bundle us into the Chevy and take off for the burger stand or a dance party. We loved Donna.'

The Alvins are quickly hooked on the music Donna turns them onto. They're soon playing in high school bands with names like Delta Pacific, The Night Shift, The Flying Cats, The Strangers, Fresh Water Bass & The Delta Rabbits. Bazz, Bateman and Gene Taylor are part of their scene. Phil and Gene start hanging out in the Mexican clubs in south Downey.

Sometimes, they sneak into the blues clubs, mixing it up with the old bluesmen. There's a place called The Ashgrove that Dave writes about on the title track of his 2004 solo album, *Ashgrove*, where they meet Big Joe Turner, T-Bone Walker, Lightnin' Hopkins and the Reverend Gary Davis.

'They were all real nice guys,' Phil says. 'But when they played, they'd get this kinda evil marijuana dancing-devil look in their eyes.'

The music they hear at places like The Ashgrove is the music they want to play. No frills rock'n'roll, stripped-down R&B, unfiltered rockabilly. The blues.

'A lot of guys in local bands got gigs in Hollywood, playing hard rock,' Phil says, visibly shuddering at the thought. 'We never went for any of that. We were always The Blasters. We were never a rock band. Rock isn't the same as rock'n'roll. Rock is the kind of thing that assholes think is rock'n'roll. Foreigner. Journey. Shit like that. Jackson Browne, even.'

Dave has joined us by now.

'Some people thought that because we played rockabilly and blues that we were a revivalist band,' he says. 'People would try to flip us out. Start yelling obscenities. They were usually a buncha dumb asshole dickheads. We never considered ourselves revivalists. This music's never been away. Maybe it hides out for a while, gets lost in the bars on the wrong side of town. But it's always there, somewhere. Sleepy LaBeef was always playing in a roadhouse somewhere. Charlie Feathers always had a steady gig at some cracker roadhouse in Memphis.'

The hip LA clubs won't book them, so they find their own gigs, hustling spots in Mexican bars, playing for bikers, hoodlums, low-rider gangs.

'The heaviest place we played was probably The Sundance Saloon,' Dave says, getting a nod from Phil. 'We played there for a long time, and every night would end in a fight. One night, Bateman got thrown on the pool table by some bikers and got the shit beat out of him. When the fighting started, we were out of those places pretty fucking quick. I never socialised too much with those guys. Phil and Gene and Bill, they'd hang out with them. I'd just go out to the van or pick up on some girls or something.'

They're stuck on this circuit for a year. What keeps them going?

'We just knew we were good,' Dave says, as Wally Hanley turns up and tells us it's time to get to that night's gig at The Hot Klub.

On our way back into Dallas, me and Janette sit in the back of the band's tour bus with Bill Bateman. Bill's telling us how The Blasters settled on their current line-up.

'The major change was Bazz replacing a guy called Mike Kennedy,' Bill tells us.

What happened to him?

'He fell in love,' Bill says.

'Did he get married?' Janette wants to know, possibly imagining a happy day full of confetti, a bride in white, church bells, giggling bridesmaids, a handsome groom.

'Not exactly,' Bill says, turning grim. 'Mike fell in love with a Long Beach hooker. He was always trying to get her to leave her pimp and marry him. One night, he went down to Long Beach and some guys killed him. Killed him three times, really. It was like they couldn't get enough of killing him. They cut his throat. Shot him in the head. Then they set fire to him.'

A pause.

'There wasn't much of him to bury when they gave him back to his mother.'

The Hot Klub's on the corner of Maple and Hondo Avenues, its name spelled out in crude wooden letters spray-painted in red and black at the back of a small stage. Years later, I find a club flyer in one of my notebooks from the trip and laugh when I see that a week after The Blasters' show, a new band from Athens, Georgia, called R.E.M. are due to play. The place seems to have been built out of graffiti, feedback and beer stains.

The afternoon The Blasters fetch up there, we find two men in suits and hats, sitting at a table, waiting for us, instrument cases at their feet, like old-school gangsters with Tommy guns. My first impression is they're hitmen on a job, here to whack someone. I put myself behind Gene Taylor, figuring his ample girth will stop anything short of a close-range shotgun blast. Instead of the expected gunfire, however, there's much backslapping and laughter, the sound of reunited friends.

Turns out this is The Blasters' horn section, just arrived from LA, which means one of them's the pre-Los Lobos Steve Berlin. The other is Lee Allen, the New Orleans sax legend who played on all the epochal early Fats Domino and Little Richard sides. He was there at the start of it all. When we're introduced it's like shaking hands with history, Lee in his mid-50s now, still an imperious figure with a wicked look. With the New Orleans music scene in recession in the mid-1960s, he moved to Los Angeles, working at an aircraft manufacturing factory and fronting a trio that brings him to The Ashgrove, where he meets the Alvins, for whom he has become a kind of mentor. I sit, biting my tongue, trying not to pepper him with questions, as he jokes around with Dave and Phil.

When Steve Berlin and Lee Allen go off to check out what passes for the band room and unpack their stuff, Dave starts talking about

191

a low point in the band's story. Gene was in Canada, playing with Ronnie Hawkins. Bazz and Bateman were playing in local bar bands. The Alvins had mostly given up on music.

'By the mid-70s, it had gone from being something that meant a lot to me to something I just didn't understand. When I was growing up, I could listen to Elvis or Bob Dylan and it was like, bam! They got you straight in the heart. Then, suddenly, it's all these arena bands. I'd go see them and there'd be a bouncer standing over every row of seats. If you got out of your seat to do anything but go for a piss, you were in trouble. The whole magic was gone.'

One night, Bazz takes Dave to La Masque, an LA punk club. He discovers The Sex Pistols and The Clash. His interest in music is almost immediately revived. The Blasters become part of an alternative LA music scene that includes X, The Gun Club, Black Flag and Los Lobos, all loosely affiliated by the idea of keeping American music out of the hands of an emerging scene of what Lenny Kaye later calls pole-dancing hair metal bands, all that virtuosity and vaudeville.

'Although I was the same age as Johnny Lydon, I couldn't write the same kind of music. Phil couldn't sing the same kinds of lyrics,' Dave says. 'So, we didn't try. The only thing we could do was play what we'd always played, but bring it all up to date, remind everyone that this kind of music is still alive. Still vital.

'We remembered what Lee Allen told us when we were kids. "Keep it short. Pack the energy." So, we didn't play long guitar solos, drum solos, any of that shit. We just made sure that we played every song with a maximum of energy and concentration.'

How much of their success is down to a recent rockabilly revival? Dave almost explodes.

'The Stray Cats should be answering that question,' he says. 'A lot of people who buy Stray Cats records don't buy them because they like rockabilly or even know what it is. They buy Stray Cats records because they think a little pimply dickhead ex-hippie like Brian Setzer is kind of cute. Or they love the way he does his hair. With us it's different. We got a guy weighs 220 pounds, balding, with a goatee beard, who plays piano. It's just unhip. You're supposed to be clean-shaven and skinny. Rockabilly's been sold in the 80s like it's fucking glam rock.'

When The Blasters are introduced the next night to a rowdy crowd at Austin's City Coliseum, no one's really interested, the crowd impatient for local hero Joe Ely. Forty minutes later, however, most of the crowd are on their feet, in the aisles, hollering. An early turning point comes with a Dave Alvin guitar solo on an electrifying version of Bo Diddley's 'I Love You So' that sounds like he's handcuffed to lightning. The place erupts.

Backstage, after the show, Dave leans against a dressing-room wall, as wet as if he's just been waterboarded.

'Sorry, man,' he says.

What's he apologising for?

'That's the second show we've played since you've been with us, and we still haven't killed it,' he says.

From where I was standing, it looked like they'd slaughtered tonight's crowd, much as they'd slayed the crowd at The Hot Klub.

'Nah,' Dave says. 'There was a couple, four rows back from the stage, in front of Phil, who didn't move. Just sat there.'

'I saw 'em,' Phil says. 'Thought they were dead.'

What does it matter that a couple of people out of hundreds didn't get it?

'It means we're not doing our job,' Dave says.

He crushes a Kool under a boot heel.

'Come on,' he says. 'Let's find that party Joe was talking about.'

Even Gene Taylor's a bit quiet on the drive the next day from Austin to Houston. The party Joe Ely invites us to turns out to be very lively. At some point, it becomes at least another couple of parties, at locations it gets hard to keep track of. At one of them, I lose Dave and find myself with Phil at somebody's place neither of us can remember getting to. Not long after this, I lose Phil, too, and end up going with Joe and a few other people back to Joe's motel. Things take a weird turn in Joe's room when someone pulls out a gun and Joe decides enough is enough and shows everyone the door.

'This is it,' Wally says, parking the band's bus in front of a two-storey building on White Oak Drive, in a north-western suburb of Houston. We're outside a place called Fitzgerald's, formerly the Dom Polski, a Polish dancehall, now one of Houston's premier alternative rock venues, with stages in upstairs and downstairs rooms. The Blasters will be playing tonight in the upstairs space.

There's a large dressing room with battered sofas, armchairs that might have been rescued from the town dump, a couple of low tables, the usual backstage scene. Bazz and Bateman are off somewhere with Wally. I haven't seen Lee Allen and Steve Berlin since the band's soundcheck. Phil and Gene put their feet up. Dave grabs a couple of beers. We take them out to the wooden stairs that run down the side of the building, sit on the top steps. It's a warm evening and from our perch we can see a crowd already gathering outside the club. The Blasters this year have taken a big step up from playing four sets a night at The Sundance Saloon, where you were as likely to get a beating from the audience as a call for an encore.

'All we ever asked for was the chance to be heard,' Dave says. 'I mean, for a long time now, you turn on the radio and it's all the same. Hard rock. Heavy metal. Fine, if you dig it. But there's more to American music than Van fucking Halen, and a lot of it's been ignored. I'm not being nostalgic. I'm not looking for a blues revival or a rockabilly revival or a whatever the fuck revival. We're talking about the music that brought us here and, man, it's as relevant as ever.'

He lights another Kool.

'It's like our song, "American Music", that's got nothing to do with any kind of flag-waving bullshit. That's about all the voices in the American choir.'

He laughs.

'That sounds a bit fucking grand,' he says. 'But I can't think of a better way to put it. There are so many depths and dimensions to American music. Jazz, rock'n'roll, country, blues, rockabilly, R&B, soul, folk. Sun. Stax. Tamla. Chess. What a history. Why ignore it? I mean, fuck. There are probably people who think American music started with REO Speedwagon and they've probably never heard of Elvis, let alone Big Joe Turner.

'But I think things are changing,' he says. 'The American public's not as dumb as everyone makes them out to be. They've just been deprived of choice. I mean, as soon as The Go-Go's got on the radio, they took off. Whoosh. And they were a band that nearly all the major labels passed on. We got on the same radio stations, and it started to happen for us, too.

'When you get played on the radio, whether it's The Go-Go's, X, The Gun Club or us, people can hear your band next to Led Zeppelin, Styx, whoever the fuck. People have a choice, suddenly. If our kind of music is stuck in clubs where everybody's fighting and getting knifed, and the audience is full of fucking bikers and maniacs and junkies, then your records are not going to chart.

'But we broke the radio. They started playing us and the record started selling. All any of us need is a chance. One lucky fucking break. We get that, we can take care of the rest ourselves.'

He finishes his beer, gets up.

'I got a show to play,' he says, flicking what's left of his Kool down the stairs. Sparks fly.

Much as they do around ten minutes later when The Blasters hit the stage of Fitzgerald's like a fireball, blowing the roof off the venerable hut with the incendiary urgencies of 'This Is It'. Dave and Phil lose their jackets. Things get hotter from there. Lee Allen brings the house down with a version of his 1958 hit 'Walking With Mr Lee', once a staple on *American Bandstand*, he and Steve Berlin improvising a little dance routine that leaves them laughing in a brotherly hug. Dave's guitar burns up everything in its airspace. Phil testifies like a hillbilly preacher at a Mississippi tent revival meeting, a man transported. Gene Taylor goes full Jerry Lee on 'Tag Along'. When the horns, guitar and Phil's harmonica blow through the unison chorus of 'So Long Baby, Goodbye' it's like an anthem for something I can't put a name to but sounds like salvation, rapture, something like that. It's a fucking great show is what I'm trying to say.

When it's over, I have to battle my way backstage. The band's dressing room is full of backslappers and well-wishers. There seem to be as many people in here as there were moments ago in front of the stage, a noisy scrum. Everyone's looking for a hand to shake. Gene Taylor comes through the crowd like a snow plough. He gives me a hug and a beer. Phil's in an armchair, looking spent enough to need an oxygen mask. Dave's across the room, steam coming off him like he's evaporating. He's got a beer in both hands, a big smile on his face that says one thing.

Job done.

THE ROLLING STONES

London, May 1982

I wake up like a fugitive from a chain gang, bloodhounds barking in a bayou. Is that hammering I can hear a posse with torches banging on a boxcar door? No. Worse than that, it's our old friend, *Melody Maker* lensman Tom Sheehan, clearly not in one of his better moods. He's standing there when I open the front door, positively fuming. Steam coming out of his ears, fire shooting out of his ass. That kind of thing. Turns out he's been banging on the door for about 15 minutes, a taxi waiting in the street behind him, its meter ticking, the driver reading a paper and contemplating early retirement from the fare he's cheerfully running up.

'Jump to it, Welsh, for fuck's sake,' Sheehan is telling me now. I stare at him in stunned amazement. What's he doing here this early on a Saturday morning, especially after the night I've had, which seems to have only recently ended. To tell you the truth, when Sheehan's infernal battering startles me from dreamless unconsciousness, I wake up wondering who I am, where I am and what calamitous behaviour may have brought me to this current bewilderment. It takes me longer than it probably should to realise I'm in my own bed. Anyway, I'm lying there, the bedroom rotating, pitching and generally moving in a way that makes me bilious, when it strikes me that the percussive hurricane of slaps, kicks and knuckle-bruising wallops that have stirred me from my stupor means there's someone at the door demanding my attention.

At which point, trying to spring gazelle-like from under the duvet, I merely fall out of bed, onto the floor, where I am no more than a crumpled heap. I get somewhat unsteadily to what I presume are my feet, giddy, dehydrated, totally fucked. And now, on top of this self-inflicted misery, here's fucking Sheehan to contend with. The furious lensman strides into the basement flat, starts marching about the place like Patton organising his troops for the audacious counterthrust that will relieve besieged Bastogne and win the Battle of the Bulge. He's barking orders, telling me we have – what? – like, five minutes, before we have to roll, get on the road to Wembley. Why? Because we are supposed to be covering The Rolling Stones at the stadium. It comes back to me now. The rash moment when I volunteered us for the gig, Sheehan unhappy from the start and telling me I'd live to regret such impetuousness. Which is what I'm doing right now, slumped and incoherent in a chair, chopping out a couple of lines. It's the only thing that's going to get me moving this morning. I offer Tom a toot. But he's surprisingly abstemious.

'Not my game, Jones Boy,' he says. 'Work comes first, and all that,' he adds reprovingly, throwing my trousers at me. 'Get those on and let's go,' he says. And then we're off.

Not much later, we're stuck in traffic in north London, somewhere near Kilburn, I think, heading towards Wembley, but not at any great speed. Sheehan's mood is by now murderous.

'Welsh,' he says, tugging at the zip of his leather bomber jacket, always a sign that he's perilously close to self-combustion. 'This is a total fucking nightmare.'

Poor old Tom. He's been buggered round all week by the Stones office, who've seemed curiously reluctant to hand over his photo pass for today's show. He is further aggrieved when he finds out they've sent his pass to the *NME*. 'I bet David fucking Bailey doesn't have to put up with this fucking nonsense,' he simmers on hearing this.

The great man's also sulking because he's spent most of the last week in Scotland, covering the first dates of the Stones tour. He hasn't enjoyed himself at all, as he's now telling a woman from one of the Fleet Street papers who we bump into at the Crest Hotel in Wembley where Tom finally gets his photo pass.

'We're talking absolute fucking herberts, love,' Tom says of the Stones, laying it on with a trowel here. 'Worst fucking band in the world. The old prancing prat whips his shirt off, everybody starts screaming their bloody heads off, the songs all sound the same. And they go on for fucking hours.'

The woman from Fleet Street thinks this afternoon's line-up is a tad curious. A mix of Black Uhuru's reggae, the J. Geils Band's blathering rock and the Stones' vintage shtick. Sheehan manfully attempts to explain the thinking, as he sees it, behind the bill.

'See, they drag in the old reggae chaps for a bit of credibility because the Stones think it's still 1975, and they get someone like J. Geils because they've just had a hit, but they're not really very good and they won't show the Stones up. Simple, really.'

It's time for us to quit the hotel for the stadium, where things will shortly kick off.

'If there isn't a bar in there somewhere,' Sheehan says menacingly as we climb towards the fabled Twin Towers, 'someone's going to get a nervous fucking coshing.'

'I think we're talking windswept dreadlocks out there,' Sheehan says as we take our seats in the Royal Enclosure, the noise Black Uhuru are making on stage reaching us on what's become quite a stiff breeze. The J. Geils Band are up next. Sheehan thinks they are noisy, American and rubbish.

'It's really good to be back in London Town,' vocalist Peter Wolf is telling the crowd. 'I'd really, really like to thank The Rolling Stones for inviting us here …'

'What a crawling fucking toady,' Sheehan says, out of his seat now and heading for the Royal Enclosure restaurant. He unloads his camera bags and takes a seat at a table from which it looks like he will not easily be budged.

'Get 'em in, Welsh,' he tells me.

I walk cheerfully to the bar.

'Four pints of lager, a couple of tequilas and a large brandy while I'm waiting, please.'

What the barman then tells me sends a chill through my very soul.

'Bar's closed,' he says.

'Bar's what?' I ask, astonished. Surely I've misheard him.

'Closed.'

'Closed?'

'That's what I said.'

I'm shocked, no other word for it.

'Closed,' I say again. 'In what way exactly?'

'Closed,' the barman says. 'As in not open.'

'There's got to be a mistake,' Sheehan says when I break the appalling news to him. He's on his feet now, heading for the bar, a little juggernaut. He raps on the bar when he gets there.

'Mein host,' Sheehan calls to the barman. He's trying to sound jovial, carefree. But there's a tightening in his voice he can't quite disguise. It's the sound of rising panic, unfettered alarm.

The barman saunters over. Sheehan tries to be tactful, something he's not well practised in.

'Look,' he says. 'There's a couple of living legends 'ere, and apparently, we can't get a drink. What's the fucking story, squire?'

'We're closed,' the barman tells him. 'That's the fucking story and this is the fucking end of it.'

He brings down the shutters on the bar with a terrifying clang, no arguing with them.

'This is the worst day of my life,' Tom says, utterly disconsolate, bereft, abandoned. 'Fact.'

We sit for a while in silence, Sheehan giving me the evil eye and probably wishing upon me eternal damnation, an afterlife of flames, torture and associated unpleasantness.

The lensman's mood is about to plummet further when there's a bit of a kerfuffle at the doors to the Royal Enclosure. In sweeps Sting, a Sun King with an adoring entourage. A small army of attendants now swarms around Sting and his party. They're escorted to a large table. Someone whips out a crisp white tablecloth, spreads it on the table. And what's this? Looks like a couple of ice buckets. Looks also like bottles of champagne in the ice buckets. Sheehan's eyes light up.

'We're not dead yet, Welsh,' he says. 'Give your old mate a wave.'

Sting's still talking to me in those days, so I do as I'm told. I give Sting a wave.

To my surprise, Sting waves back. More than this, he gets up from his table, walks over to where I'm sitting with Sheehan. He's wearing a jacket and pants made of leather that hangs on him like silk.

'How are you?' he asks me.

'He's thirsty,' Sheehan says, before I have a chance to answer.

Sting looks confused.

'They've closed the bar,' Sheehan explains, 'and we can't get a drink,'

There's an uncomfortable lull in the conversation that Tom now fills.

'See you've got some champagne, though,' he says to Sting, who's still a bit flustered.

'Yes,' he says. 'Yes, we do.'

Sheehan just stares at him. Sting finally gets Tom's drift.

'I'd … I'd send some over,' he says. 'But you don't appear to have any glasses.'

He walks off, back to his table.

'GLASSES?' Sheehan fairly shrieks at Sting's retreating back. 'Bugger the fucking glasses. Just send over a fucking BOTTLE. We'll drink out of that. Fucking glasses, my fucking arse.'

Which is about when we have to go back into the stadium to see the Stones.

What are they like?

Absolutely fucking blinding. Exactly as billed on the ticket. The greatest rock'n'roll group in the world.

CAPTAIN SENSIBLE

Croydon, September 1982

Me and the Captain's dad are sitting in the parlour watching The Monkees on TV.

'Good group. Used to like them,' says the Captain's dad. 'Nice-looking boys.'

A bit like the Captain and The Damned, I suggest.

'Not bloody likely,' says the Captain's dad, going back to his newspaper.

'Afternoon!' beams the Captain, bouncing into the room. He's spent the last hour or so being interviewed by a woman from a glossy teen magazine – the Captain in the hit parade at the moment with 'Happy Talk' – and he's just been throwing increasingly silly shapes in the garden for her photographer. He's in desperate need of a drink.

'We're going out, Dad,' he announces.

'Oh,' says the Captain's dad. 'Will you be coming back?'

'Oh, yeah,' says the Captain. 'I don't know what state I'll be in. But I'll definitely be coming back.'

'Fair enough,' says the Captain's dad, sounding like a man resigned to seeing his son turn up at all hours, often dressed as a rabbit, sometimes with the rest of The Damned in tow. Rat Scabies, wild-eyed, screaming for drugs and drink. Dave Vanian looking for the nearest coffin. That sort of thing.

'MUUUU-UU-UUUM!!!' The Captain's at the bottom of the stairs, shouting up them. 'They've gone. You can come out now.'

The Captain slams the front door behind us, strolls down the garden path.

'Me mum's dead weird,' he explains. 'Whenever a photographer comes around the house, she's frightened she's going to get her picture taken. She hides in the bedroom, locks the door and won't come out. Sometimes she's in there for hours.'

We're walking down the street now.

'Woman at the end of the road 'ere moved out after her husband died,' he tells me. 'He had a heart attack. Me and Johnny Moped were rehearsing in me dad's garden shed and he died. Everybody said it was because we were making such a noise. But we weren't that bad,' he says. 'I mean, Chiswick signed us.'

Down the pub, the Captain's interviewed by Giovanni Dadomo, a journalist from weekly music paper *Sounds* and a mutual friend. After their chat, the three of us start talking about this and that, shared adventures, that sort of thing. There are vivid memories of The Damned at the Roxy, The Damned on Stiff, when they were managed by Jake Riviera and produced by Nick Lowe. 'He just drank gallons of cider and told us to play everything as loud as possible.' There are memories, too, of The Damned on tour with Marc Bolan, The Damned terrorising New York, The Damned causing mayhem at the Mont-de-Marsan punk festival, where the Captain let off nuclear-strength stink bombs on stage when The Clash were playing, nearly poisoning an irate Joe Strummer. What larks!

The conversation, however, puts the Captain in an unusually nostalgic mood.

'Meeting you and Gio,' he says, 'it brings it all back. I've had some very dubious experiences with you both. Thinking about them makes me really nostalgic for all that. For '76 and '77. The Roxy was a dive. No doubt about it. Some people wouldn't understand what was so great about going down there. There were always fights and people being sick everywhere. I'd get pissed up and end in a scrap with Sid Vicious. The audience would beat the shit out of the bands.'

Gilded days, obviously.

'It's hard to explain what was so great about it. But back then it was the only place to go. It didn't matter that it was horrible or that you'd probably end up back at Lemmy's. He'd take you around his place. Give you loads of speed. Then you'd go stiff and collapse and when he woke you up in the morning, you'd be face down in a pile of puke. None of that mattered, because they were great days. Great times.

'What we were doing was exciting, you know. What we were doing then was fairly dangerous to your health. There were always a lot of dubious soul boys or disco kids or rockabillies waiting outside The Roxy to beat you up. Remember the rockabilly fights? If a rockabilly gang saw me walking down the road in them days, they'd shout, "*Oiiiii*! 'Ere's JOHNNY ROTTEN!" Then they'd chase me up the road and if they caught me, they'd beat me up.

'Form a punk band now and you're not really going to damage your health. But back then, it was really dangerous. The Damned were the first punk group to venture outside London,' he says, Marco Polo back from the East with tales of the Silk Road and far Cathay.

'We went to Newcastle, everywhere,' he goes on, now a breast-plated conquistador warlord with eyes on the New World. 'You came to Middlesbrough with The Damned once,' he says to me. 'We set fire to your hair. Remember that? Great days.'

The Captain's halcyon drift is taking him fairly swiftly into misty-eyed realms where unicorns possibly roam.

'There was times when you'd come out of a gig and the tyres on the van would be slashed and the windows would be smashed. People would be up the end of the road with bricks, waiting to do us. I remember one night in Lincoln distinctly. These people smashed up all the gear and we couldn't drive away because the van was wrecked. We pulled out the mic stands, and we had to fight these geezers. Pitched battle, it was. And we came out best, because Vanian destroyed them. Vanian done 'em. He went mad. Mental. Tried to bite someone. Chased the rest up the road. They just fuckin' scarpered.

'Sometimes we'd hide in the dressing rooms, under the tables, with all the lights switched off. And we could hear these people going, "Where are they? They're in one of these rooms. We'll have 'em. Smash that door in. That's the dressing room. Kill those bastards."

'It's just not like that anymore,' he sighs, a paradise lost. 'It's all a bit mild these days. I mean, most groups these days, you could take your mum to see 'em. If anyone had brought their mum to see The Damned, they'd have arrested the cunt. Locked him up or something.'

He finishes another pint.

'Do you know The Anti-Nowhere League?' he asks, veering suddenly across several lanes of oncoming conversational traffic. Giovanni and I know them slightly, not well. Anyway, why?

'The first time I ever met them, I was down The Bridgehouse in Canning Town,' Sensible says, the mists of time parting before him. 'Minding me own business in the toilet, havin' a piss. These blokes tapped me on the shoulder. I thought, "'Ere we go, Sensible. You're going to get well duffed up 'ere." And they said, "'Ere, Sensible, we're in a band. We want to support The Damned on your next tour." It was them, The Anti-Nowhere League. Just to get out of there, I had to agree.

'I phoned Rat and told him I'd found this great support band. Anyway, they turned up to the first gig and they walked into our dressing room and this bloke who was with them whacked an axe down on the table. We were just sitting around, and he whacked down this bleedin' big fuckin' axe and it stuck in the table. I thought, "Oh, fuck. If this mad cunt murders us all, Rat will fuckin' kill me." Then he pulled out this huge plastic bag full of sulphate, this bloke. Tipped it all over the table. Chucked a straw down and said, "Dip in, lads. It's going to be a great tour."

'And you know what?' the Captain says. 'It fuckin' was.'

A happy outcome, Giovanni and I agree.

'You're missing my point. What I'm saying is, there's going to be nothing like the old days,' the Captain says, talking about things that happened a mere five years ago like it was the Neolithic age, barely remembered by anyone who wasn't there at the time. 'But for a bit, on that tour, it was like it used to be. We were all mates. Most of the time, anyway. We had a right laugh. There was all that speed, too.'

Let's not forget the bloke with the big axe.

'Yeah, well,' Sensible says with what can only be described as a philosophical shrug. 'There's always going to be at least one of them. What can you do? You just keep out of their fuckin' way and hope for the best.'

JOHN CALE

London, February 1983 | Paris, April 1993

I'm sitting in an office in the London HQ of Island Records, waiting for John Cale, thinking about the last time we met, which was in the summer of 1977. I want to interview him for *Melody Maker*. He suggests we meet for a drink. Which we do, in Cale's local pub, where we spend the best part of a day, John knocking back a pint about every six minutes, me in hot and increasingly befuddled pursuit. Cale is in imperiously expansive mood, and I'm duly regaled with a succession of hilarious anecdotes, including a lot of side-splitting stories about Nico, Jonathan Richman, Iggy Pop, Patti Smith, a rib-caving set piece about the recording of The Velvet Underground's 'Sister Ray', involving Lou Reed's accidental ingestion of some kind of elephant tranquilliser.

'I don't know where he got it,' Cale says. 'It would have killed anybody else. It didn't even slow Lou down.'

There's also a hugely funny account of a recent incident at the Croydon Greyhound, when he beheads a chicken on stage with a meat cleaver.

'I don't know why everyone made such a fuss about it,' Cale says. 'The fucking chicken was dead. I wrung its neck in the dressing room before we went on.'

Cale, finishing this particular story, gets to his feet, heads for the bar to order another round of drinks. At the bar, I notice him in earnest conversation with someone I assume is a member of his road crew.

'He's not a roadie,' Cale says, returning with two pints for each of us. 'He works up the road. At the hospital. In the morgue.'

In the morgue?

'Yes,' Cale smiles. 'He's been letting me in to watch the autopsies.'

Cale must then have caught the twitch of slippery horror in my eyes and laughs. It's a hearty chuckle that soon blossoms into a throaty roar. I can still hear it rolling down the years when Cale makes his belated appearance. We're here to talk about his most recent album, *Music For a New Society*, a requiem for a burning world. It's his most extraordinary solo record to date, the result of a five-day session in New York during which he records 30 songs, most of them improvised and featuring principally only piano, guitar and that amazing Baptist tenor.

'What I was most interested in,' he says of the new album, 'was the terror of the moment. I just keep trying to be as good at this as Sam Peckinpah. Peckinpah is an expert at it, exploring the moral dilemma of people who have to choose between good and evil, because there is no other choice. Peckinpah is totally relentless about this. *The Wild Bunch* is totally unrelenting. There's no law, no religion. There's only life and death and the way people live and the way they die.'

A long rant about post-nuclear genetics that follows makes me think for some reason of Thomas Pynchon, whose name I mention.

'Pynchon,' Cale laughs, like he knows Pynchon. Amazingly, it turns out he does. 'Pynchon wanted me to write an opera based on *Gravity's Rainbow*,' he goes on, apparently unaware of my complete astonishment. Pynchon is the literary world's most notorious recluse – a genius never seen, never interviewed. Speculative tomes have been written, questioning his very existence. And here's Cale dreamily mentioning that they've met, discussed collaborative ventures. I'm absolutely fucking gobsmacked.

'He's weird, Pynchon,' Cale goes on. 'He was an aerospace engineer at Boeing. All we did was talk about aerospace engineering. We had a great time.'

Was there nothing else on the conversational agenda besides aerospace engineering?

'Oh, sure,' Cale says. 'We talked about developing new weapons systems. Things like that.'

We talk a lot about The Velvet Underground, Cale a little reluctant to engage with the legend.

'I don't feel any nostalgia for The Velvet Underground,' he says. 'I can't even remember most of what went on. It's just a blur. God, they were primitive times. Driving around in a van, being stopped by the police and being accused of kidnapping children because the girls we had with us were young and didn't have notes from their parents. We were right in the middle of Ohio, taking enormous amounts of speed, driving back from Cleveland to New York, overnight. Madness. Complete madness.'

I'm shocked when we talk about *The Velvet Underground & Nico* and *White Light/White Heat*, the two albums the VU made before Lou Reed forced him out of the band. Cale is almost entirely dismissive of them.

'They sound awful to me, in some respects,' he says. 'They're really badly recorded. The first album was done in one day, at Cameo Parkway studios. I remember they were tearing the walls down, ripping up the floorboards. The place was a shambles. They charged us $1,500 and threw in an engineer. We thought it was very reasonable of them.

'*White Light/White Heat* was all energy, the result of our experiences as a road band. We'd worked very hard on the arrangements for the first album. We used to meet once a week for about a year, just working on arrangements. When we went in to do *White Light/White Heat*, no one had any patience anymore to work on the arrangements, and it shows. We just went into the studio, turned up the amps as high as we could and blasted away. Everyone's nerves were frazzled by then. We were rabid.'

Time passes. In 1993, The Velvet Underground announce they're getting back together for a tour. I fly to Paris to talk to Cale. He meets me in the vast shining lobby of the Royal Monceau hotel. It's a lovely April afternoon outside on the sun-dappled Avenue Hoche, rich with gilt and mirrors in here. I've only been in the place five minutes, but I can feel people looking at me like I don't belong in this glittering palace. I don't want to pick anything up in case someone thinks I'm going to steal it. This makes me want to throw a chair through a window, just for the hell of it.

The hotel's burnished splendour suits Cale, however. He strides through its gleaming atmosphere, wholly at ease. He looks affluent, well-groomed, like an international arms dealer or a well-paid mercenary, a suave veteran of unspeakable violence in unnamed theatres of war, a hint about him of efficient menace. For someone who spent most of the 1970s and early 1980s on a drug and alcohol binge that could have left him either dead or mad, he also looks astonishingly healthy. Today he's sober, fit and tanned from a recent tour of Australia, where he's been promoting his live double album, *Fragments of a Rainy Season*, which quotes from an awesome body of work spanning nearly 20 years and almost as many albums.

But we are here to talk about The Velvet Underground, a band whose signature is writ large on the music of our times. Thirty years after they first unleashed their sonic revolution on an unsuspecting world as part of Andy Warhol's Exploding Plastic Inevitable, they have reformed and are about to tour, Cale working with Lou Reed, Moe Tucker and Sterling Morrison for the first time since he was effectively sacked from the group in 1968, after falling out bitterly with Lou. So, are they just getting back together for the money?

'No,' he insists, 'not at all. As far as I'm concerned, this is an opportunity to take care of some unfinished business.'

What kind of business?

'The business,' he says, 'we started when we first put the VU together. We never saw it through. We let too much get in the way. We didn't handle things very well. It was always very volatile between us, and we allowed too many frustrations to take root. There were a lot of resentments between us, too many battles, too much friction. There was so much more we could have done. I was disappointed by our inability to face up to the responsibilities that attach themselves to people who dare to be different. I think to that extent, we let ourselves down.'

Tensions between Reed and Cale become unbearable when Lou sacks early mentor Andy Warhol as the band's manager and brings in Steve Sesnick, a young Bostonian who's been hanging around them for months to replace him.

'Basically,' Cale says, 'Sesnick became an apologist for Lou. He was just a yes-man, and he came between us. It was maddening, just maddening. Before, it had always been easy to talk to Lou. Now you had to go through Sesnick, who seemed pretty practised in the art of miscommunication. We should have been able to sort out our own problems. He should never have been brought in. Things had been bad between us for a while, but when Sesnick arrived they got worse.

There was a lot of intrigue, a lot of duplicity, a lot of talking behind people's backs, a lot of plotting.'

This all climaxes with Lou calling Sterling Morrison and Moe Tucker to a meeting at the Riviera Café in the West Village.

'Lou gave Sterling and Moe an ultimatum,' Cale recalls stiffly. 'He told them that either I was out of the band or there was no band. If I didn't quit, he was going to disband the VU. We were supposed to be going to Cleveland for a gig and Sterling showed up at my apartment and effectively told me that I was no longer in the band.'

Did he think he'd ever forgive Lou for the way he was treated?

'It was the way Lou did things,' Cale shrugs, not convincingly indifferent. 'He's always got other people to do his dirty work for him. As for resentment, I don't know. Things had been pushed pretty far between us and I can't say I was entirely blameless in that situation.'

Back to the forthcoming reunion. Did he think after the tour, they'd be going into the studio to record new material?

'No,' he says, firmly. 'That's one thing I really want to avoid. Recording *Drella* [1990's *Songs for Drella*, Cale and Reed's requiem for Andy Warhol] with Lou was very difficult. There was a lot of banging of heads. It was exhilarating, and working with Lou is never dull, But I wouldn't want to go through it again. I'm much more interested in the spontaneity of playing live. I've also got three new pieces I've almost finished that I've already talked to Lou about, and he wants to do them. I think he's genuinely interested in what the four of us can do together. I don't think he wants to do anything that will sound like just another Lou Reed solo album.'

That sounds uncommonly democratic of him.

'Lou, democratic?' Cale laughs, though not totally uncontrollably. 'Let's not go too far.'

So you don't think he'll end up hijacking the entire project?

'Let's put it this way,' Cale says. 'If he thinks I'm going to turn up to play "Walk on the Wild Side", he's going to be very fucking disappointed.'

NICK LOWE

London, June 1984

We meet in a pub in Brentford, but Nick's not drinking, which is a bit of a shock.

'I knocked it on the head just before Christmas,' he says. 'It hadn't got to the point where I couldn't answer the phone or pay the milk bill, or anything like that. But it was getting in the way. I just wasn't getting anything done. I don't really feel like I've thrown away my crutches, praise God I'm cured and all that. I could happily start drinking again at the drop of a hat. But I needed to get out of that good old Basher routine. I just wasn't doing anything. I realised I was blowing it, really.

'We were meeting at the studio, and it was like a gentleman's drinking club down there. Terrific fun, of course. But the records just sounded like a lot of people getting pissed. Great for us, but not the kind of thing to inflict on anybody else.'

We've had a few adventures in between, including a trip to Texas, where we end up becoming colonels in the Confederate Air Force. But I haven't interviewed Nick for what used to be *Melody Maker* since the opening night of his 1982 tour with The Blasters. Nick had been a little maudlin at times that night, prone to the blues in his cups. His fractured relationship with Dave Edmunds seemed to weigh heavily. He brightened greatly when we talked about Elvis Costello, whose best work remains the records Nick produced for him.

'When I was in Brinsley Schwarz, he used to come and see us all the time,' Nick said. 'He was always there, looking very intense. Even when he was with other people, he always seemed to be standing apart from them. The first time I spoke to him was in a pub in

Liverpool. He was at the bar. I thought, "There he is again. I'd better buy him a drink."

'I was famous then, you see. I was in the Brinsleys, man. We were pub rock legends, earning £175 a night. We were big time. I went over and introduced myself. He just glared at me. Damned unsettling. You know the way he is. After that, whenever I saw him, we'd have a drink. I just thought he was a very intense fan. Then he moved to London, and we lost touch. Then we started Stiff, and I saw him at the local Tube station.

'He'd just been around to the office to buy a copy of "So It Goes". We started chatting and he said he'd been trying to get a record deal. He told me the story he trots out all the time now. At the time, he thought he was like someone out of those old-fashioned films where a guy walks into a music publisher's office and says, "Boy, have I got a song for you!" And he plays it on the piano and the publisher leaps up and says, "It so happens Miss Fay Fontaine is next door!" And they wheel in old Fay, and she sings it gorgeously. It's a fucking great big hit and our boy's away. Elvis obviously thought this was the way to do it.

'He'd been going around all the record companies. They'd ask him for a tape. He'd tell them he was going to sing the songs. Then he'd pull out an acoustic guitar. Of course, they were appalled. There's something very intimidating about sitting with Elvis when he's singing you something. He sings at full blast. He's got a very loud voice, and he emotes like mad.

'He'd be there emoting away like there's no tomorrow and the guy's phone would ring. It would be his wife or something. Elvis would be in the middle of some song and the guy would be going, "Eight? Yes. That'll be fine, darling. Lamb casserole? Wonderful!" Poor old Elvis would be sitting there wondering what to do. Should he carry on singing? Should he stop? Should he carry on singing, but try to be a bit quieter?

'It turned out he'd left a tape at Stiff. When I got there, Jake had already played it. He was raving about "Mystery Dance". He thought Edmunds could cover it. Then we listened to the tape again. Jake said, "No. Fuck it. This guy can make a record of his own. He's got tons of stuff here." I wasn't convinced, I must admit. The song that finally changed my mind was "Alison". I was stunned when I heard that. I'm

211

absolutely mad for a weep and when I'm in the humour, I'm hopeless. When I heard EC doing "Alison" for the first time, I wept like a baby.'

Back in the pub in Brentford, I'm explaining to Nick that I'm here to interview him for a regular *Melody Maker* feature called Shrink Rap – 'the column that straps today's pop wallahs to a couch and puts them under scrutiny by the *MM* quack'. Basically, it's a word association thing, I tell Nick.

'Sort of call-and-response?' he muses.

Bullseye!

'Let's give it a go then.'

'Bob Dylan,' I say, because Nick's got a gig coming up supporting Bob.

'I've never actually been a big fan of old Bob,' he says ruefully, lighting a fag. 'I've tried on numerous occasions. But to be honest, I never had the faintest idea what he was on about. As far as I'm concerned, he's just a job on my date sheet at the moment.'

'1977' is what I have written in my notebook as the next topic of conversation.

'Oh, the rise of punk rock!' Nick says, getting into this. 'I was involved in all that by dint of association. It was great fun, 1977. I must admit, however, I didn't see it as any kind of watershed moment. I remember doing the Damned album. I only did that because I was told to, really. I thought they were absolute rubbish. I wasn't a big crusader for that kind of music at all. I thought it was nonsense, like most people of my age. What I did like about punk was the fact it got up so many people's noses. People got really uptight and annoyed about it. I lost quite a lot of friends because I was producing The Damned and hanging around with all these ruffians.'

'Bang it down and tart it up.'

'Ah, the original production philosophy. I still think like that, although that attitude made more sense then than it does now. Most of the records we did then, like the first Damned album and "New Rose", they were just joyful rackets. I still find them more appealing than most of the records that get played at the moment.

'They don't have guitars and drums in the studio these days. It's all Fairlights, plugs and wires. I don't have a clue what's going on there. It just so happens that the kind of records I do sound better if they're a bit rough around the edges. But there is a fine line between that roughness and being too bloody untogether to do it properly. I've certainly done that in the past. Been too bloody lazy to tell the guitarist to play in tune. It's been a bit of a convenient excuse, that phrase.'

At the time, Nick is still married to Carlene Carter. I ask him about Johnny Cash and June Carter.

'The in-laws,' Nick laughs. 'Mr and Mrs Man in Black. I haven't heard from them in a while. He was very ill recently. Had a large portion of his anatomy removed, apparently. He's been in a bad way. I remember the first time he came over to stay with me and Carlene. The Man in Black in Shepherd's Bush. He was completely unfazed by it all. It was me that was getting all weird about it. The other day, we had June Carter over. She had this turban thing on, with this massive kind of brooch, like the Sultan's Eye of the Devil on the forehead, or front, of the thing. The Eye of Zoltan, or something. Anyway, she's wearing this, and these huge diamond earrings and an expensive silk blouse and when I get home, I find her with her sleeves rolled up, scrubbing the damned walls.'

Next: our old friend, Elvis Costello.

'I hardly see him these days,' Nick says. 'He's always working. Never stops, that bloke. Last time I saw him was when he produced a track on my new album. I wrote this song for Paul Carrack originally. "L.A.F.S. Means Love at First Sight". A sort of soul ballad. I can write songs for the kind of voice Paul has, but I can't sing them myself. It sounded great when Paul did it. Like Memphis-era Al Green. Elvis heard it and thought I should do it. I wasn't keen. It's quite a wet item. Not me at all.

'Elvis said, "Let me produce it. I'll put the kitchen sink on it and let's see what happens." I thought he'd forget all about it. But he didn't. So, I gave in. We did it, and it was a very funny reversal, him producing me. He runs a tight ship, old Elvis. You have to turn up, bang on time. No messing about, and sing it until it's right, all that stuff. No, "That'll do ..." That'll do doesn't occur with Elvis. It isn't in his vocabulary. He made me sing it until my face was practically purple. Very hard work indeed.'

Not long before we meet, the much-loved British comedian Tommy Cooper had died on stage during a performance at Her Majesty's Theatre. I bring the subject up.

'Well,' Nick says, chuckling at the memory of Cooper, one of the funniest men ever to walk God's earth. 'What a fucking terrific way to go. I mean, the guy's got to die at some point, therefore you can only rejoice for him. He was a great comedian and what a cracking way for him to go. Same with Eric Morecambe. He almost died on the planks as well. You couldn't ask for anything better. What a terrific end to your act. "And then I balance this huge ball on my nose, do some conjuring tricks and a spot of mind reading and then I die." I'm sure that's how they would have wanted it.

'How do I see myself going? I hope it would be doing something dangerous. Something vaguely foolhardy, at least. It would be awful just to electrocute yourself with a hair dryer or something. That would be damned embarrassing.'

Dr Feelgood

Amsterdam, September 1984

I'm off to Amsterdam to meet up with Dr Feelgood, photographer Tom Sheehan as usual in tow. Things start to go spectacularly awry from the off.

'You do know these tickets are for tomorrow?' we're asked as I hand them over to check in for the flight. I've clearly fucked up the dates. I can feel Sheehan simmering behind me, the words 'fucking', 'Welsh' and 'idiot' in uncomfortably close proximity in what he then has to say to me. I'm not sure what a gasket is, but he seems fearfully close to blowing one. I give him a weak smile. If looks could kill, the one that Tom now gives me pretty much puts me on a slab in a morgue with a stake through my heart.

Turns out, however, that there are seats available on the next flight if we want to fly a day early to Amsterdam. We decide to go. This means, of course, that no one's at the airport to meet us when we get there. I now make Tom even more furious by mentioning that I have no idea where the band are staying, but think it might be a place called Boddy's, a legendary rock'n'roll hotel, much favoured by the kind of groups whose general rowdiness is frowned upon by more conventional establishments. Sheehan and I had stayed there a couple of years ago, with Carlene Carter and her band.

We ask a woman at a tourist information desk if she can help, briefly explaining our predicament.

'You have lost your friends! This is awful,' she smiles, beaming at us like we're a couple of bedraggled orphans, tossed into her lap by circumstances too tragic to contemplate.

215

'Let us see what we can do,' she says. 'Give me the name of their hotel and I will look it up in my directory.' She brandishes a hotel directory, inches thick. She spends some time flicking through it, smiling until she starts frowning. 'There is nothing by this name. Are you sure it is in Amsterdam, this hotel?'

More or less.

'Then where is it?'

All I can tell her is that I seem to remember it being opposite a canal, which I know is hopelessly vague, but all I can come up with in the circumstances. It's too much for Sheehan.

'C'mere,' he says, grabbing the hotel directory, taking matters in hand. 'Right,' he says. 'We'll get a taxi to this place 'ere and I reckon I can get us to Boddy's from there.'

We're soon in a taxi that drops off us off somewhere in the centre of Amsterdam.

'This way, Jonesy,' Sheehan barks, slinging his camera bag over his shoulder and striding purposefully down the road into a maze of side streets. 'Down 'ere,' he decides, crossing back over a canal, vanishing up another narrow avenue. 'I remember this bar,' the photographer mutters, as if in conversation with himself. 'It must be down 'ere. Or is it over there?'

After nearly 20 minutes of this punishing route-march, Sheehan stops suddenly at a street corner, points across a canal, stands with his hands on his hips, a proud steadfast figure, mightily pleased with himself.

'THAR SHE BLOWS!' he announces, a swaggering old seadog.

And thar she certainly did blow. Boddy's Hotel! Otherwise known as the Hotel Wiechmann.

'Are we talking walking A–Z of Europe or what?' Sheehan demands rhetorically, smug now in his moment of navigational triumph, a regular Vasco da Gama, the great explorer now striding over the bridge to the hotel, where we find Feelgoods manager Chris Fenwick having breakfast.

'Jones and Sheehan,' he says, popping a boiled egg in his mouth. 'A day early and probably thirsty. Lee's already in the bar. I suppose we'd better join him.'

Lee Brilleaux is indeed in the bar. He looks like he's been here a while, actually.

'Monstrous 'angover this morning,' he says, voice as raw as stubble, before going on to tell us that the band's dates in Holland, which will climax tomorrow at a concert in front of 30,000 people at the Vondelpark, come at the end of a six-week European tour that included a residency at a club called Heartbreak Hotel in Sète, on the Golfe du Lion.

'The guvnor there said, "Here's the bar. Help yourselves," Fenwick recalls wistfully. 'I said, "I hope you're serious, because we are."'

'Very generous man,' Lee says approvingly.

'He was, too,' Fenwick says. 'I could have cried when we left.'

It turns out the only major aggravation of an otherwise agreeable tour was the long drive back through France to Holland.

'The roads were packed. Right the way through France,' Brilleaux fairly seethes at the memory. 'With caravans. I fuckin' 'ate caravans. I mean, if you can't afford to go on holiday and stay in a decent hotel – stay at fuckin' 'ome. It's just an absolute fuckin' nuisance, all these bloody people draggin' these fuckin' bungalows-on-wheels halfway around Europe. They're just pests, these people. Pests.'

Lee smacks his glass on the bar, winces as if he's just wrenched his back. He tells us he must have pulled a muscle loading the band's gear the previous night. This makes Fenwick laugh out loud, Chris telling us then that Lee had been involved in something of a scrap at last night's show.

'As it happens, there was a scuffle that needed a bit of quelling,' Lee says, draining his glass. 'Right,' he says then of his hangover. 'I think I've got this one under control. Anyone fancy a drink?'

There's a show tonight, in somewhere called Gendt; a club in a small market town that when we get there after a long drive appears to be closed, shutters down everywhere. We find a bar, a few locals scattered around in flat caps, braces, at least one of them smoking a pipe, all of them lounging around like they're waiting to be sketched by Gustave Courbet. Noble labourers at rest after a hard day in the fields, something like that. Tom and Chris Fenwick head straight for the bar. Lee's attention, meanwhile, has been drawn to what looks like an ordinary old pool or snooker table. Lee walks twice around it, stands there looking at it like it might surprise us by bursting into song.

'It's got no fuckin' pockets,' Lee says, sliding some kind of slate, puck or bit of shingle across the threadbare baize. 'If I had an 'ammer, I'd be tempted to rectify that.'

There's a noisy crowd waiting for us at the club that we have to barge through to get to the dressing rooms, where the rest of the band are already getting changed. Lee's stage duds are hanging from a hook on a wall in the far corner of the room, where there's also a table with a bottle of gin, a plastic bucket full of melting ice, a small bottle of tonic and a pint glass. Lee gets changed quickly, picks up the bottle of gin.

'Time for a quick livener before we go on,' he says. He then tips some ice into the pint glass and follows it with as much gin as the glass will hold and still have room for a somewhat superfluous splash of tonic. Lee braces himself, shoulders back, legs slightly apart, like he's leaning into a headwind on the deck of a North Sea clipper. He takes a deep breath and downs the gin in a couple of gulps, a rosy glow lighting him up even as he clenches his teeth and starts making what sounds to me like a low, growling noise.

'Gentlemen, we have lift-off,' he announces. 'Right, chaps,' he says, leading the band out of the dressing room. 'Wheels up. Let's 'ave at 'em.'

There's a great roar from the crowd as the Feelgoods plug in and blast off. Lee is by now the only member left of the original Canvey crew that blew up the London pub rock scene in 1973. Original guitarist Wilko Johnson quits in 1977 after falling out badly with Lee. Wilko's replacement, Gypie Mayo, leaves in 1981. Bassist John B. Sparks and drummer John Martin, known to everyone as The Big Figure, call it quits in 1982, 11 years of constant touring and hard living by then behind them. Lee, however, will keep at it until he dies of cancer in 1994 at the age of 41.

Anyway, tonight's the first time I see Lee with a completely new line-up behind him. There's a young guitarist, Gordon Russell, fresh from Geno Washington's band. The rhythm section is two of Lee's old Canvey schoolmates: Kevin Morris, who's played drums on the European Chitlin' Circuit with soul greats Sam & Dave, Edwin Starr and Rufus Thomas, and bassist Phil Mitchell, who's done time with Southend music legend Mickey Jupp. Nearly 30 years after Lee's death, Morris and Mitchell are still touring under the Feelgoods' banner, the band still managed by Chris Fenwick.

Tonight, in Gendt, there's enough in what they play to bring a lot of memories galloping back. Lee's presence alone is enough to fill the room with brimming history, flashbacks from dozens of Feelgoods gigs across the years superimposed on what's happening in front of me now. One night stands out. It's Sunday, 17 November 1974, at that bastion of hippie fundamentalism, the Camden Roundhouse. The Feelgoods have been booked as support to Nektar, the Anglo-German space warriors, who the rump of the hairy crowd are here to see. This is a time when the woeful indulgences of prog rock prevail. All that wank-spew virtuosity; all those solos as long as transatlantic flights, laser shows, dry ice and concept albums. Everything by now on that front given over to scale and spectacle, big gongs, capes and wizard's hats. Overall, a heartbreaking time. The Feelgoods by comparison are carnage in demob suits, a hard look that matches the raw ferocity of their music. For many in tonight's Roundhouse crowd, their music is alien, the sheer feral caw of it utterly at odds with prog's gustier inclinations. People mostly gawp at them, bewildered, unsettled by what they're listening to.

Wilko Johnson will have caught the eye of many. A gangly man in a grubby black suit that makes him look like an undertaker's assistant. His face is deathly pale beneath an institutional haircut, with the unsettling stare of Anthony Perkins in *Psycho*; someone who lives with stuffed birds, a mother in an upstairs window, briefly glimpsed against dour light. He's quickly on typical walkabout, commando-jawed, wide-eyed, like something going berserk on *Robot Wars*. What Wilko's playing and the way he's playing it is equally somewhat off-kilter. Frenetic choppy chords dispatched with savage ferocity and no solos to speak of. Their songs are too brutally short to accommodate the flashy dexterities that otherwise are the order of the day. The rhythm section, meanwhile, two burly men who look like club bouncers, drive everything forward with a relentless momentum, are only brought to heel by harsh command.

The band's singer is as lean as a whippet or car aerial, crop-haired, something predatory about him that seems genuinely threatening. He seems consumed by an unspecified anger, some seething resentment. The music the band's playing is probably the only outlet for his frustrated energies that won't involve a jail sentence. He seems coiled, as venomous as something with scales, about to strike. This is Lee, of course; until Johnny Rotten lurches into view, malice in bondage trousers, English rock's most intimidating frontman.

And here's when it all kicks off. About halfway through their set, someone in a tatty jumper and baggy jeans clambers on stage, shouts incomprehensibly into a spare microphone and blows a mouth organ, tunelessly. If something like this had happened at, let's say, Woodstock, Country Joe or John Sebastian would probably have written a song about the intrepid intruder, or given him a communal brotherly hug. Lee's reaction is altogether less benign. He first glares malevolently at the ragged-arsed stage invader and then head-butts him off stage. Lee then stands there, fists clenched, ready to take on all-comers if they fancy their chances, which nobody does. The incident isn't widely remarked upon at the time, but it's in some way like Lee's fired the first shots in the punk wars to come, sent out a message that it's time on a number of fronts for major changes. It also does much to cast the Feelgoods as John the Baptists to The Sex Pistols' savage messiahs, an advance guard for the havoc that follows, the full-on fury of punk.

We can still hear the crowd in Gendt calling for another encore when the band's van tears off into the night, Lee behind the wheel, surely not a good idea. We're now heading for Amsterdam at such speed it seems we might at any moment find ourselves airborne, even as we hurtle down largely unlit country roads, a bend or two coming up sharply enough to cause some panic in the van as Lee battles with the brakes and steering wheel to keep us out of the trees.

'Lee!' Fenwick, as white-faced as the rest of us, now shouts. 'Take it easy, mate. We've got plenty of time to get back before last orders.'

'Last fuckin' orders?' Lee shouts back at him, as the van bucks and rattles and continues to zoom down darkened lanes. 'I'm going to get us back in time for more than a fuckin' nightcap.'

He does, too, Lee finally relaxing when we end up in a bar that's happy to stay open as long as we're still standing, which we just about are when we leave as dawn is breaking, morning's pale light accompanying us on an unsteady stroll back to Boddy's.

The next afternoon, we're walking through the Vondelpark, where the Feelgoods will later be appearing. It's a bit of a grim sight, a vision of utter decay and much rot. Decrepit hippies are stretched out everywhere on grubby patches of grass, dirty piles of them.

'What an ugly bleedin' bunch,' Lee says, as we step gingerly over the bodies of assorted comatose flower children and pick our way through a maze of market stalls selling hippie trinkets and a lot of other rubbish. 'If you ask me, what this place needs is an artillery barrage to liven it up and see off this fuckin' shower. Start off with a few mortars lobbed in from close range, follow it up with a couple of Spitfires strafing the gaff just to create a sense of panic, then send in a hand-picked team of Paras to mop up. Should do the trick.'

We've been told to expect an early getaway after the Feelgoods play because they have a gig tomorrow at the Basildon Blues Festival, back in Essex, and we're going to have to make a dash to Calais for the ferry. They've barely finished their set when we're bundled into their van, Lee again at the wheel. Lee steers the van through the narrow lanes between the market stalls, the way ahead packed with dazed locals, stumbling, meandering, daydream strolling, crowding up against the van, pawing at the windows.

An egg shatters against the side of the van, annoying Lee. We can see some spaced-out hippies laughing, which annoys Lee even more, if such a thing at this point is even possible.

'If we weren't in such a hurry,' he says, 'I'd stop and have a row with that lot.'

Then we're rolling out of the park, hurtling through Amsterdam, onto the motorway. Lee starts to relax.

'Do me the honours, someone,' he says over his shoulder. I'm sitting next to Lee in the front of the van, the band, Chris Fenwick and Tom in the back.

'My pleasure,' Fenwick says. 'Pass me those glasses,' Chris says to Tom. I wonder what's going on, turn around to have a look. On the back wall of the van, there's a mounted optic, a drink dispenser, the kind they have behind the bar in pubs. Chris is even now filling a glass with brandy from it. The drink's passed forward to Lee. I ask him if he wants me to hold it for him while he's driving.

'Don't be fucking stupid,' he says. 'I want to drink it, not look at it.'

He then knocks the brandy back, all of it, straight down the hatch, no fucking about.

'That's given me a bit of a thirst, as it happens,' Lee says then. 'Keep 'em coming.'

We roar on through the night across Holland, heading for the border with Belgium.

'Are we going to stop at the Belgian border?' bassist Phil Mitchell wants to know.

'Only if they've built a fuckin' roadblock,' Lee tells him, foot hard down on the accelerator, fists balled tight around the steering wheel, a determined look in his eye. It occurs to me to ask Lee why we've undertaken such a lunatic drive to catch a ferry from Calais when most people would have sailed from the Hook of Holland, which is much nearer.

'Townsend Thoresen have ferries goin' out of Calais. Sealink sail out of the 'Ook.'

So?

'Me and Fenwick have shares in Townsend Thoresen,' Lee says. 'We can get the van, the equipment and all of us over for 'alf price. Very reasonable rates.'

Early the next afternoon, Lee hungover again, we're standing in the grounds of the Basildon Blues Festival. There's a local country and western singer on stage, tuning up for his set.

'If he starts playin' that fuckin' banjo, I'm going to have to have a very large gin,' Lee says through gritted teeth.

It's time for me and Sheehan to go. For the Feelgoods, this is just the start of another working week. They've got a few days off, then they'll be heading off for Scandinavia, or wherever else the work is. After ten years of touring, what keeps Lee going?

'The threat of bankruptcy, mostly,' he laughs. 'This is a job and a way of life. We work hard, we make a decent living. I'm just happy to be in work, as it happens. I mean, there's four million unemployed. I don't want to add to the numbers just yet. As long as someone, somewhere wants us to put on a show, we'll be there.'

'Lee!' Chris Fenwick calls from the stage. 'Soundcheck, mate.'

'Fuckin' soundchecks,' Lee moans. 'They're the worst part of it all. Fuckin' pointless. Still, better go. See you later, chaps.'

ELMORE LEONARD

London, September 1988

In 1983, looking for some holiday reading, I pick up a copy of a book called *Stick*, on a whim. It's written by someone I hadn't previously heard of: Elmore Leonard. I tear through the thing on the first day of the ensuing holiday, drink untouched, barely blinking. Who is this guy? I spend the next two weeks hungry for more. One book and his writing has turned me into an Elmore Leonard addict. When I get back, I buy everything I can find that he's written, which turns out to be plenty. I'm soon mainlining pure Elmore.

He's a habit I've had for nigh on 40 years, Leonard delivering one great book after another, one a year until age begins to slow him down. His last full-length novel, Elmore at 86 as spritely and dazzling as ever, was 2012's *Raylan*. It was based on Graham Yost's terrific TV series *Justified*, itself based on Leonard's short story 'Fire in the Hole' and the character of US Marshal Raylan Givens, played by Timothy Olyphant. Leonard died the following year.

He'd had a successful earlier career as a writer of Western novels, written when he worked in Detroit as an advertising copywriter. He became better known, however, as a crime writer. Nothing wrong with that, of course. But he was so much more than a masterful genre technician, a supremely gifted craftsman. He was a writer who created a space in American letters that was uniquely his, with a style that was entirely his own, a vernacular lowlife poetry, the magic of his dialogue making page after page of his books unforgettable.

I meet him at the stately west London hotel where he's staying at his publisher's expense. He's here to promote his new book, *Freaky*

Deaky. We sit at a table in the corner of the hotel restaurant, otherwise empty. Everything about him is as meticulous as something he's written. He almost glides across the room, moving as gracefully as a cat or James Coburn. We're soon talking about Hollywood, and its treatment of his books, which to say the least has been lacking.

Some good, even great, films had been made of his Westerns. Notably, *3.10 to Yuma* with Glenn Ford, *Hombre* with Paul Newman and *Valdez Is Coming* with Burt Lancaster. But the films based on the thrillers for which he became famous have been poor. Which is a surprise to both of us. His books – including genre-defining titles like *The Switch*, *Gold Coast*, *Split Images*, *City Primeval*, *Stick*, *Cat Chaser*, and more recent best-sellers like *Glitz* and *LaBrava* – are tough, violent, funny, fast-moving without ever seeming rushed, driven more by fabulous characterisation than gun-slick action, although there's still plenty of the latter.

It's almost a decade on, however, from the afternoon I meet him before there are reasonable movie versions of *Get Shorty*, *Rum Punch* (filmed by Quentin Tarantino as *Jackie Brown*) and *Out of Sight*, brilliantly directed by Steven Soderbergh with George Clooney in the role that basically made his movie career. Back in 1988, the most recent Hollywood botch-up of one of his books was Burt Reynolds' film of *Stick*, the book that brought me to Leonard in the first place.

'Burt Reynolds did *Stick*,' he says, unable to keep the exasperation out of his voice. 'It was terrible. It was a very bad movie. Not because it didn't follow the plot. It was just, from beginning to end, the whole thing, a really bad movie. Don't even think about watching it. With Burt Reynolds directing, it just became an action movie. It became a Burt Reynolds picture, which is not such a great thing.

'You see, I think first of all you've got to get a strong director for my stuff. Someone who understands the books. Someone who has the same attitude to them that I have. Someone who understands the humour, who understands that most of the dialogue should be delivered deadpan. A lot of the best lines are throwaway. They're sounds, rhythms more than speeches, declarations. In a film, you don't cut to other actors when one of those lines is being delivered, just to register a reaction. You let the audience react.

'Reynolds had a camera set-up that made the film look like a TV movie. Everybody was reacting wildly. It was absurd. They were reacting to every line. The camera goes in close-up for what should be a deadpan line, and they're acting the ass off it. Muscles twitching, eyes narrowing. Like they're Eastwood or Bronson.'

He stubs out a cigarette like he can see Burt Reynolds' face in the ashtray. When I read *Stick*, I tell him, I thought if it came to a movie that James Woods would have been great in it.

'He would have been good in it,' Leonard says. 'Damn good.'

Was it true that action movie maestro Walter Hill, director of *The Warriors, 48 Hrs., Southern Comfort* and *The Long Riders*, has the rights to another book, *City Primeval*, the one about deranged 'Oklahoma Wildman' Clement Mansell on a killing spree in Detroit, old-school cop Raymond Cruz on his tail, the blurb on the copy I have describing it as 'High Noon in Detroit'?

'I heard from Walter two or three years ago and that was going to be his next film. But nothing's happened,' he says, a hint of a weary shrug at this predictable pass.

'You know,' he adds then, 'the first guy who was going to do that movie was Sam Peckinpah.'

I'm agog, if that's the word I'm looking for, at the idea of the director of *The Wild Bunch* and *Pat Garrett and Billy the Kid* getting it on with Elmore Leonard. If I wasn't all ears before, I look like a fucking donkey now.

'I did about three drafts of the script and met with Peckinpah and his producers. But to be honest, I never knew what the hell Peckinpah was talking about. We'd have story conferences and Peckinpah would turn up and he'd have this girl taking notes. He'd be spouting off and it was just incomprehensible. I kept wondering what these notes the girl was taking would read back like. The guy was just not making sense.

'He came to Detroit to scout locations and then disappeared. Then he and another guy, a writer, a real hack, came back and said they'd decided to set it in El Paso, Texas. They wanted to turn it into a Western.'

He shakes his head, clearly a veteran of such eccentricities.

'Peckinpah,' he says, 'he could have handled the action sequences. No doubt about it. But his sense of humour was pretty heavy-handed, I don't think there was anything very subtle about his pictures. Outside, that is, the slow-motion dying in all of them.'

Leonard didn't fare much better with *LaBrava*, one of his biggest-selling novels, but doomed in Hollywood's incompetent hands. The rights were bought by United Artists, but when Burt Reynolds' farcical adaptation of *Stick* belly-flopped at the box office they passed the option on to independent producer Walter Mirisch, to see what he could do with it.

David Mamet had by this time read the book and greatly admired it. He passed it on to Dustin Hoffman. Now Hoffman loves it, too. He wants to film it. He also has some ideas he'd like Elmore to take on board.

'Hoffman had a lotta ideas,' he says, and if sarcasm could burn carpets we'd be sitting on floorboards. 'First of all, he wants to see the character, LaBrava, when he was a secret agent, which immediately involves a lotta flashbacks. Things that aren't in the book. Then he, Dustin, doesn't think that he, Dustin, could fall in love with a 50-year-old woman, as LaBrava does. He thinks he should have an affair with a young girl in the motel that LaBrava runs.

'I write a treatment that way. We meet a couple of times more. Dustin's just filming *Death of a Salesman* with Volker Schlöndorff, and Schlöndorff comes along to some meetings. But he doesn't last long. Then Martin Scorsese comes in. Scorsese lasts a little longer. Then he gets a deal on *The Color of Money*. So he's out, and Hal Ashby comes in. By this time, Hoffman's signed a deal with Cannon, who are advertising the deal in the trades. "WELCOME TO THE CANNON FAMILY," they're saying. Which is something I guess anyone would resent.

'Although this is taking place in New York, it's typical Hollywood. I just thought, "Well, this is just the way it is." Then, finally, I get another call from Hoffman, who tells me that he's decided he can fall in love with a 50-year-old woman. Turns out he's just met Anouk Aimée. I change it again. Then Hoffman doesn't want to do it anymore. Al Pacino gets involved for a while. Then Hal Ashby, who's got involved because of Dustin, he leaves. Then Ted Kotcheff gets involved, so the guy who did *Rambo*'s in on it. OK. Then Walter Mirisch tells me Richard Dreyfuss is interested. The only thing now, Ted Kotcheff is suing Cannon for $10 million for something I don't even know about. Who knows if it will ever get filmed.'

At the time we meet, Leonard has higher hopes for a film version of *Cat Chaser*, due to go into production shortly, directed by Abel Ferrara, one of the genuine wild men of independent American cinema, who made the grindhouse slasher classic *The Driller Killer* and goes on to make *Bad Lieutenant* with Harvey Keitel and *King of New York* with Christopher Walken.

'I like Abel,' Leonard says. 'He talks like a thug. Talking to Abel's like talking to a convict. I hear they're having trouble with the script. It's very difficult. But we'll see.'

The publicist from his UK publishers has been hovering nearby for a little while, a cluster of worries and timetables. She keeps looking at her watch like she's waiting for a bomb to go off. Now she tells Elmore it's time to leave. There's not much time for further conversation, although I could have kept him talking for the rest of the week. He's putting on his raincoat, getting ready to go, when I ask him as a parting shot if he has any advice for anyone thinking of writing a book.

'Sure,' he says, laughing. 'Keep at it and keep it simple.'

ELVIS COSTELLO

Dublin, May 1989

The Beloved Entertainer, as he calls himself on the cover of his new album, *Spike*, answers my call to his room with the dismal groan of someone waking up to the kind of hangover that might yet prove fatal. He asks me to give him 15 minutes to pull himself together. I tell him to take as long as he likes. I know exactly how he's feeling. The only thing that's currently keeping me upright is the reception desk I'm leaning on in a hotel lobby that seems to be bucking and pitching like a galleon rounding Cape Horn in a sail-shredding tempest. It feels like I've got bones growing out of the back of my head. I simultaneously have a sensation of being totally stunned, like I've just driven a snowmobile into a tree. I join *Melody Maker* photographer Tom Sheehan in the hotel bar, Tom looking as wobbly on his feet as a man trying to tap-dance in a hammock. The bar's just opened. We risk a couple of pints, find a table and wait for Elvis.

The night before, Costello was at the Irish Music Awards, performing a version of 'Dark End of the Street' with Christy Moore. After the awards, Elvis, wife Cait O'Riordan, me and Tom pile into a car that takes us to what turns out to be a lavish after-show party. It's at some hotel, country club or stately home a bit of a drive outside Dublin, the grounds lit up when we get there, a light rain falling. We hit the bar like a tidal wave and start drinking like New Jersey longshoremen at the wake of a much-loved union boss, blown up in his car on a local causeway. It's likely we're drunk before we're shown to our table.

We're hardly in our seats when more drinks arrive. Someone keeps filling my glass with wine, the glass barely empty since we got here.

The drinks aren't coming fast enough for Costello. Tom heads for the bar, returning through the crowd carrying a very big tray of drinks and moving with the careful step of a man walking a tightrope between skyscrapers. Elvis knocks back a pint of Guinness before Tom's put the tray on the table. He reaches for another pint. At this rate, we're not going to get drunk. We're going to get fucking obliterated. Bottoms up!

I go for a bit of a wander. At one point, I bump into my old friend BP Fallon, and you know how that goes. I'm wide-eyed and feeling a bit wild when I get back to our table. Elvis has shot glasses lined up in front of him with various measures of whatever they've got behind the bar in a bottle. Tom turns up with another tray of drinks. Someone fills the glass in front of me with more wine, sees the way things are going and leaves the bottle. Now Elvis is coming back from the bar with another tray of drinks, pints and shots, barging through the crowd like a man heading for a lifeboat with a baby in his arms. Then he's making us roar with laughter, an anecdote about Jerry Lee Lewis, or something. Tom comes back from the bar with another tray of drinks. Where did the last lot go? Things seem to be spinning out of control. What a great time we're having, no thought of what we'll feel like in the morning, which turns out to be very poorly, indeed.

Tom is working manfully on his second pint at the hotel bar when Elvis turns up, looking like he's arrived here after being chucked from a passing helicopter and crashing through its roof. He's wearing a big leather coat that probably cost more than the recording budget for *My Aim Is True*, but he looks somewhat derelict, like he's spent the night in a bus shelter. He slumps in a chair, seems lumpy in odd places, a shoulder pad on one side higher than the other, making him look like something glimpsed in a shadowy Notre Dame belltower.

'Drinks?' he finally asks, a bit of effort going into the one word.

'Don't mind if I do, actually,' Sheehan says. 'I think I'm coming around a bit, as it happens.'

Oh, fuck. Here we go, again.

Elvis puts three pints on the table. He looks at the drink in front of him, seems to decide that drinking it's not going to make him feel any worse – what could, short of a public disembowelment? – and knocks back half of it in a single reckless gulp. The rest of it goes down as quickly.

'Same again?' Sheehan asks, already on his way to the bar.

After a couple more, I remind Costello that I'm actually here to interview him. We reluctantly quit the bar and go up to his room. It's probably described in the hotel brochure as a penthouse suite, but it's not as grand as it sounds. There's a door, easily missed, not far from the lift on the hotel's top floor, a narrow flight of stairs, then the suite itself. A galley kitchen, a lounge with sofas, a table, a couple of armchairs, windows looking out on a balcony, a big Dublin sky beyond that.

The first thing Costello does when we get there is phone down to the bar for drinks.

'There's three of us,' he's telling someone. 'So, yeah. Six pints.'

While we're waiting for the drinks, Costello, unbidden, starts talking about when it was always like this for him. Long tours, too many drugs, too many drunken nights, a lot of regrettable behaviour. As usual, he seems to think he can talk his way out of his hangover, something I've noticed over the years I've been writing about him. I'm happy to give him the floor for what turns out to be a long afternoon.

'I really thought all that nonsense had reached a kind of peak when we were in Holland doing *Get Happy!!*,' he says, his voice chipped, tired. 'When we were literally writing songs on the way to the studio from the bar. But later, it was just as bad. Probably worse. When we were in Nashville for *Almost Blue*, there was a film crew with us, making that *South Bank Show* documentary. When they were filming, it was all very serious. I'd be making all these ponderous statements about why I was making this country album, which everyone seemed to think was a completely lunatic thing to be doing. But as soon as the cameras stopped rolling, it was, "Right. More drugs. Where's the fucking drinks?" Screaming our bloody heads off. We were so completely fucking out of it.

'A lot of people think that album sounds so depressed because I was drinking so much at the time. But there were other things that contributed to that. Things that were happening in my private life that I don't really want to talk about. It wasn't just the drinking. I mean,

I was drinking a lot in fucking 1978. But I was having a better fucking time then. It's when you're drinking and you're not happy, that's when you've got to worry. That's when it's going to affect the way you look at things. Because you're probably drinking for the wrong reasons. That's when things start to get warped, and you don't think anything through.'

There's a knock on the door announcing the arrival of our drinks.

'I remember Nick Lowe once said to me,' Elvis says, handing out pints to me and Tom. 'He said, "I just don't understand you. You fight every drink or any drugs you take. You fight them all the time. You're trying to stay straight all the way through it, whatever you're doing." I still do it. I'll never admit that I'm drunk. But we all drink. Sometimes for the right reasons. To let your mind off the leash for a while. Have some fun. Then, you don't mind if you make a bit of a prat of yourself, like last night. It doesn't matter if you end up shouting at people, or have a punch-up or whatever, as long as you wake up the same person. It's when you don't want to wake up the same person that you've got a problem.

'And I think I went through that for a while. There were times when I'd feel every moment as bad as I feel this morning. Times when you'd wake up feeling like you were knocking on heaven's fucking door and there'd be nobody there to fucking answer you. Those were the worst times.'

Some people thought you were purposely fucking up your life to give you something to write songs about.

'I think I did that for about a year,' Costello says, tired and showing it. 'At the very most. Then I began to mistrust the results. Because if you do that, it's like when they pour acid in rabbits' eyes or something. What does it prove? It proves that it hurts the animal. Very smart. It's unnecessary research. And I guess I did some unnecessary research for a while. Then I'd write something that would scare the hell out of me. Like, there's a couple of things on *Get Happy!!* that when I read them back, I scared the hell out of myself. I thought, "Uh-uh ... better not think any more about this. It's going too far ..." Because you can think too fucking much, you know, and it gets a bit fucking evil.'

Were you in these songs being too personal, too explicit, pouring too much venom, spite, rage, whatever into them?

'Maybe in retrospect,' he says. 'I can recognise sometimes where I maybe went over the line. But then again, I was never really that specific. I mean, people who really do pay too much attention for their own good have tried to peg certain songs to certain people. It's like a game, isn't it, that started in the early 70s, with people like Joni Mitchell. People always wanted to know who her songs were about. People have tried that with me, and they've always been wrong.

'The fact is,' he goes on, 'those songs were never merely confessional. Even if you're satisfying your own selfish desire to put somebody down in a song or praise them, it isn't important that everybody knows who you're writing about or the specific emotional situation that provoked it. The song should have a universal appeal, otherwise it doesn't serve any purpose. It becomes merely self-indulgent. Like, "Let me tell you some more secrets about myself ..." It's all me, me, me. And that just gets really fucking painful after a while. But then you get people saying, "Well, at least it's honest." But is it? Is it honest to go around saying, "Look at my open sores." I don't think it is. I think it's just fucking indulgent.'

Do you resent people, then, digging through the bones of your songs, looking for the autobiographical in your writing?

'I don't resent it,' Costello laughs, setting off a bout of wheezing. 'I just blame John Lennon. It's the *Plastic Ono Band*. That started it all. After that, everything was supposed to be confessional. The early 70s were full of people baring their fucking souls for public scrutiny. There were records whose authenticity depended on the confessional aspect, and if you read certain magazines and the background interviews, you knew who those songs were about.

'That for me used to spoil it. Particularly when you found out what fucking dickheads some of the people were that were being written about. I'd rather have them be like Smokey Robinson songs, which could be about anyone. I don't think it's important that people know who "Alison" was about. It's none of their fucking business. It's a song. "I Want You" is a song. It doesn't matter who it's about.'

People automatically assumed it was addressed to Cait.

'Yeah,' he says wearily. 'But it's just nonsense. It's just a song. It's a really well-written song. It's also very personal. But you don't have to know the whole story to be touched by it. It's like people might say this new record is less personal because most of it's written in the

232

third person. That's just misguided. It all came out of my head, so how can it not be personal, you know? But there are still people, yeah, who want everything I've done documented and explained.

'But we're really getting into something else here,' he says. 'It's all in the past. None of it means a damn. You can't go digging around forever in the past. It's history. Let it go. It's what I'm doing now that counts. That's what I want people to realise.'

This is Costello reminding me, of course, that we are here to talk principally about his new album, *Spike*, as if it hasn't been talked about enough already. The album was released in February to what you'd have to call a blizzard of promotional activity, unprecedented in Costello's career to date. For the first couple of weeks following the album's release, Costello was everywhere. You couldn't pick up a magazine, turn on the radio or television without finding Elvis giving it maximum verbal about the record. All this public salesmanship eventually inclined to an almost desperate attempt by Costello to revive an interest in his music that had conspicuously waned in the unforgiving 1980s, when he'd seemed increasingly marginalised. The commercial momentum that attended 1979's *Armed Forces* had been dramatically derailed by his outrageous comments about Ray Charles in an altercation in Columbus, Ohio, with Bonnie Bramlett and Stephen Stills. In these recent attempts to get it back on track, he had begun to sound, well, ingratiating.

'Fuck off,' Costello laughs, handing me another pint from the tray on the table next to him. 'I certainly didn't feel that way.' He's bristling a bit at the suggestion. 'I think it's important to remember that the last ten years with Columbia,' he goes on, 'were often really frustrating. They just didn't know how to promote me. They'd run out of ideas. By the end, I think they'd just given up. Especially after *King of America*, which they didn't have a fucking clue what to do with, and *Blood & Chocolate*, which they hated and subsequently just fucking buried.

'This is my first one with Warner Brothers and obviously you've got to accept the fact that the record company has heard nothing but horror stories from the past about you. I simply didn't want to get off on the wrong foot with them and end up having to go through the same old fucking battles just to get a fucking record in the shops.

'When the impetus came from America for me to promote the album, I said I'd do it. There was nothing ingratiating about it. As for being desperate – you can't force people to put you on the covers of magazines or on the television or the radio or whatever. That was their choice. And it just proves to me how fucking dull everything must be right now, if someone with my tenure in the business can just reappear after three years and get that kind of attention. I mean, it's no big fucking deal.

'But it amazed me, the ease with which on the one hand you can come back and command the centre stage, just by saying you're there, and secondly still be regarded as somewhat outrageous. But what else is happening? In England, there's a cult a week for some band that's going to save us all. Then you never fucking hear of them again. It's very easy and I suppose attractive to get excited and emotional about The Darling Buds or somebody. But after a while, you can't keep up with who's the latest flame.

'And who's outrageous anymore? Like, I was just in a radio station somewhere in America, in the South. Quite a mainstream radio station. This guy said, "Sometimes I just have to let my hair down and get out of here. Go over to my old college station and play as much Nick Heyward as I like." With all due respect to Nick Heyward, he's not Jimmy Reed. I mean, I think Nick Heyward's made a couple of nice records, but he's not the wild man of rock'n'roll. But he was this guy's definition of outrageous. If that's indicative of the present climate, it's maybe not so curious that I still get some attention. It's maybe why anything I do, not so much in England, but particularly in the States, seems to them to be so effortlessly weird.

'To get over to them the fact that the record isn't all that strange, you sometimes have to fill in a little of the background. You know, I've run into this a lot. People build up such preconceptions or they just associate you with one thing and they can't hear anything else you do. It's like they're looking at a painting you've done, upside down. Unless you can change their point of view, they're never going to see it.'

Costello is back on the phone to the bar for more drinks. I'm thinking about the last time I was in this room, the previous October, a few months after he and Cait moved into the suite. Elvis was frying

234

up some vegetarian sausages, the sound of sizzling coming from the kitchen. I was sitting on a couch in the lounge with Cait, talking about the film she's just starred in, a thriller called *The Courier*, in which she appears opposite Gabriel Byrne and Patrick Bergin. As soon as we've had our sausages, we're off to the premiere.

Sometime after the screening, Costello and I fetch up in some gaudy nightclub where the fluorescent throb and gash of neon drenches us in garish hues. Strobes flash, a flickering derangement. We're drinking ourselves cheerfully senseless when Bono arrives, his appearance among the heathen throng almost papal. First, the crowd parts in front of him, then gathers around him, reverent, adoring.

He settles at a table opposite us, where he's quickly surrounded by a small lapping sea of supplicants, eager to pay their respects. Kiss the hem of his coat, be touched by his presence. Blessed by his righteousness.

'It's like they're queuing for a fucking cure at Lourdes,' Costello mutters into his beer, giving Bono a bit of a wave. Bono replies with a regal nod.

Costello goes back to trying to make himself heard to me above the din of the disco. We're talking about 1986's *Blood & Chocolate*, which turns out to be his last album for a while with The Attractions. Costello's been telling me he'd been convinced this was the record people had been waiting for him to make since *Get Happy!!*, a return to the classic Attractions sound. The record that at a stroke would revive his faltering commercial ambitions, thoroughly thwarted for most of the decade.

This seems somewhat fanciful. *Blood & Chocolate* sounded for the most part like it had been ripped screaming from the clefts of bedlam, a record of conspicuous and noisy brutality. A howl from an outer darkness. When Costello tells me he thought it would return him to the mainstream, I just laugh. I don't, in fact, believe a word. Seven months later, though, in Dublin again, Costello's sticking to his story.

'I honestly wasn't being disingenuous,' he says, referring to our earlier conversation. 'I knew in America, especially, they took a huge gasp of death when we did *Almost Blue*. And although *King of America* was one of those records that got me great reviews, Columbia just couldn't sell the fucking thing. I had a notion that in the States, at least, they'd throw their hats in the air and cheer.

'I really did think it was the album they wanted me to deliver. There were elements of it that I thought were stereotypical. It was like an older, grumpier *This Year's Model*. Which I was pretty sure they'd go for. As it turned out, they did to it what they'd done to the two or three records before it. They buried the fucking thing.

'In retrospect,' Costello goes on, 'I think we underestimated how fucking harsh it sounded. But that was the mood we were in. We wanted it live. We wanted it loud. We achieved that at the expense of everything else. I mean, we tried to do a ballad on that record. A really pretty song called "Forgive Her Anything". But we physically couldn't play it. It sounded like we were playing with boxing gloves on.

'It needed too delicate a touch for the sound we'd contrived. And we got to really fighting about it. Like, "It's your fucking fault. You're playing too fucking loud." "No, I'm not. You're playing too fucking fast." It was like the fucking Troggs. But there was nothing we could do with it. That sound we had, there was just too much barbed wire in it. It was just too fucking ferocious.'

Given the subsequent split with The Attractions, was *Blood & Chocolate* meant to be a kind of last hurrah?

'Not intentionally,' he says. 'The idea was just to get together again and make a record. Originally, it was going to be an EP. A one-off thing. A bit of an undercover job, just to put the fun back into playing together. Because by then everything had got a bit askew. There was a lot of bad feeling that because of the way things turned out The Attractions ended up playing on only one track on *King of America*. The internal politics surrounding that album weren't too pleasant. And I don't think I handled it very well. But neither did a couple of the group. It just got unnecessarily ugly.

'Like, you were at the Duke of York's Theatre, the night I did the show with T Bone Burnett, and I had that row with Steve Nieve. That's the sort of thing that was happening. People were being set up against each other. I hate all that shit, and I didn't want everything to fall apart in acrimony. The main thing was to get back together instead of bickering. The thing was, I had no idea it was going to turn out to be so extreme. But I love it. I think it's one of the two or three best records we made together.'

Releasing two six-minute singles from it – 'Tokyo Storm Warning' and 'I Want You' – wasn't perhaps the most thoughtful commercial strategy. Were you just being perverse?

'No,' he says. 'I really thought they were the two best songs on the record. There were maybe a couple of others that could have been singles. "I Hope You're Happy Now" might have been a hit, or "Blue Chair". But I couldn't see the woods for the trees on that one. You know, I tend sometimes to get too self-conscious about pop music. When I've got a good pop song, I have difficulty doing it properly. I somehow want to fuck it up. And I think the idea sometimes of releasing the obvious poppy track from an album as a single is patronising.'

This sounds a bit fucking rich. The first single from *Spike* was the bouncy and irritatingly frothy 'Veronica', co-written with Paul McCartney, by some distance the album's most obviously poppy track.

'It's totally different,' Costello argues, huffing, a bit indignant. 'That track, "Veronica", it's unashamedly pop music and nothing to apologise for. With that, you know, I've come back to the way I was thinking when we did things like "Oliver's Army". I'm loath to say the word, because the moment you say something's subversive, it's not subversive anymore … But there is a trick to it, you know, where you can slip something out that takes people a while to figure out what it is you're actually singing about. With "Veronica", if people had realised straight off that it was about an old woman, they might have thought it was too maudlin and just shut it off. Whereas the whole point of the song is that there is some hope and defiance in the character. I think it's good that it sounds like it's about a young girl, instead of it being a ponderous thing about an old woman, or something self-consciously dramatic like "Eleanor Rigby". Which is a great record, but you immediately know it's about this strange person who keeps her face in a jar, you know. The idea with "Veronica" isn't to patronise the character. It's said with love. So, I like the idea that the music is really kind of bright and pretty. It's the prettiest record I've made in ages.'

'Veronica' is one of two tracks on *Spike* written with McCartney. Another of their collaborations, 'My Brave Face', has just been released as McCartney's new single; more are to follow on McCartney's forthcoming album, *Flowers in the Dirt*. At last night's party, Elvis by then drinking like someone on a rugby-club stag weekend in Prague, worked himself into a colourful lather about the jaundiced opinion some people have of the former moptop. He'd even been told, Costello complained at sozzled length, that working with McCartney had somehow soiled his own reputation. I remind him about his rant.

'That's true,' he says now. 'People actually told me that. But fuck them. They're people who wouldn't recognise a good piece of music if it boned them up the arse.'

Now that we're talking about it, what was his reaction when the summons came from McCartney? Was he flattered? Intimidated? Suspicious? Think he was onto an easy earner? What?

'It might sound facile,' he says. 'But I didn't think about it in any of those terms. I just thought, "Let's give it a go." It was all very unself-conscious. No big deal. We just got on with it. Occasionally, I'd look up at think, "Oh, hell. It's him." Because he really – don't laugh – he really does look frighteningly like him. The same was true of Roy Orbison. He's one of those people who look exactly like you expect them to.

'You know, I think of him, McCartney, like he's Buzz Aldrin or somebody. Someone who's been to the fucking moon. None of us can conceive what it must be like to have been through what he's experienced. It's a unique experience, probably, in the 20th century, to be him. And that's not making too big a thing of it.

'And the fact he's so easy-going about it all just seems to rile people. I mean, he could be a mad person. He could have reacted to what he went through in any number of ways that could prevent him now from being as straightforward and normal as he apparently is. The very fact that this guy has sort of glided through life and been very well rewarded is the cause, I think, of most of the flak he gets. It's just fucking envy. That's what it is when you get right down to it.

'And he's uncomfortably undramatic about this thing he's been through. But, you know, he has been through it all. Through more things than you could possibly imagine. So why does he have to live up to somebody else's fantasy of who he is? I think that's a completely unreasonable demand to make of anyone.

'It's like these people who criticise him for being too rich or too famous. What the fuck has it got to do with them? It's just crap. Why don't they just shut the fuck up and let him get on with his music? I also think people who criticise him for being sentimental are talking a lot of shit as well. Because in any other line of work, if a man of his age wasn't sentimental about his kids, they'd think he was a fucking sociopath. He's a married man. He has a nice life. What's the fucking matter with that? Fucking hell, just because he's famous, they want him to be at the barricades all the fucking time. It's just fucking stupid. He's just a really good musician, probably one of the best there's been in a long time. It's absolutely coming out of his fingers, you know. And if he doesn't want to use that musical talent to say world-changing things, that's his fucking business. And in any case, he fucking changed the world with The Beatles. Let's fucking leave it at that.'

Did he think when the invitation came that he was being cast in the John Lennon role in the songwriting partnership, the acerbic foil of Beatles legend to McCartney's wholesomeness?

'No,' he says, quickly. Some urgency in his voice here, a secondary concern about unsettling comparisons with John Lennon.

'Lennon's not around anymore to be fallible or great or whatever. Some bastard shot him. So, in America, I think, they're obviously fitting up a lot of people for that role. And it's a dangerous thing. In America, some really neurotic critics are trying to fit me into those shoes. And I think it's fucking irresponsible. You know, COME ON. DRAW A FUCKING TARGET ON MY BACK.'

Costello, of course, has been through all this. After Bonnie Bramlett went public with what he said about Ray Charles in their Ohio fracas, he got more than 200 death threats in less than a week.

'Don't remind me,' he says with a visible shudder. 'Just don't fucking remind me.'

On 9 March 1985, six days after the Miners' Strike ends with Arthur Scargill defeated and Thatcher triumphant, Costello anyway goes ahead with a scheduled strikers' benefit at London's Logan Hall. Billy Bragg and The Men They Couldn't Hang are also on the bill. Coming so soon after Thatcher's victory, it turns out to be a night of predictably mixed emotions. Angry desperation jostles with all kinds of rage, surly defiance. The concert ends with a heartbreakingly poignant version of 'Shipbuilding', Costello joined by the South Wales Striking

239

Miners Choir. Much throat-clearing and not a little eye-dabbing ensues.

Costello's set on the whole is especially raw. There are a lot of big hitters from his back catalogue to date, 'Watching the Detectives', '(I Don't Want to Go to) Chelsea', 'Clubland', 'Oliver's Army', 'Pump It Up'. There are welcome run outs for 'No Action', 'Alison' and 'Less Than Zero'. He also plays pointedly repurposed covers of Hank Williams's 'You Win Again', Bill Anderson's 'Must You Throw Dirt In My Face?', which Costello had first heard by The Louvin Brothers; and 'No Reason to Quit', a song originally recorded by Merle Haggard. He even throws in 'Why Don't We Try Anymore', a co-write with John Doe of X he plays tonight and at another concert a few weeks later and is never heard of again.

There are two new songs, performed for the first time. 'Blue Chair', the first of seven encores, is recorded twice by Costello. First for a single co-produced with T Bone Burnett and featuring some of the *King of America* band, then with The Attractions for *Blood & Chocolate*, produced by Nick Lowe. It never sounds as good again as it does tonight, though.

I'm even more grabbed by the other new song. The set opener. Something angry and wrathful about Margaret Thatcher. I scribble down the opening lines. '*When England was the whore of the world and Margaret was her madam ...*' I think at the time the song is called 'All You Ever Thought of Was Betrayal' and Costello records a version called 'Betrayal' with The Attractions for *King of America* that eventually surfaces on the 2005 Rhino/Edsel expanded reissue of the album. Fortunately, Costello doesn't leave it there. A massively revised version appears on *Spike*, now called 'Tramp the Dirt Down'.

The song's now an even more vicious indictment of Thatcher and the many ruinous things her government has inflicted on the country, in which Costello wishes Thatcher dead and looks forward to dancing on her grave. The song combines bitter fury with a profound sadness and is fuelled by the same righteous wrath that Dylan brought to 'Masters of War' – '*I hope that you die and your death'll come soon*' – and on release causes offence and outrage in predictable quarters. Listening to the song's uneasy sentiments, even some fans wonder if Costello's gone a bit too far.

But as Greil Marcus writes at the time: 'To make true political music, you have to say what decent people don't want to hear; that's something that people fit for satellite benefit concerts never understand, and that Elvis Costello understood before anyone heard his name.'

With the light by now fading from the Dublin sky, more beers on their way from the bar, I ask him about the song. What does 'Tramp the Dirt Down' achieve? What will it change?

'Nothing I can think of,' he says. 'I honestly don't think it will change anything. Like I said to one guy who asked a similar question, songs like that, they're like marker buoys. You know, "This is where the ship went down." The song's not a party-political broadcast, there's no manifesto. It just says, "I'll only be happy when this woman's dead."

'And some people no doubt might find that extreme. But it's meant to be. I make no apology for that song. It's an honest emotional response to events. Writing it was like casting out demons or something. The song itself is the result of a form of madness. Because when you get to that point of thinking those thoughts, actually wishing somebody dead, it really does become a form of madness.

'It's a psychopathic thought. And it's fucking disturbing to find it in your own head. But it would be cowardly not to express it. Because once it's in there, if you don't get it out, it's only going to come back and haunt you some more.

'I also think you have to remember that it's not only her that the song is aimed at. It's what she represents. The way she's changed how people value things. It's like some kind of mass hypnosis she's achieved. People are afraid to speak out. You know, one thing I thought I'd be asked when people heard it was whether I was saying it might have been a good thing if she'd died in the Brighton bombing. I don't think so. It would have made things ten times worse, because then she would have been a martyr. We would have had a dead queen. So really, in a profound sense, the song is hopeless. It's a hopeless argument. It's a hopeless situation. So, no, it's not in a large, historical sense, going to change anything.

'But I think it does have maybe an individual effect. There's always a chance it'll sneak through, somehow. Like, I sang it at a folk festival in the Shetlands, at one place that was very brightly lit. I could see the audience quite clearly. And all the way through it, there was one guy

241

nodding away, applauding every line, obviously getting into it. And on the other side, there was another guy being physically restrained from getting up on the stage and hitting me. He just fused. He really went. And I thought, "Well, I've really got a winner now." To the extent, you know, that it had succeeded in being at least provocative.'

Is that all you can ask of a song these days?

'I've never known what you're supposed to expect from a song,' he says. 'There's a danger in the very talking about it. It makes it seem like you've achieved more than you have.'

Any thoughts on a song like, say, Morrissey's 'Margaret on the Guillotine'?

'I don't know much about Morrissey,' Costello says. 'Apart from the fact that he sometimes brings out records with the greatest titles in the world that somewhere along the line he then neglects to write songs for. But I haven't heard that particular song, so I can't really comment on it. But generally, I think the best that can be achieved by songs like "Tramp the Dirt Down" is something like what "Free Nelson Mandela" achieved.

'The record didn't get Mandela released, but it did increase the membership of the Anti-Apartheid Movement, because Jerry Dammers very intelligently printed their address on the record sleeve. And the record introduced Mandela to a lot of people who maybe otherwise would never have heard of him. And there's a point where political art only works on that level – the communication of basic information.

'On a more immediate level,' Costello goes on, 'you can, I suppose, hope to annoy people, like that guy in the Shetlands. I mean, the *Sun* ran a piece a couple of weeks ago saying I'd been banned by the BBC because I said "I'm fucking sick of this" on *The Late Show*. I haven't seen the programme, but I remember swearing. I was asked something, and I remember saying, "I'm 35 years old. I'm not a boy anymore. Don't patronise me."

'It's like that Grateful Dead song "Ship of Fools" – "*It makes me wild/With 30 years upon my head/To have you call me child*". You do sometimes feel, particularly with the nanny aspect of this government, that they're treating everybody like little fucking children.

'So, the *Sun* runs this thing saying I swore on a live TV show. It was obviously pre-recorded, because I was in America when it was shown.

242

But a spokesman is supposed to have said, "Well it jolly well caused a stink around here at the BBC." And then they quoted me. "Costello said last night, I stand behind every word." Well, they must be fucking telepathic at the fucking *Sun*, because no one spoke to me about it.

'But that's almost an accolade, to get that kind of thing written about you in the *Sun*. It means you're still getting up somebody's fucking nose,' he says, laughing. 'These days, that's an achievement in itself.'

The afternoon draws on. Costello orders more drinks. When they arrive, we're talking about some of his recent collaborations. Most notably with Roy Orbison, whose version of a rewritten 'The Comedians', a song originally from *Goodbye Cruel World*, was a highlight of Orbison's posthumous *Mystery Girl* album. Before flying to Dublin, I'd belatedly caught up with the *Roy Orbison and Friends: A Black And White Night* video of the commemorative concert in Los Angeles, at which Orbison was backed by an all-star cast that put Costello close to a couple of people about whom he'd been previously less than flattering, including Bruce Springsteen.

'Let's be frank,' Costello says, laughing. 'They were people I've often been downright fucking rude about. In fact, I've usually slagged them off. Which I think is fair enough. I have my opinions about them, and they probably know what they think about me. They might get a little outraged sometimes, but I don't give a flying fuck, you know.'

How did you get on with Springsteen?

'I thought Bruce wasn't too bad,' Costello says. 'I mean, he didn't come until the day of the show. But he turned up, no entourage, no bodyguards, no manager, no roadie. Carrying his own guitar, as far as I could see. I assumed he knew all the songs so well he could just busk it. But I have this nice little image of him. We did the show at the Coconut Grove, in the Ambassador Hotel, where Robert Kennedy was shot. The Grove is in a kind of basement at the back, and the kitchen just behind the stage is where Kennedy got shot. The place was like something out of the fucking *Shining*.

'Anyway, all the boys were crammed into one dressing room. You couldn't move for all the baskets of fruit. It's Hollywood, you know, so every fucker on the show gets a basket of fruit with nuts and fucking cheese. And anyway, we're all packed in there and it suddenly reminded me of when I was a kid and I used to go to the Joe Loss shows with my dad. All the guys in the band would be standing around the dressing room in their underwear, smoking. It was great. We really were like the Orchestra. And just before we were due on, I looked around. And there's Springsteen. He's got a Walkman on, and he's got his electric guitar and he's got the chart of "Only the Lonely". He's looking really intense and worried, studying this chart. And suddenly he went, "Oh, fuck. That's how it goes!"'

More drinks arrive. We're now talking about Van Morrison.

'I think what I really admire about him,' Costello says, 'apart from the fact that he makes the most incredible fucking records, is his single-mindedness. People go on about him being difficult. But he does it his way and if you can't accept that, then go somewhere else. I don't think he's going to cry. He's tougher than that. He really is tougher than the rest. He's in a class of one and if you don't like it, then fuck off. There are only, like, two or three people with this kind of singularity left in rock'n'roll. Lou Reed, Van, Dylan.'

Tells us about meeting Dylan.

'I've met Dylan a few times,' Costello says. 'We had a strange conversation once, I remember. I met all his kids in a parking lot in Minneapolis. He came to this party with all his sons. Lined them up like they were on parade, and I had to shake their hands. He said, "This is Jesse. He knows all the words to 'Pump It Up'." I thought, "Now there's something wrong with this statement, Bob. He knows all the words to 'Subterranean Homesick Blues' is what you probably mean." Jesse was a punk fan. I don't know how old he is now, but then he was into The Clash, people like that. I think he thought his dad was a bit old-fashioned. Maybe he's since realised that his dad was a bit more happening than Mick Jones. I hope so. I mean, I love Mick. He's great. But Bob's always been a bit more happening than Mick, let's face it.'

We've been talking for so long we've missed at least two flights back to London. The next one looks like it will be leaving without us, too. It's getting dark. Tom needs to take some pictures. We go out on the balcony, Elvis standing against a glowering sky.

'Anyone fancy another?' Costello asks, back in the room, already on the phone to the bar. We've got at least another hour before the next flight. Why not?

While we're waiting, I return Costello to something we'd been talking about last night, that he'd also touched upon earlier this afternoon. The absence in today's music of provocative voices, genuinely outrageous. This had seemed to really bug him.

'It does,' Costello says. 'It does seem at the moment that there's no real willingness to test anything. But it's not surprising really. All the manners of rebellion in music seem to have been used up. You only have to look at Guns N' Roses to realise that. Cait got their album, you know, and it's fucking terrible. It's like an Outlaws record or something. "I'm goin' down the road and I'm a bad motherfucker." Fuck off, you little twat. The thing is you can't keep leaping out of the cupboard going boo to people. It's not frightening anymore.

'And the funny thing is, the real wild men are still unacceptable. I'm not talking about someone like Johnny Rotten. He's completely acceptable. He's just like Quentin Crisp. An English eccentric. But Jerry Lee Lewis, man. He's still fucking unacceptable to most people. T Bone went for a meeting with him, because he's been working on the film they're doing about him. They went to this really chi-chi Hollywood café. This little waiter comes up and goes, "My name's Christopher and I'll be your waiter for tonight. Is there something I can get you?"

'And Jerry Lee says, "Yeah. What about something blonde, 21 years old with big fuckin' tits."

'Starts straight in, you know. Someone like that, they're always going to be on the outside. He's definitely the real thing. There's really no one around who's that unique, that singular. I don't see anyone like that around anymore. I see a few interesting eccentrics. Morrissey. Michael Stipe. Johnny Lydon. Myself, maybe. But those heavy metal bands who think they're so outrageous, I just think, "Fuck off, pal. You don't even own the territory."

'Because for better or worse,' he says, getting up to answer the knock on the door that means more drinks are here, 'I look back at some of the things we've done, and it's no fucking contest. I mean, we've had our fucking moments, man.

'And they don't come fucking close.'

BOB GELDOF

London, June 1990

'Are you hungry?' he asks, tossing back a shank of hair and flicking through the menu. What the fuck is it about Geldof and feeding people? As it happens, I'm starving. But I don't want Bob writing a song about it or otherwise making a fuss. Rushing around the restaurant banging people on the head with his soup spoon.and demanding their money, that sort of thing. This is someone, after all, for whom extortion in the public good not so long ago became virtually a way of life. Five years after Live Aid, the brogue and the blarney are frighteningly intact. You feel sure he could still bully the change out of your pocket if the mood was upon him.

Turns out, though, that Geldof's less concerned with feeding me than spending someone else's money, which is obviously another of his enduring talents. We are dining at one of London's more expensive nitespots, L'Escargot, a high-profile celebrity eaterie in Soho. Phonogram, Bob's record company, are footing the bill.

'I don't know about you,' Geldof says, 'but I'm going to get straight into a seriously expensive red wine. The record company are paying,' he adds. 'Let's fuckin' go for it.'

So we do.

Meeting him again with a bottle between us for the first time in ten years is not a social occasion. Geldof is wining and dining me not merely to reminisce about mutual past adventures and sundry historical embarrassments from largely misspent years gone by. He's here as part of the promotional push for his new album, the implausibly titled *The Vegetarians of Love*. The last time we met, it was

December 1980, The Boomtown Rats still big enough for *Melody Maker*'s Christmas issue cover story. I remember him sashaying up to the bar of the pub where we were drinking with the rest of the Rats in his beret and ballet slippers and asking for a small Dubonnet on ice. A reasonable request, you'd have thought, that nevertheless makes the landlord chortle until he's red in the face, the rest of the pub, including the Rats, sniggering loudly at Geldof's embarrassment.

'When did I become such a fuckin' joke to everyone?' Bob asks, simmering in the back of a cab to the house he shares in Clapham with Paula Yates, in less troubled times for them both. At this point, I haven't seen Geldof for nigh on a year, prior to which you'd run into him everywhere, no avoiding him and the Rats, who turn out for every party, album launch or after-show jolly-up in town. They are what you might call ubiquitous, making sure they're seen everywhere and are therefore never out of the papers. Even before the hits start coming, Geldof is ever more inescapable. Then they seem to take over *Top of the Pops* for weeks on end with 'Rat Trap' and 'I Don't Like Mondays'. Bob, furthermore, is also to be found elsewhere on TV, sounding off in every direction, opinions on everything and not afraid to share them. At which point an inevitable backlash kicks in. Bob's branded a big mouth, a bag of hot air. The music press, often ambiguous about the Rats, now turns on them, vindictively. There's very little that's good-humoured about the serial pastings they get.

'It got so bad, we purposely decided to drop out of sight,' Geldof says, in the living room of his house, a Christmas tree in the corner, a tinselled concession to the coming festivities. 'I'd personally had enough of the fuckin' bollocks people were fuckin' saying about us. There were no interviews. There was no one on tour with us. We didn't want a record out. People began to think there must be something wrong, because they always suspected that we'd do anything for publicity.'

That's exactly what you fucking did, though. You brought it on yourselves.

'In a sense,' Geldof concedes grumpily. 'But it was hypocritical of the papers to criticise us for that, because they fuckin' gobbled it up. They turned around and slapped us in the face. But they encouraged us in the first place. We just did everything that was expected of us, really. Then we got very badly damaged by it. Last year, you couldn't read anything about the Rats that didn't have some horrible, snide connotations. If a journalist hated me, by extension they hated the band. They didn't listen to the music. They didn't listen to the songs. Because I'd come over as such a verbose idiot on the TV, they'd dismiss the entire band and everything we ever did.

'Somehow, when we were a young band and I was a loudmouth, shooting my mouth off and coming out with snappy one-liners, I was the arrogant young man of today, on my way to becoming the hip young man of tomorrow. I was a laugh. People would say, "Isn't it great, these young guys coming up and sticking it to whoever and isn't Geldof so articulate and witty and blahdefuckingblah?" Two years later, I'm no different. But I'm not the articulate young man anymore. I'm a facile fuckin' smart-arse. I'd probably prefer it if you didn't print this, but I just used to bawl when I picked the papers up. I'd go to bed thinking, "Christ. What have we done wrong? Are they right?"

'In the end, my self-confidence and the band's self-confidence was shattered. That's the best word for it. The others are much stronger than me. They can read the papers and just fling them away if there's any criticism. I just go to bits. A bad review can just shatter me.'

You can't blame the press for everything, though. That you didn't make it in America was entirely your own fault.

'A lot of damage was done by the things I said,' he admits moodily, and for a moment I think I'm going to lose him to a sulk. 'You ask anyone at the label in America and they'll blame it all on me not knowing when to shut up. They'll blame it on San Diego, the first gig we played. I was supposed to have insulted the radio people by asking them to take off their satin tour jackets because the glare from them was blinding me. They say I called them a shower of wankers and then turned the kids loose on them. It did hurt us at the time. And what happened at the record company was that a lot of people took offence at me calling them bastards.

'But it was just a fuckin' joke. We were set to play our first gig and so much was expected of us. We were really nervous. Lee Abrams was there. He's the guy that really runs American radio. All the programmers from his stations were staying at our hotel. They were all brought to the gig in limos, and we were supposed to travel with them. Pete Briquette is in one of the cars and this programmer goes,

"How did you get a name like The Fabulous Poodles?" The cunt thinks we're the fuckin' Fabulous Poodles. I was fuckin' livid. They didn't even know who we fuckin' were, all these people who run American fuckin' radio. I freaked. And as you know, I can't bottle these things up. I'm on stage and I can see all these people at the back, these programmers. The people who think we're the fuckin' Fabulous Poodles. These radio programmers that we supposedly have to depend on to break us in America. I thought, "Fuck it." They were sitting there while the rest of the audience was going apeshit.

'I said, "What do you think of American radio?" To the punters, you know. They were all going, "It sucks, man!" I said, "Here's a unique opportunity to tell the people who run American radio what you think of them. They're sitting over there." They turned on them, the audience. They started haranguing these bastards, who just walked out.'

Presumably that was the end of the Rats in America.

'Oh, no,' Geldof says, laughing. 'I think we may have survived that, bad as it was. It was what I said in New York about Bruce Springsteen that really killed us. Slagging Springsteen in America's like slagging God. The flak we got for that was incredible.'

Presumably you've learned your lesson and from now on you'll be keeping your trap shut.

'In your fuckin' dreams, Jonesy,' Geldof says. 'In your fuckin' dreams.'

Meanwhile, back at L'Escargot, a bottle of seriously expensive red wine arrives. Suitably fortified, I offer the opinion that *The Vegetarians of Love* is a profoundly naff title for a record he hopes will put him back in the proximity of the charts.

'Am I not allowed to be ironic?' he asks.

Call me old-fashioned, but I could find nothing ironic about *The Vegetarians of Love*. It sounded like the title of a concept album by a vegan Spinal Tap.

'It's a fuckin' joke, man,' Geldof laments. 'We're not gonna come on dressed as carrots or anything.'

After the dourness of his uniquely cheerless first solo album, the post-Live Aid *Deep in the Heart of Nowhere*, the new record is being enthusiastically touted by Phonogram as a return by Geldof to the hit-happy glory days of The Boomtown Rats. No one's falling for it, though. You can almost hear critics' knives being sharpened, honed, whatever, in anticipation of its release. Is he worried about the forthcoming reviews after the critical drubbing handed out to *Deep in the Heart of Nowhere*?

'I didn't know it got a drubbing,' Geldof completely unconvincingly says of that glum work. 'I don't read reviews. The absolute truth is I haven't read a music paper in at least seven years. Not one. Initially, it started off for defensive reasons. I was too afraid to read them. Then I just lost interest. I just assumed that album would get a fucking drubbing, because when have I not been a target for critics?'

How difficult has it been since Live Aid for him to revive his career as a pop star?

'It hasn't been hard for me,' he says, grimly. 'But it's obviously been hard for everyone else. The music press and the music industry couldn't give a toss, basically. For everybody who associated me with Live Aid, who knew me as Saint Bob, Sir Bob, Boomtown Bob, whatever Bob they wanted me to be, for those people it was very difficult. You could almost hear this sort of gasp of stifled embarrassment when I said I was going to make another record.'

In darker moments, did he think there might be nothing more to look forward to than a future on the celebrity Chitlin' Circuit? Guest spots on chat shows, presenting wildlife documentaries, fleeting appearances on charity telethons, fame's dim afterlife beckoning even as we speak.

'No!' he replies, banging the table, everything on it jumping or rattling, heads turning in our direction. 'I'd never do any of that. Never. In the wake of Live Aid, I got ludicrous offers. More writing, politics. But that never interested me. The only thing I get any satisfaction from is writing a half-decent song. And, you know, I'm not Elvis Costello. I can't go to the bog and come back with a triple album. I can't sit down and craft a song. I think that's pretty self-evident. When I come up with one I think isn't that bad – that might in my opinion even be fuckin' brilliant – it's fuckin' miraculous. It gives me a real sense of achievement.'

We are now on our second bottle of extremely expensive red wine and it's going down a lot better than I imagine *The Vegetarians of Love* will in most quarters. I think most people will listen to the album and think Geldof's taking the piss.

'Ah, fuck 'em,' Geldof says. 'I don't give a shite what people think.'

We're both surprised when we realise it's now 15 years since The Boomtown Rats made themselves chart regulars.

'A lifetime for the pop audience, quite literally,' Geldof says, suddenly wistful. 'I think most people have largely forgotten me as this guy on *Top of the Pops* doing "Lookin' After Number One" and "Rat Trap" and "I Don't Like Mondays".'

So who's the new album going to appeal to?

'I haven't a bollocks,' he says. 'Really. Fuck knows who'll buy it. I'd love to play in England and go up and down the country and play gigs and have people come and see me and think it's cool. I mean, I'm playing a gig in London in July, almost five years to the day since I last played in this country, and that was at Live Aid. And that's possibly the only thing that makes me nervous. I remember the terror when I went on the Wogan TV show, to sing for the first time in three years. I actually went out there and I just wasn't used to being a singer. I sort of shambled out there a bit sheepish and did my thing and it was completely ineffectual. I just didn't have the bluff anymore. I couldn't blast it out and give it all the fuckin' attitude like I used to. My cover was seriously blown. It was extremely difficult to get back into rock god mode.

'But aside from that, you know, I think this is a brilliant fuckin' album. I love it. It's the best I can do at the moment, thanks very much. I'd love millions of people to go out and buy it in droves. They probably won't,' he says. 'But there I be, and there ye go.'

R.E.M.

Athens, Georgia, December 1991

'What the fuck was Michael thinking?' Peter Buck wants to know as we make our way to a table at Gus Garcia's, a favourite bar on Broad Street in what I guess is downtown Athens. Buck's obviously well known here. There's a margarita in front of him before he sits down. Peter's still a bit rattled by this morning's photo shoot for *Melody Maker*'s Christmas cover, a seasonal celebration of R.E.M.'s international breakthrough this year with *Out of Time*, their seventh album, by now on its way to worldwide sales of 20 million.

The band have made some space for *MM* photographer Kevin Westenberg in their rehearsal studio in the basements of R.E.M. HQ on West Clayton Street. You have to pick your way through their fan club office to get to it, a room cluttered with band memorabilia. Leaning against a stack of cardboard boxes is the partially dismantled bike that featured in the 'Shiny Happy People' video. It was going to be thrown out until someone suggested they hold on to it and auction it for charity. This is typical R.E.M. thinking. Use everything for a good cause. Even the Christmas fan club mailout is an opportunity to make a point.

Each package being sent out contains a specially recorded Christmas single, 'Holly Jolly 1991', which consists of a cover of The Vibrators' 'Baby, Baby', backed with a Berry-Buck-Mills-Stipe tune called 'Christmas Griping'. There are calendars. Christmas cards emblazoned with the single word 'PEACE', copies of *50 Ways to Fight Censorship* by Dave Marsh (Thunder Mouth Press) and paintbrushes wrapped in a note that says 'CREATE'.

Peter at the best of times is a bit allergic to posing for someone's cameras when he could be making music, listening to records or propping up a bar. He's therefore horrified when he turns up that morning at West Clayton Street to find Michael Stipe unloading a couple of large cardboard boxes from his car that he's filled with costumes he wants the band to wear for the *MM* cover shoot. Stipe is in an extravagantly festive mood. He's got a Santa suit for Peter, some kind of bear suit for Bill Berry, an Uncle Sam top hat for Mike Mills.

'It was typical Michael,' Buck says in Gus Garcia's, introducing himself to his margarita. "Let's do this." "Let's do that." Without thinking of the consequences, you know. I mean, those pictures. Us dressed up like that. They'll haunt us for years,' he says, laughing in mock despair. 'Michael's so …'

Impulsive?

'Absolutely. He just can't stop himself,' Buck says. 'Michael is one of those people who's always ready with an idea, good or bad. It can get a little too much to deal with. If we're writing a song, he'll come up with these ideas when we're trying to figure out a drum pattern. It's always, like, "No, Michael. We're not ready for your input yet." Michael will come in and we'll play a two-chord riff and he'll go, "That's great. Now speed it up twice as fast and get rid of that second chord change and, hey, when you're at it, why don't you change the key?" And then we go, "Hey, wait a minute. What you're saying is, 'Write another song.'" And he'll go, "Well … uh … yeah."

'So we purposely try to keep Michael out of the studio while we're working up ideas. What we like to do, the three of us, me, Mike and Bill, is go into the studio on our own and just kind of bang around. We all bring in a lot of ideas and every couple of weeks we'll put them on tape. So the three of us come up with the songs and then we hand them over at some point to Michael, to write the lyrics. To get even that far, we need to keep Michael out of the studio, send him on an errand, whatever, or we'd never get anything done.'

Almost exactly a year ago, R.E.M. had just finished the final mixes for *Out of Time* at Prince's Paisley Park studio complex in Minneapolis. Their mood was strangely muted as they waited for the limo that would take them from Paisley Park to the airport and their flight home to Athens.

'It was all kind of odd,' Bill Berry says, trying to make himself comfortable on an old sofa in the West Clayton Street basement. 'We sat around chatting and making final comments about what we'd just finished. The unanimous consensus was that, even though we were proud of it, this record we'd just done was commercially going to be a flop. We thought it would probably sell a typical-for-us 40 copies overseas and do probably a half or three quarters of a million in the States. We just didn't hear a single on it.'

In a restaurant called Grits, Mike Mills, feeling reckless this afternoon, orders a carrot juice with his Orangina.

'You can never tell what people are going to like,' he says, explaining R.E.M.'s apprehension about the album's commercial appeal. 'I mean, I know what I think sounds good. But trying to predict how a record's going to sell is like trying to catch sunlight. You can't do it. At the same time, there was this feeling that the record wasn't commercial at all. Even though we had a great deal of confidence in the record as a piece of work, I'd be lying if I said I ever thought it was a sure-fire chart thing.'

All this second-guessing was part of R.E.M. facing up to pressures they'd never really encountered before. *Green*, their last album, had sold somewhere between three and four million copies. *Out of Time* was expected to top that. For the first time in their career, R.E.M. had commercial as well as artistic expectations to live up to.

'One of the nice things about being at the small level we were at more or less for nearly seven years is that no one pays that much attention to your sales,' Buck says in Gus Garcia's, working on his second margarita. 'When you're a cult band, whatever you do is what you do and that's acceptable. When you sell like three or four million records, which is what I guess *Green* did, then everyone tends to start looking at you in a business way. That doesn't affect the way we make music, but when the record's done, you start worrying about whether the fat guys in the office are going to listen to it and go, "That last one, it was a fluke! Write these people off." I don't care very much for those people and their opinions. But, on the other hand, it would make things harder to do if we were suddenly seen as washed up. Which is what would happen if we put out a record that didn't sell.

'In the end, *Out of Time* sold real well. But, at the time, having made the record we'd made, we weren't sure that, in 1991, given the musical climate and what was being played on the radio, that it was obviously commercial. It was essentially an acoustic record and the lead instrument on the first single ['Losing My Religion'] was a fucking mandolin, and that was going against this whole dance groove, you know. So we said, "OK, we're not going to sell any records." Fuck it, you know. You do what you think is right and stand by it.'

Did they actually set out to make a record that wilfully ran against the musical drift of the times?

'Not really,' Mike Mills says. 'We never said, "Let's make this an acoustic record to go against the grain of what's on the radio these days." It's great that it turned out the way it did, but what happened was that, basically, after all the touring we did in '89, Peter was tired of playing guitar. And from such small things do records come. I guess that some people can conceive of this grand notion of what their record is going to sound like. But I can't imagine that at all. You just have to wing it and hope it turns out OK. That's what we do, anyway.'

'I don't think we ever consciously set ourselves in opposition to anything except maybe ourselves,' Buck says. 'We always try to get as far away as possible from sounding like R.E.M., although we never get as far away as we want it to be. I mean, given Michael's voice, which is very distinctive, and my guitar playing, which, because of my own limitations, is what it is, you know, we have to work really hard not to sound like us.'

R.E.M. didn't tour to promote *Out of Time*, which was a surprise to everyone but themselves.

'If we'd gone out, we might've sold another two million records,' Mike Mills says. 'But, shit, you don't want to be a pig about it. The record did great without us touring. And, although I think we would've done well if we'd toured, because people do like to come out and see us, it was not, in the end, a bad year not to tour.'

'As far as not touring,' Bill Berry says, 'I think we made the right decision. No doubt about it. With the recession the way it is, nearly everybody that went out stiffed. Tours were being cancelled and if they weren't cancelled, they were moving into smaller venues. And, shit, if we'd toured, we'd just be winding down about now. We'd be absolutely weary and just plain tired of seeing each other. And it would be another two years before the next record came out. As it is, we could do a new record right now. We've been working for the last three months on new songs. We're almost ready to go.'

'We knew at the end of the *Green* tour that we wouldn't be going back out for a while,' Buck says. 'It just wasn't the right time to tour. We all understood that. Of course, you look at it financially and you think, "Gee. We could've been raking in the bucks." But money's no reason for doing anything. See, I don't want to sell something I would give away. If you're doing it just to make money, then you're selling it. And there's something wrong with that.'

What was the label reaction when they found out R.E.M. weren't going to tour behind the new album. Warner Bros had, after all, signed the band for $80 million or something and must have been keen on seeing a quick return on their investment.

'They weren't thrilled,' Bill says with a smirk. 'That's for damned sure.'

'They shouldn't have been surprised,' is Mills's opinion. 'They knew when they signed us that we make our own decisions about things like that.'

'Michael and I were pretty adamant about not touring with this album,' Buck says. 'But we didn't tell the record company straight off. You can't broadcast your plans that far in advance. That gives them time to try to convince you to do things their way. And you can talk almost anyone into doing anything. In the end, we thought, "Well, we've got a manager. We'll get him to give them a call. That's his job." We kind of kept our heads down at that point.'

'We see a lot of bands,' Bill says, 'and the record company tells them to do this, do that. And even if their gut instinct tells them not to, they go ahead and do it anyway because they think the record company knows best. And they still don't sell shit. Their tours still flop. We've always worked the other way around. Warner Brothers knew what they were getting when they signed us. We're not very predictable. They know that we don't just buckle down to what they think the bottom line is. We do things the way we want to. I think our fans appreciate that and the record company accepts the fact that the fans buy the records.'

After the epic *Green* trek, had the fun simply gone out of touring?

'The fun was still there,' Buck says. 'But sometimes finding it was a pain in the ass.'

'When we announced we weren't going to tour,' Bill says, 'I think a lot of people thought, "Oh my God, R.E.M., the band that pretty much lived on the road and made records once in a while as a secondary thing, they don't like to play anymore." The truth is, the monster had got too big. It's like a military operation now. You need all this money and organisation upfront just to get going. And when you get going, you've got to keep going or you don't break even. It's insane. The costs involved are enormous. There's a lot less money to be made from rock'n'roll tours than people think. I remember when I was a kid, I'd go to concerts and drive away thinking, "God, those guys in the band are backstage right now, counting piles of money, girls hanging from their arms, champagne popping …"

'And it's not like that at all,' Bill continues, sounding utterly and possibly permanently disenchanted by the disappointments of life as a member of a top pop group.

R.E.M. have by now been together for ten years. How have they changed in that time?

'I think everybody's pretty much the same, a bit calmer, maybe,' Mike Mills says. 'Otherwise, I don't know. It's been such a gradual thing.'

'It's uncanny how much we haven't changed,' Bill says. 'Peter's still cynical. Mike's still a great sports fan and Michael still eats roots and seeds and stuff.

'We're all a few pounds heavier and some of us are a little thinner on top. But really, we haven't changed at all.'

'There have been definite changes,' Peter says. 'Most of them for the better. When we started the band, I think I was the oldest. I was like 24 or 25 when we did *Murmur* and I think Michael was 21 or something. We were really young and musicians don't do a lot of things that normal people do. I had friends who, when they were 24 or 25, already had like two kids and a real job and knew what it was like to be an adult. When I was 24, I was still sleeping on people's floors, living in vans. I didn't have a job. I hadn't even been paid by cheque for a job in six or seven years. It was all under-the-table work. I think since then we've all learned a lot about life and how to work with each other. All of us were real stubborn, but we've learned how to bend and compromise in ways I think most people never do. For me, it's all been real good. Because I used to be totally impatient,

257

and I really had to have my own way all the time. Now, I don't feel that way. The world still goes on. No matter how pissed off I feel on Monday, there's always Tuesday to come and I know now I'll probably feel different.'

What's kept them together all this time?

'Two things,' Mike says. 'One, we all have things to do that don't involve each other. Two, we're all friends. It's not like we're people who merely tolerate each other. The fact that we're friends is the main key, I think, to why we're still together.'

'It also didn't happen too fast for us,' Bill says. 'That can be the kiss of death. I like to pride myself that we're pretty level-headed guys. But, hell, at 23, if we'd had the success we've had now, I'd probably be shooting up drugs and not getting a whole lot done, except getting in trouble and stuff. Ours has been such a slow, steady rise that we've been able to keep tabs on it. If someone had handed me $3 million when I was 23, I'd probably have gone to LA and bought a mansion and a Rolls-Royce, and I don't know what I'd be doing now.'

'Not being in the music business spotlight,' Peter says, 'we always had this feeling that it was us against the world. It always felt to us that we were on the outside and we had to work that much harder to get anywhere. And that made us much tighter as friends and as people. There was this big showbiz world that we were never really a part of, and we're still not really a part of. We had to prove ourselves on our own terms.'

What if *Murmur* had been as successful in 1983 as *Out of Time* was in 1991?

'I honestly don't believe we would have made a second album,' Buck says, turning a bit grim. 'We wouldn't have gotten that far. I can't imagine that we would have been able to function.'

Do you really think you would have got that fucked up?

'Oh, yeah. Definitely. No doubt about it,' Buck says. 'I think so. I think it would have been bad for all of us. I think it's real good for your career if you're not successful until you're ready for it.'

Before the break from touring they've taken in 1991, R.E.M. had been on the road for as long as they'd been together. Were there any nostalgic pangs for days gone by, the band piling into the back of a van and taking off somewhere? Did they wake up in their own beds, wondering why they weren't in a Holiday Inn in Tuscaloosa, Gothenburg, Madrid, Glasgow?

'Travelling with six people in the back of a van is not something I could easily go back to,' Mike says. 'I loved every second of it. But it's a lot easier when you're 20 than when you're 30-something.'

'You get the occasional nostalgic pang,' Bill says. 'But it passes. They were great days. But right now, I don't want to be in a van with four guys with dirty clothes and equipment falling on you and shit. I'm 33 years old. It's not really what I want to do.'

'Those days make for great memories,' Buck says as the light fades on Broad Street. 'I don't mean to sound like someone out of *The Last Waltz*, but I think I squeezed every little bit of experience I could have out of those days. And now, whatever nostalgia I have for that time is tempered by the fact I remember never being warm, never having enough to eat, not washing for weeks, sleeping on people's floors.

'If I was still doing that, I'd either be dead soon or trying to kill someone. The past is a friendly place, but I don't want to go there much. Occasionally, in the right circumstances, over a couple of drinks,' he says, polishing off another margarita, 'I like to sit around telling road stories, you know ...'

I signal to the waitress for another round, ask a seasonal question. Did R.E.M. ever tour at Christmas?

'What? In the snow and stuff? Sure. We've done our share of bad-weather driving. Nothing ever stopped us. I remember in the Green Van days, the first van we ever had, for some reason the tyres kept blowing out. Bill and I were always the night drivers because we always had ... uh ... insomnia, and everybody else would sleep. And the tyres always seemed to pop at like five in the morning. We got to the point where we could unload the van, change the tyre and get back on the road in like three and a half minutes. Sometimes the tyre would blow and the people asleep in the van wouldn't even know. We were like a race team.

'It's real funny,' Peter says as the waitress hands him a margarita and the sound of Christmas bells reaches us from Broad Street, 'I look back on those days and think about these totally out of their minds, barely past teenagers running around the country. We were insane. They were beautiful days. But I'm glad they're over.'

A pause. Peter starts shredding a cocktail napkin, head down.

'Those pictures of us in the costumes,' he says finally. 'You're going to use them, aren't you?'

I give him an innocent shrug that makes him laugh.

'Fucking Michael,' he says, shaking his head, a long-suffering martyr to Stipe's whims. 'What would we do without him?'

LAMBCHOP

Nashville, July 1996

They are in the basement of the house on the corner of Sweetbriar Avenue and Belmont Boulevard, waiting for us with music, mind-blowing moonshine whiskey, good weed and strong beer. When every-one who's able to show up tonight is here, there will be six of them. They will look like they've dropped by to fix the plumbing, mend the roof or lay a floor, which are among the things they do when they are not writing or recording some of the most beguiling and beautiful music I've ever heard.

They are Lambchop and that's bandleader, vocalist and songwriter Kurt Wagner over there, just to the right of where I'm sitting on a banged-up flight case, Kurt surrounded by notebooks and scraps of paper with lyrics scrawled on them. He's playing guitar and singing, his voice not much more than a cracked whisper in the shadows of this small, cluttered room. Who else is here?

Panning from left to right, Jonathan Marx is on cornet, a preppy little dude. Next to him is Allen Lowrey on drums. Squatting behind a hanging frame of spanners, wrenches, things like that, the contents of a toolbox, basically, is C. Scott Chase, beating time on a lacquer-thinning can. The guy with the beatnik goatee and Peter Tork haircut is bassist Marc Trovillion. Pedal steel virtuoso Paul Niehaus has made a little space for himself against the far wall, where he's hemmed in by an amp on one side and a monitor speaker on the other. The most notable absentees are sax player Deanna Varagona and keyboard player John Delworth.

The gig the band had scheduled for this evening at a local bar for the benefit of their visitors from what used to be *Melody Maker* has been cancelled at short notice. It was Kurt's idea to put the show on here, Lambchop playing for an audience of two, me and Tom Sheehan. What these unlikely, unassuming people are playing tonight, down in this dimly lit basement, is mostly improvised, songs plucked as it were out of the air. Kurt usually starts, the lyrics murmured as much as sung, hard to catch, the rest of the band joining in when they have something to add to whatever's taking shape. One of the things they play that sticks with me goes on to become 'The Gettysburg Address' on 2002's *Is A Woman*. Listening, anyway, to the music unfold is akin to being a witness to the rituals of magic, being brought under a spell, mesmerised.

You will know what this music sounds like if you've heard either their 1994 debut, *I Hope You're Sitting Down/Jack's Tulips*, its January 1996 follow-up, *How I Quit Smoking*, or the just-released mini-album, *Hank*, the first breath-taking stirrings of what would become a hallmark mix of country, burnished Southern soul, psychedelia, gospel hallelujahs, orchestral pop, feedback psychosis, far-out funky strutting, languid introspection and engulfing ballads. Kurt's songs on these and the albums that follow find him mostly looking at the world in quiet wonder and wondering in turn at its inconsistencies and variables, the fragile perishability and impermanence of things particularly troubling to him. Hence the celebration in his songs of the so-called ordinary, everyday rituals and routines, the stippled repetition of reassuring household chores. The talismanic virtues of the morning hug, the barking dog, a dreaming bird, the creak of familiar floorboards, the unfolding universe.

Whatever, we're back in the basement now and what with the heat and the beer and the moonshine and the weed and the narcoleptic swirl and eddy of the music, I begin to drift, spellbound.

Pretty soon, Tennessee is not the only state I'm in.

The next afternoon, Kurt is sitting in the front room of his new house. Outside, it's punishingly hot, Nashville burning in high summer heat, no air to breathe. In the quiet of Kurt's house, it's blessedly cool, an air conditioner humming, blinds drawn against the day's bright glare. Kurt tugs at the peak of his baseball cap, sips beer, lights another Vantage cigarette, tells me how he ended up coming back to

Nashville after adventures elsewhere and started writing the songs that Lambchop would go on to record.

'I'd been living in Chicago for about a year and a half,' he says. 'Then a series of traumatic incidents brought me back to Nashville. A friend of mine had been living in New York and had gone through a series of similar disasters. He moved back here around the same time and did nothing but listen to Hank Williams and write these incredible country songs. And it suddenly dawned on me that I could do that, too. That's when I started writing.

'It was pretty strange. I'd played in what I guess you'd call experimental bands at art school in Chicago and punk bands in Memphis. I'd never really considered playing so-called "country music". Growing up in Nashville, you obviously couldn't escape the music. But it was always uncool. Country music represented everything that was conservative and kind of right-wing. It was a different world, the 1960s in Nashville. It was a very strange time, a very redneck town. I was 16 and had hair down to my butt, which meant I was subjected to quite a bit of abuse, police harassment. The kind of thing that was happening in most Southern towns.

'And the music I associated with the people who were throwing beer bottles at me for having long hair was country music. Country music was emblematic of these real redneck attitudes, which to an extent it still is. I'd say that's where the money is, the redneck dollar.

'So, it wasn't like country music was in my blood or anything. It was just something I drifted towards. What happened was, that bar we were in last night, The Springwater, I started going there. It was an amazing place. They used to have this thing called The Working Stiff's Jamboree. It was like the Misfits' Opry. All the misfit songwriters, the oddballs of Nashville, used to get together there. And for me, that was the most interesting music in town. No doubt about it. It was totally unpredictable. Just amazing moments of beauty and wonder.

'That's where, I guess, Lambchop started. We never actually sat down and said, "Let's form a 13-piece band that plays weird country music, with a drummer who plays wrenches and an oil can." We were just friends, and it was a case of whoever turned up and stayed, they became part of the band.'

I imagine you were immediately embraced by the country tradi-tionalists who no doubt took you to their hearts, their collective heav-ing bosom.

'Not quite,' Kurt laughs, a gulp of beer nearly choking him as he chuckles. 'In fact, not at all.

'They thought we were a joke. We started getting a reputation for being real oddball, and I wasn't comfortable with that. I don't think I'm odd. I think I'm a real normal guy. Really. But I'd meet these other songwriters and they'd introduce me to people, and they'd say, "This is Kurt. He writes some real wild, weird stuff. He's pretty left-field." That's how they would describe me and what I did and that, to me, wasn't very encouraging. Because it was different to what they were doing and I approached things differently to them, by definition, what I was doing was weird and odd. But it was nothing I strove for. It's all relative, anyway,' he says, shrugging, coming back from the fridge with another couple of life-saving beers. 'As they say, one man's strange is another man's genius.'

Turns out we have Superchunk's Mac McCaughan to thank for bringing Lambchop to our attention. He heard a single they'd recorded for a local indie imprint, encouraged them to record an album and then put it out on Merge, the label he co-founded in Durham, North Carolina, in 1989. The album was the 17-track *I Hope You're Sitting Down*, also sometimes known as *Jack's Tulips*, and cost $1,500 to make.

Cue international acclaim, or something a bit like it.

'You've probably noticed we're not the most self-promoting people in the world,' Kurt says. 'We were amazed at the amount of atten-tion the record got. We really didn't think we'd done anything to deserve it. Nearly all the press was favourable – especially the reviews in Europe. We couldn't believe it.

'I'm still a little fuzzy about how many copies it's actually sold. But the important thing is it sold enough for us to be able to make a second one, which in turn sold enough for us to make a third one. So, it's all pretty cool.'

Have you made enough money yet to give up your day jobs, to concentrate fully on music?

'No,' Kurt says, deadpan. 'We're a strictly non-profit-making organisation. Whatever we earn from record sales goes straight into financing the next one. If there's anything over, we might take the band out to dinner, or we'll buy a bunch of beers and have a barbecue. Pretty exciting, uh?'

You were saying earlier that you'd make more money if you weren't so reluctant to tour.

'I guess we could,' he says. 'People want us to play, and I love playing. But the logistics and expense of, like, 10 or 12 people on the road are pretty frightening. And I don't think touring is real conducive to leading a normal life. We all have regular jobs and wives and kids. I'd like to preserve that.

'Also, I don't subscribe to the received wisdom that when you put out a record you've got to tour for months to promote it. Yeah, we'd probably sell more records, make more money. But so what? Being on the road forever is no kind of life. And it's not that I need that much more money. I mean, it's not like I have this huge swinging lifestyle to maintain. I'm a construction worker. I lay hardwood floors. I make a modest amount of money, but it comes in every week. And with what we earn from record sales, it's enough.

'Basically, I like having a life and I think I'd be reluctant – I am reluctant – to sacrifice it to endless touring. Writing and recording, those are the priorities. Also, the idea of going out, night after night, playing the same material, it's stifling. It can kill a band. Imagine if painters had to go out and tour. Hang up their paintings every night, stand around talking about them. Take them down, load them up into the van and go on to the next town and do it all over again. Hanging the paintings, talking about them. It wouldn't happen.

'So, I think we'll keep our distance from a lot of that. And as long as we're able to remain masters of our own fucked-up little universe, I'll be happy.'

According to the front page of that morning's edition of one of Nashville's newspapers, Southern skies are aflame again. Black communities in Alabama, Tennessee, Texas and the Carolinas have watched their churches burning, 32 of them in the last 18 months. Local government agencies have denied these are racist attacks – as if! – but there's a 200-man FBI task force in the field and for a lot of people terrible memories of the Ku Klux Klan have been revived.

'What's been happening is incredible,' Kurt says. 'It reminds me of 30 years ago. I can't believe they don't have the National Guard posted at every Southern church from here to out west. They have the manpower. I'm not talking about tanks on the lawn, just a couple of guys. They don't even have to be armed. They'd just have to be there. Some of these places are so isolated, in the middle of nowhere, out in the country. And when it's dark out there, it's very dark and there's nobody around for miles, so they're perfect targets. It's the same kind of small-minded nonsense that's been going on for years. It's real disturbing that it's boiled over again. But maybe not totally surprising.'

We are talking about such things because the conversation has turned to a song on *How I Quit Smoking*. It's called 'The Militant', and it describes a spooky encounter with the KKK.

'It's a true story,' Kurt says. 'I was working out at this house where a fireplace had been recently built. The concrete had just been poured and was still soft. Someone had carved the initials KKK in really big letters. It's common graffiti on building sites around here and getting more prevalent. I found this particularly disturbing, because the cement was so fresh, and I could hear voices upstairs. It was a bunch of house-painters and there was a pretty good chance they were responsible. And I was going to have to be working all day with them in the house. I was a little unnerved.

'But I found it really offensive. I scratched it out. I guess there was always the chance they'd come downstairs to admire their handiwork and discover I'd undermined it, which could have led to a certain unpleasantness.'

This is the classic dichotomy of the Deep South, what it pretends to be and what it is. On the one hand, the South prides itself on its sense of courtesy and chivalry, its patrician airs and graces. On the other hand, it's neck deep in a history of slavery, lynching, burning crosses and white supremacy.

'That's very much the story here,' Kurt says. 'You're always running into the most gracious, kind and polite people. They'll treat you very graciously, with big smiles on their faces. But underneath that, they're bigoted and bitter. It's something I've grown up with, from storekeepers to teachers to classmates. It's part of the culture, an old story. In the recent cases, it's motivated as ever by ignorance. I think bigotry is based on nothing but ignorance and it's an ignorance that's been handed down from generation to generation. Taught to their children by people who don't know any better. I guess like the way folk music and folk art is passed on, so this bigotry is passed on.

'A lot of people think these are individual incidents, not evidence of a conspiracy. Some people think these people are incapable of organisation. But at one time the KKK were a powerful and extremely well-organised force in this country. Then they went underground. A lot of the smart ones, anyway. And they're the scary fuckers. The ones that write stuff in restrooms and on the job sites where I work, those guys are just idiots who think it's probably funny. But I'm pretty concerned about the whole situation. It really reminds me of a long time ago. And I don't think we need to go back to that. It should be taken care of swiftly. It should never have been allowed to drag on as long as this. We should be making a more serious effort to control it.'

There are fireflies on the front lawn, a long day coming to an end. Time for one last question.

Why the fuck Lambchop?

Kurt laughs, takes a big swig of beer.

'The first single we put out was under the name of Posterchild,' he says. 'And a highly paid lawyer from Warner Brothers sent us a letter asking us to cease using the name because it was perilously close to the name Poster Children, who were a band signed to Warner Brothers. My point of view was that it wasn't. One was obviously singular. The other was obviously plural. We tried to ignore him for a while, but the guy was persistent. Finally, it became clear that we were going to have to change our name. I thought we should call ourselves R.E.N. Because those letters are the difference between Poster Child and Poster Children.

'Of course, we then figured there might be further complications with R.E.M. My own feeling was that we should have done it. Then we could have made a career of hiding out under all these different names and being discovered by lawyers and being sued and graciously apologising and throwing ourselves on the mercies of the small claims court. I think they wouldn't have bothered us, but you never know.'

But why, of all things, Lambchop?

'It was just something Marc came up with when we were driving to work one day,' he says. 'He was spouting off, as he's wont to do, talking to someone in the van. And I heard him say this word. I don't even remember the context. By then, the whole process of finding a new name had been going on for months. I didn't want to think about it anymore. Lambchop didn't seem any more stupid than any other name and I thought it was neat that all the letters were different. Then I got my wife to say it and she looked so cute. And most pretty women, when you ask them to say "Lambchop", they always kind of smile when they say it and they look beautiful.

'Try it when you get home and see if it works,' he says.

I did, and it does.

JOHN CARPENTER

London, September 1996

John Carpenter is in Room 103 at the Dorchester. Kurt Russell's in a suite two doors down the hall, as if the two of them together would be too much cool for one room to hold. They're in town to promote their new film, *Escape from L.A.*, a belated sequel of sorts to 1981's *Escape from New York*.

Carpenter's dressed in LA casual. A surprisingly blousy shirt, the sleeves rolled up, pockets on the front big enough to stuff puppies into, crisp, pleated slacks. Despite the debonair togs, he's got a lean, angry look and the exasperated air of someone who's been asked too many times to explain himself. Something pent up about him almost crackles and if detonated could blow a hole in the ceiling. As we cut to a close-up of Carpenter lighting a cigarette, however, the crusty director isn't giving us a promotional pitch for the new movie. He's getting hot under the collar on the subject of movie violence, which as the man who made *Assault on Precinct 13*, *Halloween* and *The Thing*, he knows more than a little about.

'It's interesting you bring this up,' he rasps, a two-packs-a-day man I'd guess. 'There's been a lawsuit recently filed in America under the production liability laws, and what it means is that for the first time in history a movie is being sued for causing real-life copycat violence.'

Carpenter's talking about the case recently brought against Oliver Stone by best-selling author John Grisham. A friend of Grisham's named Bill Savage was shot dead in Mississippi by two teenage runaways from Oklahoma. They'd gone on a killing spree after multiple viewings of Stone's film *Natural Born Killers*. Grisham blames the

269

film for the death of his friend. The film he contends was made 'with the intention of glorifying random murder'.

He furthermore holds Stone personally responsible for what happened to Bill Savage. Citing US product liability laws, under which manufacturers can be held responsible for any injuries or deaths caused by their products, Grisham wants Stone and Warner Bros, the studio that financed the movie, fined, preferably massively, for what he describes as their part in what happened to Savage.

'There was a fascinating article recently in the *LA Times*,' Carpenter says. 'It was written by a psychiatrist who said it was inevitable there will be more cases like this and just as inevitable one of them will succeed. They'll win. This psychiatrist went on to explain why. Basically, you have a segment of the population or the audience that is simply delusional. They apparently can't tell the difference between fantasy and reality. How you identify that segment, I don t know. Is it a drug-inflamed fringe group? I don't know. Do they look a certain way? Do they act a certain way? I don't know. Neither did the psychiatrist. Which means you can't identify them to keep them from seeing this kind of movie but as a filmmaker you're still responsible for their actions.'

What can you do?

'Well,' Carpenter says, disappearing in a cloud of cigarette smoke, 'the Director's Guild just called me up recently and invited me to join a group of ten directors who're going to be meeting with the heads of all the major Hollywood studios. I'm going to propose that our movies carry disclaimers. Like you have on medicine bottles. That say watching moving pictures may cause certain members of the audience to identify with certain characters and incidents and that the producers assume no responsibility for anything that happens in their lives.

'We'd better spell it out,' he goes on, getting into it now. 'Because some of these idiots can't tell the difference between reality and what they see on screen, which is fantasy. It's things like this, you know, that make me really fear for society. Truly and honestly fear that we've rounded a corner of real stupidity. I really don't know what more to say.

'Poor Oliver Stone. He's the one getting all the flak. He's been singled out as this monster of depravity. I give him such ultimate credit, though. He's standing up and fighting back. He's even put out his director's cut of *Natural Born Killers*, which includes a lot of stuff we didn't see in the original version. And if you see what he's put back in, you realise he was really laying it on the line in that picture. He really went all out and satirised all kinds of violence. He satirised our love of violence and showed what it does to us. Nobody's pretending it's pretty. But these idiots don't get the point. What I don't understand is why they don't just blame the perpetrator of the crime. People commit crimes, not movies.'

What you're saying is that Stone shot a movie, not Grisham's friend.

'Exactly,' Carpenter says. 'But it's Stone that's getting blamed.'

I take it he didn't agree with Dustin Hoffman's recent outburst at the Cannes Film Festival, when the diminutive star blamed violent movies for violence in society.

'Dustin Hoffman?' Carpenter splutters. 'If Dustin Hoffman walked in here right now, I'd kick his ass around the room.'

We talk about Snake Plissken, the sociopathic anti-hero played with nihilistic panache by Kurt Russell in *Escape from New York* and now in *Escape from L.A.*

'Snake went further than even, say, Dirty Harry,' Carpenter says. 'Even Dirty Harry cared for the victims, spoke for them. Snake doesn't care about anybody but himself. He's totally self-centred. He doesn't care if he kills you. He doesn't care if he saves you.'

Did Carpenter think he had anything in common with Snake?

'Oh, sure.'

What are the things you have in common?

'Arrested adolescence,' he says. 'The questioning of authority. A refusal to take orders.'

Could he elaborate? He could.

'I have a simple philosophy. If you ask me to do something, I'll do anything you want. I will. I'll do it. However, if you tell me to do something, it's over. I'm gone, man. I love collaboration. If someone has something to say that's worth listening to, I'll listen. No problem. Just don't treat me with contempt. Don't discount me. Don't put me down. If you call me a shit-heel, I won't budge. Don't do that. I'll be obstinate. I'll be ornery. I won't give a damn what you do. I'll piss on your campfire. I'll bring it all down.'

He now sounds uncannily like Snake.

'Well,' he says, laughing. 'There are similarities.'

Carpenter bristles at the suggestion, made elsewhere, that *Escape from L.A.* is a satire of America's political right.

'We decided early on that it would be too easy to just attack the right,' he explains, but you can tell it's tedious for him, all this self-justification. 'Although since Reagan there definitely have been shifts towards fascism in America. There's more racism. Unrestrained capitalism has taken over. But there's also the tyranny of the left. All this political correctness. Those people are nuts. This whole business about not being able to smoke anywhere. I can't even begin to tell you what I think about that. And it comes from the dear old left. What is it with these people? Do they think their shit doesn't stink?'

What about the *Washington Post* critic who thought *Escape from L.A.* was a hymn to America's anti-government militias? Did he agree with him?

'God, no!' Carpenter laughs derisively, a seal barking on a rock. 'The militias are idiots. Scam artists who don't want to pick up the bill. When they say they are against the government, they don't realise we are the government. We're electing these idiots to office. If we're going to be that stupid, we deserve everything we get.'

He takes a drag on his cigarette that brings the burning tip down to the filter in one go. When he blows out the smoke, it looks like the room's been teargassed.

'You know, it's funny,' he goes on, although he clearly thinks it's anything but, every muscle he's got and a few he hasn't all seeming to go tense at once, like he's just been injected with starch. 'The way people tend to react to these movies.

'I had this gal in France,' he says, an exasperated memory, 'who was convinced I'd based the character of Snake on the Unabomber. I mean, Christ almighty.'

He grinds out what's left of his cigarette like he's trying to bore a hole in the ashtray.

'And now this *Washington Post* guy with his hymns-to-the-militias bullshit,' he says, jaw working like he's chewing a chair leg.

'What's the matter with these people?'

He lights another cigarette.

'*Escape from New York* is a comedy Western, guys,' he says, sucking on his fag and making a noise like he's snorkelling in liquid nicotine. 'Relax before your stupidity kills me.'

OLIVER STONE

Dallas, May 1998

Oliver Stone, standing in American sunlight.

'Do you see that building over there?' he asks, pointing to the Dallas skyline, which is full of them.

'That's where we stayed when we shot *JFK*.'

I give him a bit of a look at this.

'I'm talking about the movie, of course,' he smiles, and it's a tense little grin, a flexing of muscles, a tightening of lines around the mouth and eyes. A series of spasms, almost. An effort, you guess, not a reflex, as if he's had to think hard and quickly about the legitimacy of a light-hearted response. But the grin is there, however hard-won. And it's good to see, because you don't want Stone to be wholly the earnest demagogue of Hollywood legend, in whose annals he too often comes across as Bono with a Steadicam.

It's late afternoon in Dallas, the sun starting to set. We're on the balcony of The Mansion, the hotel in Turtle Creek where Stone is staying tonight before flying tomorrow to Toronto.

Trying to make conversation while *Uncut* photographer Phil Nicholls prepares his camera set-ups for a brief photo-op with Stone, I mention that the day before, Phil and I had been in downtown Dallas, a couple of blocks from Dealey Plaza, where in bright winter sunshine in November 1963 John Kennedy was murdered, America going into shock, a trauma from which, for many, it has never recovered.

We had been picked up by a crusty old cab driver named Charlie. I asked Charlie if he was in Dallas when Kennedy was shot.

'No, sir!' Charlie says with some gusto. 'I was not. And I have an alibi. I was working at a convenience store in Galveston.'

Charlie had been in Dallas, however, when Stone was here on location for his film, *JFK*.

'I was on what they called Stone Watch,' Charlie said. 'Whenever we saw the film crew, we'd call the local TV station and they'd come a-running with their cameras and what-all.'

I mention this to Stone, standing there on the balcony of his hotel overlooking Turtle Creek, and immediately cause a great deal of unintentional confusion.

'You were following me?' Stone asks Phil, quite sharply, suddenly twitchy, scanning the horizon for snipers, sunlight gleaming off telescopic sights, people who shouldn't be there taking up positions on a grassy knoll.

'I wasn't following you,' the startled photographer replies.

'Didn't you just tell me he was on something called Stone Watch?' Stone asks me.

Phil wasn't following you, I try to explain. It was a cab driver.

'A cab driver was following Phil?'

No. He was following you.

'Phil was?'

No. Charlie.

'Who's Charlie?'

He's a cab driver.

'And Charlie was following me?'

Yes.

'Today? When? What's going on? Who are these people you know who are following me?'

This is like something out of the fucking Marx Brothers. All we're missing is Margaret Dumont and a fucking harp solo. It's been like this since we arrived at Turtle Creek about an hour ago.

The face being so familiar, you would recognise Stone anywhere, and we did. Stepping into the lift on our way to meet him in the suite at The Mansion where he's set up a temporary production office, he passes us going the other way – at some speed, let it be said. We are in the lift by now, the doors closing too quickly for introduction. We wonder where he's going at such a determined lick, face screwed up, a knot of concentration, lost in thoughts we can't at this distance even begin to identify. We merely watch him disappear around a corner.

274

We are received at the door of Stone's suite by his assistant, Annie Tien. She tells us Mr Stone is running to an extremely tight schedule today, offers us soft drinks or water and then wonders what Mr Stone might be doing in the lobby when we tell her we've just seen him downstairs.

We make polite conversation, a lot of it. There's no sign of Stone. Annie Tien makes some calls, sorts out piles of papers, notes, letters. You can imagine her always being this busy around Stone. He exerts a kind of kinetic force even when he's not here in person, the bulk of his personality a physical absence, but still somehow a looming, imminent presence. I keep looking at the door, waiting for it to come off its hinges with his arrival. Annie Tien is opening and shutting cupboards and drawers with an impatient urgency.

'I'm looking for a fax machine,' she explains.

I ask her what Stone is doing in Dallas.

'I can't say. You'll have to ask him about that,' she says, guardedly. You get the feeling that electrodes and a cattle-prod wouldn't get the information out of her without Stone's consent. Which confirms an impression that he is someone who commands a fierce protective loyalty from the people around him.

The next thing we know, Stone is on the phone to Annie Tien, calling from God knows where.

'He'll be another ten minutes,' she tells us.

When he finally turns up, he couldn't be friendlier.

'How have you been, Allan?' he asks, as if we've known each other for years but haven't seen each other for at least a couple of them. '*Salvador*, right?'

I tell him we haven't met before, but he doesn't seem convinced. I've lost his attention, anyway, a fuss now being made about his shirt, which he suddenly decides is the wrong colour and which he announces he will change, disappearing then into the bedroom. Twenty minutes and a shirt change later, he's had his picture taken, banished Phil from the suite, and is settling himself opposite me on a large couch, telling me he's ready to talk.

While I'm getting my tape recorder out of my bag, I casually ask him about the reaction to his new film, *U Turn*, a ferocious desert-noir starring Nick Nolte, Sean Penn, Powers Boothe, Billy Bob Thornton, Joaquin Phoenix and Jennifer Lopez.

'How did *U Turn* do in America?' he asks, laughing to himself at a joke I don't get. 'That's your first question?'

I guess it is.

'The movie died over here,' he says, and he's not laughing now. 'It was killed by indifference and critical stupidity. The box office was terrible. People said it was a film about nothing. That it was violent, meaningless and nihilistic. It's five weeks since it was released, and you can't see it anywhere. You can't even find it at a drive-in. It's gone. It's sad. But if you make a movie with no obviously sympathetic characters, it's a given fact you're going to lose 30 to 40 per cent of your audience. There are certain people who just walk. These are the people looking for happy endings to assure them life's just fine. And what *U Turn* tells them is that life isn't fine. Anything but, in fact.'

Outside, it's dark, and getting darker still in here.

'What,' asks Stone, 'was your second question?'

These are some things you may want to know about Oliver Stone.

He was born into upper-middle-class affluence. His father, Lou, with whom he had a turbulent relationship, was a stockbroker. His mother, Jacqueline, was French and beautiful. Stone was privately educated at schools in New York and Pennsylvania. In 1961, when he was 15, his parents divorced. Stone's reaction was typically understated. Declaring himself abandoned and betrayed, he tried to enlist as a mercenary in the Congo, where a civil war was raging. The military demand for adolescent prep school students was virtually non-existent – even in a slaughterhouse like the Belgian Congo. Stone had to wait another four years, one of which he spent restless and unhappy at Yale, before he made a decisive break with his entitled past and went looking for his future in Southeast Asia.

In June 1965, Stone arrived in Saigon, taking up a teaching post at the Pacific Institute in Cholon, the Chinese quarter. He was 18 and watched fascinated as American troops poured into the city, Marines and the US 1st Infantry among them, as the war he would eventually join loomed around him. Stone taught for two terms at the Pacific Institute before signing on in 1966 as a deckhand on a US merchant ship bound for Oregon. His next stop was Guadalajara in Mexico, where he began feverish work on a novel, a vast hallucinatory epic, inspired by Rimbaud, Conrad, Joyce and Norman Mailer. The novel,

400 pages of which had been handwritten in a furious burst of creative energy in Mexico, was finished the following year in New York. It was by now over 1,400 pages long and rejected by every publisher to whom it was submitted.

In a moment of the deepest despair, Stone threw several sections of the original manuscript into New York's East River. He was tempted to follow the pages into the seething water. Instead, he decided to return to Southeast Asia, this time as a soldier. He volunteered for the army. After training at Fort Jackson, South Carolina, he was shipped out to Vietnam. It was September 1967. Stone was 21.

'At that time, in real life, it was clear that I couldn't kill myself, but the army could. And I was willing now to go the last step. I enlisted. I insisted on combat. I insisted on the jungle. I didn't want to miss the war. I didn't want to be an officer. I just wanted to be an infantry soldier and see the war upfront. And either I would survive the war – which I didn't think I would – and it would be like something out of Hemingway, a rite of passage, or a Conradian rite of cowardice. Whatever. Some kind of will had to be tested before I died. Which, as I said, I thought I would.'

So you went to Vietnam not as a gung-ho young patriot, but as a young man looking for death.

'Yes,' he says. 'I was a very complicated boy. I was looking for death. I don't think I have to clarify it any further.'

Stone served a 15-month tour of duty in Vietnam. He was wounded twice, winning a Bronze Star for combat gallantry after singlehandedly charging an enemy foxhole, from which the NVA had been pinning down his platoon with machine-gun fire. It was where he was turned onto marijuana, acid, Motown and rock'n'roll, his life changing beyond recognition in the process.

'I think if you've ever been in a war,' he says, 'the way you think about life is forever different. Forever fucked and twisted. I think once you've seen what the people who went to Vietnam, for instance, saw, nothing is ever the same. You look at the world. It's not the world you used to know. That world in many ways has gone forever.'

By the time he was shipped back to America, he'd abandoned plans to be a novelist. He enrolled at the New York University Film School, where he was encouraged by Martin Scorsese, one of his tutors there.

'I learned an incredible amount from Marty,' Stone says. 'When I went to film school, I had no idea how to make a movie, how to hold a camera. Marty would hold these amazing classes where he never seemed to stop talking. He introduced us to these great directors, all the great movies, this great tradition we would become part of. It was a great experience. He'd bring people like John Cassavetes down to talk to us about filmmaking, which was an education in itself.

'Marty was always massively encouraging. Very charming then, as he continues to be very charming today. He had a talent for telling you what was wrong with your work without dismissing it or saying it was a piece of shit. It's not a talent I have, no. I have a talent for turning up the heat, and I've gone toe-to-toe with people in positions of power and I've been burned for it, no doubt about that.

'Marty, though, encouraged us to make films from and about our personal experience. This was an important lesson. I made a film called *Last Year in Vietnam*. It was shown to the class, and he said, "This is the work of a filmmaker."'

How did that make you feel?

'Vindicated.'

Stone had to wait until 1986 to direct the film he'd been burning to make since graduating from film school. During this time, he had through bloody persistence and a few lucky breaks become one of Hollywood's top screenwriters, developing in the process a major cocaine habit. His screenplay for *Midnight Express* earned Stone an Oscar, a Golden Globe and Writers Guild of America Award. His scripts for *Scarface* and *Year of the Dragon* won him a reputation for lurid excess and eye-popping violence. A reworking of the Howard Hawks gangster classic, directed by Brian De Palma, *Scarface* starred Al Pacino as Cuban refugee Tony Montana cutting a bloody swathe through a Miami drug world full of chainsaws, rocket launchers and enough cocaine to fill several landfills. It's since infiltrated the culture. At the time, it was reviled.

'It stalled my career. It didn't set it back, but it certainly put it in neutral for a while. It got terrible reviews. No one liked that movie. Everyone attacked it. People thought it was sick, repulsive, had no morals. No one wanted anything to do with me for a while. I went off and directed a movie called *The Hand* that nobody ever forgave me for.'

What did you think of De Palma's direction? How different would it have been if you'd made it?

'I thought Brian did a marvellous job. It's like grand opera. I couldn't have directed it at the time. I didn't know how. Brian wasn't interested in the street aspect of the story. I would have placed maybe more emphasis on that. Where Tony came from and the people around him. Brian always saw it as a genre movie, a gangster movie. I always thought there was more to be brought out of it. But Brian was more interested in the clothes, people looking in mirrors at themselves and what they're wearing. It's a perfectly valid perspective, but there were other aspects of the movie I think could have been developed. I remember taking Brian down to Miami to these clubs that were full of guys like Tony. He talked to them, but you could tell he wasn't really interested.'

How much personal research did you do into cocaine-taking?

'Good question,' he laughs. 'I'd already done my research, in a way. Cocaine was everywhere in Hollywood in the late 70s. I did my share in a big way.'

His big break as a director came with *Salvador*, an angry indictment of interventionist US foreign policy in Central America, basically the bankrolling of dictators, based on the real-life adventures of war correspondent Richard Boyle, played with an unhinged sweaty panache by James Woods. It was headstrong, seething and won Oscar nominations for Best Screenplay and Best Actor. Stone next poured a version of his Vietnam experience into *Platoon*, with Charlie Sheen as his screen surrogate. It was nominated for eight Academy Awards, winning four, including Best Director and Best Picture, even as it was breaking box office records.

The films that followed – *Wall Street* (1987), *Talk Radio* (1988), *Born on the Fourth of July* (1989) – continued an award-winning hot streak of box office winners. For as long as his films were successful, Stone was bomb-proof. But critical resentment was growing into an intolerance of what many detractors saw as his bombastic, overheated, increasingly manipulative and politically motivated style of filmmaking. To the added irritation of these critics, Stone appeared to be dedicated to the idea that he should use his position as one of

Hollywood's most influential players to chronicle everything America had been through since the 1960s, that decade of assassination, riots, acid and war.

Their cawing derision went into overdrive, however, when in 1990 Stone announced his most ambitious project yet – *JFK*, a film he claimed would finally tell the truth about what happened in Dallas on 22 November 1963. The official verdict delivered by the Warren Report concluded that Kennedy had been killed by a single gunman. Lee Harvey Oswald was an ex-Marine. Allegedly a Castro sympathiser, a disturbed loner, a perfect fit for the president's assassin. Stone flamboyantly announced that *JFK* would prove that Kennedy was the victim not of Oswald acting alone, but of a vast conspiracy involving Washington, the military–industrial complex, anti-Castro Cubans incensed by Kennedy's betrayal of them at the Bay of Pigs, the FBI, rogue elements of the CIA and the Mob. In fact, the only people who weren't at some point incriminated were the Salvation Army, the Lawn Tennis Association and the original London cast of *My Fair Lady*.

Stone was hardly alone in believing there was a conspiracy to murder Kennedy. A poll at the time found that 77 per cent of Americans doubted the findings of the Warren Commission. But what to him looked like a coordinated smear campaign portrayed Stone as a paranoid fantasist with a tenuous grasp of reality, a conspiracy freak, a crank. An early draft of the screenplay was stolen, published and ridiculed.

'It was like surviving an onslaught of the most vicious derision,' Stone says, tightening at the memory, back in Dallas for the day on unexplained business before flying on to Toronto. 'I was, in a sense, outlawed because of *JFK*,' he goes on. 'I crossed a line with that film. It set up the idea that I had somehow passed beyond film into the public arena, into the political arena. The film itself, the style of *JFK*, the craft that went into its making, has very rarely been discussed. What people talked about and wrote about was me, and my ideas, what a nutcase I was. How screwy my politics were. It's been about that ever since. No one looks at the films themselves anymore.'

I mention a couple of typical headlines, from the *Washington Post* and *Newsweek*. 'Dallas in Wonderland: How Oliver Stone's Version of the Kennedy Assassination Exploits the Edge of Paranoia'; 'Why Oliver Stone's New Film Can't Be Trusted'.

'That sort of thing certainly came up a lot,' he says. 'I was gratuitous. I was a fraud. I was brainwashing the young. I was an intellectual sociopath.'

Do you think a lot of the hostility was provoked by the fact that at some point you seemed to assume a provocative sense of mission, that you were going to tell America the truth about itself?

'I never stated that as my mission,' he insists. 'I keep seeing the words "self-appointed" being used by people who don't like my work. But I never made that appointment. All I do is what I do.'

And yet people question the truth as you see it, or perhaps find the telling of it overblown, exaggerated, even far-fetched.

'But why?' he wants to know, a geyser of exasperation. 'Is it the fact that Kennedy could have been killed by a cabal? Is that so upsetting? What's so difficult to buy about that? What if he got in the way of some power structure and he was removed? Simply removed. As so many leaders have been.

'I do believe he was killed by a cabal. I believe it was an inside job, if you like. I believe there was military involvement because of the way it was carried out. It was a classic military ambush. I'd seen these things in Vietnam. It was the way these things were done. It was the ultimate black op.'

'I'm going to treat myself to a glass of wine,' Stone suddenly announces. 'It's the twilight hour. Will you join me?'

I thought he'd never ask. He gets on the phone to room service, orders a bottle of Californian Chardonnay.

'I'll leave the vintage to your discretion,' he tells whoever he's talking to. 'Just make it quick. I'm an alcoholic.'

He settles back on the couch opposite me.

'Looking back,' he says, resignation giving way to something like self-pity. 'I was lucky to get as far as I did. I had my moment in the sun with *Platoon* and *Born on the Fourth of July*. I won Academy Awards. The films were extremely popular. I had a wonderful run of success, of a kind few filmmakers ever enjoy, right up to *JFK*. All that changed after *JFK*, however. I saw it coming. It was coming for years. I felt it coming on *Nixon*, which was one of my most mature movies. There are certain things in there that are amazing. But no one ever talked about them. They were overlooked, ignored.

281

'And this is what hurts,' he says. 'What's happened to me is that there has been so much easy dismissal of the work I've done. Any other filmmaker, having made the movies I've made, would probably be taken a bit more seriously. I don't know why that is. But there's something going on and I would trace it back to *JFK*. I've really paid a price for that film. There's been a lot of rejection since.'

Stone settles into a grim silence that's broken by a knock at the door that startles us both.

'Who do you think that is?' Stone asks, looking at the door like he thinks it's about to be blown off its hinges, a Glock-wielding Phil Nicholls marching in at the head of a black ops death squad.

I take a wild guess and suggest it's room service.

'What do you think they want?' Stone asks.

I imagine they've turned up with the wine Stone ordered, Californian Chardonnay, the vintage left to the wine waiter's discretion.

'Yes, of course,' Stone says, getting up to answer the door, but ready it looks like to make a bolt for it if he opens it and someone in a ski mask tries to wrestle his head into a sack.

The phone's been ringing for the last couple of minutes. Stone finally answers it. It's Annie Tien. She apparently needs him to finish the interview as soon as possible. Stone has a meeting this evening with Michael Tolkin, author of the brilliant Hollywood satire, *The Player*, filmed by Robert Altman. Tolkin's already downstairs, waiting for Stone. He also has an interview to film to preface a Channel 5 screening that coming weekend of *Natural Born Killers*.

'We still have a little more time,' he says, unruffled by Annie Tien's urgency, pouring more wine, 'and you look like you've got another four days' worth of questions there.'

I do, too. Let's press ahead, then, before Stone is whisked away by the briskly efficient Annie Tien. We're soon talking about the controversy surrounding *Natural Born Killers*, that anarchic ultraviolent romp, *Duck Soup* directed by Sam Peckinpah.

'That was a different kind of controversy to *JFK*,' he says. 'I think it's important to remember that. *JFK* provoked a much broader controversy because it was about the recent history of my country, America, and it brought to the surface a lot of things that had been widely talked about but systematically ignored. Facts that were obvious were being disputed, and it was an attempt to clarify those facts. The ramifications, the implications of what that picture had to say, were much larger than *Natural Born Killers* and obviously and intentionally so.

'I have said this before and taken flak for it, and I'll say it again and expect to take more. *Natural Born Killers* was intended as satire, in the tradition of Swift and Hogarth. I thought people would get it. Not all of them did. In fact, as it turned out, a lot of people didn't get it. But I wanted to hold up a fun-house mirror to this country and say, "This is what America is like."

'Stylistically, the film was intended to reflect the lurid sensationalism of so much of our news coverage, the fascination of our culture with violence and sensationalism, the way killers become celebrities, commercial products. It's about violence as a commodity, a commercial industry. The controversy around it was much more limited than *JFK*. It had a narrower focus. But it was in some ways just as bad. And then of course, I had to put up with the bullshit of people like John Grisham.'

Ah, John Grisham. Stone's self-declared nemesis, whose accusations in a legal action that NBK purposely glorified random violence had so incensed John Carpenter.

'That was such a cheap shot,' Stone says, angry enough to pop an eye. 'And the way the press set me up – it was ludicrous. They sided with him even though they knew his case was bullshit, because they knew it would get me going. He cast himself as a victim. Fuck him. Who does he think he is, the fuck? Setting himself up as a judge, deciding himself what's responsible, what's irresponsible. That's how Hitler and fucking Stalin got started. Social responsibility? Get the fuck out of here. I would never have given in to that shit. That's why they hate me.'

What about the idea that *NBK* inspired copycat killings?

'Again, bullshit,' Stone says. 'No connections were ever proved. In every case, these people had serious histories of drug abuse. They didn't think they were Mickey and Mallory because they saw *Natural Born Killers*. They were already fucked up. But, hell, I can't win. If I make a film that's factually based, I'm accused of distorting history. If I make a film that exaggerates stylistically the violence of the society we live in, I'm accused of glorifying the violence I'm condemning. Give me a fucking break.'

He pours another glass of wine, as if a drink will calm him down, sinks into a silent funk, the exhaustion of someone who's recently been losing more battles than he's been winning.

Annie Tien's just called again, pressing Stone to wrap things up and get downstairs, where you imagine her impatiently prowling the lobby.

'I have to go,' Stone says. 'Let's finish this tomorrow,' he adds then. 'In Toronto.'

Toronto?

'Fly up tomorrow and meet us there,' he says. 'Speak to Annie Tien. She'll give you the address of our hotel. Meet us there.'

I tell him I can't just fly off to Canada on a whim. I have to get back to London, where there are things to do. Deadlines to meet, a magazine to get out. It's all irrelevant to Stone, who clearly now expects me to meet him tomorrow in Toronto. He's on his feet, getting ready to go downstairs to meet Michael Tolkin and Annie Tien.

'You know,' he says, jacket going on, pockets being patted for something that's missing that turns out to be his phone, 'you could very easily use this interview to make me sound extremely paranoid.'

He's heading for the bedroom now, me following, tape recorder in hand.

'It's happened before,' he says, moving piles of what look like film scripts from a desk, still no sign of his phone, although he appears to have found his wallet on a chair. 'I just hope this hasn't all sounded like one long complaint. But the setback of *Nixon* and now *U Turn* definitely has hurt me. Hurt my ability not only to finance films, which my critics are probably very happy and exalted about, but also hurt my personal confidence. I wonder if I'm making sense anymore. That's the deepest implication. That's what concerns me most.'

He finds his phone, finally, under the shirt he'd discarded for being the wrong colour for the pictures with Phil.

'The thing is,' he says, making for the door, 'you have to have confidence to make movies. You have to go out there and believe in yourself. You have to convince actors to work in a certain way, directors of photography, editors. You have to convince a large body of people, and then you have to go through the editing process, the financial

284

process, the marketing process. It's exhausting. And every time you suffer a defeat, believe me, it resounds through your system.'

We're in the hotel corridor now, Stone steering me by an elbow to the lift.

'It means it will take another year or two years of effort to make another one, and inevitably right now, there's a hopelessness about any effort I would make.'

The lift arrives, announced by a brightly declarative ping. We step inside, Stone still talking. To himself as much as me.

'If I continue to make films,' he says, 'I'll make them for myself. I'll be my own audience. Because if people continue to dismiss what I do so lightly, without any real thought, then what's the point of making films for them. To have your work dismissed as my films have been, that's a heartbreaker.

'But that seems to be my filmic destiny right now. And that's a tough place to be. A very tough place to be,' he says as the lift reaches the ground floor and the doors open onto the glare and hubbub of the hotel lobby, someone at the reception desk, presumably Tolkin, giving Stone a cheery wave as we step out of the lift, the doors closing behind us.

'Toronto,' Stone says. 'Tomorrow,' he adds, shaking my hand like we've just made a pact, a blood oath. He heads off with his arm around Michael Tolkin's shoulder, Tolkin laughing at whatever Stone is telling him as they disappear into the crowd heading for the hotel restaurant.

The next morning, I fly back to London.

A few nights later, I'm working late in the *Uncut* office. The phone rings, odd at this hour. Turns out it's Annie Tien. What the fuck?

'Allan Jones?' she says, 'I have Oliver Stone for you.'

She does, too, although I don't remember giving either of them my number. And how did he know I'd be here this late?

'We were expecting you in Toronto,' he says.

I repeat the need for an urgent return to London, but he still sounds a bit put out, failure to follow a Stone instruction likely something he rarely tolerates. But why's he calling?

'Unfinished business,' he says. 'You seemed to have a lot of questions left that I didn't have time to answer in Dallas. There was something about Scorsese and *Taxi Driver* you were keen to talk about.'

There was. I grab a notebook. When Stone went to film school, he was just back from Vietnam and drove a cab to pay his college fees. I wanted to know if when he saw *Taxi Driver* he identified with Travis Bickle?

'Oh, God, yes,' Stone says. 'Totally, yeah. It was amazing. I couldn't believe it. That was me. I was Travis Bickle. I thought I must have given Marty the idea. But it turned out that Paul Schrader, who I didn't know, had been working along parallel lines to my own thoughts. I thought it was a great film, *Taxi Driver*. You know the flak jacket Travis wears, driving the cab? I wore one exactly like it. It was the jacket I had in Vietnam, and like Travis, I wore it when I was cab-driving. It was extraordinary for me to see a character like Travis on screen.'

Is it true you were obsessed when you got back from Vietnam with the idea of assassinating Nixon?

'I wasn't obsessed,' Stone says. 'That's the wrong word. I came back from Vietnam, where I had been in combat, in the front line. I'd been a soldier. I'd seen the war, close-up. And I was appalled when I got back. It was like a fever. And all these anti-war protesters, the peace movement people, I thought they were full of bullshit. Not because they were against the war. I just thought they were hopeless. There was a point to their opposition to the war, but merely protesting didn't seem to me to be a very likely way of bringing the war to an end. So, I was consumed by this raging frustration. I was just out of combat, and I thought the only way they were going to achieve anything was by direct action.'

Of what kind?

'I thought they should get armed, storm Washington and take Nixon down with gunfire,' Stone says, and nothing about him suggests he's joking. 'At the time, I think I had more in common with the Black Panthers,' he goes on. 'I had more of a Panther mentality. I was a combat veteran, older, more cynical. I thought something should be done, and that was the way to do it. Park the fucking tanks on the White House Lawn.'

There's a long pause.

'We had our moment to get rid of the clowns,' he says at last. 'But we fucking blew it.'

CHRISSIE HYNDE

London, March 1999

Chrissie Hynde, nudging 50 and comfortable with it, is sitting somewhat primly in a suite at a private members' club north of Oxford Street, dressed for business in a pinstripe suit and a shirt sprouting frills at the collar and cuffs. The Pretenders have a new album out soon, ¡*Viva El Amor!*, their seventh, and she's here for an interview with *Uncut*, a cover story on her life, career and music to date. There's a lot to talk about, therefore, before we even get to the new record. As usual, there isn't a question she doesn't answer, nothing she doesn't remember.

Her story ranges from Akron, to Cleveland, Mexico, London, Paris, Tucson, and back to London, where after many setbacks and disappointments, much frustrated effort, she finally puts together The Pretenders, her dream band. As you join us, she's describing how she recruited Pete Farndon, just back from Australia, where he'd been playing bass in a band called The Bushwackers. Pete in turn brings in guitarist Jimmy Honeyman-Scott, also from Hereford. When things don't work out with the drummer they've been working with, Jimmy suggests they try out Martin Chambers, a drummer from Hereford Jimmy's played with in a band called Cheeks. Martin's now in London, working as a driving instructor and living in Tufnell Park. They bring him in for a rehearsal.

'We plugged in and started playing "Precious",' she recalls. 'I remember clearly, I had to turn around and face the wall. I was laughing so hard, because as soon as Martin started playing with us, I knew that was it. We had the band.'

It doesn't happen immediately for them. Their first two singles – 'Stop Your Sobbing' and 'Kid' – barely make the Top 30. But their third, 'Brass in Pocket', is a number one. For months, you can't go anywhere without hearing it. Released on 11 January 1980, *Pretenders*, the band's by-now long-awaited debut album, goes straight in at number one. Now things are happening for them at a gallop.

'We were hot,' she says. 'We were ready to go. We were a great band. I'd been working my ass off to get this far. I was ready for it. I'd put a lot of work into this thing. I mean, I read stories about girls who say they fucked their way to the top. Man, if only it was that easy.'

The album sells over half a million copies in America before they've even set foot in the country. When they finally tour there, it's to sell-out crowds everywhere. Their popularity escalates, even as there are signs that the pressure of sudden, dizzying fame is having an unravelling effect. In Memphis, towards the end of the first of probably too many tours, Chrissie, drunk, gets into an argument with Darrell Sandstrom, manager of a club called TGI Fridays. She takes a swing at his head with a chair. The cops are called, arrest her and throw her into the back of a squad car. She kicks out two of the car's windows, spends the night in the cells.

In New York, not much later, by all accounts even drunker, she gets up on stage with Johnny Thunders' Heartbreakers. She grabs Johnny's microphone, tells the audience they're 'Qualuuded-out-hippies – stupid assholes who wouldn't know a good rock band if you saw one. I'm glad that now I'm a rich rock star, I don't have to put up with people like you.'

She spends the next set face down on the stage, occasionally getting up to throw beer bottles at the crowd. It's an ominous portent of darker things to come for the band, the beginning of the end for the original line-up. Within a couple of years, two of them are dead.

'We were a great rock'n'roll band,' Chrissie says, looking back, ruefully, painfully. 'And we loved rock'n'roll. But in the end, it was rock'n'roll that killed us. Dave Hill was real smart,' she says of the band's former manager. 'He got us over to America and we toured our asses off over there. Obviously, it burned the band out and killed us in the end. But we did those tours and you documented at least one of them, so you know what it was like.'

San Francisco, September 1981, *Pretenders II* just out and screaming up the charts, the band in town for two shows at The Warfield
Theatre, the opening dates of another long US tour. Backstage, on
the first night, everyone seems on edge, tantrums in the air. Chrissie's
locked in her dressing room, refusing to see anyone. Dave Hill's trying to keep things cool. Pete Farndon wanders around, dressed as a
samurai, his stage gear for the tour. Jimmy's already half in the bag,
on his way to being very drunk.

The corridors back here are full of people who seem to have nothing much to do with the band, milling about, bumping into things,
generally getting in the way. Most of them appear to be drug dealers.
Everyone's high. There's cocaine everywhere.

'Well, that was the thing,' Chrissie says. It's all coming back to her
now. 'Those assholes could always use cocaine as a calling card to
get backstage. I hated them for that. It pissed me off big time. But
Jimmy and Pete, they couldn't get enough of that shit. I didn't mind
the drugs. I just minded the assholes. I hated people using drugs as a
way of getting close to the band. I never liked that. I always went off
on my own. But, yeah, there were a lot of drugs. Like I said, Jimmy
was a bit of a speed freak – cocaine was too expensive for us when we
started. And there was always that smack element hanging around.

'When Johnny Thunders and The Heartbreakers came over to
London, smack really became the cool thing. Pete was absolutely mesmerised by Johnny Thunders. When Johnny Thunders left a blood-
stained tea towel in Pete's kitchen, that to Pete was like an example
of rock'n'roll genius. The writing was on the wall from then on, I'm
afraid.

'I mean, everyone, you know, dabbled. Me, I was always a dabbler.
But I never let anything get a grip on me. My complete focus was on
the music. But, you know, when I look back on it – hey! These were
just guys from Hereford. They didn't know what hit them. Like you
say, it was probably too much too soon for them. But for me – I'd
been crawling in the gutter for years. It wasn't too soon for me at
all. But, shit. They'd never even been to America. And when they got
there, there's limos and stuff, crazy parties. Of course, they thought it
was the greatest.'

Back to San Francisco. There's a party at the band's hotel after the
second Warfield show. Chrissie's been in surprisingly high spirits on

the drive back from the gig, but her mood soon changes. We're standing in the hotel lobby when Chrissie's called over to join a heated conversation Pretenders tour manager Stan Tippins has been having with Pete Farndon. In a radio interview that afternoon, Pete's apparently mentioned the party and invited any local bikers or biker gangs who happen to be listening to pop along if they fancy a jolly-up.

Stan's just heard that a convoy of riders from the Oakland Chapter of the California Hells Angels is even now on its way to the hotel in a synchronised Harley-Davidson roar. Chrissie's furious.

'The fucking Hells Angels. Pete?' she says, seething. 'Are you out of your fucking mind?'

'They'll be cool,' Pete tells her, sounding not entirely confident in his own prediction.

'Fuck, Pete,' Chrissie says. 'Did you ever hear of fucking Altamont?'

She stands there, glaring at Pete, who shifts uneasily under her merciless gaze.

'You invited them, you fucking take care of them,' she tells Pete, before storming off in an enormous strop.

The Hells Angels duly arrive, seven of them, swaggering into the hotel, mostly fiercely bearded, wild-haired, burly men with more leather between them than a tannery or Lemmy's wardrobe. I scan their ranks for anyone familiar from *Gimme Shelter*, but no one seems to be wearing an animal's head as a hat. They're a tough-looking crew, though, led apparently by a bald little dude in a beret, an earring and motorcycle gauntlets shoved through the epaulettes of his leather jacket. His name's Paladin, according to Stan. He gives us a little wave from across the lobby.

Pete suddenly wants nothing to do with them.

'Take this,' Pete says, handing me a plastic bag he pulls from the inside of his coat like a conjuror producing doves from an enveloping cape. The plastic bag's full of cocaine. 'Make sure they're sorted,' Pete tells me, nodding towards Paladin and his people. 'Have as much as you like, just keep that lot happy.'

Which is how I find myself, not much later, sequestered in a downstairs toilet cubicle, a queue of Hells Angels outside, waiting in turn for a toot or two of the ferociously good cocaine Pete's given me to vibe them up. They come in, one at a time, a succession of very large, tattooed men with crushing, soul-brother handshakes and their own rolled-up dollar bills. Sticklers for cocaine etiquette, the Angels insist that I help myself to a line, sometimes two, before they tuck in themselves. There's a lot of hooting and hollering when the beak hits the spot, much thunderous backslapping that leaves me first breathless then bruised. They seem on the whole a friendly lot. A couple of them actually tip me! I feel like I'm on my way to becoming a cartel kingpin. Say hello to my little friend, and all that. Paladin's the last one in.

'Hit me again,' he says, a couple of toots already making him kind of visibly tingle.

'See you later, kid,' he says, squeezing out of the cubicle even as a big chap with a wild look and a pirate's grin pushes his way in.

'You Pete's buddy?' he asks. Is Farndon upstairs, selling fucking tickets for the show down here? I get the bag of coke back out.

'After you,' the feller says, something distantly familiar about him. I'm banging out a couple of lines when I realise with a bit of a whoop that the hulking chap here is Commander fucking Cody, of Lost Planet Airmen fame! I make them big ones. We then have a couple more, for no better reason than he's Commander Cody, and a couple after that. By the time we make it back to the party, we're holding onto each other like we're on a plane about to go down in flames or a couple of sailors on shore leave rolling down the Reeperbahn. The Commander's telling me something, but I can hear only the whooshing noise in my head and he's not making much sense, anyway, so we end up cackling like the witches in *Macbeth* about nothing at all. What a bloke! What drugs!

We run into Pete and Jimmy who are well on their own way to being truly ripped. Sheehan appears from somewhere, lines us up like Can-Can girls and nearly blinds me when his flash goes off like a solar death ray. Pete and Jimmy wander off with Commander Cody, to mug it up for Tom's camera.

I now find myself in a corner of the bar with Paladin, capo of the visiting Hells Angels, who's completely off his tits. Even in my own spectacular disorientation, it's clear Paladin doesn't have both oars in the water. No matter, we're soon deep in conversation, even as the drinks keep coming and the cocaine runs amok in our systems. Paladin has some possibly homegrown theories about what he calls static mobility and dynamic mobility that he's keen to share, a noticeable lisp or something making him sound like he's talking in excitable bursts of static. I turn on my tape recorder, tell him to talk into it.

'Shince my words're being recorded for poshterity', he says, in what turns out to be a barely decipherable speed-slur, 'it putsh a sher-tain shtatus on 'em. But, as I continue to shpeak, thish is an example of dynamism. I'll give you two real exshamples of shtatic vershus dynamic mobility.

'Now,' Paladin goes on, an arm around my shoulder. 'In aynshient times, the pyramidsh of Egypt were a clashic exshample of shtatic mobility. A pyramid, it stands there forever. It moves through hishtiry, but you have to go to Egypt to shee one. Dig what I'm shaying.'

I do. I do.

'But,' Paladin announces with a flourish. 'The VIKINGS, the fuckin' Vikings, man, with the dynamic mobility of their longshipsh, they'd row up to your fuckin' front door, man, and rip you off for your sheep and your gold and your women and kill all your priests of the foul Christian religion. You diggin' this, man?'

I am. I am. Amen!

'And in modern timesh,' Paladin roars on. 'The car is perfectly shtatic when itsh standing shtill. But a motorcycle will tip over until it gets up a good head of shteam and it starts BOOOOGIENG down the highway.'

He pauses, sermon, or whatever it is, delivered.

'And thatsh all,' he says, giving the bar in front of him a hearty slap, 'and I mean ALL I've got to shay on THAT! I'll just leave it on the table for you think about it.'

Paladin makes a sign to the rest of his gang that it's time to go. The Hells Angels head for the exit, a few of the boys giving me a cheery wave and a couple of thumbs up as they head for their choppers, hogs, whatever. I can hear their bikes revving up and tearing away from the hotel, onto Post Street and back to their Oakland clubhouse, even as in London, 20 years later, I ask Chrissie Hynde if she ever tried to talk Pete and Jimmy into cutting back on the drugs, putting a brake on the partying?

'No,' she says. 'I didn't care what they were doing. As long as we made great records, who cared what drugs they were doing. I didn't. And I wasn't exactly Mary Poppins, myself. But things did get weird.

There was a weird vibe with Pete, especially, and it put a big strain on things.'

When did Pete's drug-taking get completely out of hand?

'On that last tour ...' she says, getting a little distant. 'Also, when I started going out with Ray Davies, that put a bad vibe on the band. There was a punch-up between Ray and Jimmy after one of the shows one night ...'

What was that about?

'You'd have to meet Ray to understand,' she says, a little wearily, as if a mere mention of Ray somehow depletes her. 'There's friction between him and anyone. Jimmy couldn't fucking stand Ray. The guys all hated Ray because Ray was driving a wedge between me and the band. Ray just didn't like me being in this band. He had his own problems.'

Did he want you to quit the group?

'He didn't say so in specific terms. He was just one of those guys who made it very hard for me. I no longer had my spontaneity and my freedom and my joie de vivre with the band. Because Ray gave me a hard time, all the time. And those guys hated him for it. Because instead of the band being the most important thing in the world to me, I had this guy who was ... well, basically abusing me and keeping me from the band and being the bandleader.

'Pete specifically didn't like me being with Ray, because I'd gone out with Pete in the very early days. When we split up, Pete would have all these girls on the coach in America. I didn't care. I just thought it was tacky. But if I was with someone, Pete would start going into toilets and shooting up and stuff.'

That time in San Francisco, the tour just a few days old, she had already seemed disillusioned, dejected. I recall us driving from Santa Barbara to Los Angeles, the band flying on ahead, Chrissie complaining about feeling trapped in what for her had become a relentless, unhappy routine.

'Remember,' she says now, 'there was a lot of travelling. We always travelled by coach, and I couldn't sleep on the coach, so there was always a lot of alcohol. And all these people wanted to meet us because we were like this new wave band from England, and I went from this skanky chick that no one wanted in their band to being like America's darling renegade. I guess I didn't know what hit me,

293

either. When you combine that with all this really intense touring, something's gotta give. Like, we'd tour for ten months at a time. Even I threw a TV or two across the room. Sometimes, you just have these psychotic episodes, because you've been travelling so long, then you're put in this tiny room and, Jesus, it gets intense. You have to learn how to deal with that stuff. And the only way you learn is from experience. And while you're getting that experience, it's burning you out. It's killing you.

'By the time we finished that second tour, after our second album, Pete was getting pretty unreasonable. We weren't communicating very well. Now, I regret that. I realise I wasn't very nice to Pete. But he was acting like a total asshole. When we came off that last tour, we took a few months off. Everyone was burned out and didn't want to see each other, that's for sure. Then I had a meeting with Jimmy and Martin – and Martin will back me up on this, it's not just how I remember it – and I kinda wanted to give Pete a second chance. But we all knew we couldn't work with him anymore. He'd become impossible to work with. He'd degenerated badly.

'At that meeting, Jimmy said, "Look, if Pete's in, I'm out." Jimmy didn't care that Pete Farndon got him in the band, or that they were both from Hereford or that Pete had gone out with his sister. Jimmy just cared about the music and when Pete started making the music unworkable, he wanted Pete out. Jimmy was ruthless that way. He wasn't gonna let anyone fuck up the music for him. In that respect, Jimmy was hard – but only in that respect. Anyway, the bottom line was that Jimmy was simply not gonna work with Pete again. He couldn't. Pete was just a junkie. That's all. And it was cowardly and shitty the way we fired him. We didn't even meet with Pete. Everybody was too disgusted with him. Dave Hill called Pete on the phone and just said, "You're out." And I sat in my little flat in Maida Vale and waited for the phone to ring and sure enough Pete called me, and he was in tears, saying, "What's going on?" And I said, "Well, that's it. We can't work with you." Pete was devastated. I never spoke to him again.'

And he really couldn't see it coming?

'No. He was a junkie. All he could see was this junkie lifestyle. And he and I – to be honest about it – we were ex-lovers and now there was an animosity between us. I was clearly the leader of the band.

I wrote the songs. He resented that, and he didn't like it when I went out with other people. He didn't like it when I was with Ray Davies. And I was mean to him, because he was acting like a tough guy. But he wasn't a tough guy. He was just like a kid. I can be a not very nice person. I wouldn't want to be on the end of my ill will. But Pete was. But it wasn't just something between me and him. None of the guys in the band wanted to work with Pete. He'd become extremely belligerent.

'One of the last dates we ever played was in Australia. There was an old man at the side of the stage, one of the janitors. When we went back on for the encore, Pete, as usual, lit up a fag and had it dangling out of his mouth, looking really stoned, putting on this real junkie pose. And this old man told Pete he couldn't take a cigarette out on stage and Pete just punched the guy.

'I think that was really it for all of us. We just couldn't deal with this guy. Not even Jimmy – who was just the most irreverent guy you ever met in your life, as you know. You couldn't work in Germany with Jimmy, for a start. He'd be goose-stepping all over the place doing Nazi salutes. Jimmy could be an absolute fucking riot. But at the same time, there was something about Jimmy that made him a sad character. He wasn't very healthy. He was a burned-out speed freak when I met him. But I still didn't see the writing on the wall with Jimmy.'

Her mood is quietly ominous now, recalling what happened in the aftermath of Pete's sacking.

'Two days after we fired Pete,' she says, 'Jimmy went out to this benefit. I think it was at The Venue in Victoria, for Ronnie Lane. And in the morning, he was dead on some girl's sofa. One day I'm in the greatest little band in the world, and like three days later it's just me and the drummer. Dave Hill called me in the morning, and he said, "I've got some very strange news. Jimmy died." And that was it. Martin went over to this girl's house and walked in and saw Jimmy on the sofa and that was the end of The Pretenders, really.

'But in a way,' she says, wondering how to put this, 'in a way, I couldn't let it end there. Because I didn't want it to be Jimmy's fault. I loved Jimmy so much and he was my musical right hand. I knew the last thing Jimmy would have wanted would've been for the music to stop. Because he really was The Pretenders' sound. That's why I refused to go solo. Because The Pretenders wasn't my sound. I don't sound like that. When I met him, I was this not very melodic, punky, angry guitar player and singer and Jimmy was the melodic one. He brought out all the melody in me. He was what even Ray called "the hook man". He had all these great guitar hooks. Jimmy was really the musical one, not me. And I realised I couldn't let the music die. Jimmy wouldn't have wanted that. I mean, he fucked up and died, but he didn't want the music to die. That's why I kept the thing together.'

She remembers the day they buried Jimmy. Beach Boys music playing in the church. A sky full of rain. Pete Farndon staring at her, still bitter at his sacking.

'I felt terrible about the thing with Pete,' she says. 'But he was in bad shape. He was really not someone you could work with. What do you do with someone who's a junkie, you know? No one wins. Everyone suffers. And the last time I saw him was at Jimmy's funeral. He just looked at me from across the church and I know what he was saying to me. He was going, "If I'm so fucked up, how come I'm not in that box."'

The irony being, of course, that less than a year later, on 14 April 1983, Pete ends up in his own box, found dead in the bath after shooting up a mixture of heroin and cocaine lethal enough on its own to have killed him, if he hadn't passed out first and drowned.

'Dave Hill called,' Chrissie Hynde remembers. 'He just said, "Farndon." One word. I knew straight away. Pete was dead.'

ROBERT PLANT

The Green Man Festival, Wales | Birmingham, August 2007

When a trip to Spain to see him play at a festival in Alicante falls through at the last moment, Robert Plant summons me down to the Green Man Festival in the Brecon Beacons. He's by now made it a condition of talking to me about his new album that I see him with his band, Strange Sensation, although they are not on the new album, and he won't be playing anything from it. The Green Man festival is the last date on their recent tour. He expects me to be there. I pass on a message to say that I'll be on holiday that weekend, spending time with some friends who're flying in from San Francisco to see the Stones at the O2 Arena.

Plant, clearly used to people doing his unquestioned bidding, replies by telling me he's sending a car that will take us down to Wales to see him headline the festival with Strange Sensation and bring us straight back to London. How can we now refuse?

So that Saturday night, you find us trudging through a veritable sea of mud towards what passes for the backstage area of the Green Man festival site, where Plant will later meet us. It's a forlorn place, a few people milling about, shoulders hunched in the persistent drizzle, a row of connected tents, flimsy flapping things. I think I can hear Richmond Fontaine on the main stage.

My friend Leslie and her daughter Lola are wet and cold, so I poke my head inside one of the tents and someone asks me if I'm part of what he calls 'Planty's crew'. I tell him we are. He invites us inside.

'Is this Robert's dressing room?' Leslie asks, sounding vaguely dismayed, as if she's stumbled upon some old friend, fallen upon hard times. She looks around the tent's bleak interior, which is evidence, as she might see it, of the reduced circumstances of the former rock'n'roll Sun King. There's not much to look at – a trestle table, a fridge full of ale and cider, a few plastic chairs, rough matting. How, Les might be wondering, did Plant go from Zeppelin's annihilating roar to this dismal circumstance?

There's a bit of a commotion about now, when an SUV lurches into the backstage area, wheels churning through the mud. Plant fairly bounds out of the front seat almost before the vehicle's come to a stop, clearly fit at 59, hair a messy tangle, bewhiskered, a jacket on against the cold, khaki shorts that can't be keeping his legs below the knee at all warm, the chill from the mud we're standing in beginning to bite to the bone.

We're introduced and in turn I introduce him to Les and Lola. As soon as he hears they're from San Francisco, he descends upon them with all his shaggy charisma and is soon regaling them with tales of bygone days, about festivals he played when he first went to America with Led Zeppelin – 'a group I used to be in' – when they shared bills with, for instance, Janis Joplin, about whose legendary drinking he's now telling Les and Lola.

'They were the Dancing Days,' he's telling them. 'Fantastic times. Fantastic.'

He's talking to me, I now realise.

'Have you heard the new album?' he asks, which I have. *Raising Sand*, a brilliant excursion into the fantastic heart of Americana, recorded with Grammy-winning bluegrass singer and fiddle player Alison Krauss and producer T Bone Burnett, is the reason I'm here.

'Incredible, isn't it?' he goes on, and it is. It's also the last thing I'd have expected after all those years with Led Zeppelin, squawking like something in a rain forest. It goes without saying, I think it's the best thing he's done, certainly in the nigh-on 30 years since Zeppelin disbanded, following first the death of his son Karac and then the passing of John Bonham.

'It's like nothing I've ever done,' he says of the album, on which he and Krauss cover songs by, among others, Gene Clark, Tom Waits, Townes Van Zandt, The Everly Brothers, Doc Watson, Mel Tillis and Little Milton.

'I wasn't even sure I could do it, you know. Neither was Alison. It was a step into the unknown for both of us. I remember when we came to do that track "Rich Woman", Alison took me aside and said, "I can't sing this, I'm too white." And I said, "Listen, baby, I've been fucking white all the way through, and I've been groaning nonstop. Just groan, baby." So, we groaned, and she got it. We both went to a new place with this record. I can't tell you how proud of it I am – that we actually pulled it off, you know.'

The rain's falling again, and he's asked to give his attention to tonight's setlist, someone who turns out to be Justin Adams, his long-serving guitarist and musical collaborator, holding out a flapping sheet of foolscap for Plant's attention.

'No,' he says of the song list he's reading, making some scribbled changes. 'We should maybe start with "Friends", what do you think?'

It's time for him to go, so I wish him a good gig and hopefully a dry one.

'Thanks,' he says. 'I have it from a higher authority that it won't rain. I spoke to the Dark Lord earlier.'

The Dark Lord? He must mean Jimmy Page, surely. Has he just spoken to Jimmy? Current rumours about an imminent Led Zeppelin reunion are, as they say, rife. There may be a scoop in the offing here.

'Jimmy?' he laughs. 'No. I wasn't talking to Jimmy.'

Turns out, he's referring to a conversation he's apparently had with an even more abstract and elemental force than the former Zep guitarist. Evidently some kind of satanic weatherman with whispered forecasts. It's all turning a bit *Excalibur*, frankly.

'The Dark Lord,' Plant says now, head back, taking in the turbulent heavens above, the cosmos beyond, whatever's out there. 'He promised me: no rain, baby.'

We're standing beneath a starless, Bible-black sky. It's too dark for me to see what I hope is a mischievous twinkle in his eye or a light smirking smile on his lips, and now he's walking away, things to do before he plays.

The rain, meanwhile, yeah, it appears to be easing off.

A few days later, I'm standing outside the Hyatt Hotel in Birmingham, waiting for Plant, who duly arrives behind the wheel of a very smart

Mercedes, his 16-year-old son Jesse in tow. Plant gets out of the car, a cheery handshake for the hotel staff, all of whom he seems to know by name, moving among them like a much-loved mob guy. Popular with everyone, dropping in at a favourite place.

He walks over to where I'm standing, introduces me to Jesse. I tell him I'd met Jesse the previous Saturday at the Green Man festival, where we talked about his band, Aura, for whom he plays drums. Jesse's friend Dave, Aura's lead singer, had given me the group's business card.

'Well played, Dave,' Plant says, laughing heartily. 'Actually, you should hear some of their stuff. It's amazing. I've got a CD in the car.'

He leads me across the hotel parking lot to his gleaming Merc. We get in the car, and I settle back in the front seat. To which I am quickly pinned when Plant turns on a CD player that turns out to be probably more powerful than the sound system Led Zeppelin used when they last played Madison Square Garden. It's heavy stuff. Plant beams, the proud father, as it blasts out, deafeningly, from the speakers.

Walking back towards the hotel, Plant asks me if I have any music business contacts that I could put Aura in touch with. This makes me look at him somewhat askance, amazed that he thinks I know more influential people than he does, and then watch him disappear into the hotel bar.

I ask Jesse if his dad gives him a lot of advice, invaluable musical tips and the like.

'Not really,' Jesse says. 'He's not a bad singer. But he's a terrible drummer.'

We find a table in the bar, where Plant talks at length, illuminatingly, about the record. Before we finish the interview, though, there's something else I need to bring up, which he might be touchy about.

Namely, what's currently happening with Led Zeppelin.

Zeppelin played their last show in what was then still West Berlin, on 7 July 1980. Since then, the bellowing yell for the surviving members to get back together has grown nothing but louder, with often unimaginably vast sums being offered to them for a reunion tour, which they have so far fiercely resisted. Plant's reluctance to entertain the notion of a full-scale reunion has been especially conspicuous, the singer preferring at one point touring Welsh pubs with Priory of Brion to going on another world tour with Page, and then famously refusing to turn up at the 2005 Grammys in Los Angeles, where Led Zeppelin were given a Lifetime Achievement Award. The occasions to date when the band has played together are events he looks back on unhappily.

When we meet, the din of rumour about a reunion show this year – maybe around the release of the *Mothership* two-CD Zep best of on 11 November – is becoming deafening. Plant's notoriously fractious perspective on Zeppelin and what by the time they finally split they'd become – 'the psychosis of Led Zeppelin', as he puts it – and the intransigence that has so often infuriated and frustrated Jimmy Page, makes me think he'll be grimly tight-lipped on the topic of the reunion. The use of seriously unpleasant interrogative techniques, it strikes me, may be the only way to get a word out of him on the subject. In fact, he comes quickly to the point.

'There'll be one show,' he says, confirming an appearance by Led Zeppelin, with Jason Bonham replacing his father on drums, at the O2 Arena on 21 November, a benefit for a charity founded by Ahmet Ertegun, who looms large in Zep mythology as label boss of Atlantic Records.

'Ahmet was a friend and sidekick,' Plant says. 'He was yet another member of the Zeppelin entourage who came to us to fulfil his dreams of craziness or whatever. He was doing that as well with John Coltrane and Ray Charles, you know, which is even more amazing. He was a fucking incredible character and personality, with great wit and humour. They were great people, Ahmet and his widow, Mica. When she approached me, I told her I'd do anything for her, for Ahmet.'

And will the O2 show be followed by a full-on 2008 reunion tour?

'No, absolutely not,' he says, shaking his head and stroking his beard for emphasis, and a bit of a silence follows. 'There'll be one show, and that'll be it. We need,' he goes on, 'to do one last great show. Because we've done some shows, and they've been crap.'

But if the show goes spectacularly well, and the thrill of playing again as Zeppelin returns, won't there be a temptation to go back out for a worldwide last hurrah?

'Not for me,' he says. 'I can't speak for anyone else.'

Don't you look at, say, The Who or the Stones, bands you used to be in competition with to be the biggest band in the world, and think you could reform and go out there and possibly blow them away?

'We weren't in competition with anybody,' Plant says, and there's a flash of insolent haughtiness in his reply. 'We were Led Zeppelin. We were at that time the biggest band in the world. There wasn't anyone else. There was no one near us. We were out there on our own. And blowing everybody away isn't the issue anymore. Blowing myself away is the issue. That's what it's all about now.

'If you think about it, what I'm doing now is hearty and in its own way and in its own declension it's soulful and if it was anything else, I'd be redundant. I'd be on the pile. I'd have to be following the same tour schedule as The Rolling Stones, in some sort of incubator.'

What do you think of the Stones and The Who, touring endlessly into their dotage?

'They're doing what they're doing,' he says, not altogether approvingly. 'It keeps them off the streets, I suppose. Actually, I just heard a very plummy Radio 4 news bulletin before I met you that said the local council who govern the O2 Arena area didn't receive any complaints as two members of The Rolling Stones smoked onstage last night. And I went, "Fucking hell, so they stood up for two hours and smoked." I don't know. You put so many people together at that age and it threatens to turn into a comedy show – a cocoon on ice, or "Stairway to Heaven on Broadway".'

I wonder if he merely felt too old for a lot of cock rock squawking, and he laughs.

'That's not really it,' he says. 'I know I'm getting on and I do come back from touring, and I'm shocked to find a lot of my mates tend to be going to bed far too early and that means I should probably be doing the same. Maybe I should stop having a good time and get old.

'But there's no chance of that quite yet. I'll carry on until I just implode, which I will one day. Until then, I'll just keep going. There's really not that many things I want to do that I can't because of my gathering years. I play soccer every Boxing Day in the local village, and everybody laughs when you fall over, because it takes so long to get back up, but there are other parts of my life that I find have way improved and I don't feel threatened or impaired.

'The simple fact is that when I lost my son, when Karac left us, I really changed. I mean, there's nothing on the planet to equal that kind of grief ... it still makes me shudder,' he says. 'No matter how good you are or how capable you are or how strong you are or how well-intentioned you are, you don't get over anything like that. And from then on, I found the juggernaut lifestyle I went through with Zeppelin had to be modified and that's what I've done. And there are some places and situations I just won't go back to.'

Where, for instance?

'The very places I was playing with Jimmy when we got back together, with the Egyptians,' he says, referring to the 1995 tour he did with Page and a 16-piece Egyptian orchestra. 'We had the music, and we had the aura, but because of the ticket demand and because we had this production where if you want to make it work you've got to play to at least 15,000 people a night, you end up playing some grubby faceless basketball arena in Mannheim, Germany, and it just doesn't go with the music. I very quickly on that tour began to resent having to play those places and I don't want to go back to them, simple as that. My life has taken me in a different direction.'

I mention to Plant that in 1977, not long before 'God Save the Queen' comes out, I spend an eventful afternoon with The Sex Pistols, during which Johnny Rotten, as he then was, launches into a windy rant, Zeppelin in his demonology responsible for most of the world's woes with Plant especially singled-out as a target of his sneering wrath. Plant's amused that 30 years later, he's making some of the best music of his career while Johnny's living in acidic exile and is most recently famous for gurning on reality TV.

'He was very vicious about us,' Plant says. 'He said he hated us. But he took his chance, he did the right thing. I don't blame him at all. The irony is, a few years later when he was in Public Image, he contacted me for the lyrics of "Kashmir" and I wrote them for him on the back of a breakfast menu from a Holiday Inn somewhere.

'That was an odd time,' he goes on. 'We'd been endlessly lauded and adored and suddenly there were all these kids who wanted us gone, who wanted to get away from Floyd and Zep and groups like us. And who could blame them? I wanted to, as well. So did Pagey. So did all of us.'

There are people signalling to me across the Hyatt bar that time's just about up, Plant needing to get on with the rest of his day.

'It's strange, really,' he says, offering his final few thoughts on Zeppelin and their history. 'It's like going into a room that's quite dusty and the afternoon light is in that room and there's a door that opens now and again and you walk through it and look around and there's all that work from that time standing there proudly and you know it's been repositioned to retain something, to say, "Hey, don't forget – this is great." And that's my vision of the whole Led Zeppelin thing: don't forget it, because it was great and remember the imagination that went into those songs and how natural the process was.

'It may have been chemically induced at times, later on especially. But it was still very, very, very good. Actually, it's an outstanding collection of stuff, the Zeppelin repertoire. But now I suppose we really are more like curators than creators. I was 32 when Zeppelin died, nearly half a lifetime ago.'

Was that a fearful moment for you, did you think you'd spend the rest of your life regretting the band's passing?

'No. I simply changed the locks on the doors of my heart. I was gone. It was a brilliant time, and we made some brilliant music. But when it was over, it was over. My view now is that the past should look after itself.

'I go on, undaunted.'

JOHN CALE

Los Angeles, December 2009

Someone mentions it's coming up to 45 years since John Cale met Lou Reed, surely an opportunity for an *Uncut* cover story on The Velvet Underground. Cale agrees to an interview. I call him in Los Angeles, where he's just finished a long night in the studio.

'*Sut dach chi*, Allan,' he says, a familiar Welsh greeting. 'What's on the agenda today?'

The Velvet Underground, I remind him. The whole story this time, from the beginning, not scraps, anecdotes, disconnected flashbacks. Imagine it's your last chance to give a full account of the band, something like that, I suggest. He laughs at this.

'A full confession,' he says. 'That's an interesting proposition. Let's give it a go,' he decides, and for the next two and a half hours I'm often a mute witness to his elaborate testimony, a light hand on the conversational tiller keeping Cale on course as he navigates an extraordinary history.

Their dark alliance begins in November 1964 and starts like this.

'Lou was still under care at the time, working as a hack songwriter for Pickwick Records in Long Island City and living at home with his parents who kept a close eye on him. They'd already put him through this terrible barbarism when they committed him to the state mental institution for electric shock therapy when he was in high school, to "cure" his homosexuality. So, he was still very fragile. But there was also a lot of playfulness. Albeit playfulness on a razor's edge.'

Cale is talking about the first time he met Lou Reed, with whom he shortly forms The Velvet Underground, named after the title of a

305

racy paperback discovered appropriately in a New York gutter by a friend of Cale's. The Velvets go on to take rock'n'roll to places it had never been before, along the way changing it forever. Nothing after them is the same.

'They are not the reason rock'n'roll exists,' Richard Williams, who in the pages of *Melody Maker* is one of their earliest UK champions, writes years later of their influence. 'But you could call them the reason it sounds the way it does and not get laughed at.'

Cale at the time is 22, a classically trained musical prodigy, originally from Garnant in South Wales. He's been in America for just over a year and recently completed a postgraduate course in Modern Composition at the Berkshire Music Center in Tanglewood, Massachusetts, to which he had won a Leonard Bernstein scholarship. At Tanglewood, as Cale discovers, anything goes unless it goes too far. Which in Cale's case it does. The faculty flees his last performance there when he starts laying about him with a hatchet.

Now, he's deeply embedded in the avant-garde scene of New York's Lower East Side, a community of experimental musicians, out-there composers, poets, pranksters, performance artists and filmmakers. He's a member principally of La Monte Young's fearsomely experimental Theatre of Eternal Dreams, and its offshoot The Dream Syndicate. Young is the radical composer of testing pieces that explore the possibilities of drones and repetition. In performance, they are prone to sustain single notes for up to two hours at a time. On at least one occasion, La Monte's performance consists of not much more than screaming at a plant until it dies.

'No one had heard anything like it,' Cale says, with some understatement. 'No one else in the world was doing anything like it.'

Cale's living at the time in an apartment at 56 Ludlow Street with Tony Conrad, who also plays with La Monte. They're invited by a mutual friend to a party where they meet someone who's looking for a band, to back a young singer he knows who's recorded a song called 'The Ostrich', which looks like it may be a hit. There's a TV show coming up, live dates maybe to follow.

'He said, this guy, "You are musicians. You've got a crazy beatnik look, why don't you be the band?" The song was just a cash-in, but what really impressed me was that it had been written by tuning all six strings of the guitar to one note. I thought, "What the hell's going on here?" We went out there the next day, I think, to Pickwick. That's when I first met Lou.'

Lou Reed, also 22, is a graduate of Syracuse University, where he's studied English Literature and been befriended by the poet Delmore Schwartz, a lifelong influence, sold drugs and hosted a late-night radio show called *On a Wobbly Rail*, named after a song by jazz pianist Cecil Taylor. Lou loves early rock'n'roll, doo wop, R&B and free jazz. He's been a staff writer at Pickwick since September.

'We hit it off straight away,' Cale says. 'We started talking about literature and what was the riskiest kind of writing available. What prose most gave off the stink of threat. Lou said, "You've got to read Hubert Selby Jr's *Last Exit to Brooklyn*." We went roaring off into the sunset together.

'Anyway, we did the TV show as The Primitives. We even did a few gigs. There was Lou, me, Tony Conrad and a friend of ours, Walter De Maria, a sculptor who also happened to play drums. It was obvious nothing was really going to come out of what we were doing, and Pickwick weren't really interested in the songs Lou was writing. He already had "I'm Waiting for the Man" and "Heroin". But Pickwick were only interested in these crazy pop songs, cash-in stuff. Actually, one of the first things I remember at Pickwick was Lou shoving these lyrics in my face, but I wasn't interested.

'He'd play them to me on an acoustic guitar and it sounded like folk music. They were like Joan Baez songs. I hated folk music, so I was very sceptical. But when he sat me down and read me the lyrics, I realised how well-crafted these songs were. I was caught up in their rhythms and what they were about. I was flabbergasted. I'd never heard anything like them. They seemed a long way from "Be-Bop-A-Lula".

'I began to think there was an opportunity here to do something that was different to everything else that was going on. I thought if we combined Lou's literary side and my classical training and what I'd been doing with La Monte with the excitement of rock'n'roll and put the furthest reaches of these propositions together, it would take us where no one else had been and no one else was going.

'La Monte had this piece, "Draw a Straight Line and Follow It", which was designed to find out if the universe is finite or infinite. If the universe is curved, you come back to where you started, because space is finite. If it's infinite, you'll never come back. I thought that would be an interesting place to be.

'I kept thinking of Bob Dylan writing these 15- or 16-verse songs, and I thought, "We can do that. But let's bring in some of the stuff I've been exploring with La Monte, the drones and repetition. That's where we'll be different. We'll do these songs and never repeat the same thing twice." Never repeating the same thing twice was really important. I mean, for an avant-garde musician, the idea that you would play the same piece exactly the same every time you played it was not where it was at. You had to do something different every time. Establish a new performance with every performance.'

And Lou bought into this?

'He was wary at first,' Cale says. 'And I don't think he understood the intellectual tradition these ideas came from. But he was as ambitious as me. Here we were at 21 or 22 with the chance of going at these ideas with an absolute vengeance. I was hell-bent on doing something that had never been done before. So was Lou. We wanted to be the best band in the world. Did we want to take things further than The Beatles? Certainly. Did we want to take things further than Bob Dylan? Absolutely. And we did.'

When Tony Conrad moves out of 56 Ludlow Street, Lou moves in. What he and Lou find out they have in common, beyond music: a hunger for sex, although Cale resists Lou's advances, and also a taste for hard drugs, principally amphetamines and heroin. Cale is squeamish about needles, so Lou shoots him up. How important were drugs to their relationship?

'They killed some of the boredom and got us focused on the music,' he says. 'I mean, I was always focused on the music, but I thought they definitely helped creatively, too. Unfortunately, I still thought they helped about 20 years later, until I lost my sense of humour and thought, "To hell with this. It's time to sober up."'

How would the VU's music have sounded without drugs?

'It's difficult to say. All they did, really, was break the ice. We had a good time. That was part of it all, too. It was a great experiment. I don't know that the music got any better after drinking or taking hypnotics or whatever. On the road, later, it became very destructive. Everything suffered, then. There was just too much of it.'

There are only two of them for the moment, but as far as they're concerned, they are a band and therefore need a name. They call themselves The Falling Spikes. Cale's seeing a woman named Elektrah at the time. She briefly joins them on guitar, which instrument she strums until her fingers bleed. Even by their standards, she's deemed unstable, and she's soon gone.

They're looking for another guitarist when by chance they run into Sterling Morrison, who Lou had known at Syracuse. Sterling is studying English Literature at City College. He also plays guitar, likes the same music as Lou, who wants him in the band. Cale isn't so sure.

'He had such a chip on his shoulder, I didn't know what his problem was,' Cale says. 'I kept saying to Lou, "I don't know what's wrong with Sterling." He had this real edge to him. We met him on the subway. This derelict came up to Lou and he's going, "Hi, Lou. How are you doing, man?" He had this beard, no shoes. I sort of stepped back, you know, like, "Who is this and how does he know Lou?" It turned out to be Sterling.

'Slowly, we got to know each other and the more you heard his guitar playing, you realised there was a thinking brain at work. I think I didn't hit it off with him originally because he was so fiercely irascible and would continue to be so. It was one of the things I liked so much about him, eventually. But at first, I just kept saying to Lou, "What's wrong with him? What's his problem?" And Lou said, "You've got to remember, Sterling is an orphan. He's been an orphan all his life. He doesn't have anyone. He's never had anyone." I thought, "OK, I'll keep out of his way and see how things go." He turned out to be a great guitarist.'

Quickly rechristened The Warlocks, they're joined for rehearsals at Ludlow Street by drummer Angus MacLise, another Dream Syndicate veteran. Their basic repertoire starts to take shape, and in July they demo six songs, four of which will be re-recorded for their debut album, including 'Heroin', 'I'm Waiting for the Man', 'Venus in Furs' and 'All Tomorrow's Parties'. Through the summer, they play occasionally at the Film-Makers' Cinematheque, where from behind a gauze curtain, they improvise soundtracks to underground movies, including Barbara Rubin's *Christmas on Earth*. Rubin is well connected on the Manhattan arts scene. She's appeared in Andy Warhol's *Kiss*, introduced Dylan to Allen Ginsberg. More crucially to the band who have by now become The Velvet Underground, she knows the influential music writer Al Aronowitz.

Aronowitz is famous for introducing Dylan to The Beatles in 1964 and currently fancies himself as a rock manager with a New Jersey group called The Myddle Class. Rubin persuades him to check out the nascent VU at one of their soundtrack gigs. He takes his friend Robbie Robertson with him. Robbie walks out after the first number. Aronowitz stays and after meeting the band offers them a gig, opening for The Myddle Class at Summit High School in New Jersey, at which point MacLise inconveniently quits.

They need a new drummer, fast. Lou and Sterling remember that a friend of theirs from Syracuse, Tony Tucker, has a sister, Maureen, who plays drums. Lou decides to get in touch. Moe's a big fan of Bo Diddley, the Stones, her playing inspired by the album *Drums of Passion* by the Nigerian percussionist Babatunde Olatunji. The kit she has at the time cost her mother $50 and consists of one snare, a bass drum, a floor tom and a cymbal the group will declare superfluous. What she now brings to the Velvets is as crucial as anything in their musical armoury.

'I didn't want her in the band at first,' Cale admits. 'We'd had our tails whacked by Elektrah and I just didn't want another woman in the band. But she turned out to be incredible. No cymbals, brilliant. She was perfect because she understood the value of simplicity, the unadorned beat.'

The Velvet Underground as they now exist make their debut on 11 December 1965, playing to a crowd that's initially baffled and swiftly appalled, which is an audience reaction that quicky becomes typical. Did they thrive on the hostility that pursued them?

'Maybe we did,' Cale says. 'We were out there with nobody. But if we seemed sinister and nasty and unfriendly, it was mainly a form of protection. I mean, we weren't unfriendly to what fans we had.'

And what were they like, these early Velvet Underground fans?

'There was a group of girls from New Jersey,' Cale says, laughing at the memory. 'They used to show up for concerts and they'd stand huddled together in the corner with their eyes wide open, staring. When you saw the four of them together, it was like looking out at the Children of the Damned.'

Aronowitz next secures the VU a December residency at the Café Bizarre in Greenwich Village, where the stage is too small even for Moe's minimal drum kit, and they play six sets a night for $5 each. They're sacked before the end of their scheduled run, but not before Barbara Rubin persuades Gerard Malanga and Paul Morrissey, close associates of Andy Warhol, to check them out.

By coincidence, Morrissey, who acts as business manager for Warhol's studio, the fabled Factory on East 47th Street, is currently looking for a house band for a club Warhol has been invited to put his name to in Queens. He thinks The Velvet Underground might be what he needs. The next night, he's back at the club with Warhol and an entourage including Barbara Rubin, doomed socialite Edie Sedgwick and Malanga, who is very soon jiving erotically to the band's dark music.

Warhol evidently likes them well enough for Morrissey to cut a deal for Andy to become, but not in any conventional sense, their manager. In what's become a momentous month for them, The Velvet Underground are also featured on the New Year's Eve edition of CBS News, filmed at 450 Grand Street, where Cale and Reed are now living. It's for a report on underground filmmaking in New York. Cale, Lou and Sterling are bare-chested, faces smeared with make-up. Moe is there, too, in a bridal gown, along with experimental filmmaker Piero Heliczer, dressed as a priest, and his crew who are filming the Velvets, the lot of them looking like something out of a Fellini movie.

They go in what seems like an instant from Lower East Side poverty to Andy's swish universe, sucked into the world of The Factory. If New York at the time is Andy's Kingdom, The Factory is his Camelot, home to his silk-screen studios and various waifs, strays and self-styled superstars. What was it like for them, one minute starving on Ludlow Street, the next thing being whisked from party to party, glitzy premieres. Gallery openings, the world of celebrity, glamour and rampant hedonism?

'Well,' Cale laughs, 'we were still starving, but perhaps not quite so hungry. But The Factory, from the minute you got there, the great thing about it was you felt there were people who understood what you were trying to do. They got us. All of a sudden, we weren't just four people fighting everybody else. You felt you were part of what was a pretty good army. We went all over Manhattan in a swarm.

311

It was an endlessly entertaining scene to be around. Something was always happening. And what a parade of stars you saw coming through.'

Did you ever feel overawed being there?

'A little bit, yes. Until you got used to it and started to know how to deal with what was going on. I mean, there were several different layers to life at The Factory. There was the gay community, for a start. Lou understood that and enjoyed it. He threw himself into it, in fact. He had a lot of fun. Sterling and I, less so. Moe just tut-tutted a lot.'

Although the band are shocked when he first suggests it, they're enough in thrall right then to Warhol to agree to his suggestion that they add to their original line-up the startling European beauty and quintessentially 1960s scenester Nico. Brought up in wartime Germany, Nico's worked as a model, been cast in a small role by Fellini in *La Dolce Vita*, recorded a single for Andrew Loog Oldham's Immediate label, had a son with Alain Delon and affairs with Brian Jones and Bob Dylan. She's been introduced to Warhol by Gerard Malanga, and Warhol thinks she'll be perfect as a singer with the VU. Lou promptly falls in love with her, as does Cale, who has already had a brief, intense affair with Edie Sedgwick.

'I was just getting over the fact we had Moe in the band,' Cale recalls. 'Did we really need another woman? Then it struck me that this was great PR on Andy's part. She had this blonde-bombshell look. People couldn't take their eyes off her.'

In January 1966, they play their first Warhol-sponsored show, at Delmonico's, the ritzy Manhattan hotel. Andy's been invited to address the New York Society for Clinical Psychiatry. He doesn't speak. Instead, he puts on the Velvets. They play 'Heroin' to a crowd of slack-jawed shrinks. A film of a man tied to a chair, being tortured, is projected on a screen behind them. Malanga and Edie Sedgwick dance. Barbara Rubin films the audience, shouting obscenities at them as the camera rolls.

The Velvets are then stars of Warhol's Up-Tight, a series of shows at the Cinematheque, out of which choreographed lunacy grows the Exploding Plastic Inevitable, an extravaganza involving music, lights, film and dancing. They take over The Dom, a Polish dancehall in the East Village. The shows become part of their legend. Cale thinks they never played better than they did there. The great English music writer and broadcaster Charlie Gillett is a student at the time at New York's Columbia University. One night in April, he goes to The Dom, where downstairs there's a disco he's been to before. This particular night, he notices a sign advertising an event being held upstairs, somehow involving Andy Warhol and a group called The Velvet Underground that he's never heard of. He decides to take a look.

'I was virtually the first person there,' he remembers when I speak to him, only a few months before his death in March 2010. 'Two films were already being projected on the walls on either side of the stage. One of which was *Empire*, the other *Kiss*. Nothing much happens in either. A cloud moves across the sky in *Empire* and then suddenly goes back and starts over again. In the case of *Kiss*, one of the kissing faces presses harder than the other so one head moves slightly across the screen and then suddenly it flicks back and does the same thing again, indefinitely. So that's all that was happening, for quite a long time.

'After a while, at the back of the stage, another film started to be projected which was of a band playing on stage and in front of the band a woman and a man come on stage, and she lazily strokes the man with a whip. It was all very gentle. There was nothing violent about it. And there's no sound, just the pictures. After some time, a band wanders on stage, evidently the band that is shown in the film. And they shambled on stage – that would be the word – bit by bit, one by one. I've always been a bit naive in not recognising when people, obviously to everyone else, are under the influence of whatever drug it might be they're on. The whole thing about being on stage is such a responsibility that the idea anybody would do it while under the influence of drugs was just so far from my puritanical mind, I couldn't imagine such a thing.

'So, there was no particular explanation for me as to why this band was just so uncommunicative. They just played like zombies. Most startling was when the song slowed down and appeared to be about taking heroin and I didn't notice there was anything negative about it. It seemed to be pretty much an advert for taking heroin, as far as I could tell.

'I was mostly appalled, is the truth. I was not the right person to be thrilled by this thing. It just sounded amateurish and shambolic. It was extraordinary to discover later how well developed their musical skills were. And I think there was something quite deliberately perverse in them and they would have been quite happy with my befuddled reaction. It wasn't like they were trying to impress somebody like me. I never saw them again. I came back to England a week or two later. I got the album when it came out and felt some of the things about it that I felt when I saw them. Although I could hear there were tunes that hadn't been apparent in the live performance, songs that if they'd been performed as well live as they were on record, I would have understood better what was going on.

'But I really don't think they cared. I think they were all very high on whatever each of them was on. As I say, it was like watching a performance by a group of zombies. It didn't cross my mind that this was the beginning of anything. I was aware it was a big sidestep from anything I knew about. But it really was a new beginning. If people are looking for new beginnings, they're really hard to find. Normally, you can step back from something and say, "Ah, that was the precursor. That came before this." But even with all the wisdom I have now, I don't think that there was anything that was a precedent for that record. Its influence has been absolutely enormous.'

Scepter Recording Studios, West 54th Street, April 1966. This is where The Velvet Underground record the bulk of their debut album in four days, with a total recording time of ten hours at a cost of $1,500, split between Warhol and Columbia sales executive Norman Dolph, who also engineers the sessions. Warhol will eventually be credited as producer, but if that's what he is, it's in the sense of a movie producer. He's set this up, financed it, made it somehow possible. But his active involvement in the making of the record is minimal. Sometimes he's there, sometimes he's not.

'We did it quickly, yes,' Cale says of the album. 'But why should it have taken any longer? We'd been rehearsing those songs for a year and a half. We knew exactly what we wanted the record to sound like, which was how we sounded live and just as loud. The only problems we had were with the engineers, who kept telling us to turn it down, that everything was going into the red and distorting. We said, "That's how it's supposed to sound." We were never going to turn it down. They kept saying, "This won't work." To which my response was, "Make it work, or get out of our way." We only ever did things our way. We were arrogant, perhaps, in thinking we knew best. We were also right. We did know best.'

While Norman Dolph hawks around the acetate of the album to mainly uninterested, sometimes openly hostile labels, the entire Exploding Plastic Inevitable crew, including Warhol, fly to Los Angeles. It's May, 1966. They've been booked into The Trip on the Sunset Strip for two weeks. The Mothers of Invention, with whom they almost immediately fall out, open for them. In the audience on the opening night are Sonny and Cher, John Phillips and Cass Elliot, The Byrds, Ryan O'Neal and Jim Morrison, who goes on to become another of Nico's smitten lovers. The next night, the club's virtually empty. On the third, it's closed by the police following complaints that the Velvets' performance is 'pornographic'. For contractual reasons, they have to stay in LA for the duration of the original booking to collect their full fee for the cancelled shows. They hate it there.

'The West Coast was too flowery for words,' Cale says, still aghast at the memory. 'I mean, Flower Power? Fuck off. We hated the bands. We hated their music. We hated their politics. And we certainly hated the way they dressed.'

The band spend at least two days in TTG Studios with producer Tom Wilson, who's worked with Dylan and Simon & Garfunkel and wants to sign them to MGM/Verve, which he does, although he's more interested in Nico, whose solo album, *Chelsea Girl*, he subsequently produces. They re-record three songs from the New York sessions: 'I'm Waiting for the Man', 'Venus in Furs' and 'Heroin'.

Lou now rewrites the opening line of 'Heroin', which ever since they started playing it has been: '*I know where I'm going …*' Lou changes this to '*I don't know where I'm going …*' It's an amendment that excites Cale's considerable wrath.

'I thought he blew it completely,' Cale says, steam coming out of his ears a lifetime later. 'It was a good song once. The whole song was much more powerful with the original opening line, that positive statement. '*I KNOW where I'm going.*' You're committed when you say that. When he sang, '*I DON'T know where I'm going*', it was like Lou was stepping back into folk music, turning into Joan Baez again. I was furious. I just went on a rant. He said, "You'll get over it." That's something else he got wrong. I never did.'

315

March, 1967. Almost a year after it was recorded, *The Velvet Underground and Nico* is released, its belated appearance attributed variously to inept management, MGM's jitters about what they consider the record's explicit content, and the manipulative influence of Frank Zappa and his manager Herb Cohen, who successfully push for the label to release The Mothers of Invention's *Freak Out!* first. There's also the small matter of Andy's cover design, with its peel-off banana, which is hugely expensive and causes myriad manufacturing problems.

'MGM weren't really interested in us,' Cale says. 'I think they only picked us up in the first place because of Andy. They said, "We're not going to promote the record. The promotion money's going to Frank Zappa. Why do you need money? You've got money and Frank needs help." Everywhere we went, it was the same. They thought we had more money than we ever had because of Andy.'

The album is poorly reviewed, barely scrapes onto the *Billboard* chart and gets no airplay. There's a further calamity when MGM have to withdraw it from sale after Warhol superstar Eric Emerson demands payment for the use of an image of himself on the sleeve that has to be airbrushed out. Things are starting to come apart for them.

In May, they sack Nico. It's been coming for a while. When she turns up typically late for a show at the Boston Tea Party, which has become their favourite venue, they won't even let her on stage.

'At the same time, Andy was losing interest in us,' Cale remembers. 'He was getting into films. That was the new thing for him. Then he had a meeting with Lou about what was going to happen next, and Lou fired him. When Lou pulled that stunt with Andy, I couldn't believe it. The only way I can look at it is that to be prepared for success you first of all have to have a stable personality, which Lou didn't. Neither did I, to be fair. So we were never ready for success. Not that we had any,' he laughs. 'Let's not fool ourselves. What we got was a lot of publicity from our association with Andy, because of which people thought we must be successful on some level, which of course we never were.

'I'm sure it ate away at Lou that the VU was Andy's group to a lot of people who didn't really know us and thought that Andy had put the group together and was pulling the strings, which was enough in the end for Lou to sack him. I don't think Andy was much bothered.

There was more money in films for him and as soon as that door opened for Andy, he ran through it like someone was chasing him.'

September, 1967. Mayfair Sound Studios, 7th Avenue. It's nearly 18 months since The Velvet Underground were last in the studio and they are not in good shape when they get there to record their second album, *White Light/White Heat*.

'By then, we were basically uncontrollable,' Cale says. 'In some respects, we weren't even a band anymore. When Lou sacked Andy, he brought in this guy, we've talked about him before, Steve Sesnick,' Cale adds with the menacing sibilance he brought to the hissing asides on 'The Black Angel's Death Song'. 'He'd been around for a while, trying to get his foot in the door. He just manipulated things to everyone's detriment. Eventually, even Lou saw through him, but by then he'd really driven us apart.

'There was a lot of turmoil. Even by our own standards we were unstable and there were a lot of drugs. We'd been on the road, not writing so much, just coming up with things at soundchecks. I don't think we even had a rehearsal room after we left The Factory. It was very different to the first album, which we'd really prepared ourselves for. There was no one to tell us to stop all the nonsense and focus on the music. We thought we were beyond needing to be told anything.'

They've got some songs in the style of the limpid ballads that graced *The Velvet Underground and Nico*, but concentrate instead on the most volatile and poisonous things they can cook up. And so *White Light/White Heat* is the sound of the slaughterhouse, the nastiest, dirtiest, most frenzied and unhinged rock music yet made, its serial derangements still largely unequalled. The album's centrepiece is the 18-minute 'Sister Ray', a series of sordid vignettes about sex and drugs that sounds like something snatched from the pages of *Last Exit to Brooklyn* and set to the kind of music you might hear in hell, or one of its many chambers, one of those rooms guarded by a dog with two heads. The track quickly becomes a battle for supremacy between Cale's scalding Vox organ and Lou's screaming guitar, the pair of them tearing chunks out of each other in climax after climax, goading themselves to further and further extremes.

'It was carnage,' Cale says. 'We were falling apart, and we didn't even know it.'

By late September, the tensions within the band have come to a head. Even Sterling is exasperated by some of Cale's recent ideas, which apparently include the recording of their next album with their amplifiers under water. Lou calls Sterling and Moe to a meeting at the Riviera Café on Sheridan Square. He gives them an ultimatum. If the group is to go on at all, it will go on without Cale. If Cale stays, Lou says he'll break up the band right there and that will be the end of it. Sterling is dispatched to break the news to a stunned Cale.

'Typically, Lou couldn't come and tell me himself that I was out of the band,' he says in bristling retrospect. I can feel the heat of a distant simmer. 'I thought that was simply cowardly.'

The Velvet Underground continue, with Doug Yule as Cale's replacement, going on for another two years. They record two more albums, make more great music, some of it as good as anything they have done with Cale. But with his departure, their sound is changed forever. For Cale, it's an opportunity lost. There are places even further out than they've been that he wanted to take them. Nico's solo album *The Marble Index*, which he soon arranges and provides all the music for, is perhaps one of them. How in a word would he describe his relationship with Lou at the point he was sacked?

'Irretrievable,' he says, a voice booming from a distant pulpit, like one of the ministers of his youth in the Welsh valleys.

15 June 1990. Lou Reed and John Cale, who two years earlier have collaborated for the first time in 20 years on *Songs for Drella*, their requiem for Andy Warhol, have been invited to play at the opening of a Warhol exhibition at the Fondation Cartier, in Jouy-en-Josas, France. Along for the ride are Moe Tucker and Sterling Morrison, who end up on stage with them. According to Moe Tucker, the moment had not been planned. She just remembered Cale at one point running over to her and asking, 'Do you have any mallets with you?'

They play a ten-minute version of 'Heroin'. It's the first time they've been on a stage together, all four of them, since September 1968. There's immediate talk of an official reunion, but that doesn't happen for another two years, when they start a European tour at the Edinburgh Playhouse, where they play two nights on 1 and 2 June 1993.

I meet Cale in Paris, a month before the tour. He sees the reunion as a belated opportunity to take care of what he describes as 'unfinished business'. There's talk of new music, three pieces he's started writing that Lou's agreed to work on. He imagines there will be a lot of improvisation. There's none of this, however, on the tour that follows, apart from a fairly desultory new song, 'Coyote', that possibly no one now remembers. When I see them in Edinburgh and at the London Forum a few days later, I'm elated, although by the second show some things have already begun to jar. The fan in me, however, is thrilled to finally see them and I also get to meet Sterling Morrison, who is already ill with the non-Hodgkin's lymphoma that in 1995 kills him, silencing what Lou Reed calls in posthumous tribute 'the warrior heart of The Velvet Underground'.

The tour goes on through Europe. There are festival shows, stadium dates opening for U2, an appearance back in the UK at Glastonbury Festival. By now, old tensions are resurfacing, and Lou is often travelling separately from the rest of the band. The last show of the tour is at the Stadio San Paolo in Naples. Bono joins them for a version of 'Satellite of Love' from Lou's *Transformer*. They will never play together again.

There's been talk of a US tour, an MTV special. But Lou now makes it a condition of any future work they do that he will produce it, basically have the final say over everything. Cale is incandescent at Lou's high-handedness. His mood worsens, if that's possible, when he gets wind of an insulting message Lou has sent to Moe.

'It was unbelievable,' he fumes on the phone from Los Angeles. 'He'd sent Moe this really withering fax and treated her so poorly I couldn't let it go. Moe had dealt with all the bullshit between us over the years and always with such great heart and then he comes along with this venomous, spiteful letter to her that I saw. I knew then that it was over between us.'

Cale fires off a nine-page fax to Lou, effectively ending their relationship.

'I told him that when he was shooting holes in his arm, Moe was bringing up, single-handed, three beautiful children and he has the gall to treat her like this. I wanted to write him something he wouldn't get up from, and he hasn't.'

Did he now regret the reunion and his part in it?

'We showed what we could do, although Moe was pretty appalled that Lou could not do the songs as well as he used to,' he says. 'But it was all pretty cheerless. Lou approached that project differently to the rest of us. He didn't want to be a part of the band like we did. He made that fairly clear. He was Lou Reed, and we were there at his indulgence.'

Why put up with it? Why not just walk out?

'I had an opportunity very early on in the process to quit,' Cale broods in LA, a dark mood on the end of the line. 'About the second week we were rehearsing, I realised what we were doing was just regurgitating the catalogue. Which wasn't what the project was about as I originally understood it. When we first talked about the tour, we said we could do whatever we wanted. We could stand on our heads out there and improvise. It didn't happen, of course. And I quickly felt I was being shut out, punished for some reason or another. I saw it happening and I thought, "You can walk, or you can see it through. But if you walk, it will all be on your head. The tour will be gone. The U2 thing will be gone." The tour meant a lot, financially, to Moe and Sterling. I stayed. We did it. End of story.'

Their signature is writ large on the music of the times, but how would he like The Velvet Underground to be remembered?

'As horrible as the first two albums sound to me now,' he says, 'the ideas are all still there and they'll always be there, the sparks we threw out. That's what I think will survive, what I think will endure.'

WILKO JOHNSON

Westcliff-on-Sea, April 2013

If you catch the train out of London from Fenchurch Street, Westcliff is nearly at the end of the line. This seems appropriate, because so is Wilko Johnson, who I'm here today to meet. Last month, it was announced that the former Dr Feelgood guitarist had been diagnosed with terminal cancer of the pancreas. He's refused chemotherapy and therefore been given less than a year to live, during which time he apparently plans to record a last album and, health permitting, play a farewell tour.

On hearing the news, memories of fans who saw the band in their incendiary early prime likely turned quickly to those legendary nights in 1973, when the Feelgoods first tore up London's pub rock scene, mad dog Canvey Island R&B monsters whose ferocious live shows were quickly the stuff of legend. Everyone who sees them has a hard time remembering when a British rock'n'roll band sounded so fucking wild, most people agreeing that you'd have to go back to the 1960s club heydays of The Who and The Rolling Stones.

Back then, Wilko and the Feelgoods blew a gaping hole in the day's musical fabric, through which a few years later the punk hordes would pour, partly inspired by their no-nonsense example. Their 1976 live album *Stupidity* makes them briefly the biggest band in the UK, but it's almost all over for the original line-up. During fractious sessions for its follow-up, *Sneakin' Suspicion*, Wilko falls out with vocalist Lee Brilleaux, bassist John B. Sparks and drummer The Big Figure, and walks out on the band. The Feelgoods carry on without him and, with replacement guitarist John 'Gypie' Mayo, have their biggest hit with 1979's 'Milk and Alcohol', produced by Nick Lowe.

Wilko's subsequent solo career is less illustrious. He forms The Solid Senders, who release an album on Virgin but never really catch on. Following a spell with Ian Dury's Blockheads, he makes for many years a steady if unspectacular living on the club circuit here and in Europe and even Japan, but he's become a somewhat overlooked figure. The Feelgoods, too, for just as long, seem to be forgotten, their vital early role in the punk insurrection that followed them largely ignored. Julien Temple's 2009 documentary *Oil City Confidential* redresses the balance somewhat, and 2012's *All Through the City* four-CD boxset, meanwhile, is a startling reminder of what the band had been, which at their best was pretty much as good as it gets. Wilko's career simultaneously had taken a wonderfully unexpected turn when he was cast as grim-faced executioner Ser Ilyn Payne in HBO's *Game of Thrones*.

And now, he's dying. But not so fast that he can't find time for one last interview with *Uncut*, in which over a couple of hours he looks back unsparingly at his time with the Feelgoods, their days of glory and eventual falling-out. He talks at length also about facing up to the illness that has promised to claim him.

He's in the garden having his picture taken when I arrive, standing against a wall in the black suit he seems to have been wearing since at least 1973. Someone else who's just dropped in, an old friend from the Canvey music scene, answers my knock on the front door of a terraced house on a quiet Westcliff street and leads me through a hallway full of clutter into a large living room even more given to mayhem. There's a bike against a wall, some amplifiers on the floor, guitars, a table piled high with notebooks, papers, books. There are more books – on astronomy, history, music – haphazardly stacked on sagging shelves.

There's a step down to a lower living-room area, where there's a large coffee table, its surface scarred and scorched, a couple of arm-chairs that look to have taken a few beatings over the years, into one of which Wilko, pictures taken, now sinks. He starts rolling a joint. For an old dog supposedly on his last legs, there's still a lot of wag in his tail. I remember trying to interview him one night after a show with The Solid Senders in Hemel Hempstead, his departure from the Feelgoods still a raw seething memory. He was sullen, angry, distracted, clearly unhappy and without much to say about anything. Today, mellowed by a little weed, death apparently looming, he's in remarkable good humour, eager to talk. I'm happy to listen.

'I got the diagnosis about the cancer just before Christmas,' he says, taking a hit of the joint he then hands to me. 'My son, who was over from Manila, noticed I was pissing blood. I would have ignored it, but he took me into the local A&E. Forced me to go, actually. They examined me and said, "You've got this mass in your stomach." I'd been aware of it for some time, but I'd just ignored it. I first noticed it last summer. I thought it might have something to do with the fact that after being teetotal all my life, in my dotage, I've taken up drinking. We had a night out and I started drinking absinthe, quite a bit of it. In the morning, I could feel the lump again and I'm like, "What's this? I know. It's my liver." Years ago, when I was in India, I had hepatitis. I was told I should never drink again. Of course, it had nothing to do with that.

'Anyway, they did these tests. Shortly after that they did a biopsy, which is an experience I wouldn't want to go through again. It's a bit freaky. Then, we went in just before Christmas for the results. In the meantime,' he laughs, 'we all had a go at the diagnosis. The consensus was that it was a cyst and they'd just cut it out. So, when we went in for the results, I wasn't expecting them to say it was cancer. But the doctor said, "This mass in your stomach. It's cancer and it's inoperable." My son cracked up. I was absolutely calm. I just nodded. I went, "OK."

'When we left the hospital,' he goes on, 'I felt elated. That's the word. You never know what your reaction is going to be and at the best of times I'm a miserable so-and-so. I've suffered from depression all my life. Since my teens, at least. So, feeling like this was a bit unusual. But this elation remained all day and it was still there when I woke up the next day. I realised there's nothing to be hung up about, because the present, the future: it doesn't mean anything. So, this elevation of spirit remained. You walk down the street just tingling, man. You feel so alive. You notice every little thing – every bird against the sunlight, everything – and just feel absolute calm. At times, it amounted to euphoria.'

Were you surprised by your reaction?

'Yes, totally,' he says, skinning up another joint. 'It's been over a month now. Normally, I don't keep a feeling, especially a good feeling, for more than a few hours. Usually, I find something to mess it up. But it's remained. It's like you've been given the ability to exist in the moment you're in, without bothering about the taxman, or anything. You realise what a marvellous thing it is to be alive. When the illness hits me, I don't think I'll be quite as jolly. I'm a complete wimp when it comes to illness and suffering. But right now, I'm feeling fine. And I'm hoping this feeling will last a while longer.'

The conversation turns to Canvey Island, which looms so large in his life and the legend of Dr Feelgood. What was it like growing up there?

'You need a movie to tell the Canvey story,' he says, taking a big hit off the joint he's just finished putting together, drifting a bit as he looks back. 'It's a place that keeps on changing. When I was a lad, it was more or less rural. Canvey Island is reclaimed marshland, you know. It was constructed in the 17th century. They got Dutch engineers across, because they were good at draining land. They built a sea wall around it and made it this island.

'Oh, it was mysterious then,' he says, grinning at the magic of it all. 'It was all unmade roads. People were living in shacks and railway carriages. There were a few proper houses, but it was a bit of a shanty town. When I went to the grammar school, up here in Westcliff, because there isn't a grammar school on Canvey Island, I met people who didn't dare go down to Canvey. They used to say, "Goodness knows what kind of chainsaw massacres take place down there." In fact, it was a nice place. There was a disastrous flood in 1953, which is one of my first memories. Looking out the back window and seeing the sea where there used to be a field. There were waves rolling up to our back door.'

There was no music scene to speak of on Canvey when he was growing up.

'Like any small town,' he says, the world he's describing a palpably monochrome post-war place, 'you'd go down the local youth club and there'd be half a dozen bands practising. But the real scene was in Southend. There were a couple of very good clubs there and there were two great groups. The Paramounts with Gary Brooker and Robin Trower, and Mickey Jupp's band, my favourites, The Orioles. Mickey Jupp could sing like Elmore James and his guitarist Mo Witham remains one of the best I've ever seen. I used to go along there and plonk myself in front of Mo and hope I could maybe learn something. That was where the music scene was.

'By the time the Feelgoods got going, there was a series of yacht clubs along the river, and you could get gigs there. There were youth clubs, the occasional wedding. But you couldn't call it a music scene. The Orioles and The Paramounts were into American rhythm and blues. They were a great introduction to a lot of great music. First of all, though, there was The Rolling Stones. Everything about them was exciting. The music they played, the way they looked. And you knew your parents hated them. In the aftermath of the Stones making their mark, the record shops in Britain became full of blues material – Johnny Otis and the like – and you'd just stand in the record shop, flicking through the racks of records, loads of them. You thought they'd go on forever. Do you remember? There was so much to discover. It just seemed magical.'

He can't remember ever thinking seriously then about being in a band, music as a career, earning whatever you might call a living from playing guitar, writing songs, making records, touring.

'I've never, ever been serious about music as a career,' he says, not even bothering with a shrug, 'I got into it completely by accident. When I was about 18, I had quite a good R&B band. I also had a jug band. We'd go down the seafront, wait for the pubs to come out and we'd play some songs. "You Are My Sunshine" or "Irene, Goodnight". One time, we were playing, and three boys came up. We were 18 and they were about 14 – a big gap when you're that age. But the leader of these boys, he was so intense. This was Lee Brilleaux. I saw him occasionally over the next two or three years whenever I'd come back from university.

'Then I went to Kathmandu and when I came back, I was living on this housing estate and thinking, "Well, it's own up time. I need a proper job or something." My mother got me a job as a teacher. Around that time, I'm walking down the street and who's this coming the other way, but Lee Brilleaux. He was a solicitor's clerk by then, and he had a sharp haircut and sideburns and was wearing a pinstripe suit. I thought, "He don't half look mean." I just looked like a sloppy hippie. I go, "How's your band?" And he goes, "The guitar player's left and we're looking for a new one." I'm thinking, "I wonder if he's going to ask me to join?" But he didn't. Later that day, Sparko comes

325

knocking and says, "Will you join our band?" I just went, "YES!" It started there, and for two years, it was just a local band.

'We got a regular gig at a disco on Canvey Island. Every Thursday night. The best one was called The Esplanade, down Southend. It was 10p to get in and we kept all the money. I knew from the start that Lee was a star. I had a lot of belief in him. The whole Dr Feelgood thing developed around him. This style of music we wanted to play, it was not fashionable. So, we were somewhat scorned by local bands, but we carried on doing our thing. That went on for a few years. Occasionally, we'd spend an afternoon around someone's house learning a few new numbers, but that was about it. We never rehearsed or discussed what we should look like or what we were going to do. It all grew naturally out of who we were.

'We were all such great friends then and we had so many good times,' he says, but you would not describe him particularly as misty-eyed at whatever he's remembering. 'It did get ugly in the end. There was terrible animosity. We ended up in a position where they were all drinking a lot, and I wasn't drinking at all. Which is not as flippant as it sounds, because when you're on the road you'll be stuck in your room, and they'll be in the bar. And who are they talking about? Let me think.

'I was growing apart from them, really,' he says with a bit of a sigh, all that water under the bridge possibly making him think of the 1953 Canvey floods. 'I tried very hard to involve Lee in the songwriting as he was a very witty guy. But it never happened. I was doing the songs and they never realised how hard it was. They didn't know about the times you'd end up beating your head against the wall trying to come up with a new one. If you've had a bit of success, obviously, your next thing has to be better. It's a bloody strain. If you're the only one doing it, it worries you. It did make me pretty intolerable at times, I have to admit. I can't blame it all on them.'

Before it all started to come apart, things happened for you very fast when you first started playing London dates.

'We found out about this London pub rock thing, which was a term I hated, and we were quite keen to get in on it,' he remembers. 'The first London gig, though, that was a bit of a let-down – filling in for Ducks Deluxe or someone and not many people being there. But quite soon, we were playing The Kensington on a Saturday, The Lord Nelson on a Thursday, and occasionally The Hope & Anchor and

Dingwalls. After that, it happened very fast, the record deal, all that. We'd come from nowhere and some of the bands on that scene had been around for ages. But it was us things started happening for. It wasn't a surprise to me that we became popular so quickly. There was no one else like us. No one sounded like us. No one looked like us.'

How important was the look you had?

'What a band looks like is always important,' he says, sounding a bit surprised that this is even under debate here. 'But again, it wasn't something we thought about too much. Lee always dressed like that, very sharp. Also, we found you could go down York Road market and buy a suit for 30 bob. It really worked for us, because people could identify with us. You didn't have to dress up in a cape and a pair of tights to see Dr Feelgood. It wasn't like going to see Kiss. We had a really strong connection to our audience because of the way we looked and also through our songs.

'At the time, there was a lot of stuff about hobgoblins, rubbish really, that had nothing to do with anything. My first inspiration was the blues, but I realised I couldn't write songs about freight trains and chain gangs. There weren't any on Canvey. So, I tried to keep it all in Essex, to get the landscape, the oil refineries into the songs. Lee brought frustration and pent-up anger to them. That's what connected us to punk. If we'd stayed together, we'd have fitted in perfectly with punk. In fact, we'd have walked all over punk. But by then, it was all blowing up in our faces. People were more interested in the Pistols and The Clash. They weren't interested in this band splitting up because of some obscure row. And in the excitement surrounding punk, we were forgotten.

'We'd had a number-one album with *Stupidity*, and, I don't know, maybe the band thought I was taking over. I'm sure that had something to do with what happened next, which was basically them plotting to get me out. Before we went to Rockfield to record the fourth LP, Lee and I went to Atlanta to meet Bert de Coteaux, who was going to produce it. We had three days together. We were friends again, hanging out. But as soon as we got to Rockfield, it was clear they wanted me gone. Suddenly, there was a real animosity. Lee was one of the greatest people I've ever known. But at the end, there was a lot of bad feeling. It got nastier and nastier. I was completely isolated from the band. And then one day, I was out.'

Bitterness ensued, you'd have to imagine.

'I didn't want to be bitter about Dr Feelgood, because it was the greatest thing in my life,' he says. 'I was confused more than bitter at the time, I didn't know whether to carry on, in fact. But I'd been in the music business for five years by then and it's a pretty good business to be in. I thought, "Well, I'm going to have to try to carry on." But I attracted the worst people in the world around me and we carried on and ruined it. The whole business did no good to either side. They lost it and I didn't have it. I'm quite good at what I do, and I was holding my own. Then Ian Dury asked me to join The Blockheads. Ian was great – one very unusual person. I did really like him. Also, I found him to be the most offensive person I've ever met. Dear, oh dear. That guy could be so offensive. A lot of my time was taken up by smoothing over the frightful situations that had arisen when Ian had had one too many.'

Did you keep up with what the Feelgoods were doing? The albums with Nick Lowe, for instance?

'No,' he says emphatically. 'Whenever I took interest, I wished I hadn't. Everything was crap.'

There was no reconciliation with Lee. Even when Lee was dying, Wilko found ways to ignore him.

'We met by accident a couple of times, but we had nothing to say to each other. When he was dying, my brother went to see him, and he expressed a wish to see me. I said, "Well, they'll have to send someone over to take me. I'm not going to just turn up and knock on his door." Nobody ever bothered to call for me.

'There were two occasions when we nearly got back together in the year after the band split that didn't work out. One of them nearly did. I was up in town, and I met a mate and he said, "Guess who I've been talking to?" I said, "Is it Lee Brilleaux?" He said, "I had a long talk to him, and he'd like you back in the band. He really, really would." I said, "Would he?" Because I was thinking the same thing. A few months later, this guy said, "I've gone so far as to make an arrangement for you to meet in The Ship, in Wardour Street, tomorrow afternoon." Then I met this girl and spent the next 48 hours with her. I missed the meeting with Lee and never really spoke to him again. That's just the way things happen.'

So what's next for Wilko, the clock ticking, time running out?

'We're playing some dates in France that were scheduled before I was diagnosed and we're doing an album. Because of my current circumstances, it's going to be a quick one. No time for fiddling about with them knobs. We'll just bloody record it, the way they used to make records. Then when we come back from France, we'll be doing the farewell UK tour, which, obviously, I hope I'll be fit enough to do. I'm not going on stage ill. I don't want people to see me like that. But I've got every reason to hope I'll be fit enough to do those dates.

'If I can, it would be a consummation dearly to be wished,' he says with an almost wistful finality. 'I'll be happy then.'

I get the train back to London wondering what will appear first in print, the feature I'm due to write for *Uncut* or Wilko's obituary. The farewell tour goes ahead, fans all over the country bidding him an emotional farewell. He also finds time to make a new album, *Going Back Home*, with The Who's Roger Daltrey, whose release he's sure he won't live to see. But he doesn't die, as predicted. In fact, an oncologist named Emmanuel Huguet at Cambridge's Addenbrooke's hospital declares his cancer is operable, although there's only a 15 per cent chance he'll survive the surgery. In a nine-hour operation he has a tumour 'the size of a football' removed. He also loses his pancreas, spleen, part of his stomach and intestines. By October 2014, the cancer is gone. At the time of this writing in early 2022, he's back on the road. The cancer gets him in the end, of course, when it returns fatally in November 2022, by which time he's made the most and more of his incredible reprieve. And until then, Wilko's story has a happy ending. And you can never have too many of those.

THE CLASH

London, September 2013

The last time I was in a room smaller than Brixton Academy with The Clash, we were in an all-night diner in Washington DC, where at four in the morning Joe Strummer was trying to persuade the rest of the band to join us on a trip to the White House. It was February 1979. The Clash were just over a week into their first American tour, newly arrived in DC after an overnight drive from Cleveland through one of the worst blizzards in local memory.

More than 30 years later, Strummer dead since 2002, two of the surviving members of The Clash are grappling with menus not much smaller than a broadsheet newspaper in the plush restaurant of a private members' club near Marble Arch. The third is on his way to join us to talk about *Sound System*, a new box set that collects the band's first five albums plus three discs of rare and unreleased material and houses them in a box designed to look like a boom-box stereo. It's astonishing to think all this music was made in just five intense years of relentless creativity that produced 16 sides of long-playing vinyl and 17 singles during a time the band toured virtually without a break.

'It's an incredible legacy,' Topper Headon says, as Mick Jones scans the menu. 'Double albums, triples, tons of singles. We were out there on our own. No one else was doing anything like it.'

Topper at 58 looks fit enough to beat a Kenyan in a marathon. After the many unhappy years that followed his sacking from The Clash in 1982 – including a long period of heroin addiction and a spell in prison – he's trim enough to still fit the clothes he was wearing that night in Washington, which can't be said of the rest of us.

'We had something that few bands have,' Topper goes on. 'That's why the music still stands up and deserves to be heard. It's all as relevant today as it was when we made the original records.'

Mick Jones, meanwhile, is now wondering whether to have the watercress velouté, whatever that is, for lunch. At 58, Mick is not quite the snake-hipped rock god of yore. He cuts a rather jollier figure these days, as disarmingly charming as ever, what's left of his hair swept back from the top of his head. He's often to be seen crisply turned out in pinstripe suits and matching accessories. Today, he has the slightly crumpled look of someone who's fallen asleep on a couch watching the Weather Channel. He has the raffish air of a venerable actor, popular on TV chat shows for his hilariously indiscreet yarns of thespian wassailing, long weekends spent quaffing and carousing with legendary hell-raisers from another time, Burton, O'Toole or Richard Harris. In another light, while we're at it, he might remind you of an old-school football manager from the days of sheepskin coats, untipped cigarettes and car-park bungs.

Mick seems about to make a decision about the watercress when there's a bit of a commotion and he and Topper are suddenly on their feet. Paul Simonon's belated arrival is the cause for much hugging, backslapping and good-to-see-you laughter. The same age as Mick and Topper, Paul, like Mick, is no longer the lanky, leather-clad colt of the band's charismatic heyday, when he would often smoulder in photographs in the manner of a particularly moody young method actor, sometimes posing with a cigarette dangling from his lips. This afternoon, he's dressed in black jacket, shirt, trousers and boots, a small straw hat quickly removed to reveal thinning hair cut brutally short. He looks like he's stomped across a field to get here. The three of them settle down, Paul wondering if they have egg and chips on the menu, which makes Mick laugh.

Now that everyone's here, the conversation turns to *Sound System* and how long it took to put together.

'Three bloody years,' Paul sighs, as if he hasn't had a day off since the idea came up, although it was Mick who put in the studio hours.

'I listened to everything we ever did.' Mick looks wan with weariness, thinking about it. 'I got all the CDs, and all the tapes, to see what we had and what we could do with it. Did we want to put out everything we did, find a place for everything, all the odds and sods, bits and pieces? Just pile it all on? That didn't seem to me the way to do it.

'There's been a trend over recent years, especially with box sets and legacy editions, to pile on so many extras they become overdone. And they're usually not much cop, to be honest. I mean, how many alternative versions do you need of one song? Who needs, like, 27 takes? This is much more about the recorded works of The Clash, our musical legacy, rather than a collection of off-cuts, out-takes, rehearsal tapes. Things we never put out, and usually for a good reason. You're missing the point of this box set if you moan about the fact it isn't full of stuff like that.

'What this box set does in a way is carry the name of The Clash forward, you know? So The Clash and what we did lives on. It was also a way of bringing Joe with us as well, as his words are so strong, so powerful. They live on. We never thought when we started out that what we'd do would end up having such significance, but that's happened and that's something else the box set celebrates.'

What was it like listening to, say, the first album again?

'Pretty cool, actually,' Mick says, sounding a little as if this had surprised him. 'At the same time, I feel a bit removed from it, to be honest with you. It's all so long ago now and I kind of look back on it as a fan as much as anything. And I followed the band's story through the music, rather than the mythology that sometimes surrounds the history of The Clash.'

How large does the legend of The Clash continue to loom in your lives? It's 30 years since you split. Has there been a defining experience in your lives since to match it?

'None,' Mick says. 'There's been nothing like it. Being in The Clash was a defining moment in our lives and I'd be lying if I said I'd gotten over it.'

'Personally, I find it easy to put things behind me and move on,' Paul says. 'I can shake off sentimental attachments. I'm only reminded of The Clash when things like this box set come up or someone puts in a request to use one of the songs for a commercial or whatever. Other than that, it's behind me, really.'

'The Clash was a fantastic thing to have been part of, but it was 30 years ago,' Topper says.

Are your feelings about The Clash coloured by the way it ended for you?

'Not really, no,' Topper says. 'It was my fault it ended the way it did. There's no blame attached to anyone else. I'm just grateful for the fantastic memories I have. At the same time, the experience was so intense it couldn't have lasted much longer anyway. The Clash had to explode or implode or whatever. I'm totally surprised it lasted as long as it did. It was always, "Bloody hell! We've made it through another week."'

What was the extent of your ambition then?

'From the beginning,' Paul says, 'it was like there was no point in being in a band for the sake of being in a band. There has to be more to it than that. In our case, it was to match and go beyond the bands who'd come before us. Reach the same heights, but on our own terms.'

'There was a great naivety about The Clash,' Topper says. 'We wanted to be the biggest band in the world. But there were conditions. We weren't going to play seated stadiums. We weren't going to do this. We weren't going to do that. We're going to do a double album. We're going to do a triple album. We're going to be the biggest band in the world, but we won't do anything that will make that easy. In fact, we're going to make ourselves a pain in the arse. You had all these other groups who also wanted to be the biggest band in the world, and they'd do anything the record company told them if they thought it would bring them the success they were so desperate for. We'd go on tour with these fantastic support acts, and we'd still find ways to piss off the record company. We couldn't do it like all those other bands.'

'That's why we were The Clash,' Paul says.

And what were Mick's ambitions?

'I just wanted to be in a band,' he says. 'I grew up in a time when that's what everybody wanted. But I was a lot more serious about it than a lot of people. I studied every band I went to see. I studied every band that came before us. I studied their songs, how they were arranged. I analysed everything about them. What they sounded like. What they wore. I'd check out all their moves. Whatever looked or sounded good, I'd nick.'

'Pete Townshend and Wilko from Dr Feelgood were the ones who were really great on stage,' Paul says. 'That's what I wanted to be like.

333

That was a bit difficult, though. You're supposed to have a guitar to do all that stuff. That's why I didn't really want the job of being the bass player. Because if you were the bass player, you were the one who stands in the back, like John Entwistle or Bill Wyman. I didn't want the job of standing in the back, so I used to pretend I was playing Mick's parts.'

When you recorded your first album, how ready were you?

'We were absolutely as ready as we would ever have been,' Paul says.

'We were just desperate to get on with it,' Mick says. 'We'd been waiting long enough for the chance.'

'It didn't seem a problem that we weren't at some kind of musical pinnacle in terms of our professionalism or ability,' Paul says. 'That didn't seem the point. Being able to play at some elevated level of competence or our musical ability generally wasn't important. We didn't need to be super-efficient at playing. We were an expression of the times and our age and experience. We weren't polished. We weren't slick. I think it gave a certain sincerity to what we were doing.'

What did you think of punk, Topper? Joe, Mick and Paul were obviously already central to what was happening, but before you joined them you had your own scene going.

'When I joined the group, I loved the way they looked,' Topper says. 'The three of them were very charismatic and seemed wonderful. The only thing that worried me was whether it would last. The punk thing seemed destined to be short-lived. But in The Clash, we had a scene of our own. We were living our own lives. We were The Clash, and nothing else mattered. Being in The Clash meant everything to us. As Joe used to say, the chemistry between the four of us was incredible. If I have any regrets, I think it would be not appreciating at the time what we had between us. The pity is I took it for granted. Maybe we all did, unfortunately. I mean, for Mick and Joe to write those songs and Joe to come up with those lyrics, what a team. There were so many great songs. Mick and Joe were an amazing songwriting team and, you know, Joe, in so many ways, has been with us through this whole thing.'

'You knew Joe before any of us,' Mick says to me. 'In Newport. You were at the art school when Joe was there. What was he like?'

I trot out a by-now familiar story. How Joe – or Woody, as we knew him then – turns up at my digs, keen to hear some of the music

I've been bellowing about as an alternative to the kind of thing we regularly watch on *The Old Grey Whistle Test* on the banged-up old TV in a room at the student union building on Stow Hill, presenter Bob Harris murmuring adoringly about Camel or Wishbone Ash, bands like that. How Joe had not been impressed by most of what I play him. Including The Velvet Underground, MC5, David Bowie, Roxy Music, The Stooges, Joe hilariously once describing Lou Reed as a decadent slut.

'Joe said that about Lou Reed?' Mick asks, with a look that suggests that if he'd known anything about this, Joe would still be playing The Red Cow with The 101'ers.

'It's a terrible thing to say,' Paul adds. 'But I couldn't stand Bob Harris. When I heard Sid Vicious attacked him, I was really happy.'

'That was at The Speakeasy, wasn't it?' Mick says, The Speakeasy a club made famous by the 1960s rock aristocracy and still a place to be seen in the 1970s. 'It used to be really cool to go there. When I was really young and had long hair and that, I used to go and wait outside to see who would turn up. We also used to hang around outside Tramps nightclub, if the Stones were playing. I'd go down there and wait for them and get in by joining the back of Billy Preston's entourage, as if I was part of it, just swan in. The Speakeasy was where all the bands hung out. That thing with Bob Harris happened just before it closed down, just after all the punks started going there. There was a brief crossover between the dinosaurs and young punks coming in.'

Did you really think of them as dinosaurs? As Robert Plant's reminded me more than once, he was only 29 when punk hove noisily into view.

'Some of them, yes,' Mick says. 'The problem with those bands was they left you as they found you. They did nothing to change you. Some of them barely even acknowledged their fans. I think we did more than most to break down the barrier between the audience and the group. There were a lot of good groups before us. I'm not talking about some of the more severe cape-wearing progressive groups. I'm talking about the Big Five. The Stones, Who, Beatles, Kinks, Small Faces. They were great, and so were some of the other groups from that era. Everybody else got what they deserved.'

'We did admire those bands, but it was time for a change,' Paul says. 'You had to be brutal. You had to say, "It's Year One, now. Everything

335

starts again and we want you out of the way. Your time is over." That said, we had a lot of time for some people. Like Pete Townshend. He was one of the few people who came to our shows. He showed his support by coming to see the band. It meant a lot. It was fantastic, in fact. I don't recall anyone else doing that. Bob Dylan came in the later stages, but Townshend was around a lot. I can't think of anyone else of his standing that came to see us when the shows were, to put it mildly, very rough and tough.'

'Pete Townshend was wonderful to me after The Clash,' Topper says. 'He rescued me. He sent me for treatment in LA and paid for it himself. He'd had his own problems, so he knew what I was going through. He was no stranger to any of it. I was working with Pete Farndon, who'd just been kicked out of The Pretenders. He died of a heroin overdose. Pete came up and said, "You're next. Carry on like this and you'll be the next to go." He'd just got clean at the time. He was brilliant.'

'And of course, we toured with The Who,' Mick says. 'It was their last tour for a long time, and it was almost like they were handing the mantle to us.'

Some disgruntled fans thought you became at that point what you'd set out to replace.

'I think we did OK, given the contradictions we had to deal with,' Mick says. 'Whatever some fans thought, it was interesting to see if we could play places like Shea Stadium, environments like that. It was a challenge. That's what we were always looking for.'

It was as if to be a proper punk The Clash wouldn't play anywhere larger than The Roxy.

'Or sign to CBS,' Paul says, grinning.

'The day punk died!' Mick laughs, fanning himself with a napkin, like a Southern belle with a touch of the vapours.

Punk fundamentalists were also outraged when they discovered Joe had gone to a minor public school, when they would have preferred him to have been brought up in an orphanage on a diet of mouse droppings, and hadn't as they would have preferred been forced up chimneys as a child. Suddenly, he was inauthentic, a middle-class poseur playing at being a punk, not the real thing.

'That totally pissed me off,' Paul says, angry and showing it. 'I've never been to one of those schools and it doesn't matter, anyway. I'm from a working-class background, right, but I was furious with that criticism of Joe. It was pathetic. When I first met Joe, he didn't have two pence to rub together. He was living in a squat. The most important thing was that I liked him, and he liked me. We communicated well. That was what was important to me. It was all I needed to know about him. What school he went to was totally unimportant. We just enjoyed a really good friendship and what I learned from it was that your background, that's irrelevant. It's who you are that counts.'

Do you think some of Joe's more extreme rhetoric was an over-compensation for his background, a way of distancing himself from privilege? I'm thinking of his ill-judged tendency to romanticise so-called revolutionary groups like the Baader-Meinhof gang and the Red Brigades.

'Yes, I think so,' Mick says. 'That's very possible.'

'I think that Joe was just trying to work things out. He was always looking for something to believe in,' Paul says. 'The Red Brigades, he realised that whole issue was a hand grenade and didn't want to go near it when he thought things through. We never wanted to align ourselves to any political party, even though we were obviously very much of the left.'

So what did The Clash stand for?

'Humanity and compassion,' Paul says. 'Personal politics, not party politics. We treated fans as human beings,' he adds. 'That was quite new.'

Since they are now so sainted and their reputation hallowed, it's perhaps too easy to forget what a rough ride The Clash even in their heyday were given, often by their own fans. Their punk credentials seemed to be under constant scrutiny by punk's Taliban. Critics were frequently harsh, even mocking. Their idealism made them easy to ridicule. Strummer's rebel posturing was a particular target.

'You just got used to it,' Paul says. 'We got all kinds of criticism. Everybody had something they wanted to take issue with. In the end, it was like, "It doesn't matter what anyone thinks. This is our band. We'll play the music we want to, and just get on with it. If you don't like us, form your own band."'

'*London Calling* was the point, I think, when we started doing things for ourselves and stopped worrying what anyone else thought,' Mick says.

'When we recorded *London Calling*, we loved each other's company, and we were pretty inseparable,' Topper says. 'The camaraderie was amazing. We were just great friends. Being in a band can be a fabulous feeling, but being in The Clash was even more special, particularly at that time.'

'People used to look at you when you came through the airport,' Mick remembers, sounding wistful. 'We really made an impression as a group. You couldn't miss us. We really stood out. We looked great. We were great.'

'Well, we were the fucking Clash,' Paul says.

These were halcyon days. A year after *London Calling*, in December 1980, they delivered *Sandinista!*, six sides of music that again tested fans and critics, for whom the triple album was less evidence of the band's broadening musical horizons than gross self-indulgence. They remained defiantly single-minded.

'There was just no stopping us,' Mick says. 'We were fanatical about what we were doing because it really does take fanaticism to work at that level. I can't imagine now trying to maintain that level of energy and intensity. It would be impossible at our age,' he laughs. 'But at the time, we pushed everything as hard as we could. The Clash was our life, and we were dedicated to it. We lived every moment to the full.'

'We lived it, simple as that,' Paul says. 'Twenty-four hours a day. What you wore onstage, you wore offstage. There was no difference. We went from playing the shows straight into the studio. There was no stopping us. We couldn't even stop ourselves.'

'We paid the price for it all, though,' Mick says. 'None of it was without its cost, as Topper unfortunately knows.'

By 1982, Topper's heroin addiction was out of control. He made it through the *Combat Rock* sessions, but before the album was released, he was sacked. Terry Chimes, who'd played on *The Clash*, replaced Topper for an American tour with The Who, then quit in early 1983, worn down by the rancour between Joe and Paul on one side and Mick on the other. Pete Howard was drafted in for the US Festival in California, which The Clash headlined with Van Halen and David Bowie. The Clash played on 22 May. It was Mick's last appearance with them. In September 1983, in a putsch mounted by Joe and Paul, he was sacked from his own band.

'I knew realistically that groups split up,' Mick says. 'I mean I was heartbroken when Bowie split the Spiders. When you've got your own band, though, you don't think that's going to happen to you. When Topper went, something of me went with him. I didn't want him to go, but there didn't seem like an alternative at the time. That's just the way things were. He'd become a problem and had to go. As I was about to find out, I was next.'

Joe said later you'd become as difficult to deal with as Elizabeth Taylor in unfettered diva strop.

'Well, my mum was a bit like Elizabeth Taylor. Maybe I got it from her,' Mick says, his humour for the first time faltering at these unhappy memories. 'It might have seemed to Paul and Joe that I was acting too much like a rock star, but I didn't see it that way. I do admit that I'd maybe become a bit too possessive of the music. I was too precious with what essentially and for the best, really, was a group thing. I got too much into myself. That could have caused problems.'

Paul, how much of a problem had Mick's behaviour become for you?

'Quite a major problem, actually,' Paul says, sombre now, too. 'For me and Joe, it was like there was so much to do, we needed to get on and do it. We'd been putting up with Mick for six years. Mick is Mick and he gets up at a certain time and at first that was OK. But you get to a point where you're not a teenager, you're a man of 27 and it's still, "Where is he? Why isn't he out of bed? We've got shows to do." After a while, it wears you down. In the end, we got bloody-minded. You think, "Sod it. He's got to go. We can't go on like this."'

'In my defence,' Mick says, 'I was being pushed into an uncomfortable place with the return of Bernie [after being sacked as manager, Bernie Rhodes was reinstated in 1981].'

'Yeah, but Bernie was unaware of what was going to take place,' Paul says. 'When we said we wanted you out of the band, he didn't know anything about that when he came back. Bernie was shocked. He said he knew something was going to happen. But he didn't know me and Joe were going to sack you.'

'I felt I'd been stitched up,' Mick says.

'You were,' Paul says. 'But not by him.'

'I was amazed when I read Mick had left the band as well,' Topper says. 'But that was so typical of The Clash and the way we did things.

The downside of making all that music and touring as much as we did was that we lived together for five or six years. Every morning I'd wake up and know I was going to see Paul, Mick and Joe. And like in any other relationship, things when they're so intense are going to sour. You get fed up with each other. I just think The Clash ran its course and couldn't have gone on much longer. It was just too intense.'

The table's being cleared. A car is waiting for Mick and Topper. Paul's got his hat on, ready to stomp back across the field or whatever he crossed to get here. One more question. What would the young Clash have said if someone had walked into an early rehearsal or their first recording sessions at Beaconsfield and told them that in 30 years they'd be sitting in a private members' club and talking about the music they hadn't yet made in the context of a career-spanning, multi-disc box set, designed for posterity.

'Laughed, probably,' Paul says, following Mick and Topper out the door.

The 101'ers

July 2014

Joe Strummer in the house! I mean, really. The hammering you heard an hour ago? That was Joe at the front door of the flat I've just moved into on Riffel Road in Willesden. This would make it March 1976. Joe's unexpectedly turned up from I don't know where, making an enormous noise, bugles and drums the only things missing from what otherwise sounds convincingly like the noisy announcements of an army arriving to lift the siege of a beleaguered garrison. His mood, you could say, is urgent.

'I've got something to play you,' he says, following me up the stairs to the mildewed untidiness of the rooms I've only recently rented, unpacked boxes everywhere, full of records and books, wallpaper yellow with age, no furniture to speak of. 'Have you got anything to play this on?' he asks, producing from a pocket a C60 cassette with a bright orange label. We're quickly listening to 'Keys to Your Heart', the song by now a regular highlight of sets by Joe's band, The 101'ers. The version Joe's playing me has just been recorded for the fledgling independent label, Chiswick, who, Joe confirms almost unbelievingly, want to put it out as a single. He looks electrified at the thought, like he'll never have better news to tell anyone.

We play the tape nonstop for over an hour, awash with excitement. Later, down the pub, Joe is still lit up. This is a moment of possible vindication, after all. The pay-off, maybe, for nigh on two years of backbreaking slog. The 101'ers might yet be on the verge of something you could describe as a breakthrough, a chance perhaps to reach a wider audience than the one that has so far barely sustained them. Which is how, back in my Riffel Road digs, 'Keys to

Your Heart' playing over and over, Joe describes the things he hopes will happen next for the band, an unwritten future taking shape in his imagination. What neither of us realises then is that by the time 'Keys to Your Heart' comes out in May, The 101'ers will be over and Joe will be a member of The Clash.

The next time I see him it's June, at a showcase for Charlie Gillett's Oval Records label at the Royal College of Art. He initially avoids me, ducking into the crowd when we spot each other. He then suddenly turns up next to me at the bar they've set up in a courtyard or garden. He's got a new haircut that doesn't include much hair, his rockabilly thatch trimmed brutally short and dyed blond. He's got some new duds, too. A leather jacket so fresh off the rack, it audibly squeaks, biker boots, the beginning of a fabled look. He keeps glancing over his shoulder, like he's afraid we might be seen together.

'I wanted to let you know what was happening,' he says finally. 'But I was told not to talk to you. I didn't know what to do. Everything's real different now.'

The sound of Joe saying sorry for something becomes familiar over the years. You couldn't pass an evening with him at times in the late 1980s without drink making him maudlin with self-pity about his part in destroying The Clash. He took all the blame and deserved most of it. He's wrong, though, there in the grounds of the Royal College of Art, if he thinks I believe he's made a mistake by walking out on The 101'ers. The ship he jumped was already sinking. Anyway, it's not me he should be apologising to. It's his former bandmates. Since joining The Clash, Joe's comments about The 101'ers have been callous and dismissive. He's basically written them off at the instruction of Clash manager Bernie Rhodes, who's recently been busy scrubbing away Joe's past to present him anew as the punk rock warlord of future legend.

As far as Bernie's concerned, Joe's past is there only to be ignored, denigrated, denied. Which is what Bernie, with the scowling face of an enraged toddler given to foot-stamping, bed-wetting and much infernal squealing, is now making clear to both me and Joe. He's stormed through the crowd after seeing us together and now forces himself between us like a referee trying to separate a couple of boxers. He's clearly furious at Strummer, who's apparently been repeatedly told not to engage with anyone from his former life in the squats, the pubs, The 101'ers. Joe's head drops as Bernie rages.

'Start fucking listening, will you?' he shouts at Strummer, spit flying, 'Just do what you're fucking told.'

He turns to me, no sign of the puffed-up blowhard calming down just yet. What he wants me to know is that I'm an uncomfortable reminder of a part of Joe's past Bernie wants no further reference to. I'm therefore unwelcome at any forthcoming Clash shows. Banned from them, in fact. Prohibited, too, from writing about the group. Bernie communicates all this with great seriousness, like he's delivering a papal excommunication to an especially troublesome German heretic. In his bitter opinion, The 101'ers were a crap pub rock band Joe is well rid of and in Bernie's emerging version was never really part of.

I'm not sure if laughing at the fatuous little fuck will help defuse the moment, so I'm not entirely surprised when a noisy chuckle makes him yet angrier. For a moment, he seems close to throwing a punch. He'll go home missing at least one of his cars, if he does.

'Let's go,' he says to Strummer, Bernie heading off in a fearful strop. Joe hurries to catch him up, slowed down a little by the tail between his legs but clearly keen to be at his master's side, punk's rebel hero brought to obedient heel. Bernie doesn't get very far, however, before he stops, Joe bumping comically into him. Bernie turns around, walks back to me, pokes a pudgy finger at me. He's close enough that I can feel his breath on my face, a fuming heat.

'If I haven't made myself clear,' he says, as if addressing not just me but an imaginary crowd, Danton whipping up the mob, 'let me say it again. The 101'ers, they never existed, right? Give it a month and no one will even remember them.'

Hastings, nigh on 40 years later, one night at the end of July 2014, storm clouds gathering, rain on its way. A pale-coloured Porsche pulls out of the station car park, Clive Timperley at the wheel. The last time I saw Clive, who these days is a driving instructor here on the south coast, he was lead guitarist in The 101'ers, author of the firestorms over which Joe Strummer, especially in the band's latter days, raged. We're on our way to Clive's rather swish pad in a converted Victorian school, where he now wonders how much he'll be able to remember about the times I've asked him to talk about.

'It's all a bit jumbled, frankly,' he says. 'The early 70s were a bit of a mess. There were a lot of drugs.'

Clive, however, is soon recalling 1971, the year he lived in Ash Grove, Palmers Green, sharing a house called Vomit Heights with a bunch of art students, one of whom is the young Johnny Mellor, who everybody already knows as Woody and in due course becomes Joe Strummer.

'Woody was a bit bonkers, as I recall, a bit off his head,' begins Clive. 'But he was funny and even then, he had this charisma, if you like. He'd come into a room, sit down and immediately there'd be people gathered around him. People wanted to talk to him. He was an interesting guy.'

Clive at the time is in a group called Anaconda, signed to Shel Talmy's production company, for who they recorded an album, never released. He has no idea then that Woody is interested in music, so after losing touch with him when Woody heads to South Wales, fetching up in Newport, Clive is surprised in September, 1974, to discover that Woody's back in London and in a band who are making their debut at a pub called The Telegraph in Brixton. They've been booked to support Dennis Bovell's Matumbi at a Chilean Solidarity Campaign benefit that on a whim he decides to go to.

The band he sees are billed as El Huaso and The 101 All Stars and their line-up that night is Woody on rhythm guitar, Simon 'Big John' Cassell and Alvaro – El Huaso himself – a refugee from Pinochet's Chile on saxophones. Patrick Nother's on bass. His brother Richard – who becomes Richard Dudanski – is on drums, a last-minute stand-in for the band's errant original drummer who he eventually replaces. He's been playing drums exactly a week.

'I was just dragged into it,' Richard recalls from his home in Spain, where he's lived in Granada since 1988, after a post 101'ers career that included stints with Bank of Dresden, The Raincoats, Basement 5 and PiL (he's the uncredited drummer on *Metal Box*). 'Woody said, "Just keep the beat. It doesn't matter if it gets faster, just make sure it doesn't slow down."'

'They were terrible,' Clive laughs. 'Patrick played bass with his back to the audience, like Stuart Sutcliffe with The Beatles. He couldn't play and was desperately nervous. They only seemed to know about four songs, and they played them all at least twice. Big John was singing lead on most of them, but Woody did a couple of Chuck Berry numbers. I remember thinking they were rubbish.'

In January 1975, however, Clive sees them again, at a pub called The Chippenham, in Shirland Road, just off Elgin Avenue in west London, in an upstairs room the band have named The Charlie Pigdog Club.

'It was still pretty raw, most of them were still learning their instruments, they had speakers made out of kitchen cabinets and it was still a bit of a shambles,' he remembers. 'Most of them were living in a squat at 101 Walterton Road, about five minutes from The Chip. It was all unbelievably basic.

'But they'd obviously been practising like maniacs. Woody was suddenly this mad guy with a light-blue suit and a leg that was shaking uncontrollably. I was really impressed. I thought, "Blimey, he's giving it a lot of energy, he's fantastic." He didn't know how to play the guitar, but he had so much energy, it was amazing just watching him. Later, he became an absolutely relentless rhythm guitar player, to the point where he'd break strings, end up with bleeding fingers. The more blood there was on the guitar at the end of the night, the better the gig had usually been.'

Clive's got his own band at this point, Foxton Flight – 'an acoustic, Steely Dan-type thing' – but they aren't really getting anywhere. He brings his guitar to a couple of 101'ers rehearsals, jams with them on some tunes and fits in well enough for Woody to take him aside one night. 'He said, "I've had a word with the boys" – those were his exact words – "and we'd like you to join the band." And I'm going, "Oh, so it is a proper band, then?"

'I mean,' he says, 'at that point they were still pushing their gear around in a pram.'

The Chip, as they used to call it, is still there, rebranded now as The Chippenham Hotel, signs outside promising 'accommodation' and 'en suite rooms'. There's a large screen in the bar, golf being played in foreign sunshine, the bar itself otherwise empty on a sweltering recent afternoon. Frank Sinatra's on the sound system, singing 'Young at Heart', which makes me laugh, thinking of Joe at 22 in 1975, standing in this room with The 101'ers, none of them much older than he was then.

The band's old digs at nearby 101 Walterton Road are long gone, the derelict row of houses that included their squat demolished in the late 1970s to accommodate Abinger Mews, a gated community of pricey townhouses and equally expensive flats. Standing where we are now 40 years ago, you might have heard from what used to be the band's rehearsal room at number 101 the thumping sound of them practising, perhaps for a gig that night at The Charlie Pigdog Club, which is where I see them first in February 1975.

Joe is an old friend from Newport, where I'd been a student at the art school before moving to London in July 1973 and then joining *Melody Maker*, where one afternoon I get a call from him. The gist of the chat that follows is that he's apparently in a band. They've got a gig coming up at a place in Ladbroke Grove if I fancy going. Joe, still Woody then, had played in a couple of art school bands – The Rip-Off Park All-Stars and The Vultures – who had been rowdy fun, so I go, not expecting too much of the band but thinking it'll be good to see Woody again. As it turns out, The 101'ers are raw, but also sensational, blasting out mostly R&B covers, the staple repertoire of what's known back then as pub rock. Joe himself is a revelation, amazing even then, clearly already on the road to legend. At times, there are too many of them to count in this early line-up – bass, guitars, drums, four or five saxes, Joe's recent busking partner and later Clash collaborator Tymon Dogg on violin. There's also a skinny little dude in sunglasses named Julian Yewdall who plays occasional harmonica and briefly manages the band, before settling on a career as a photographer whose many pictures of The 101'ers are later collected in the book *A Permanent Record*. The set ends with a roaring version of Van Morrison's 'Gloria', Joe playing on even as the police arrive to close things down, oblivious, in thrall to the mayhem of the moment. Later, the band drives me home to south London in their newly acquired hearse, which seems impossibly cool.

This is the first of many great nights that follow, mainly at The Elgin, a pub in Ladbroke Grove, just south of the Westway, where they start a residency in May that runs through to the following January. By now, they're a four-piece, with Joe on guitar and vocals, Richard on drums, Clive on lead guitar and Marwood 'Mole' Chesterton on bass, and they're on fire every time they play, their set now peppered with the songs Joe's recently started writing, including crowd favourites 'Keys to Your Heart', 'Letsagetabitarockin'', 'Motor Boys Motor', 'Rabies from the Dogs of Love' and the pile-driving 'Steamgauge 99'.

'We rehearsed all the time, three or four times a week, for hours,' Clive remembers, 'and every Thursday we played the Charlie Pigdog Club. Everyone got better really quickly, especially Richard who became this powerhouse drummer, absolutely fantastic. And Joe went from strength to strength as a frontman, especially after he saw Bruce Springsteen at the Hammersmith Odeon in November. He was very impressed. After that he totally modelled himself on Springsteen. He thought Springsteen was where it was at. That's what Joe wanted to be like on stage, he was absolutely inspired by seeing someone that hard-working and just turned into this incredible showman.'

A series of shows with Eddie and The Hot Rods brings them to the attention of Dr Feelgood producer Vic Maile, with whom they cut six tracks at his studio in Rickmansworth. They never hear from him again, but their despondent mood lifts when they're approached by Ted Carroll and Roger Armstrong who run the Rock On second-hand record stall in Shepherd's Bush. They want to record The 101'ers for their fledgling independent label, Chiswick. Ted sees them at Dingwalls in January 1976, just after Mole has been replaced by Dan Kelleher, who's actually played with a very early version of the band.

'Ted came down to the market and said, "I've just seen this amazing band. The lead singer is a real star. They're called The 101'ers",' Roger, now the MD of Ace Records, recalls, sunlight streaming through the windows of his Harlesden office. 'I realised I'd already seen them at The Elgin. I was with a friend, and they were playing in the other bar and sounded a bit of a shambles. I remember thinking they were a bit weird, because they had a trumpet player. So, Ted and I went to see them at Imperial College. There was no stage. The band just set up in a corner of the room. There was me, Ted and maybe 40 people in the bar and no more than ten of them watching the band. But Joe delivered this performance like he was playing Glastonbury. He had the big white suit by then, the Little Richard suit. When he moved, the suit went one way, and he went the other. He really was a knockout.'

347

On 4 and 10 March, they're at Pathway Studios in Archway, where Nick Lowe records most of the early Stiff records, and emerge from the sessions with a version of live favourite 'Keys to Your Heart' Chiswick plan to release as a single in May. Almost as soon as he's run off a cassette of the tracks, Joe brings them around to my digs in Willesden, lit up with enthusiasm and much excited chat about what suddenly looks like a brighter future for The 101'ers. By the time the record comes out, however, Joe's left the band.

'I was at a Jam gig at the Windsor Castle, at the bar,' Roger Armstrong recalls. 'The place was half empty, it was early evening. Joe stood next to me and said, "Have I done the right thing?" I said, "What the fuck are you talking about, Joe?" He said, "I've started a band with this guy." And there was this skinny, long-haired kid standing in the background, Mick Jones. Joe said, "I've left The 101'ers. We've split up." I just said, "What the fuck ..." Of course, it was a shock, with the single just coming out. In the end, we just said, "Well, good luck to you, fair enough, off you go." It was disappointing, yes. But we didn't feel especially betrayed. You just moved on. At that time, people were forming and leaving bands all the time and there was always another band around the corner.'

What's happened is that by now Joe has seen The Sex Pistols, who support The 101'ers on 3 and 23 April at The Nashville Rooms. What looks like a blatantly put-up scrap at the second gig ends up with the Pistols and manager Malcolm McLaren in mid-brawl on the cover of *Melody Maker*, with no mention of The 101'ers. I'm standing at the bar with Joe, Clive and Dr Feelgood's Lee Brilleaux when the Pistols appear the first night. None of us really get what's happening, apart from Joe, who looks like he's seen a future he desperately wants to be part of.

'The Sex Pistols were getting the kind of attention Strummer was craving at that time,' Dan Kelleher says from his home in Shaftesbury, the picturesque Dorset village made famous by a 1973 Hovis TV ad. 'He'd been thrashing his arse off for the last couple of years and he'd had very little recognition. Things were happening for The 101'ers, but obviously not fast enough for Strummer. He could see the way the wind was blowing.'

Strummer is smitten with the Pistols, but Clive and Richard are less impressed.

'I remember standing with you at the bar of The Nashville, the night of the so-called fight, at the second show,' Clive says, 'and we looked at each other as if to say, "What the fuck is this?" I liked the Pistols a lot as people, but the whole scene around them seemed totally fake.'

'Joe was getting more and more uncomfortable,' Richard recalls. 'Things weren't going well in rehearsals between Joe and Clive and Dan. Joe wasn't very happy. He'd be out a lot, drinking heavily, spending a lot of time down the 100 Club when the Pistols played there. Then Clive got the boot because Joe off his own bat thought that Clive should be moving around more on stage and should sharpen up his image. That wasn't Clive at all. Maybe if we'd said to him, "Look, cut your bloody hair and put on some drainpipes", maybe he would have done that. But he wouldn't have moved around more, that's for sure.'

'I didn't leave The 101'ers,' Clive says, able to laugh about it now. 'I was urged to resign. Joe came around to my squat and he kept going on about "Maximum Impact", which sounded like a phrase he'd picked up from someone, probably Bernie Rhodes, who'd started appearing at gigs. He wanted me to perform more, to come out of myself. But that's just not me. There was no way I was going to start wearing crazy clothes, get a spiky haircut and go bonkers. So, it was like, "OK, we'll wrap it up then." Dan always maintained Bernie Rhodes had already stolen Joe from The 101'ers in order to manufacture his version of The Sex Pistols.'

Rhodes, one-time Malcolm McLaren lieutenant, has already in fact made an approach to Joe, on 25 May, at a Pistols show at The 100 Club, inviting him to meet Mick Jones, Paul Simonon and Keith Levene, his future bandmates in what becomes the first line-up of The Clash. On 30 May, Bernie turns up at The Golden Lion in Fulham where The 101'ers are playing and gives Joe an ultimatum, 48 hours to decide whether he's going to join or stay with The 101'ers.

'I noticed some people hanging around the gig,' Richard recalls, 'and when Joe disappeared with them, I had a feeling something odd was going on. I think that was two nights before he told me it was all over. I was in bed at the squat in Orsett Terrace. I remember Joe shaking me awake, saying, "Wake up, Snakes. I've got something really important to tell you. This is the end. We've got to talk about it." I said, "In the morning, Joe. We'll talk about it then." I'd had this feeling something was up. He'd been very taciturn since the Golden Lion gig. Anyway, I went downstairs the next morning and there was Bernie, who I remembered from the Golden Lion. He started spewing out all this stuff about how crap The 101'ers were and how punk was going to happen. It was a totally one-way conversation.

'Then he said he wanted me to be the drummer in the new band, to stick with Joe. Bernie was the main reason I didn't join The Clash. If there'd been a different manager, I might have thought about it. But there was no way I was going to have this guy telling me what to do.

'I went to see The Clash at The Roxy and I couldn't believe how Joe had changed. He wasn't Joe anymore. He was someone else. His identity had changed entirely. I just thought, "What happened to this guy?"

'Some of the things he went on to say about The 101'ers were very hurtful. And some of it was just rubbish, like saying we'd taken our name from Room 101 in George Orwell's *1984* to make it sound more political. That was ridiculous, a bit sad. But for that first year or two he was in The Clash, he was in another place.'

'I think that was Strummer's way of interpreting the new narrative,' says Dan Kelleher. 'Everything that had gone before was crap. We became the fall guys for Strummer having been as it were led astray. It must have been especially hard for Clive and Richard because they'd been with him from the start. Mick Jones is supposed to have said that Strummer was brilliant but The 101'ers were crap, musically, which was rubbish. Clive went on to great success with The Passions and 'I'm In Love With a German Film Star'. And within months, Richard was playing with Johnny Rotten, in PiL. The whole idea that The 101'ers were a crap band was ludicrous.'

The 101'ers play their last show at The Clare Halls, Haywards Heath, on 5 June, with Clive appearing for 'Gloria', played one last time as their final encore.

'It was all very sad in the end,' Clive says, who sees Strummer for the last time at a benefit for Mole, who died in 1999, 'but I always thought from very early on, Joe had an idea in his mind about where he was going to go and I don't think there was much that would have stopped him, including breaking up The 101'ers. It was a shame, really, that we didn't go on. I saw The Clash at The ICA and to be honest, I thought they were kind of rubbish. Musically, they weren't as good as The 101'ers would have been if we'd stayed together.'

'It was like everything came to an end at once,' says Julian Yewdall of the band's final days. 'Joe announced the band was over, that he was leaving to join The Clash. At the same time, the whole street where we had our last squat in Orsett Terrace was given its eviction notice. So the band was falling apart, the house was falling apart. Previously, we'd always moved as a group. We moved from one squat to another, always together, as a unit. Now it was every man for himself. Joe had already made his move. He knew The 101'ers were going to be left behind and he got on the punk bandwagon. However agonising it was, he knew what he had to do, and he did it.'

Many years after the scattering of The 101'ers and their squatter clan from these streets, I'm back in Ladbroke Grove, for so long the band's stamping ground. It's Record Store Day, April 2015. There's a new version coming out of *Elgin Avenue Breakdown*. This is the compilation of 101'ers tracks that Richard first puts out on his Andalucia Records in 1981 and updates for release by EMI in 2005, when it's expanded to include studio cuts and live tracks, five of them from a great gig at The Roundhouse in April 1976, when The 101'ers support prog rock titans Van der Graaf Generator ('Shakespeare crossed with Uriah Heep,' as Strummer later describes them). Bernie Rhodes threatens spiteful legal action to prevent the 1981 release. Strummer, however, intervenes and Bernie backs down. Joe even joins Dudanski for a *Melody Maker* interview to promote the album, reconciled finally with his own past.

Richard and Clive have agreed to mark the 2015 edition of the album by playing a 101'ers set outside Rough Trade West, in Talbot Road, just off Portobello Road in Ladbroke Grove, not far from The Elgin, site of their Thursday-night residency in a long-ago time. There's a drum kit, amplifiers, microphones, guitar stands and other stuff set up in the street outside the shop, where there's also a small crowd. There's also much hugging and laughter when I bump into Richard coming out of the Rough Trade shop.

Amazingly, Dudanski looks as trim as he was the last time I saw him, 40 years ago. He introduces me to his son, Giggs, who's going to be playing bass this afternoon. We're joined by Clive, who's wearing a wide-brimmed hat and the kind of garish Hawaiian shirt that would have had Strummer ranting about Maximum Impact and trying to get him into a pair of bondage trousers. A mate of Clive's, Todd Sharpville, one of his old guitar pupils, a stocky dude with a touch about him of Steve Marriott's youthful cockiness, has the fairly thankless task of standing in for Joe.

They run through some old 101'ers favourites and make a grand racket. 'Motor Boys Motor'. 'Letsagetabitarockin''. A couple of minutes into a raucous version of 'Keys to Your Heart', the song that Joe had played me a lifetime ago in my Willesden digs the night The 101'ers recorded it, there's a hand on my shoulder. At the end of it, grinning, is former *NME* writer Chris Salewicz, Joe's long-time friend and biographer, dapper as ever. We might both be thinking the same thing. How great it would be to turn around and see Joe duckwalking along Talbot Road in his baggy white Little Richard suit. But the street beyond the small crowd is full of shoppers, tourists, people drinking outside the pub on the corner, not a ghost in sight.

The 101'ers outside Rough Trade West are now getting stuck into 'Gloria', always their closing number, going back to the Charlie Pigdog days. There's a version of it on *Elgin Avenue Breakdown*, prefaced by a long Strummer rap about being inspired by recently seeing Patti Smith that fades out after six minutes although it sounds like it's still got plenty in it. It was recorded at their last show.

'G-L-O-R-I-A!'

Something you could call a convenient narrative link draws me across Portobello Road, down Blenheim Crescent to Ladbroke Grove, where a sharp right quickly brings you to The Elgin and the rocking din The 101'ers used to make there.

'G-L-O-R-I-A!'

Time bends and twists, taking us back, measured out in snare cracks and backbeats. One big boogaloo.

'G-L-O-R-I-A!'

The 101'ers go for it one last time. A final chorus that brings us back to somewhere near the start of the story now coming to an end.

'G-L-O-R-I-A!'

In that other world, it's getting late. The band's packing up. This place is closing. They've called last drinks at the bar. One by one, the lights are going out. But there's always somewhere else to go, even if you think you've been everywhere. A basement, a garage, a backroom where another band is getting ready to play, amps humming. The night's wide open. There's got to be a town that will take us. We can listen to Big Star on the way.

'G-L-O-R-I-A!'

Grab your coat. Let's get out of here.

THE AFTERSHOW

It's a bitterly cold night at the back end of October 2021. I'm making my way along Coombe Lane, a largely unlit road in the suburban outback of Raynes Park in southwest London, somewhere between Wimbledon and Kingston upon Thames, by the look of it a place that hasn't changed much since they built the first houses and planted the first allotments. In the dark it has an especially forgotten look. I'm keeping an eye out for somewhere called The Cavern, where an old friend is unexpectedly playing tonight. Somewhere along Coombe Lane, there's a lot of growling thunder, a flash of lightning. It starts to rain. Now I'm wet as well as cold. What fucking joy. It crosses my dampening mind that if things had gone to a different plan, I'd be lounging in Texas sunshine right about now, in Austin for a wedding, on a trip that in its original planning involves looking up some familiar faces from a far-off carousing past.

Former Fabulous Thunderbirds guitarist Jimmie Vaughan is still in Austin, playing most Fridays at a place called C-Boy's Heart & Soul on South Congress. I'm sure Kim Wilson's eyeballs are getting soft most mornings somewhere in town. I'll look them up. The original date for the wedding is September 2020 and is cancelled when the world goes into lockdown. If I'd gone then, I might also have caught up with The Blasters' Gene Taylor, who moved to Austin in 1993, when he joined a late line-up of the Thunderbirds fronted by Kim and his pliable eyeballs. That part of the plan goes to shit when Gene's found dead at his home from hypothermia in February 2021, after severe storms cause a state-wide power failure, and millions in Texas are isolated in sub-zero temperatures without water, food or heat. This puts a big dent in the reunion jalopy, but come a second invitation to the delayed nuptials, and a possible reunion looms with another old Austin crony.

Joe 'King' Carrasco has been based for many years in Puerto Vallarta, a beach resort in Jalisco, Mexico, where he has a long-standing residency at somewhere called Nacho Daddy's. He still plays regularly in Austin and across the southwest, though, no doubt raising all kinds of hell along the way. With a bit of luck, he'll be in Austin or somewhere near when I'm there. As the rearranged wedding date approaches in October 2021, continued travel restrictions and sundry Covid concerns mean that I don't make it to Austin for the wedding or anything else and it looks like my chance of catching up with Joe for the first time in 40 years is gone.

Around the time I should have been packing, though, a post on Joe's Facebook page announces he's in the UK. In fucking Carlisle, of all places. He's up there in Cumbria rehearsing with a young band called Hardwicke Circus, who I know are managed by Dave Robinson, who as Stiff supremo in 1980 signs Carrasco to the label. There are dates coming up, apparently. A friend sends me a link to one of them, which is tonight's show in Raynes Park. What the juggling fuck is going on? How did Carrasco end up with this date on his gig sheet? I feel like I'm surely hallucinating. Carrasco in Raynes Park? It's so outlandish, it must be true. Back-channel enquiries eventually make some sense of it all. From what I can gather, Dave was in Austin hustling some gigs for Hardwicke Circus at the annual SXSW Festival, mostly a showcase for new talent. When Covid strands him in Austin, Dave holes up with Joe and plots his first UK dates since 1982, with Hardwicke Circus backing him. Dave probably figures that if they can handle a couple of weeks on the road with Carrasco, they'll be able to handle anything.

Meanwhile, I seem to have arrived at The Cavern. It's in the middle of a parade of shops and may have been two buildings once, now knocked up into something more imposing. There's a low red-brick wall outside, tables and chairs under an overhanging canopy. The windows are all lit up, like it's already Christmas inside. It's flanked on the right by an opticians, a Turkish restaurant and a nail parlour. To the left, there's another Turkish restaurant and a Korean community centre. There's a Korean community in Raynes Park? What else goes on here? Is it one of those places where human sacrifices are made to a god who looks like a goat, or am I thinking of Purley Oaks? Next door to The Cavern is Matheou's Fish Bar & Restaurant, basically a chip shop.

I'm about to go into the pub when someone comes flying out of the chippie dressed as if for a cattle round-up. A weathered cowboy hat, a bandana around his neck, a kind of keffiyeh scarf over that, a khaki topcoat with a Western cut, Ray-Bans on a leather strap. It's Carrasco.

'Buddy!' he shouts through suddenly thickening rain, arms flung open for a hug. He's carrying two plastic bags.

'Dinner for the band,' he says. 'Man, you got to meet them. They're all, like, 18 or something. They haven't eaten all day and ain't got a dollar between 'em.'

As ever, Joe has the excited, somewhat dazzled air of someone who's just driven a hovercraft into a bridge. The rain hits us in a sudden squall. We go inside before we're swept downstream. I follow Joe into a large, bright room. Every available inch of wall space is filled with framed pictures and posters of The Beatles that take them all the way from Hamburg's leathers and quiffs to the fur coats and beards of their rooftop adieu. To our right, there's a stage in a corner that's clearly too small for Hardwicke Circus's gear. Sax player Andy has set up his bits and pieces on the floor next to it, at the foot of the narrow stairs that take us to the band's dressing room.

Joe pushes open a door at the top of the third or fourth flight of stairs, and we step into a big attic space that looks like the storeroom of a junk shop, where they keep all the junk that even people who shop in junk shops don't want. I think of all the band rooms just like it that I've been in over the years, from Lapland to Bondi Beach, each one almost identical to the others. At least this one has some heating. The band, anyway, seem to have made themselves at home. Keyboard player Lewis Bewley-Taylor is unpacking the fancy suit he wears onstage and might be looking around for an ironing board and an iron to go with it. Guitarist Zack McDade and bassist Joe Hurst, who looks no older than 12 but has actually just turned 17, give Joe a wave and go back to whatever they were talking to Dave Robinson about before we arrived.

Singer Jonny Foster and his drummer brother Tom are sitting at a low table that might be a door held up by some bricks. Joe empties the carrier bags onto a couple of plates, rips open the paper wrapping. The group gather around. Eyes widen.

'There you go,' Joe says and as if he's just fired a starting pistol, the band dive in like they've been locked in a barn for a fortnight with only corn husks and bat droppings to eat. I nip downstairs and order some drinks.

'Don't fucking spoil them,' Dave Robinson says as a couple of barmen arrive with the drinks. 'I don't want them getting used to room service.'

Jonny and Tom want to know how long I've known Joe. I tell them since 1980, which I suspect is at least 20 years before any of the band were born. I feel suddenly lucky I've still got my own teeth and enough hair to not yet have to wear a hat. How do I know him?

'Hell, he was at the Battle of Helotes!' Joe tells them, although this means nothing to them at all. 'He came out to Texas and wrote about us in *Melody Maker* when nobody outside Texas had even heard of us. We had a hell of a time.'

Between mouthfuls of cod, Jonny and Tom start talking about a documentary they've recently seen about Quincy Jones, and Michael Jackson's part in it. I ask them if they know that Michael Jackson sang backing vocals on a track called 'Don't Let a Woman (Make a Fool Out of You)' on Joe's 1982 album *Synapse Gap*. The cod chewing stops in an instant. Jonny and Tom couldn't have looked more surprised if I'd just introduced them to Jimi Hendrix.

'He was in the studio next door to where we were recording,' Joe tells them. 'I kept thinking, "Man, I've got to get him on my record." Whenever we saw him, he was usually surrounded by managers, bodyguards, people who kept him away from everybody. But one day, I saw him sitting in this reception area, staring into space, on his own. I said, "Hey, Mike, why dontcha come sing on my record?"'

Jonny and Tom look at Carrasco like he's pulling butterflies out of his ears.

'And I just kinda made off with him,' Joe says. 'When his managers came back and found him in the studio with us, they freaked out. But the track was down, and we had Michael Jackson singing on the damn record.'

Jonny is still staring open-mouthed at Joe when he's called away to attend to some technical hitch with the band's gear. Joe is telling me about his recent weeks in Cumbria.

'I love it up there, man,' he says. 'It's pretty wild. We've been staying in this real run-down hotel. I mean, really run-down. Kinda place you could imagine Bukowski holed up in. Some real interesting characters live there. A song behind every door, you know?'

Dave Robinson tells us Hardwicke Circus are about to go on. I leave Carrasco and follow Dave down the stairs. Hardwicke Circus turn out to be a blast. There's a lot of E Street Band in there; some Tom Petty; a little Costello. The Boomtown Rats come more than once to mind, as do Van Morrison, Dexys Midnight Runners and The Clash. In the late 1970s or early 1980s, they'd have been signed to Stiff, getting good reviews in *Sounds* from Chas de Whalley and Pete Silverton, decent mentions in *NME* from Roy Carr and Charles Shaar Murray, but probably ignored by Nick Kent unless a couple of them turn out to be major smackheads. It's easy to imagine a larkish on-the-road feature by Carol Clerk in *MM*, hopefully a story that doesn't end with the band and Carol being banned not from a bar or hotel, but an entire country. Which is the case when Carol goes to Israel with Hanoi Rocks and things get so out of hand they're deported and upon their noisy exit told never to return. Oh, those roiling days.

The weekly music press as I remember it when it was still a bit wild out there is, of course, long gone. Even the people who used to write for it then are getting worryingly thin on the ground. Carol Clerk left the building in 2010. She's since been followed out the door by an entire staff block of names familiar to anyone who grew up reading the weeklies back then. Alan Lewis. Roy Carr. Andy Gill. David Cavanagh. Dele Fadele. Gavin Martin. Pete Makowski. Fred Deller. Nigel O'Brien. Dave Jennings. Tommy Udo. Norman McLeod. Stephanie Jones. Colin Irwin. Some days all you can see are people who are no longer there.

Carrasco hits the stage, joining Hardwicke Circus in a flurry of coyote yips and excited chat. He plugs in his guitar, makes what appears to be a crucial adjustment to the tilt of his hat and quickly turns a southwest London boozer into an exotically lit borderlands cantina, full of old school Tex-Mex rock'n'roll, R&B and garage band classics. A version of 'Hey Joe' takes it back to The Leaves. Hardwicke Circus suddenly sound like they've learned to play by listening to nothing but Lenny Kaye's *Nuggets* collection. A carnival atmosphere soon prevails.

Carrasco of course is in his element. He's on a stage. It doesn't matter where or how many people are in the audience. It could be just me and your dog. We'll look like multitudes to Carrasco. He's soon amok among the crowd, playing his guitar behind his head, Andy following him on sax, up some stairs to a raised area at the other end of the pub where unsuspecting punters are startled by Joe's sudden appearance at their tables. The last time Joe played in London, at the Half Moon in Putney, in 1982, he ended up dodging traffic on the Lower Richmond Road. Tonight, on his way back to the stage, he makes a detour out of The Cavern, onto the veranda. There's enough rain coming down to allow Noah a valedictory smirk. Coombe Lane is awash, a flood tide streaming downhill from Wimbledon. Joe's soon back inside, limbo dancing with his guitar balanced on his head, arms outstretched, surely one of the last of his kind, a roadhouse warrior running out of road. He makes it back onstage for the last chorus of 'Little Queenie'. Everyone's laughing, and it's all a bit of a riot.

You think of other times, a hundred places like this. The years peel away, time in retreat. It comes back to you then, all of it. The music, the girl on your arm. Small rooms, lit up with guitars, feedback, love and laughter. All those bands, all that beautiful noise. A guitarist with a bandaged hand and blood on his guitar strings. The nights you never wanted to end that you were lucky to get home from in your own lifetime, especially if a cat like BP Fallon was involved. Where did they all go, and so many people with them? Talk about smoke through a keyhole.

We're back in the band's dressing room, the gig over. Everyone's packing up their stuff for a long drive through tonight's storm. Tomorrow's show is at HM Prison Werrington, a juvenile offenders centre near Stoke. They're going straight there, leaving soon. Joe is telling me how they're all travelling on a converted double-decker bus, which sounds wildly cool.

'Come with us,' Joe says, laughing, but only half-joking.

'Always room for one more,' says a passing Jonny Foster.

Forty-five years ago, something like that, when we were young, reckless, thin and up for anything, I would have jumped on the bus without a second thought. Driven off into the night, stopping somewhere at an off-licence, picking up Tom Sheehan along the way. Even now, I'm tempted, some cackling witch in my head telling me to go, why not? I could go downstairs, get on the bus. Find a seat. Settle in and wait to see what happens next.

Such are an old cowboy's dreams, anyway.

There's a blast of thunder. I look out from the attic window of The Cavern at the pounding rain. If I don't leave now, I'll need a canoe to get to the station. I make my way back up Coombe Lane, past the opticians and the Turkish restaurant and the nail parlour towards Raynes Park station, in the battering rain, the unforgiving wind. There's a moment on the platform when the witch in my head starts cawing again. Go back. Get on the bus. It will be one last adventure. Not quite the old days, but near enough.

There's a train coming, lights barely visible in the downpour.

More thunder. A hardening rain gusts down the platform, washing away the cowboy dream of a final round-up, a last sunset to ride into. When the train pulls out of the station, I'm on it.

By the time you read this, I'll be nearly home.

A NOTE ON THE AUTHOR

Allan Jones is an award winning British music journalist and editor, who joined *Melody Maker* in 1974 as a junior reporter and features writer. He was editor of *MM* from 1984 to 1997, then launched *Uncut* magazine and for 17 years wrote a popular column called 'Stop Me If You've Heard This One Before', based on his experiences as a music journalist in the 70s and 80s, the legendary heyday of the UK music weeklies. His previous book, *Can't Stand Up For Falling Down*, was the *Sunday Times* Music Book of the Year 2017.

A NOTE ON THE TYPE

The text of this book is set in Linotype Sabon, a typeface named after the type founder, Jacques Sabon. It was designed by Jan Tschichold and jointly developed by Linotype, Monotype and Stempel in response to a need for a typeface to be available in identical form for mechanical hot metal composition and hand composition using foundry type.

Tschichold based his design for Sabon roman on a font engraved by Garamond, and Sabon italic on a font by Granjon. It was first used in 1966 and has proved an enduring modern classic.